The Slave's Narrative

CHARLES T. DAVIS

AND

HENRY LOUIS GATES, JR.

Oxford   New York
OXFORD UNIVERSITY PRESS

Oxford University Press

Oxford   New York   Toronto
Delhi   Bombay   Calcutta   Madras   Karachi
Petaling Jaya   Singapore   Hong Kong   Tokyo
Nairobi   Dar es Salaam   Cape Town
Melbourne   Auckland

and associated companies in
Berlin   Ibadan

Library of Congress Cataloging in Publication Data
Main entry under title:
The Slave's narrative.
1. Slaves—United States—Biography—Addresses,
essays, lectures.   2. Slavery—United States—Condition
of slaves—Addresses, essays, lectures.   3. Slavery—
United States—History—Sources—Addresses, essays,
lectures.   4. Autobiography—Addresses, essays, lectures.
I. Gates, Henry Louis.   II. Davis, Charles T.
(Charles Twitchell), 1918-1981.
E444.S575   1984   973'.0496   83-3950
ISBN 0-19-503276-4
ISBN 0-19-503277-2
ISBN 0-19-5066561 (pbk.)

Material in AUTOBIOGRAPHICAL ACTS AND THE VOICE OF THE SOUTHERN SLAVE by Houston A.
Baker reprinted from THE JOURNEY BACK, Chapter Two, pp. 27-52, by Houstin Baker, Jr., by permission of The University of Chicago Press.

USING THE TESTIMONY OF EX-SLAVES: APPROACHES AND PROBLEMS by John Blassingame reprinted
from JOURNAL OF SOUTHERN HISTORY, Volume 41 (November 1975), pp. 473-492. Copyright ©
1975 by the Southern Historical Association. Reprinted by permission of the Managing Editor.

I WAS BORN by James Olney was written for AFRO-AMERICAN LITERATURE: THE RECONSTRUCTION
OF A LITERARY HISTORY which will be published by The Modern Language Association.

I ROSE AND FOUND MY VOICE by Robert Stepto is reprinted from FROM BEHIND THE VEIL by Robert
Stepto, courtesy of the University of Illinois Press.

HISTORY FROM SLAVE SOURCES by C. Vann Woodward is reprinted from AMERICAN HISTORICAL RE-
VIEW, vol. 79, 1974, pp. 470-481, courtesy of the author.

Material from TEXTS AND CONTENTS OF HARRIET JACOBS' INCIDENTS IN THE LIFE OF A SLAVE GIRL:
WRITTEN BY HERSELF by Jean Yellin is reprinted from AMERICAN LITERATURE 53:3, pp. 479-486,
copyright © 1981 by Duke University Press, Durham, N.C.

The version of article, TEXTS AND CONTENTS OF HARRIET JACOBS' INCIDENTS IN THE LIFE OF A
SLAVE GIRL: WRITTEN BY HERSELF by Jean Yellin which appears in this volume, copyright © 1983,
Jean Yellin.

4 6 8 10 9 7 5 3
Printed in the United States of America

. . . when we get a little farther away from the conflict, some brave and truth-loving man, with all the facts before him . . . will gather from here and there the scattered fragments, my small contribution perhaps among the number, and give to those who shall come after us an impartial history of this the grandest moral conflict of the century. [For] Truth is patient and time is just.

Frederick Douglass, 1891.

. . . unless the descendant of the slave writes an exhaustive book from his standpoint, [U. B. Phillips's *American Negro Slavery*] might be the last word on the subject.

Mary White Ovington, 1918.

Let the study of the Old South be undertaken by other scholars [than U. B. Phillips] who have absorbed the viewpoint of modern cultural anthropology, who have a feeling for social psychology (a matter of particular importance in the study of a regime in which status was so vital), who will concentrate upon the neglected rural elements that formed the great majority of the Southern population, who will not rule out the testimony of more critical observers, and who will realize that any history of slavery must be written in large part from the standpoint of the slave—and then the possibilities of the Old South and the slave system as a field of research and historical experience will loom larger than ever.

Richard Hofstadter, 1944.

The authors wish to dedicate this book, with admiration and affection, to John Wesley Blassingame, Sr., who restored the black slave's narrative to its complex status as history and as literature.

"Things for the Abolitionist to Do,"

1. Speak for the Slave, . . .
2. Write for the Slave, . . .

"They can't take care of themselves."

The New England
Anti-Slavery Almanac
for 1841

Preface

The Slave's Narrative, a collection of essays and reviews addressing the autobiographical narratives written or dictated by ex-slaves of African descent in the eighteenth, nineteenth, and twentieth centuries, has a two-fold purpose: to demonstrate the nature and function of the interpretation of this curious genre of literature and to explicate the structure of the world these narratives represent. We have chosen these commentaries carefully. These contributions from scholars of different disciplines demonstrate remarkably diverse methodological approaches to narrative studies. We undertook this project—the collection of representative examples of two hundred years of speculation upon the nature and function of the narrative of slaves—simply so that a fair sample of historical analysis and literary criticism of this body of compelling texts, would be readily accessible in one volume.

Where in the history of human slavery does there exist another literature of this ironic sort, consisting of the imaginative reconstruction of human bondage narrated by hundreds of former chattel slaves? One dares not imagine the broad implications that this amount of written accounts from antiquity, for example, would inevitably have had upon our recreations of Graeco-Roman history. The integrity of those texts would have been inescapably apparent by revealing in particular detail the shape of a substructured world we have come to know only through the musings of the aristocratic and essentially solipsistic slave owners. Moreover, where in the history of narration does there exist a literature that was propelled by the Enlightenment demand that a "race" place itself on the Great Chain of Being primarily through the exigencies of print? Viewed generally with uncritical acclaim by the antislavery advocates, and viewed with suspicion or disdain by slavery's proponents, the slave's narrative did not elicit a calm response from its contemporary critics, or in scholarly comment a century later. As "authentic" it was suspect because of the direct political uses to which abolitionists put those unremitting indictments of the "peculiar institution." And only within the last two decades have historians begun to turn sufficiently to the texts to discern the contours of slavery, as represented, in language, by the slaves.

The slave's narratives are veritable repositories of the ontological and epistemological concerns of human beings enslaved in antebellum America. Even though in this genre even the extreme examples have more in common with one another than they do with other forms of narration, still, the slave narrative does share resemblances to other narratives, especially the picaresque, the sentimental novel, and the spiritual autobiography. In light of the broad concerns of the commentators in the essays included in our volume, it is remarkable that scholars of literature only recently have turned to these narratives to "read" them closely and perhaps for the first time to "allow" them to yield their implicit logic and explicit concerns through approaches and methodologies as various as is the critical imperative itself.

We have, in a sense, given a priority to the discrete uses of language. By taking the language of the narratives as the most common, if not obvious, feature of the texts, scholars of all disciplines may interpret these slave narratives through the peculiar concerns and demands of their particular disciplines, while taking verbal textures as a starting point. And what does this "literary" bias yield? It confirms convincingly the hermeneutical principle that the tools with which we read largely determine what it is possible to discover in a text; and, second, that despite the attention and energy of these more than two dozen essayists, the black slaves' narratives retain their integrity and are as compelling as they were before these scholars and reviewers turned their attention upon them.

The reviews and essays published between 1750 and 1982 that are collected here record the history of the interpretation of the slave narrative. Their chronological arrangement is designed to reveal the progressive consideration of these narratives over two centuries. We have tried to choose essays that challenge the assumptions of one another in order to provide a record of the debate about the nature and function of these narratives which historians and critics have been engaged in for the last half-century—and more heatedly so during the past decade. The book is designed to be a convenient and useful coda to these debates, and to serve as an hermeneutical analogue to works such as John W. Blassingame's *The Slave Community* and *Slave Testimony*. We have, with some regret, relegated our extensive array of essays on Frederick Douglass to its own collection, to be published separately. It is an accident of literary history that our book appears two years after Marion Wilson Starling's pioneering book, *The Slave Narrative: Its Place in American History,* which since its completion as a dissertation at New York University in

1946, has been the often unacknowledged source of accepted knowledge about the narratives in the works of major historians of slavery. It is our privilege to be in such splendid company. Finally, this collection is intended to demonstrate the multi-disciplinary scholarly uses to which the genre can be put, and to demonstrate the role of metacommentary in Afro-American studies.

*　*　*

Charles T. Davis died just two weeks after this book was contracted. We were able, however, in his difficult last months, to complete most of its planning and editing. I hope that this collection can, in part, stand as a testament to Davis's vision as a critic. The final decision we made about this book was to dedicate it to our colleague and friend, John Wesley Blassingame, Sr., to honor what we termed the revolution in historiography he effected in *The Slave Community*. Blassingame's work relates to our work in criticism, in an ideal relation of text to context.

I would like to thank David A. Curtis, Nicola Shilliam, Mary McFarland, and Darby Tench for their excellent research assistance and admirable stamina; Susan Rabiner, Mary Polo-Wander, and Naomi Schneider for their impeccable editorial advice; Alice Poindexter Fisher, and Robert Burns Stepto, for enabling me to participate in a Modern Language Association summer seminar on Afro-American literary theory; Kai Erikson for asking me to write about Frederick Douglass for the *Yale Review;* the Program in Afro-American Studies for its unflagging support; my colleagues Houston A. Baker, Jr., Kimberly W. Benston, Hazel Carby, John Brown Childs, Michael G. Cooke, Geoffrey H. Hartman, Robert Hemenway, Fredric Jameson, Barbara Johnson, J. Hillis Miller, Robert O'Meally, Nancy Stepan, and Susan Willis for sharing with me, generously, their ideas about the critical activity; Mrs. Gwendolyn Williams for meeting unreasonable deadlines, and Jeanne Curtis Davis and Sharon Adams for their love.

New Haven, Connecticut   H.L.G., Jr.
November, 1984

Contents

3. *The Slave Narratives as Literature*

Illustrations follow page 146

Introduction
The Language of Slavery

There may be humane masters, as there certainly are inhuman ones—
there may be slaves well-clothed, well-fed, and happy, as there surely are
those half-clad, half-starved and miserable. . . . Men may write fictions
portraying lowly life as it is, or as it is not—may expatiate with owlish
gravity upon the bliss of ignorance—discourse flippantly from arm chairs
of the pleasures of slave life; but let them toil with him in the field—sleep
with him in the cabin—feed with him on husks; let them behold him
scourged, hunted, trampled on, and they will come back with another
story in their mouths. Let them know the *heart* of the poor slave—learn
his secret thoughts—thoughts he dare not utter in the hearing of the white
man; let them slip by him in the silent watches of the night—converse
with him in trustful confidence, of "life, liberty, and the pursuit of happiness"; and they will find that ninety-nine out of every hundred are intelligent enough to understand their situation, and to cherish in their bosoms
the love of freedom, as passionately as themselves.

Solomon Northup, 1853

. . . there is not yet a picture of the institution [of slavery] as seen
through the eyes of the bondsman himself.

L. D. Reddick, 1937

No written text is a transparent rendering of "historical reality," be
that text composed by master or slave. The slave's narrative has *precisely* the identical "documentary" status as does any other written account of slavery. Whereas its presuppositions tend to differ dramatically
from those of texts written by non-slaves, both sorts of texts are of the
same order as historical documents and literary discourse. If this volume
can serve to demonstrate this obvious, yet generally ignored, first principle, then we shall have succeeded in our endeavor. Historians who
work so painstakingly to establish verifiable records have, until recently,
treated these texts either with an alarmingly irresponsible naïveté, or

else with a pernicious double-standard, finding "bias" in the slave's text and "objectivity" in that of the master. As many of the essays included here demonstrate, historians can no longer remain unaware of the marvels of close textual analysis, if they seek to employ texts as documents in their own "fictions" of "history." Textual "resurrection," as it were, at which the historian is so very adept, enables the literary scholar to compare the discrete uses of language by an author at several places, so that the clash of voices, between the well-intended prefatory or appended attestations of abolitionists about the author's integrity (or indeed his or her intelligence) and the voice of the slave subject, can be more clearly overheard and interpreted.

Literary critics, however, have been guilty of ignoring both the historian's methods of verification of authorship and of events depicted in a text, two key features of John W. Blassingame's use of the slave narratives to reconstruct a history of the antebellum South from the slave's stance. Nevertheless, scattered literary scholars, increasingly aware of the determining influence these narratives have had upon the Afro-American novel, have, at least since the mid-1920's, devoted various studies to the "literariness" of these picaresque and confessional texts. But rarely has a volume attempted to analyze these texts as narrative discourses as important to criticism for their form and structure as they are important to historiography for the "truths" they reveal about the complex workings of what Blassingame calls "the slave community."

Ignored for too long, the Afro-American slave narratives as a whole form one of the largest bodies of literature produced by any group of slaves in history. Using a certain "structural" approach that allows scholars of various disciplines to address one common subject, we intend this volume of critical essays for historians, literary critics, economists, folklorists, anthropologists, sociologists et al. It stands as a record of the history of the interpretation of, and a necessary step in the academic revaluation of the slave narrative. And, finally, we hope that *The Slave's Narrative*, in addition to adding something to our knowledge of the nature and function of interpretation, also well serves those eighteenth and nineteenth century texts through which the black slave first proclaimed himself a human being.

The written and dictated testimonies of the enslavement of black human beings are what we mean by the phrase, "the slave's narrative." Rather arbitrarily, we have defined as a slave narrative only those *written* works published before 1865, after which time *de jure* slavery ceased to exist. We treat *dictated* works in essays on the oral slave narratives collected in the 1930s by the Federal Writers' Project. We have assigned this end date simply for literary reasons: the very structure of the narratives, their rhetorical strategies as a genre, altered drastically once the milieu in which they were written and read altered drastically. Once slavery was formally abolished, no need existed for the slave to *write* himself into the human community through the action of first-person narration. As Frederick Douglass in 1855 succinctly put the matter, the free human being "cannot see things in the same light with the slave, because he does not, and cannot, look from the same point from which the slave does." The terms of the opposition here are "slave" and "free human being," not black and white. The nature of the narratives, and their total rhetorical strategies and import, changed once slavery no longer existed.

A simple exercise in close reading indicates that Douglass's claim is true. Booker T. Washington's *Up from Slavery,* published in 1901, bears a revisionary, or signifying, relation of intertextuality to Douglass's 1845 *Narrative.* The first paragraphs and first chapter of *Up from Slavery* refigure Douglass's models. Nevertheless, what we might think of as the sheer "weight" of cultural and political experience, which accumulated in the intervening fifty-six years between 1845 and 1901, seems to force Washington's mimetic narrative strategy to crumble. Douglass's neatly structured, uncompromising antitheses and his multiple uses of the trope of chiasmus become qualified in Washington's saga by curiously compromising and demeaning parenthetical "explanations" of his assertions. "My life had its beginnings in the midst of the most miserable, desolate, and discouraging surroundings," Washington assertively enough begins his second paragraph. Then he qualifies this: "This was so, however, not because my owners were especially cruel, for they were not, as compared with many others." Furthermore, in his first paragraph Washington transforms Douglass's magnificently determinant rhetorical gesture into a poor attempt to amuse. Douglass writes, "I was born in Tuckahoe, near Hillsborough, and about twelve miles from Easton, in Talbot County, Maryland. I have no accurate knowledge of my age, never having seen any authentic record containing it. By far the larger part of the slaves know as little of their ages as horses know of theirs, and it is the wish of most masters within my knowledge to keep their slaves thus ignorant." Washington's revision confirms the presence of a drastically alerted rhetorical principle: "I was born a slave on a plantation in Franklin County, Virginia. I am not sure of the exact place or exact date of my birth, but at any rate I suspect I must have been born somewhere and at sometime." Washington's would-be slave narrative could not have been written before 1865: Washington rends Douglass's rhetorical antitheses asunder with the apologetics of the parenthetical. That Washington turned to the form of the slave narratives, however, attests to a black intertextual or signifying relationship, upon which any meaningful formal literary history of the Afro-American tradition must be based.

Once thought to be only a kind of ephemeral, politically motivated writing, the slave narrative continues to command the attention of scholars, a full century after slavery was abolished. Whereas these narratives initially were the province of historians and then literary critics, now they are of importance to anthropologists and folklorists, historians of art and musicologists, sociologists and political scientists, linguists and psychologists, philosophers and legal historians, and economists and theologians. We have tried to bring together for this collection among the best and most representative scholarship concerned with the slave narrative, including essays on the Federal Writers' Project's oral narratives, now edited by George P. Rawick and published by the Greenwood Press in forty-one accessible volumes.

One indication of the continued scholarly and popular interest in this genre is the number of full-length studies published with relative regularity. Since 1969 alone, the following titles, among others, treated aspects of these works: Gilbert Osofsky, ed., *Puttin' on Ole Massa: The Slave Narratives of Henry Bibb, William Wells Brown, and Solomon Northrup* (1969); John F. Bayliss, ed., *Black Slave Narratives* (1970); Norman R. Yetman, ed., *Voices from Slavery* (1970); Abraham Chapman, ed., *Steal Away, Stories of the Runaway Slaves* (1971); John W. Blassingame, *The Slave Community* (1972); George P. Rawick, *The American Slave: A Composite Autobiography* (41 vols. 1972, 1978, 1979); George P. Rawick, *From Sundown to Sunup: The Making of the Black Community* (1972); Stephen Butterfield, *Black Autobiography* (1974); Sidonie Smith, *Where I'm Bound: Patterns of Slavery and Freedom in Black American Autobiography* (1974); Robert S. Starobin, ed., *Blacks in Bondage: Letters of American Slaves* (1974); John W. Blassingame, *Slave Testimony: Two Centuries of Letters, Speeches, Interviews and Autobiographies* (1977); Frances Smith Foster, *Witnessing Slavery: The Development of the Slave Narratives* (1979); Paul D. Escott, *Slavery Remembered: A Record of Twentieth-Century Slave Narratives* (1979); and Maron Wilson Starling, *The Slave Narrative: Its Place in American History* (1982). Indeed, this collection of essays published between 1750 and 1982, indicates the interest shown in these peculiar tales for over two centuries. It is especially significant that the slave narrative has become the basis of both slave historiography, particularly with Blassingame's 1972 publication of his re-creation of the fabric and texture of life in the slave quarters, and of Afro-American literary history, with John Herbert Nelson in 1926 and Vernon Loggins in 1931 arguing for the narrative's central role not only in the birth and shape of Afro-American fictional narrative forms, but also in the subsequent developments of black autobiography. In 1966, Arna Bontemps put the matter well in a statement about black literary ancestry that has influenced Afro-American literary history ever since.

> From the narrative came the spirit and vitality and the angle of vision
> responsible for the most effective prose writing by black American writ-
> ers from William Wells Brown to Charles W. Chesnutt, from W. E. B.
> DuBois to Richard Wright, Ralph Ellison and James Baldwin. . . .

Indeed, from 1760 to the present, almost *half* of the Afro-American literary tradition was created when its authors and their black readers were
either slaves or former slaves. Have there ever been more curious origins
of a literary tradition? The slave narrative arose as a response to and
refutation of claims that blacks *could* not write.

Nelson and Loggins's suggestive, if problematic, claims were echoed
in scattered writings of the 1930s by critics such as Sterling A. Brown.
This revisionary history of the nature of Afro-American literature parallels similar revisions in American slave historiography. John McCade in
1935, L. D. Reddick, in 1937, and Richard Hofstadter in 1944, each challenged the established convention within American slave historiography
of attempting to re-create an image of slavery primarily from the records
of the planters, the masters. As Hofstadter said, "Let the study of the
Old South be undertaken by other scholars . . . who will realize that
any history of slavery must be written in large part from the standpoint
of the slave." This is an obvious enough sentiment now, yet it was a bold
challenge to the presuppositions implicit in Ulrich B. Phillips's unsubtle,
proslavery, nostalgic fictions of a South that simply never existed. Indeed,
it is a simple exercise in close reading to show that Phillips derived his
representation of black people, not from their own words or cultural institutions, but from the established racist stereotypes common to the
genre of the "confederate romance."

Since the status of the slave narrative as history and literature seems
self-evident to us, how could the narratives have been "lost" to us for
such a dark period, when the apparent "silence" of the slave was drawn
upon by a host of commentators as "evidence" of either the total brutal
environment of slavery or else of an inherent mental deficiency within
the slave? After all, slave narratives were extraordinarily popular texts.
Arna Bontemps found their closest analogue in this century to be the
Western. I think rather the genre of detective fiction is a more apt formal
analogue, since the plots of all the slave narratives turn upon the resolution of a mystery, already resolved in fact by the first-person "detective"
narrator. Both forms, moreover, share conventions of realism (verisimilitude), despite the fact that the slave narratives also shared contradictory
characteristics with the sentimental novel (florid asides, strident polemics,
the melodramatic imagination).

The narratives had an appreciable market. Here is a sampling of how
well they sold. Charles Nichols and Arna Bontemps have informed us that

Frederick Douglass's *Narrative* (1845) sold 5,000 copies in the first four months of publication. Between 1845 and 1847, the *Narrative* sold 11,000 copies; in Great Britain, nine editions were printed in these two years. And by 1860, 30,000 copies had sold. Solomon Northup's narrative sold 27,000 copies in its first two years of publication. Moses Roper's text went into ten editions between 1837 and 1856. Equiano's narrative went to thirty-six editions between 1789 and 1850. And William Wells Brown's book reached its fourth edition in its first year of publication. *Truth Stranger than Fiction,* one of Josiah Henson's narratives, had an advance sale of 5,000 copies. As John A. Collins, general agent of the Massachusetts Anti-Slavery Society, wrote to William Lloyd Garrison in 1842, "The public have itching ears to hear a colored man speak, and particularly a *slave.* Multitudes will flock to hear one of his class." The slaves' writings were often direct extensions of their speeches, and many ex-slave narrators confess that their printed texts are structured formal revisions of their spoken words organized and promoted by anti-slavery organizations. This then provides an ideal opportunity for critics to study the complex relation between oral and written forms of narrative, and especially the trope of orality itself which remains central in much of contemporary black fiction. The popular acceptance of the figure of the black was determined, to this extent, by his or her mastery of words.

We can achieve an idea of the role that the words of ex-slaves were able to play in the fight against slavery by considering the following comments published between 1845 and 1855. Lucius C. Matlock, in 1845 wrote that

> Naturally and necessarily, the enemy of literature, [American slavery] has become the prolific theme of much that is profound in argument, sublime in poetry, and thrilling in narrative. From the soil of slavery itself have sprung forth some of the most brilliant productions, whose logical levers will ultimately upheave and overthrow the system. . . . Startling incidents authenticated, far excelling fiction in their touching pathos, from the pen of self-emancipated slaves, do now exhibit slavery in such revolting aspects, as to secure the execrations of all good men and become a monument more enduring than marble, in testimony strong as sacred writ against it.

In that same year, Wendell Phillips wrote that

> I am glad the time has come when the "lions write history." We have been left long enough to gather the character of slaves from the involuntary evidence of the masters. One might, indeed, rest sufficiently satisfied with what, it is evident, must be, in general, the results of such a relation without seeking further to find whether they have followed in every instance.

Ten years later, in a review of Douglass's second slave narrative, *Putnam's Monthly* said that

> Our English literature has recorded many an example of genius struggling against adversity,—of the poor Ferguson, for instance, making himself an astronomer, of Burns becoming a poet, of Hugh Miller finding his geology in a stone quarry, and a thousand similar cases—yet none of these are so impressive as the case of solitary slave, in a remote district, surrounded by none but enemies, conceiving the project of his escape, teaching himself to read and write to facilitate it, accomplishing it at last, and subsequently raising himself to a leadership in a great movement on behalf of his brethren.

The curious and direct relation between reading and writing, on one hand, and legal freedom, on the other, was evident to both the slave narrators and to their reviewers.

Sales figures alone do not attest to the popularity of the form. A reviewer of Henry Bibb's narrative wrote in 1849 that "This fugitive slave literature is destined to be a powerful lever. We have the most profound conviction of its potency. We see in it the easy and infallible means of abolitionizing the free States. Argument provokes argument, reason is met by sophistry. But narratives of slaves go right to the hearts of men." An 1852 review of Randolph's *The Cabin and the Parlor* refers to "that surfeit of 'nigger' literature, which now sickens the popular taste." A more revealing indication of the extensive readership is, perhaps, the scores of pro-slavery confederate romances published to rebut the slave narrative's collective realism, as well as critical admonitions to Southern writers and readers to support such fictions. "Let the people of the South make it a point to buy and read the writings of their own men," a writer in the *Southern Quarterly Review* put it in 1854, "even to the exclusion of all others." The *Southern Literary Messenger*, two years later, printed an even bolder and more desperate plea: ". . . as literature has been the most powerful weapon which the enemies of African slavery have used in their attacks, so, also, to literature must we look for the maintenance of our position, and justification before the world." The editorial continued, "Let Southern authors, men who see and know slavery as it is, make it their duty to deluge all the realms of literature with a flood of light upon the subject. . . ." Such hostility signifies the presence of a black discourse both popular and compelling, one which even informed and helped determine the shape of its narrative antithesis, the plantation novel; the two forms seem to have been locked together in a bipolar moment, as it were, or a signifying relationship.

How could these narratives with such broad readership simply "disappear" for sixty years? One reason was suggested, prophetically, by Frederick Douglass in an editorial he printed in 1856, "Opposing slavery and hating its victims has come to be a very common form of abolitionism." Once legal slavery disappeared, a more subtle form of subjugation, as we know, displaced it in a relation of *de facto* to *de jure*. The concomitant economic, political, and social conspiracy, between 1876 and 1915, most certainly had profound literary ramifications. Within American society, the literary presence of the speaking black subject was replaced by the deafening silence of his absence; essentially as an object, a figure in the fictions of nonblacks, did the black then "exist" in mainstream literature. Blacks, of course, continued to publish poetry, fiction, autobiographies, essays, and letters between 1865 and the turn of the century, but primarily in black periodicals. With the end of slavery, however, the black seems to have lost his great, unique theme until Jim Crow racism and segregation recreated it. The stilling of the black "voice" assumed myriad forms, not the least distressing of which was the effective destruction of black arts and letters existing before 1865. Only with great devotion and diligence have we even begun to restore the fragments of the lost records of the Afro-American mind. And who can estimate what these losses have cost the development of literature and art?

II

Since the New Negro Renaissance, literary scholars have been wrestling with the question of the influence of the slave narratives on the form of subsequent Afro-American literary works. That the matter is still alive is perhaps best illustrated by the divergent opinions on this question expressed by Ralph Ellison and Arna Bontemps, two Afro-American creative writers and critics whose works are central to the Afro-American canon.

On the one hand, in a 1978 interview with Ishmael Reed, Steve Cannon, and Quincy Troupe, published in *Y'Bird*, Ralph Ellison responded at length to Cannon's question about certain structural similarities between *Invisible Man* and the slave narratives. Ellison's considered response bears repeating:

> Cannon: [*Invisible Man*] reads very much like a slave narrative, doesn't it? Would you say you've borrowed the techniques?
> ..
> Ellison: No, that's coincidental. And, frankly, I think too much has been made of the slave narrative, as an influence on contemporary writing. Experience tends to mold itself into certain repetitive patterns, and one

of the reasons we exchange experiences is in order to discover the repetitions and coincidences which amount to a common group experience. We tell ourselves our individual stories so as to become aware of our *general* story. I wouldn't have had to read a single slave narrative in order to create the narrative pattern of *Invisible Man*. It emerges from experience and from my own sense of literary form, out of my sense of experience as shaped by history and my familiarity with literature.

Because the Afro-American historical experience incorporates patterns of northern and western migration, Ellison continues,

> . . . the movement from South to North became a basic pattern for my novel. The pattern of movement and the obstacles encountered are so basic to Afro-American experience (and to my own, since my mother took me North briefly during the Twenties, and I came North again in '36), that I had no need of slave narratives to grasp either its significance or its potential for organizing a fictional narrative. I would have used the same device if I had been writing an autobiography.

Invisible Man, of course, is a fictional autobiography of a nameless protagonist, which both embodies and transcends almost two centuries of repeated black narrative strategies. As Robert B. Stepto and James Olney have argued in fine detail, these strategies were first employed in the slave narrative. Nevertheless, Ellison's perceptive claim—that this pattern of South-to-North migration is "so basic to Afro-American experience"— raises as many questions as it resolves, precisely because historical experience and textual experience reinforce each other in a dialectical relationship so complex that the identification of origins is, at best, rendered problematic.

This is not to say that the Afro-American historical experience can be characterized by vertical migration (or "elevation," the nineteenth-century keyword that "migration" supplanted), simply because this recurs as one of the black textual tradition's repeating tropes. Rather, Olney and Stepto argue that a crucial feature of the structure of *Invisible Man* placed it, at its publication in 1952, at the "end" of a narrative tradition of figuration that had commenced in English in 1760 with Briton Hammon's slave narrative. For the literary critic, this textual fact is what is important to literary history. That Ellison would have "used the same device if I had been writing an autobiography," seems to strengthen the critics' argument, since their histories of narrative ignore certain arbitrary distinctions between "fiction" and "non-fiction." Ellison's final word on the subject inserts "consciousness" as a substitute for intention, which is one reason critics qualify any author's account of their own origins. Ellison concludes:

> All this is not to put down the slave narrative, but to say that it did not
> influence my novel as a *conscious* functional form. And, don't forget, the
> main source of any novel is other *novels;* these constitute the culture of
> the form, and my loyalty to our group does nothing to change that; it's
> a cultural, literary reality. (Emphasis added)

The key sentence in this exchange is Ellison's observation that "the pattern of movement and the obstacles encountered are so basic to Afro-
American experience." It is precisely this pattern of movement that the
art of the slave's narrative willed to the black textual tradition, making it
possible both for us to transcend the chaos of individual memory, since
these collective texts constitute the beginnings of the Afro-American
canon, and for the trope itself to inform black novels, which emerged in
the nineteenth-century directly from the slave narrative. Arna Bontemps
makes this argument for the key place of the narrative in Afro-American
literary history: that both fictional and autobiographical forms, as con-
flated in James Williams' *Narrative* (1836), Harriet Wilson's *Our Nig*
(1859), in Richard Wright's *Black Boy* (1945), and in *Invisible Man,*
emerge from the ex-slave's tale. Bontemps would concur with Burton's
dictum from *The Anatomy of Melancholy* "Our style bewrays us." As
Bontemps stated in 1966:

> *Consciously* or *unconsciously*, all of [the major black writers] reveal in
> their writing a debt to the narratives, a debt that stands in marked con-
> trast to the relatively smaller obligations they owe the more recognized
> arbiters of fiction or autobiography. (Emphasis added)

Ellison reverses Bontemps' claim about the narratives, detail by detail.
Perhaps anticipating an Ellisonian revision of this formal relationship
between black fictional and non-fictional forms, Bontemps implies that
the structural patterns implicit to the slave narrative were simultaneously
formal *and* cultural; and, whereas relations of content are readily imitated, borrowed, or derived, relations of form are not only implicitly ideological, but also shared, or "collective," despite the intention or conscious
desires of an author. "If not all of them had read slave narratives," Bontemps continues, "they had heard them by word of mouth or read or
listened to accounts these had inspired. Thus, when they put pen to
paper, what came to light, like emerging words written in invisible ink,
were their own versions of bondage and freedom." Bontemps argues that
the evidence is to be found in these texts themselves. Where Ellison,
curiously, places a priority upon "experience," Bontemps maintains that
we know "experience" through our canonical texts, which, taken together,
will to the tradition what we might think of as received *textual experience.*

If Bontemps and Ellison serve as convenient emblems of two modes of thinking about the narrative's role in Afro-American literary history, then Theodore Parker's reflections upon the status of American literature at mid-point in the nineteenth century and his opinions of the slave narrative, help us to understand the milieu in which these narratives were written, published, and distributed. Parker was a theologian, a Unitarian clergyman, and a publicist for ideas, whom Perry Miller described as "the man who next only to Emerson . . . was to give shape and meaning to the Transcendental movement in America." In a speech on "The Mercantile Classes" delivered in 1846, Parker laments the sad state of "American" letters:

> Literature, science, and art are mainly in [poor men's] hands, yet are controlled by the prevalent spirit of the nation. . . . In England, the national literature favors the church, the crown, the nobility, the prevailing class. Another literature is rising, but is not yet national, still less canonized. We have no American literature which is permanent. Our scholarly books are only an imitation of a foreign type; they do not reflect our morals, manners, politics, or religion, not even our rivers, mountains, sky. They have not the smell of our ground in their breath.

Parker, to say the least, was not especially pleased with American letters and their identity with the English tradition. Did Parker find any evidence of a truly American discourse?

> The real American literature is found only in newspapers and speeches, perhaps in some novel, hot, passionate, but poor and extemporaneous. That is our national literature. Does that favor man—represent man? Certainly not. All is the reflection of this most powerful class. The truths that are told are for them, and the lies. Therein the prevailing sentiment is getting into the form of thoughts.

Parker's analysis, of course, is "proto-Marxian," embodying as it does the reflection theory of base and superstructure. It is the occasional literature, "poor and extemporaneous," wherein "American" literature dwells.

Three years later, in his major oration on "The American Scholar," Parker at last found an entirely original genre of American Literature:

> Yet, there is one portion of our permanent literature, if literature it may be called, which is wholly indigenous and original. The lives of the early martyrs and confessors are purely Christian, so are the legends of saints and other pious men; there was nothing like this in the Hebrew or heathen literature, cause and occasion were alike wanting for it. So we have one series of literary productions that could be written by none but Americans, and only here; I mean the Lives of Fugitive Slaves. But as these are not the work of the men of superior culture they hardly help to pay the scholar's debt. Yet all the original romance of Americans is in them, not in the white man's novel.

Parker was right about the originality, the peculiarly *American* quality, of the slave narratives. But he was wrong about their inherent inability to "pay the scholar's debt"; as the essays here attest, scholars had only to learn to *read* the narratives for their debt to be paid in full, indeed many times over. As Charles Sumner said in 1852, the fugitive slaves and their narratives "are among the heroes of our age. Romance has no storms of more thrilling interest than theirs. Classical antiquity has preserved no examples of adventurous trial more worthy of renown." Parker's and Sumner's views reveal that the popularity of the narratives in antebellum America most certainly did not reflect any sort of common critical agreement about their nature and status as art.

One section of this book treats the "twice-told tales" of slavery recorded and transcribed by the Federal Writers' Project during the Depression; the rest of the volume deals with slave narratives published before 1865 and abolition—texts that were, explicitly and implicitly, polemical, discursive acts against human bondage. For although hundreds of Afro-American authors after 1865 published memoirs and autobiographies representing their pre-1865 years of bondage, after 1865 the generic expectations of these autobiographies altered drastically, as did, accordingly, the black autobiographical form itself. Essentially, the slave narrative proper could no longer exist after slavery was abolished. This use of the absolute abolition of slavery as the cut off point for this genre was not made without much debate between us. Questions of intention and context, of course, should not alone be used to define a period or a genre in literary history. The matter of defining this genre is complicated by the many novels, printed before 1865, which *imitate* the form of the slave narrative, and pretend to be first-person accounts of bondage in the South. Though an anathema to the historian, these are the very delight of the literary critic, since they enable him more readily to discern both the repeated structure of the genre itself and the pervasiveness of these texts as literary models. Pastiche or parody, in the strictest sense of imitation or mimesis, depend upon profound familiarity with the parodied original, that is, with the missing term of the simile. For the slave narrative to be used as a model for a novel suggests its widespread literary influence, which we are only just beginning to understand. Accordingly, although an historian may yearn for the sheer purity of the "authentic" tale told by the ex-slave, the literary critic seizes upon the "slave narrative novel" as a sub-genre of American, English, French, and Spanish fiction, and as evidence of intertextual relations of a subtle, yet profound sort. Once fully explicated, these novels will help us to determine if the slave narrative, as a genre of literature, can be identified without our having to resort to the sanctions of factors outside the structure of the texts themselves, factors such as those rules of evidence used so faithfully and rigorously by Marion Wilson Starling and John W. Blassingame. Even these "rules," however, are not fail-safe, as Jean Fagan Yellin's convincing essay on Harriet Jacob's authorship of her own narrative, long a matter of dispute, makes clear.

Beginning with a 1750 review of the case of Job Ben Solomon, and a review of Equiano's narrative published in 1789, in this book we attempt to document the chronological development of these writings about the slave narratives. For the ensuing two hundred years, critics have been aware of, and commented upon, these documents of human bondage. Perhaps the most remarkable facet of the texts of the slaves in the South is the copious corpus of narrative that the black slave wrote "Himself," or "Herself," as the narratives subtitles attest. When, in the history of slavery, have the enslaved reflected upon his own enslavement by "representing" its hideous contours through the spoken and the written arts? Representing the institution of slavery, in the sense of mimesis, implies indictment, but it also implies something of the representativeness of the slave narrator himself vis-à-vis his "experience" of slavery as well as his relationship to other slaves. To the day of his death, for example, Frederick Douglass was fairly popularly known as "The Representative Colored Man of the United States." Just *how* "representative" was Frederick Douglass? The unmentioned term in this Emersonian description, however, was "most"; Douglass apparently was held by his fellows to be most representative, because he was most "presentable." And he was most presentable because of his unqualified abilities as a rhetorical artist. Douglass achieved a form of *presence* through the manipulation of rhetorical structures within a modern language.

We must understand this correlation of language-use and *presence* if we are to begin to learn how to read the slave narrative within what Geoffrey H. Hartman calls its "text-milieu." The slave narrative represents the attempts of blacks to *write themselves into being*. What a curious idea: through the mastery of formal Western languages, the presupposition went, a black person could become a human being by an act of self-creation through the mastery of language. Accused of having no collective history by Hegel in 1813, blacks responded by publishing hundreds of individual histories. As Ellison defined this relationship of the particular to the general, to Steve Cannon, "We tell ourselves our individual stories so as to become aware of our *general* story."

Since the Renaissance in Europe, the act of writing has been considered the visible sign of reason. This association has been consistently invoked in Western aesthetic theory when discussing the enslavement and status of blacks. Writing in *The New Organon* in 1620, Sir Francis Bacon, confronted with the problem of classifying the people of color which a sea-faring Renaissance Europe had discovered, turned to the arts as the ultimate measure of place in nature: "Again," he wrote, "let a man only consider what a difference there is between the life of men in the most civilized province of Europe, and in the wildest and most barbarous districts of New India; he will feel it be great enough to justify the saying that 'man is a god to man,' not only in regard to aid and benefit, but also by comparison of condition. And this difference comes not from soil, not from climate, not from race, but from the arts." Eleven years later, Peter Heylyn, in his *Little Description of the Great World,* used Bacon's formulation to relegate the blacks to a sub-human status. The black African, he wrote, lacked completely "the use of Reason which is peculiar unto man; [he is] of little Wit; and destitute of all arts and sciences; prone to luxury, and for the greatest part Idolators." And all subsequent commentaries on the subject were elaborations upon Heylyn's position.

By 1680, Heylyn's keywords, "Reason" and "Wit," had been reduced to "reading and writing," as Morgan Godwyn's summary of received opinion attests:

> [a] disingenuous and unmanly *Position* had been formed; and privately (*and as it were in the dark*) handed to and again, which is this, That the Negro's though in their Figure they carry some resemblances of manhood, yet are indeed *no* men . . . the consideration of the shape and figure of our *Negro's* Bodies, their Limbs and members; their Voice and Countenance, in all things according with other mens; together with their *Risibility* and *Discourse* (man's *peculiar* Faculties) should be sufficient Conviction. How should they otherwise be capable of *Trades,* and other no less manly imployments; as also of *Reading and Writing,* or show so much Discretion in management of Business; . . . but wherein (we know) that many of our own People are *deficient,* were they not truly Men?

Such a direct correlation of political rights and *literacy* helps us to understand both the transformation of writing into a commodity and the sheer burden of cultural imperatives that both motivated the black slave to seek his text and that defined the "frame" against which each black text would be read. The following 1740 South Carolina statute was concerned with making it impossible for blacks to become literate:

> *And whereas* the having of slaves taught to write, or suffering them to be employed in writing, may be attending with great inconveniences;

> *Be it enacted,* that all and every person and persons whatsoever, who shall hereafter teach, or cause any slave or slaves to be taught to write, or shall use or employ any slave as a scribe in any manner of writing

whatsoever, hereafter taught to write; every such person or persons shall, for every offense, forfeith the sum of one hundred pounds current money.

Learning to read and to write, then, was not only difficult, it was a violation of law. That Frederick Douglass, Thomas Smallwood, William Wells Brown, Moses Grandy, James Pennington, and John Thompson, among numerous others, all made statements about the direct relationship between freedom and discourse only emphasizes the dialectical relation of black text to a "context," defined here as other, racist texts against which the slave's narrative, by definition, was forced to react.

By 1705, William Bosman, a Dutch explorer, had formed Peter Heylyn's bias into a myth, which the Africans he had "discovered" had purportedly related to him. It is curious insofar as it justifies human slavery. According to Bosman, the blacks "tell us that in the beginning God created Black as well as White men; thereby giving the Blacks the first Election, who chose Gold, and left the Knowledge of Letters to the White. God granted their Request, but being incensed at their Avarice, resolved that the Whites should ever be their masters, and they obliged to wait on them as their slaves." Bosman's fabrication, of course, was designed to sanction through mythology a political order created by Europeans. It was David Hume, writing at the mid-point of the eighteenth century, who gave to Bosman's myth the sanction of Enlightenment philosophical reasoning.

In a major essay, "Of National Characters" (1748), Hume discusses the "characteristics" of the major divisions of people in the world. In a footnote added to his original text in 1753, Hume asserted with all of the authority of philosophy, the fundamental relationship among complexion, character, and intellectual capacity:

> I am apt to suspect the negroes, and in general all the other species of men (for there are four or five different kinds) to be naturally inferior to the whites. There never was a civilized nation of any other complexion than white, nor even any individual eminent either in action or speculation. No ingenious manufacturers amongst them, *no arts, no sciences.* . . . Such a uniform and constant difference could not happen, in so many countries and ages, if *nature* had not made our original distinction betwixt these breeds of men. Not to mention our colonies, there are Negroe slaves dispersed all over Europe, of which none ever discovered any symptoms of ingenuity; . . . In Jamaica, indeed they talk of one negro as a man of parts and learning [Francis Williams, the Cambridge-educated poet who wrote verse in Latin]; but 'tis likely he is admired for very slender accomplishments, like a parrot who speaks a few words plainly.

Hume's opinion on the subject, as we might expect, became prescriptive. Writing in 1764 in his *Observations on the Feeling of the Beautiful and the Sublime,* Immanuel Kant elaborates upon Hume's essay in the fourth section entitled "Of National Characteristics, as far as They Depend upon the Distinct Feeling of the Beautiful and Sublime." Kant first claims that "So fundamental is the difference between [the black and white] races of man, and it appears to be as great in regard to mental capacities as in color." He, moreover, is one of the earliest major European philosophers to conflate "color" with "intelligence," a relationship he develops with dictatorial surety. The excerpt bears citation.

> Father Labat reports that a Negro carpenter, whom he reproached for haughty treatment toward his wives, answered: "You whites are indeed fools, for first you make great concessions to your wives, and afterward you complain when they drive you mad." And it might be that there were something in this which perhaps deserved to be considered; but in short, this fellow was *quite black* from head to foot, a clear proof that what he said was *stupid.* (Emphasis added)

Kant refers to the correlation of "blackness" and "stupidity" as if it were self-evident.

What is curious about Kant's correlation of physical and metaphysical characteristics is that traces of this "figure" recur in black texts themselves. I mean by figure the sign of blackness as negation, and the curious, arbitrary, so-called relation between the speaking subject and his common humanity with the European.

Black people responded to these profoundly serious allegations about their "nature" as directly as they could; they wrote books: poetry, autobiographical narrative, political and philosophical discourse were the predominant forms of writing. Among these, autobiographical "deliverance" narratives were the most common, and the most accomplished. Accused of lacking a formal and collective history, blacks published individual histories which, taken together, were intended to narrate, in segments, the larger yet fragmented history of blacks in Africa, then dispersed throughout a cold New World. The narrated, descriptive "eye" was put into service as a literary form to posit both the individual "I" of the black author, as well as the collective "I" of the race. Text created author, and black authors hoped they would create, or re-create, the image of the race in European discourse. The very *face* of the race, representations of whose features were common in all sorts of writings about blacks at that time, was contingent upon the recording of the black *voice*. Voice presupposes a face but also seems to have been thought to determine the contours of the black face.

The recording of an authentic black voice, a voice of deliverance from the deafening discursive silence which an "enlightened" Europe cited as proof of the absence of the African's humanity, was the millennial instrument of transformation through which the African would become the European, the slave become the ex-slave, the brute animal become the human being. So central was this idea to the birth of the black literary tradition in the eighteenth century that four of the first five eighteenth-century slave narratives drew upon the figure of the voice in the text as crucial "scenes of instruction" in the development of the slave on his road to freedom. James Gronniosaw in 1770, John Marrant in 1785, Ottobah Cugoano in 1787, Olaudah Equiano in 1789, and John Jea in 1815, all draw upon the figure of the voice in the text. Gronniosaw's usage is worth quoting here.

> My master used to read prayers in public to the ship's crew every Sabbath day; and when I first saw him read, I was never so surprised in my life, as when I saw the book talk to my master, for I thought it did, as I observed him to look upon it, and move his lips. I wished it would do so with me. As soon as my master had done reading, I followed him to the place where he put the book, being mightily delighted with it, and when nobody saw me, I opened it, and put my ear down close upon it, in great hope that it would say something to me; but I was very sorry, and greatly disappointed, when I found that it would not speak. This thought immediately presented itself to me, that every body and every thing despised me because I was black.

That the figure of the talking book recurs in these four black eighteenth century texts says much about the degree of "intertextuality" in early black letters, more than we heretofore thought. Equally important, however, this figure itself underscores the established correlation between silence and blackness we have been tracing, as well as the urgent need to make the text speak, the process by which the slave marked his distance from the master. The voice in the text was truly a millennial voice for the African person of letters in the eighteenth century, for it was that very voice of deliverance and of redemption which would signify a new order for the black.

Despite the presence of the black voice in the slave's literature, writers intent upon casting aspersion on the "nature" of the black either ignored these texts completely or else criticized them harshly. Thomas Jefferson, Kant, and Hegel provide examples of revisions of Hume's strictures against the public black mind. In "Query XIV" of *Notes on the State of Virginia*, Jefferson maintained that "Never yet could I find that a black had uttered a thought above the level of plain narration, never see even an elementary trait of painting or sculpture." Of Wheatley, the first black to publish a book of poetry in English (Juan Latino, a black slave of Granada, published three volumes of verse in Latin between

1573 and 1576), Jefferson wrote: "Misery is often the parent of the most affecting touches in poetry. Among the blacks is misery enough, God knows, but not poetry. . . . The compositions published under her name are below the dignity of criticism." That same year, Kant, basing his observations on the absence of published writing among blacks, noted (as if it were patently obvious) that "Americans [Indians] and Blacks are lower in their mental capacities than all other races." In 1813 in *The Philosophy of History*, echoing Hume and Kant, Hegel noted the absence of history among black people and derided them for failing to develop texts indigenous to Africa or even to master the art of writing in modern languages.

Hegel's strictures on the African about the absence of "history" presume a crucial role of *memory*, of a collective, cultural memory, in the estimation of a civilization. Metaphors of the "childlike" nature of the slaves, of the masked, puppetlike "personality" of the black, all share this assumption about the absence of memory. Mary Langdon, in her 1855 novel *Ida May; A Story of Things Actual and Possible*, says that "but then they *are* mere children. . . . You seldom hear them say much about anything that's past, if they only get enough to eat and drink at the present moment." Without writing, there could exist no *repeatable* sign of the workings of reason, of mind; without memory or mind, there could exist no history; without history, there could exist no "humanity," as was defined consistently from Vico to Hegel.

This purported connection between the act of writing and the "rights of man" did not escape the notice of the slave. Sojourner Truth, in her frequently quoted speech about Women's Rights, describes her opinions about the relationship in this way:

> "Den dey talks 'bout dis ting in de head—what dis dey call it?" "Intellect," whispered some one near. "Dat's it, honey. What's dat got to do with woman's rights or niggers' rights? If my cup won't hold but a pint an' yours holds a quart, wouldn't yet be mean not to let me have my little half-measure full?"

Nevertheless, it is difficult for us to understand the profound importance that the mastery of literacy had for the slave. Almost all of the narratives refer to literacy in three ways: they recount vividly scenes of instruction in which the narrator learned to read and then to write; they underscore polemical admonishments against statutes forbidding literacy training among black slaves; and they are prefaced by ironic apologia, in which the black author transforms the convention of the author's confession of the faults of his tale, by interweaving into this statement strident denunciation of that system that limited the development of his capacities.

William Wells Brown, in a lecture delivered in 1847 before the Female Anti-Slavery Society of Salem, said that

> If you have not liked my grammar, recollect that I was born and brought up under an institution, where, if an individual was found teaching me, he would have been sent to the State's prison. Recollect that you have come here tonight to hear a Slave, and not a man, according to the laws of the land; and if the Slave has failed to interest you, charge it not to the race, charge it not the colored people, but charge it to the blighting influence of Slavery,—that institution that has made me property, . . .

Rather cleverly, accepted convention and indictment merged, in one rhetorical act.

Reading and writing was no mean thing in the life of the slave. Learning to read and write meant that this person of African descent took one giant step up the Great Chain of Being; the "thing" became a human being. No one puts this more aptly than Thomas Smallwood, in his 1851 slave narrative, which even the most diligent historians have forgotten.

> When that [ability to read and spell] became known to his neighbours they were amazed at the fact that a black or coloured person could learn the Alphabet, yea, learn to spell in two syllables. I appeared to be a walking curiosity in the village where I then lived, and when passing about the village I would be called into houses, and the neighbors collected around to hear me say the Alphabet and to spell baker and cider, to their great surprise, (which were the first two words in the two syllables of Webster's Spelling Book). This may afford the reader a glimpse into the abyss of intellectual darkness into which the African race in America has been so long purposely confined, to serve the avarice and envies of their tyrannical oppressors, and to get out of which, by the aid of their friends, they are now struggling against many obstacles; prejudice on the part of the whites being among the most potent.

The pervasiveness of this equation of the rights of man with the ability to write affected those vehemently opposed to slavery. In 1832, an essayist for William Lloyd Garrison's *Liberator*, a journal started the year before expressly to agitate for the abolition of slavery, wrote that "till [the blacks] are equal to other people in knowledge and cultivation, they will not and cannot rank as equals." Emerson, speaking in 1844 on the Anniversary of the Emancipation of Haiti, summarized the challenge facing blacks determined to end their own enslavement: Nature, he said,

> deals with men after the same manner. If they are rude and foolish, down they must go. When at last in a race a new principle appears, an idea— *that* conserves it; ideas only save races. If the black man is feeble and not important to the existing races, not on a parity with the best race, the black

man must serve, and be exterminated. But if the black man carries in his bosom an indispensable element of a new and coming civilization, for the sake of that element, he will survive and play his part. . . .

This "idea," of course, could be communicated only in written form.

Without his own written "idea," a slave was a "thing." We tend to read assertions such as this as metaphors; no metaphor, however, could have such deleteriously literal effects, enjoying the sanction of law. Harriet Beecher Stowe, we sometimes forget, submitted to the *National Era* in 1851 the first chapter of her novel entitled *Uncle Tom's Cabin or The Man that Was a Thing*. These black objects could become subjects only through expression of the will to power as the will to write. As Ishmael Reed says in *Flight to Canada*, the slave who was the first to read and write was the first to run away.

Calvin Fairbanks, in his *Autobiography*, presents an anecdote that helps to explain this relationship between the absence of selfhood and enslavement.

> It was a morning in April, sharp, crisp and clear, and we were rounding a bend in the Ohio River just below Wheeling when I caught sight of a strapping darky, an ax flung over his shoulder, jogging along on the Virginia bank of the river, singing as he went.
>
> "De cold, frosty morning make a niggah feel good,
> Wid de ax on de shoulder he go jogging to de wood."
>
> "Halloo, there! Where are you going?" I called to him. "Gwine choppin in de woods!" "Chopping for yourself?"
> "*Han't got no self.*"
> "Slave, are you?"
> "Dat's what I is."
> (Emphasis added)

Marion W. Chapman, in a letter to Mary A. Estlin, discusses the relationship between the use of language and human identity. "It is a dangerous doctrine that it lay aside any of its armour in order to be more at home in the world," she wrote. "But to lay aside the *sword* of the spirit, which is the word—a man," she concludes, "makes himself *no-body* who does it." It is the presence made valid by the immediacy of the voice that Chapman is talking about. In *Past and Present* Thomas Carlyle wrote,

> This speaking man whom have we to compare with him? . . . The Speaking Function, this of Truth, coming to us with a living voice, nay, in a living shape, and as a concrete practical exemplar; this, with all our Writing and Printing Functions, has a perennial place. . . .

Douglass, echoing Carlyle, speaks of "the living human voice" as that which is required to speak against the evils of slavery.

This relationship between "voice" and "face," appears frequently in nineteenth-century writings; it is an idea received from the Enlightenment. Bronson Alcott wrote in his *Journal* in 1847 that "Our friend the fugitive" possesses "many of the elements of the hero. His stay with us has given image and a name to the dire entity of slavery," bringing before us "the wrongs of the black man and his tale of woes." Austin Seward, a slave narrator, wrote that he "sends out this history," his *Twenty-Two Years a Slave and Forty Years a Freeman*, "presenting as it were [my] *own body*, with the marks and scars of the tender mercies of the slave drivers upon it, . . ." It was the face of the race that the slave narrators painted, so as to give it a voice, Gronniosaw's voice in the text. It is this notion of the presence of voice and self-creation through representation, transferred to writing through the metaphor of voice, which motivated the ex-slaves to produce hundreds of testimonies of their enslavement, rendered in painstaking verisimilitude.

There are well over one hundred book-length slave narratives, authorized and documented, printed and reviewed by proponents of the abolition of slavery in England and America, France and Germany, Cuba and Brazil. The documentation of these, moreover, occurred *during* slavery. Also we now have authoritative texts of the oral and written testimony of thousands of ex-slaves, recorded between 1865 and 1940. But the slave narratives of which I speak were written and published as a *genre* before slavery was legally abolished in the United States. Why, then, have contemporary historians and, recently, literary scholars felt the need to "resurrect" these "lost" texts, and to employ them, for the first time as data and evidence in the writing of history and as objects of literary explication and interpretation?

As late as 1939, an historian, John S. Kendall in response to his own rhetorical question, "What was it like to be a slave?" could answer only that:

> We do not know. The slaves themselves never told. There were always . . . negroes who had secured their freedom. . . . But they had no literary gift. If they were capable of self-analyses to the degree of distinguishing their sentiments in one estate from those in the other, they have omitted to set down the result in writing. Still less have we the story of a slave—of a slave who was nothing but a slave.

Kendall did not know his historiography. By 1939 a number of historians had drawn upon the narratives of ex-slaves as historical data, despite the powerful strictures against their credibility rendered by the historian's historian, Ulrich B. Phillips. In 1918, Phillips wrote in *American Negro Slavery* that "books of this class are generally of dubious value." In his *Life and Labor in the Old South* (1929), Phillips expanded his opposition to the historian's use of the narratives: "ex-slave narratives in general," he polemicized, "were issued with so much abolitionist editing that as a class their authenticity is doubtful."

Despite Phillips's claims against the "authenticity" of the slave narrative, however, a few scholars not only argued for its use in history making, but they also employed it as evidence. Among these historians and their works are: James Ford Rhodes, *History of the United States from the Compromise of 1850* (1904); Harrison A. Trexler, *Slavery in Missouri, 1804-1865* (1914); Frederick Bancroft, *Slave-Trading in the Old South* (1941); and J. Winston Coleman, Jr., *Slavery Times in Kentucky* (1940). Marion Wilson Starling's 1946 dissertation, not published until 1982, led directly to Kenneth Stampp's use of the narratives in his *The Peculiar Institution: Slavery in the Ante-Bellum South* (1956), which in turn perhaps influenced Chase C. Mooney's use in *Slavery in Tennessee* (1957). Benjamin A. Botkin's essay on the results of the collection of the oral narratives by the Federal Writers' Project, entitled "The Slave as His Own Interpreter" (1944), and Richard Hofstadter's splendid refutation of "U. B. Phillips and the Plantation Legend" (1944), were works which have informed all historical debate about the status of the narrative since the end of World War II, as has Carter G. Woodson's careful review of Botkin's *Lay My Burden Down*. Despite dozens of articles published since 1945, as late as 1970, Howard Zinn, in *The Politics of History*, could still deem it urgent to call for a "slave-oriented" history of slavery, in which evidence would be "drawn from the narratives of fugitive slaves." Despite two important attempts to re-create slavery from the vantage point of the slave (I refer here to Charles H. Nichols's *Many Thousand Gone: The Ex-Slaves' Account of Their Bondage and Freedom* (1963) and Stanley Feldstein's *Once A Slave; The Slave's View of Slavery* (1971)), it was not until John W. Blassingame published *The Slave Community; Plantation Life in the Ante-Bellum South* (1972) and George P. Rawick Published from *Sundown to Sunup; The Making of the Black Community* (1972) that Zinn's call for a profoundly revised account of slavery was responded to in fine and sustained detail.

It is to record this adventure in the interpretation of slavery, always of interest to the literary critic, and to resurrect from the footnotes of the historians some of the more crucial pieces in the puzzle of slave historiography, that we have edited this book. We have brought together arguments among the historians with accounts of the structure of the narratives by literary critics in order to emphasize that—*whatever their "veracity"*—

the narratives of ex-slaves are, for the literary critic, the very generic foundation which most subsequent Afro-American fictional and non-fictional narrative forms extended, refigured, and troped. This is as true of Booker T. Washington's *Up from Slavery* and of *The Autobiography of Malcolm X* as it is of Zora Neale Hurston's *Their Eyes Were Watching God,* Richard Wright's *Black Boy,* and Ralph Ellison's *Invisible Man.* Ishmael Reed's novel, *Flight to Canada,* a formal parody or a structural signification upon the conventions of the slave narrative, makes this implicit literary relationship apparent. As many of the literary critics included here argue, the Afro-American literary tradition, and especially its canonical texts, rests on the framework built, by fits and starts and for essentially polemical intentions, by the first-person narratives of black ex-slaves. This is curious for literary history—where else is such the case?

Literary scholars have analyzed the narratives extensively. John Herbert Nelson in 1926, in what without casting aspersion we may call a racist text, devotes one full chapter of *The Negro Character in American Literature* to "The Heroic Fugitive." Lorenzo Dow Turner in 1929 called slave narrative "the index of [the slaves'] inner life, and of their habits of thought." And Vernon Loggins in 1931 in *The Negro Author and His Development in America* not only undertook and completed much of the detailed and restorative bibliographical research needed to establish the texts and variants of the slave narrative, but also included in his impeccably compiled bibliography fictional slave narratives. Out of a silent past, Loggins resurrected the texts of scores of narratives printed before 1865. Indeed, Loggins's chapters of analysis of the slave narrative no doubt influenced the Federal Writers' Project which collected the oral narratives of living ex-slaves. That well-known and controversial project (directed by the Folklore Division of the Federal Writers' Project rather than the Project's Office of Negro Affairs) is the oral counterpart of Loggins's establishment of the written texts. We reprint in this anthology Sterling A. Brown's memorandum on the transcription of language in these interviews, which is the thoughts of a master poet whose works were informed by black vernacular language patterns.

Brown's refined literary sensibility, his distinguished place in black literary history, and his repeated praise of the narrative as a genre no doubt account in part for three successive dissertations on the slave narrative as literature, completed at major universities between 1946 and 1954. Marion Wilson Starling at New York University, Charles H. Nichols at Brown, and Margaret Young Jackson at Cornell, all analyzed the slave narrative as literature in their dissertations in English literature. And Arna Bontemps's critical and fictional work, done between 1940 and 1970, also contributed much to bringing to the attention of creative critics and writers the conventions of the narratives as history, folklore, literature, and data for the social sciences. The slave narrative, then, has withstood the exigencies so often fatal to occasional genres of literature, and it continues to enjoy its unique status as textual evidence of the self-consciousness of the ex-slave and as the formal basis upon which an entire narrative tradition has been constructed.

The Slave's Narrative

1. Written By Themselves: Views and Reviews, 1750-1861

The writings of the once enslaved, of the captive and his or her boldly effected escape, have long enjoyed an especial readership in Western cultures. Arna Bontemps compares the genre of black slave narratives to that of the Western; he could just as appropriately have compared the genre to detective fiction. The recently published narratives of the Iranian hostages, the detailed and impassioned stories of the American citizens imprisoned in Iran, are merely generic extensions of the slave narratives, which, in turn, were fundamentally related structurally to the Indian captivity tale, so popular in the late seventeenth- and early eighteenth-centuries, some of which have been collected by Richard Van der Beets in *Held Captive by Indians: Selected Narratives, 1642-1836.*

This section of our book reprints several reviews of slave narratives to begin to recreate a sense of the critical reception these books received at the time of publication, and a sense of their role in the anti-slavery struggle. As many of these attest, the writings of the slaves were used to prove the common humanity and the intellectual capacities that persons of African descent shared with Europeans and Americans. Because of this polemical use of the narratives, many of these reviews appear in anti-slavery newspapers, such as *The Liberator,* edited by William Lloyd Garrison in Boston between 1831 and 1865. Moreover, as the two reviews of James Williams's narrative attest, the veracity of the slave's narrative was an object of close scrutiny by friend and foe alike. It was as important that the slave wrote his or her own story, as it was that that story was true. From the 1750 account of Job Ben Solomon's release from slavery because of James Oglethorpe's discovery of his literacy in Arabic, to the 1861 review of the narrative of Harriet Jacobs ("Linda Brent"), which Jean Yellin's essay printed in Part Four demonstrates to be authentic, these reviews—a tiny sample of scores of others—reveal the extensive interest of the reading public in the formal uses of language by the black slave.

The Life of Job Ben Solomon

ANONYMOUS

Job Ben Solomon was a person of great distinction in his own country. In the year 1731, as he was driving his herds of cattle across the countries in Jagra, he was seized and carried to Joar, where he was sold to capt. *Pyke,* commander of the ship *Arabella,* who carried him to *Maryland,* and sold him to a planter. Here *Job* lived about a year without being once beat by his master; at the end of which he had the good fortune to have a letter of his own writing in the *Arabic* tongue conveyed to *England.* This letter coming to the hand of Mr. *Oglethorpe,* he sent it to *Oxford* to be translated; the translation pleased him so much, and gave him so good an opinion of the man, that he directly ordered him to be bought from his master. But soon after setting out for *Georgia,* before he returned from thence, *Job* was brought to *England;* where waiting on the learned *Sir Hans Sloane,* he was found to be a perfect master of the *Arabic* tongue, by translating several manuscripts and inscriptions upon medals into *English,* of which he had acquired a competent knowledge during his servitude and passage to *England;* this gentle man recommended him to his grace the duke of *Montagu,* who being pleased with the sweetness of humour and mildness of temper, as well as genius and capacity of the man, introduced him to court, where he was graciously received by the royal family, and most of the nobility, from whom he received distinguishing marks of favour.

After he had continued in *England* about fourteen months, he wanted much to return to his native country and his father, to whom he sent letters from *England.* He received many valuable presents from Q. *Caroline,* the D. of *Cumberland,* the D. of *Montagu,* the E. of *Pembroke,* several ladies of quality, Mr. *Holden,* and the royal *African* company, who ordered their agents to show him the greatest respects. He arrived safe in *Africa;* and Mr. *Moor* in *his travels* met with, and gives some farther account of him.

Gentleman's Magazine Vol. XX (1750) 272

The Interesting Narrative of the Life of Olaudah Equiano, or Gustavus Vassa, the African; Written by Himself.

ANONYMOUS

We entertain no doubt of the general authenticity of this very intelligent African's interesting story; though it is not improbable that some English writer has assisted him in the compilement, or, at least, the correction of his book: for it is sufficiently well written. The narrative wears an honest face: and we have conceived a good opinion of the man, from the artless manner in which he has detailed the variety of adventures and vicissitudes which have fallen to his lot. His publication appears very seasonably, at a time when negroe-slavery is the subject of public investigation; and it seems calculated to increase the odium that hath been excited against the West-India planters, on account of the cruelties that some of them are said to have exercised on their slaves; many instances of which are here detailed.

The sable author of these volumes appears to be a very sensible man; and he is, surely, not the less worthy of credit from being a convert to Christianity. He is a Methodist; and has filled many pages, toward the end of his work, with accounts of his dreams, visions, and divine impulses; but all this, supposing him to have been under any delusive influence, only serves to convince us that he is guided by principle; and that he is not one of those poor converts who, having undergone the ceremony of baptism, have remained content with that portion, only, of the Christian Religion: instances of which are said to be almost innumerable in America, and the West-Indies. Gustavus Vassa appears to possess a very different character; and, therefore, we heartily wish success to his publication, which we are glad to see has been encouraged by a very respectable subscription.

Monthly Review Vol. 80 (June 1789), 551-2.

The Life and Adventures of a Fugitive Slave

ANONYMOUS

Slavery in the United States: a narrative of the life and adventures of Charles Ball, a black man, who lived forty years in Maryland, South Carolina, and Georgia, as a slave, under various masters, and was one year in the navey with Commodore Barney during the late year. Containing an account of the manners and usages of the planters and slaveholders of the South, a description of the condition and treatment of the slaves, with observations upon the state of morals amongst the perils and sufferings of a fugitive slave, who twice escaped from the cotton country.

It has sometimes been made a question whether more truth can be communicated in real or fictitious narrative. The latter, certainly, has the advantage of selecting from a wider field of incident, and though its facts may none of them have ever actually occurred, yet they may be more strictly analogous to the great body of those which do actually occur, than the events in the life of almost any one individual. Sometimes, however, an individual is found whose history, unaided by fiction, correctly illustrates the history of his class. Through the well written life of such an individual, we can look in upon the character, condition and habits of his class with as much clearness and confidence as through a window. The fictitious narrative may afford us a view of the same objects, equally distinct and vivid, but after all it is only a mirror, and may leave upon the mind a doubt whether it has not practiced some distortion as well as reflection upon the direct rays of truth. Whether the narrative, whose very prolix title we have placed above, is real or fictitious, we think its reader will not retain, through many pages, a doubt of the perfect accuracy of its picture of slavery. If it is a mirror, it is of the very best plate glass, in which objects appear so clear and "natural" that the beholder is perpetually mistaking it for an open window without any glass at all. We are led to this remark, not because we feel ourselves at liberty to doubt the genuineness and reality of the whole, but because the book itself does not answer a number of preliminary questions which the public will not fail to ask.

Of the plan of the work we cannot give the reader a better idea than by quoting from its preface.

"The narrative is taken from the mouth of the adventurer himself"; and if the copy does not contain the identical words of the original, the sense and import, at least, are faithfully preserved.

Many of his opinions have been cautiously omitted, or carefully suppressed, as being of no value to the reader; and his sentiments upon the subject of slavery have not been embodied in this work. The design of the writer, who is no more than the recorder of facts detailed to him by another, has been to render the narrative as simple, and the style of the story as plain, as the laws of the language would permit. To introduce the reader, as it were, to a view of the cotton fields, and exhibit, not to his imagination, but to his very eyes, the mode of life to which the slaves on the southern plantations must conform, has been the primary object of the compiler.

"The book has been written without fear or prejudice, and no opinions have been consulted in its composition. The sole view of the writer has been to make the citizens of the United States acquainted with each other, and to give a faithful portrait of the manners, usages, and customs of the southern people, so far as those manners, usages, and customs have fallen under the observation of a common negro slave, imbued by nature with a tolerable portion of intellectual capacity. The more reliance is to be placed upon his relations of those things that he saw in the southern country, when it is recollected that he had been born and brought up in a part of the state of Maryland, in which, of all others, the spirit of the 'old aristocracy,' as it has not unaptly been called, retained much of its pristine vigor in his youth; and where he had an early opportunity of seeing many of the most respectable, best educated, and most enlightened families of both Maryland and Virginia."

It is due to the writer to say, and perhaps a higher compliment could not be paid him, that he has accomplished his very important and difficult object, in a manner that would have done credit to the author of Robinson Crusoe. He has traced his hero through all the vicissitudes of slavery, with a minuteness of detail that is truly astonishing, while at the same time the interest of his narrative is ever fresh and growing. The book is not merely readable. It has charm and potency about it. It is one of those books which always draws the reader on by the irresistible magnetism of the next paragraph to the unwelcome appearance of "The end." It may be supposed that we speak as a partizan; however this may be, the book is not a partizan book. Though it comments with just severity upon some of the atrocities of slavery, it broaches no theory in regard to it, nor proposes any mode of time of emancipation. While it does not strive to palliate or conceal any of the dark things, it fairly displays those flashes of sunbeam, which are sometimes called the bright side of slavery, but which are in reality only the kindly workings of human nature, bursting out in spite of slavery. We rejoice in the book the more, because it is not a partizan work. An abolitionist, if he were to be sent through the southern states, with safe conduct, and full of power to investigate, would, of course, be so much alive to the bitter evils of slavery, that he would be apt to search them out and note them down, to the exclusion of those alleviating ingredients, with which God's blessed constitution of things always strives to sweeten the cup of human woe. On the other hand, an anti-abolitionist, whose theory binds him to set down to *the credit of slavery* every particle of happiness, or even common comfort, of which he may find the slave possessed, would be filled so full with the discovery of good fruit, that he would find no time or disposition to look beneath the surface, into the working of the iron machinery of motive, which, for the most part, animates the system of southern labor. Our narrator has much better satisfied the demands of truth, by exhibiting both the inside and the out,—by showing the worm at the root of the tree, and the consequently diseased and rotting condition of the trunk, and the green leaves which nevertheless continue to adorn and comfort its branches. There is a common sense consistency in his whole picture, which shows us a giant sin battling against the impregnable bulwarks of God's pain; it is not the creation of an over-enthusiastic brain, in which we see God dishonored by the complete triumph of that sin. . . .

Believing, as we have privately good reason to do, that this book contains, in the language of a faithful interpreter, a true narrative which has fallen from the lips of a veritable fugitive, we have only to regret that there is not an appendix of some sort, containing some documentary evidence to that effect.

Quarterly Anti-Slavery Magazine Vol. I, No. IV (1836), 375-393.

Narrative of James Williams

ANONYMOUS

Amid the strange characteristics of mankind, no one of their moral features is more unaccountable than their complex credulity in some cases, and in others, their marvellous unbelief. This general position is illus-

trated in an astonishing manner, upon the subject of slavery. It seems as
if our northern citizens had determined to resist all evidence respecting
the practical concerns of slaveholding, until they are ocularly convinced,
while they have resolved never to witness *Life in the Negro Quarters*. It
is yet more perplexing, that many of our anti-slavery friends are incredu-
lous respecting the facts which are stated by professed eye-witnesses,
and the few competent narrators of slavery as it exists in our country.
Thus the only citizens, who personally know what slavery is from their
own observation, and who are sufficiently independent to disclose the
truth, are not only disbelieved, but are suspected of untruth, or re-
proached with falsehood, by the silly statement—"I will not believe it;
it cannot be true."

I select one instance, out of many others which might be adduced.
The notorious facts—that is, *notorious in Virginia*—which are detailed
in Bourne's *Picture of Slavery*, have been told by him in many places for
more than twenty years past, as exact delineations of slaveholding society, as he himself witnessed it. Some of these facts were publicly admitted as the ordinary traits and operations of slavery in Virginia, twenty
years ago, by slaveholders themselves, in the General Assembly of the
Presbyterian Church; as Thomas Shipley frequently attested, who used
to declare, that they were true by the acknowledgement of the parties;
and yet many of our anti-slavery friends either doubt or deny the authenticity of those statements, and impeach the veracity of the historian.

One circumstance will elucidate this point. It was at the time when
the American Anti-Slavery Convention met in Philadelphia, December,
1833, if I am not mistaken. Amos A. Phelps mentioned the mode of torturing slaves by whipping them, and then tearing them with the *claws of
a cat!* John C. Whittier requested Mr. Phelps not to tell that story, for
nobody would believe it. When our friend Whittier afterward saw the
same fact stated as undeniable on Page 130 of the *Picture of Slavery*, he
doubted whereunto that thing would grow. After having heard James
Williams tell the same story, and after having recorded it in his own
graphical painting, in the fifty-second page of his *Narrative of James
Williams*, it is worthy of inquiry, whether the poet thinks the heart-
rending tale is now fit to be told and meriting belief.

The testimony in the case is more remarkable, because the fact which
Mr. Bourne relates, occurred in Virginia before Williams was born; and
the murder which the latter unfolds happened in Alabama in 1834;
twenty years after the story in *The Picture of Slavery* was first told, and
even after thousands of that volume had been scattered throughout New
England.

There is a circumstance related on pages 61, 62, 63, and 64, respecting the murderous scourging of a young woman, which, it is alleged, cannot be true. But a similar tale is narrated in the *Picture of Slavery*, page 122, and the latter can be verified by the Clerk of the Court of Rockingham County, Virginia, if he will give the record concerning the case. The latter story was denied by two Doctors of Divinity in the General Assembly of the Presbyterian Church in 1818, who both declared, that they had never heard of that fact; although it happened in the same county where two brothers of one of them resided, and he as well knew of that murder and trial, as he knew that he himself was a slave-driver.

The *Narrative of James Williams* is an important addition to the documentary evidence representing the secrets of the slaveholder's prison-houses, which cannot be more accurately described than in the language of holy scripture—Psalms 71:20: "dark places of the earth, full of the habitations of cruelty." Mr. Birney has avowed his disbelief of the *Narrative of James Williams,* from his own acquaintance with Alabama; and so many persons can be adduced to testify to the accuracy of his statements respecting Virginia, that I am convinced no man of any class will dare to contradict him; except in points where his ignorance of letters renders a mistake almost unavoidable.

One great advantage which will follow from the publication of the *Narrative of James Williams* is this: it will aid to destroy the scepticism which so much prevails upon this subject. It is an invincible argument in favor of our common Christianity, that the apostles preached through Jesus, the resurrection of the dead, in spite of prisons, beating, shame, and threatened stoning. Now the testimony of some of our original anti-slavery brethren was given amid persecution, which, for twenty years, has been as unrelenting as it has been continual. Why, therefore, shall the testimony be discredited? A few more such personal narratives as the life and experiences of James Williams will render the boasted "southern domestic institutions" as loathsome, as they are cruelly malignant and criminal.

There is nothing in the *Narrative of James Williams* which more convinces me that he has exhibited the scenes that he actually witnessed, than his portraiture of "the wife of Master George." No slave could have depicted such a complex and contradictory creature, if he had not closely watched the living reality. One fact alone is so striking, that its strangeness, improbability, . . . determines the truth of the history.

I have no doubt that multitudes of northern women will be ready to cast away the whole book as a fiction, from disgust at the account, which Williams gives of *"the wife of Master George,"* page 36, and of her girl Frances. The *Narrative* says—"I have seen her take her by the ear, lead her up to the side of the room, and beat her against it. At other times, she would snatch off her shoe, and strike the girl on her head and face with it." There are persons in New York who have often seen that lady-like mischief executed; and the manner in which the slipper or shoe was pulled off the foot for the sake of battering the slave's face, was not the least memorable part of the slave-driving show!

Now I maintain that no *man* could have invented that story; and more, I am convinced that the notion never entered the head of any northern young woman, single or married, to take off her shoe, and smite the head and face of a female domestic with it, until she was tired of her own inhumanity. The *Narrative of James Williams*, therefore, is incontrovertibly true; and is additionally valuable, because it so powerfully corroborates other evidence and facts which have been published. I hope that it will be universally read, and although I presume the names are not accurately spelt yet the parties will easily be identified. One thing is certain; some of the persons designated by Williams, were so living as described by him at the periods and in the places specified; whence it may be presumed that he is not mistaken respecting the barbarous functions of a slave-driver.

The Liberator VIII (9 March 1838), 39.

Narrative of James Williams

ANONYMOUS

A wide circulation has been given by the Abolition papers to a narrative of a person calling himself James Williams, filled with statements of the most inflammatory and improbable character, in relation to the owners of slaves, at the South. We regretted the diffusion of this libel, as we do that of every publication calculated, like it, to excite angry feelings among our Southern brethren, and thus obstruct that union among good men in all quarters of the Union in philanthropic enterprises of a practical character. We also regarded the circulation of such a paper by the Abolitionists as being exceedingly impolitic, on the assumption that they sincerely desire the cooperation of the South in the extinction of slavery; for surely nothing has a less tendency to that result than accusations of the most atrocious description against Southern citizens. We abstained, however, from animadverting [sic] on the narrative, and therefore did not notice the official admission of its falsehood; which, after a considerable interval, and then not very cordially, was made by the Executive Committee of the Anti-Slavery Society.

It was with utter amazement that we observed, the other day, in the "Philanthropist," the leading Abolition newspaper in the West, published at Cincinnati, by the Executive Committee of the Ohio Anti-Slavery Society, advertisements, under date of May 7 and May 21, 1839, of the renowned narrative for sale. Among the works advertised in the "Philanthropist" of that date for sale, "at the Ohio Anti-Slavery Depository," is the "Authentic Narrative of James Williams, an American Slave"!! As the Abolitionists are thus active in circulating what they have, in the most formal and solemn manner, repudiated as false and libellous, we deem it due to truth and justice to copy the official statement referred to. It is as follows:

(From the *Emancipator*) Statement authorized by the Executive Committee

About three months ago, the Executive Committee of the American Anti-Slavery Society appointed the undersigned a special committee to investigate, and report on, certain allegations, published, together with the testimony to support them in the Alabama *Beacon,* against the credibility of the "Narrative of James Williams." This they have done with the most cautious circumspection, inasmuch as the party whose veracity was called in question was absent from the country, and his aid in the investigation could not be had. The investigation was given to the public in the *Emancipator* of August 30th. It will be remembered that the objections taken were not so much to the force and applicableness of the testimony as to the loose and suspicious form in which it was presented in the *Beacon.* The material bearing much of it was denied, provided the actual entity and the credibility of the witnesses (of which the committee knew nothing) could be made to appear, in such a manner as to remove from them all reasonable ground of doubt or impeachment.

That the editor of the *Beacon* might be advertised of what—in the eyes of others less excited by the subject than he appeared to be—was wanting to his testimony, the deficiencies were pointed out, and an opportunity thus afforded him of correcting any error, or supplying any omission, that might have occurred in the preparation of his cause.

Immediately on the publication of the statement, the undersigned individually addressed letters of enquiry to between forty and fifty persons residing in Virginia, Alabama, and elsewhere. Some of the letters were written in such a manner as not to disclose to those to whom they were directed the object of the writers in seeking the information requested, or their connection with the anti-slavery cause. Where these letters have been answered at all, it has been done, as it is thought, without any knowledge, on the part of the respondents possessed by the undersigned, to show that full confidence may be reposed in the sincerity with which their answers have been given. Other letters were written to persons who were made fully acquainted with the object of the writers and their anti-slavery connection. Where those have been replied to, it has been done in a manner not only equivocal and direct, but respectful and courteous.

Letters have been received from the following persons in Virginia: From Dr. John Brockenbrough, who has resided in Richmond forty years, and been long and extensively known as among the most respectable and intelligent of its citizens.

From John Ruthford, Esq. Mr. R. was born in Richmond, and has resided there ever since, with the exception of two or three years years spent at Princeton College, where he was a classmate and friend of one of the Committee, and where he was considered, in every way, a young man of unusual worth. It is believed that he has maintained this character in his native place unimpeached up to this time.

From Thomas Miller, Esq., two letters have been received. It will be remembered that two communications from Mr. M. appeared in the *Beacon.* It was in this that the committee first became acquainted with his name. They take pleasure in stating—and in doing it explicitly—that they have ascertained, from various sources, that Mr. M. is not only all he represented himself to be in the communications referred to, but that, in Virginia, his standing is very high, as an upright and intelligent citizen.

From Hon. John Scott, judge of the sixth circuit court, residing in Fauquier County.

From William J. Dance, clerk of Powhattan County Court.

From James Roy Micou, clerk of Essex County Court.

From James R. Micou, father of the one last mentioned.

From John L. Pendleton, clerk of Caroline County Court.

The Committee know no reason for impeaching or suspecting the testimony of these witnesses, apart from the fact that they are slaveholders, and interested in the system whose enormities are exposed in the narrative.

The Committee abstain from any detail touching the credibility of the greater part of the narrative that would unnecessarily protract this statement. They will only present the substance of the testimony furnished by the letters above cited.

1. There is an estate in Powhattan County, of but little value, called Mount Pleasant, but it has not been owned or possessed, in the memory of the existing generation, by any one bearing the name of Larrimore, or any other name resembling Larrimore.

2. No such man as the Larrimore described in the narrative, or any other

of that name, has been known, at any time, to have resided either in Powhattan County, or in any of the neighboring counties or in Richmond, either in summer or winter. There is but one family named Larimer (none named Larrimore) known as having resided in Virginia. This consists of two brothers only; one of them, a few years back, removed to Florida; the other is George T. F. Larimer, of Essex County—the same whose letter was published in the *Beacon*.

3. There has been no intermarriage between the Larrimores and Roanes, Brochenbroughs or Scotts, for the last fifty years, if ever.

4. The late Mr. Brochenbrough, of Charlottesville, never held a slave who was brother to James Williams.

5. Neither John Smoot, described in the narrative as a planter of Powhattan, nor John Green and Benjamin Temple, as administrators on the estate of the elder Larrimore; nor John Gatewood, as the master of Williams' wife, and as living about four miles from Mount Pleasant, are known as having at any time resided in said country or elsewhere.

6. Neither is such a man as Stephen Ransdel known ever to have resided in Caroline County.

7. Nor has John Scott, a respectable merchant of many years' standing in Fredericksburg, ever resided in Richmond.

There is but little, if anything, set forth in the narrative, and denied in the letters, that can fairly be considered as matters merely of opinion, about which a person of hasty or weak judgement might have expected unconsciously to err. The statements are of facts on the one side, met by absolute denials misrepresented, is placed beyond all doubt. The committee, called on, in the discharge of their duty, to say which, in coming to a decision, have scrupulously guarded themselves against the influence of the prevailing prejudice, which would lead them to decide, of course, or hastily, against a black, where his testimony was contradicted by a white. Thus prepared, as they feel themselves to be, for impartially weighing all the circumstances of the case, they have been drawn fully to the conclusion that the statements in the narrative so far as they are cited above, and contradicted by the writers of the letters, are wholly false, and therefore they cannot with propriety ask for the confidence of the community in any of the statements contained in the narrative.

Without waiting longer for answers to letters that have been addressed to several persons in Alabama, the undersigned presented, at the last meeting of the Executive Committee, a report in accordance with the opinion expressed above—whereupon, it was

Resolved, that the said special committee prepare, as soon as may be, a statement in relation to said narrative, to be inserted in the *Emancipa-*

tor; and that the publishing agent be directed to discontinue the sale of the work.

In accordance with this resolution the foregoing statement is submitted.

James G. Birney
Lewis Tappan, Committee

African Repository Vol. XV, No. 10 (June 1839), 161-66.

The Narrative of Juan Manzano

ANONYMOUS

Poems by a Slave in the Island of Cuba, recently liberated; translated from the Spanish, by R.R. Madden, M.D.; with the History of the Early Life of the Negro Poet, written by himself to which are prefixed Two Pieces descriptive of Cuban Slavery and the Slave-Traffic, by R.R.M.

We opened this volume rather from curiosity than with any great expectation that the verses of a Cuban slave would possess much poetical merit. *Not* indeed that we are converts to the philosophy that He who made of one blood all nations to dwell upon the earth, created the inhabitants of one quarter of the globe with such inferior powers of intellect that, like brute animals, they were intended only to be the thralls of their more favored brethren. Mr. Lawrence, in his infidel Lectures on Physiology, attempted to prove that a negro "cannot be a religious animal;" or vie either in morals or intellect with "the white varieties of mankind." To suppose so, he says, would be "as unreasonable as to expect that the greyhound may be taught to hunt by scent like the hound, or the mastiff rival in talents and acquirements the sagacious and docile poodle." And as for religion, the well-meant labours of missionaries must be futile; for "organization is too strong for Christianity." And yet, if it were true, as he contends, that the notion that mankind possess souls,— an immaterial, immortal principle,—is a fable; the unconverted African would really shew his good sense, not his stolidity, in not embracing a

faith of which this is an essential element. We, however, who believe
that God has given to all the tribes of mankind both souls and brains,
see nothing to prevent negroes being either Christians or philosophers.
The Abbé Gregoire wrote a book, in which he shewed, by a great number of examples, that the African race, notwithstanding the many disadvantages under which they have so long laboured, have produced
many men of considerable genius; and we well remember the reply of
Dr. Beattie to Hume, who had maintained the same opinion as his
brother infidel Lawrence. He said:

> Mr. Hume argues nearly in the same manner, in regard to the supe-
> riority of white men over black. His assertions are strong, but I know
> not whether they have anything else to recommend them. The inhabit-
> ants of Great Britain and France were as savage two thousand years
> ago, as those of Africa and America are at this day. To civilize a nation
> is a work which it requires long time to accomplish; and one may as
> well say of an infant that he can never become a man, as of a nation
> now barbarous, that it never can be civilized. That a Negro Slave who
> can neither read nor write, nor speak any European language, who is
> not permitted to do anything but what his master commands, and who
> has not a single friend on earth, but is universally considered and
> treated as if he were of a species inferior to the human; that such a
> creature should so distinguish himself among Europeans, as to be talked
> of through the world as a man of genius, is surely no reasonable expecta-
> tion. To suppose him of an inferior species, because he does not thus
> distinguish himself, is just as rational as to suppose any private Euro-
> pean of an inferior species, because he has not raised himself to the
> condition of royalty.

Our curiosity therefore was not elicited by the fact that a man of
dark skin and African blood should write poetry; but that he should
have done so under the withering influences of slavery. That he was
able, or had the desire, to cultivate his mind, or to pour forth the affections of his heart in tuneful numbers, alternating with the stocks, the
lash, and the prison-house, may well excite wonder.

The authenticity of the work is the first point to ascertain. For this
Dr. Madden, who has spent several years in Cuba, and is well known
for his zealous labours for the abolition of slavery, vouches.* He dedi-

---

* Dr. Madden lately addressed to the Pasha of Egypt a most able and faithful remon-
strance upon the atrocious slave-trade carried on in his dominions. He had presented
in person to the Pasha last year, an address from the "Anti-slavery Convention" held
in London, signed by Mr. Clarkson the Chairman, in the name of four hundred
delegates, expressive of their gratification at his having prohibited manstealing, and
also paying his troops in slaves, and urging him utterly to extinguish the slave-trade
and slavery itself throughout the territories under his sway. Ali Pasha (who levies
taxes upon the traffic) listened attentively to his arguments, but we fear that he
advanced in return little beyond courteous words; for we find Dr. Madden summing
up the present afflicting circumstances of the Egyptian slave-trade as follows:

cates his work to his fellow-labourer in the cause, Mr. Sturge; and he has deposited the original manuscripts in the Spanish language for inspection at the office of the "British and Foreign Anti-Slavery Society." He says that a collection of poems, written by a slave recently liberated in the Island of Cuba, was presented to him in the year 1838, by a gentleman at Havanna, highly distinguished for literary attainments. Some of these pieces had found their way to the Havanna, and attracted the attention of the literary people there, while the poor author was in slavery in the neighbourhood of Matanzas; in consequence of which the gentleman alluded to, with the assistance of a few friends, redeemed the writer from slavery, and enabled him to publish such of his poems as were of a publishable kind in a country like Cuba, where slavery is under the especial protection, and knowledge under the ban, of the censors of the press. Dr. Madden has not translated any portion of his volume; the contents of which we are not acquainted with. The pieces which he has translated, and "put into English verse," are a few which were unpublished or unpublishable in Cuba. These pieces are but few, the bulk of the book being taken up with other matter; but they are extraordinary compositions for a Cuban slave; and Dr. Madden asserts that he has given the sense of the writer as plainly as he could, but that he "has not done justice" to them. He adds the testimony of "a very distinguished Spanish scholar" to their poetical merit. He has prefixed to them a "Sketch of the Cuban slave-trade merchant and planter in verse," which we must pass over in favour of his hero, and also of his own prose illustrations of the atrocities of the slave-trade and slavery in Cuba. He further states that the author of the poems is now living at the Havanna, but his name he thinks it advisable not to publish. He is now in his forty-second year. He was born in Cuba, where his father and mother lived and died in slavery. He was about thirty-eight years of age

---

"In conclusion, may it please your higness, I would beg leave to recall the facts to which I have endeavoured to direct your attention.

"1. At the expiration of nearly fifteen years I have visited Egypt for the second time, and I find slavery and the trade in slaves unchanged in their character, and unrestrained by any measures of your higness adopted for their suppression.

"2. I find the slave-markets glutted with negro women and children as heretofore.

"3. I find the exportation of slaves from Alexandria for Turkey, on board European vessels, carried on openly at the present time.

"4. I find the prices of slaves actually lowered by the increase of the numbers brought down to Alexandria and Cairo, and those slaves, children and women, selling from 600 piastres to 1500 a-head, or from six pounds sterling to fifteen pounds each.

"5. I find the slave-hunts are carried on by your people, and even by your soldiers, as usual, and the only prohibition that has been issued, is one given in the presence of certain European consuls at Fezaghan, that never has been carried into effect.

"6. I find the same evils arising from this nefarious trade, and the same barbarous monopoly in mutilated beings permitted as heretofore, and even encouraged by your authorities in Upper Egypt."

when he obtained his liberty. The price paid for it was 800 dollars. He obtained employment as a tailor for some time after he procured his freedom. Subsequently, he went out to service—then tried the business of a house-painter, and was not successful—was advised to set up as a confectioner, and lost all his money in that line, and now gains his livelihood as an occasional servant. The gentleman who was mainly instrumental in obtaining his liberation from slavery, induced him to write his history. It was written in two parts—the second part, Dr. Madden says, fell into the hands of persons connected with his former master, and is not likely to be restored; the first part Dr. Madden has translated and printed; and it contains, he says, the most perfect picture of Cuban slavery that ever has been given to the world.

From this narrative we will extract a series of passages; in order to illustrate what slavery is, even in its milder forms; for Spanish slavery has always been boasted of, and even our own emancipationists described it, as more lenient than Dutch, or French, or Portuguese, or United States, or our own West Indian slavery; and the subject in the present instance was not a predial slave, but the favoured attendant of opulent gentlemen of polished manners, and ladies so delicate and sensitive, that we might have feared they could not curb the ferocity of such barbarians as our poet with their gentle tenderness.

And why do we open up such scenes? Not assuredly because they present agreeable pictures; but because the slave-trade and slavery still exist;—because they are flourishing and rampant; and have hitherto defied and scorned all the entreaties and remonstrances of justice, humanity, and religion, to stop their guilty and blood-stained career. England has a special interest in the question: she has exerted her zealous influence, and lavish millions upon millions of treasure, to put an end to the slave trade; she has set the Christian example of abolishing slavery in her own colonies, at the cost of twenty millions of money; and yet, she witnesses these dire and desolating scourges sweeping away their victims with the most afflicting and wide-spread barbarities. . . .

The Christian Observer, Vol. 41, No. 37 (January, 1841), 43-61.

*Narratives of Fugitive Slaves**

EPHRAIM PEABODY

America has the mournful honor of adding a new department to the literature of civilization,—the autobiographies of escaped slaves. We have placed below the titles of these narratives of this description. The subjects of two of these narratives, Douglass and Henson, we have known personally, and, apart from the internal evidence of truth which their stories afford, we have every reason to put confidence in them as men of veracity. The authors of the remaining accounts are, for anything we know to the contrary, equally trustworthy. We place these volumes without hesitation among the most remarkable productions of the age,—remarkable as being pictures of slavery by the slave, remarkable as disclosing under a new light the mixed elements of American civilization, and not less remarkable as a vivid exhibition of the force and working of the native love of freedom in the individual mind.

There are those who fear lest the elements of poetry and romance should fade out of the tame and monotonous social life of modern times. There is no danger of it while there are any slaves left to seek for freedom, and to tell the story of their efforts to obtain it. There is that in the lives of men who have sufficient force of mind and heart to enable them to struggle up from hopeless bondage to the position of freemen, beside which the ordinary characters of romance are dull and tame. They encounter a whole Iliad of woes, not in plundering and enslaving others, but in recovering for themselves those rights of which they have been deprived from birth. Or if the Iliad should be thought not to present a parallel case, we know not where one who wished to write a modern Odyssey could find a better subject than in the adventures of a fugitive slave. What a combination of qualities and deeds and sufferings most fitted to attract human sympathy in each particular case! . . . .

* *Narrative of Henry Watson, A Fugitive Slave. Written by Himself* (Boston: Bela Marsh, 1848). *Narrative of the Sufferings of Lewis and Milton Clarke Among the Slaveholders of Kentucky* (Boston: Bela Marsh, 1848). *Narrative of W. Brown. A Fugitive Slave. Written by Himself* (Boston: The Antislavery Office, 1847). *Narrative of the Life of Frederick Douglass, An American Slave, Written by Himself* (Boston: The Antislavery Office, 1845). *The Life of Josiah Henson, Formerly a Slave, Now an Inhabitant of Canada, as Narrated by Himself* (Boston: Arthur D. Phelps, 1849).

One of the many unanswerable arguments which show how unfounded the assertion is that the blacks are naturally incompetent to bear the responsibilities of freedom, is derived from the fact that in so many of them there exists this intense longing to possess it,—a sense of its value which all the appliances of slavery have not been able to crush out. Most men at the North have seen numbers of fugitive slaves. In a single town of New England with which we are acquainted, there are more than two hundred, and there cannot be less than thousands scattered through the different cities and villages; and they constitute, to say the least, as orderly, intelligent, and useful a portion of the population as the great body of foreign immigrants.

These biographies of fugitive slaves are calculated to exert a very wide influence on public opinion. We have always been familiar with slavery, as seen from the side of the master. These narratives show how it looks as seen from the side of the slave. They contain the *victim's account* of the working of this great institution. When one escapes from the South, and finds an opportunity of speaking and has the power to speak, it is certain that he will have attentive listeners. Not only curiosity, but a sense of justice, predisposes men to hear the testimony given by those who have suffered, and who have had few among their own number to describe their sufferings. The extent of the influence such lives must exert may be judged of, when we learn the immense circulation which has been secured for them. Of Brown's Narrative, first published in 1847, not less than eight thousand copies have been already sold. Douglass's Life, first published in 1845, has in this country alone passed through seven editions, and is, we are told, now out of print. They are scattered over the whole of the North, and all theoretical arguments for or against slavery are feeble, compared with these accounts by living men of what they personally endured when under its dominion.

These narratives are for many reasons worthy of attention. The statements they contain may be partial and prejudiced, but are not likely to be more so than are the estimates formed of slavery by those who profit from its continuance. At any rate, in forming a just judgment of this institution, it is quite as important to know what it is to Henson the slave, as what it is to McDuffie the master.

These narratives, however, do not give a full and complete view of the whole subject. There is one point of great moment, which they tend to make us forget, instead of bringing it forward into the light. We refer to the position of the antislavery men of the South. These books give the impression that the Slave States constitute one vast prison-house, of which all the whites without exception are the mere keepers, with no interest in the slaves further than they can be made subservient to the pleasure or profit of their owners. But this is far from being the case. It may not be, certainly it is not, a common feeling, but there is nowhere a more settled and bitter detestation of slavery than is sometimes met with at the South. Strange as it may seem, so entangled is the whole subject, so complicated the relations and powers of the several States and of the Union, that though the slave may find the most sympathy personally at the North, our main hope of the abolition of slavery as an institution depends on the efforts of the enemies of slavery at the South.

Of the narratives at the head of this article, the first four possess no especial interest beyond what must belong to the life of almost any fugitive slave. They are records of degradation on the part of both blacks and whites,—of suffering and wrong and moral corruption. They give, doubtless, a just idea of what slavery is to the slave. But, on the other hand, while we have no reason to question the truth of particular facts respecting individuals, we have no doubt that they convey an altogether erroneous idea of the general character of the masters. The best qualities of the master are likely to appear anywhere rather than in his connection with the slave. And except it be an easy kindness, the slave is in no position to estimate aright the virtues of one who, towards himself, appears simply as a power whom he cannot resist. They stand in such utterly false relations to each other, that their whole intercourse must necessarily be vitiated, and the worst qualities of each, and these almost exclusively, must be perpetually forced on the attention of the other. But human society could not long exist were the great body of slaveholders like those whom these narratives describe. . . .

These narratives, without any such intention on the part of the writers, reveal incidentally, but very vividly, some of the necessary evils of this mournful institution. The white children, in great part, grow up uneducated; for schools cannot be sustained in the country by the scattered population which alone slavery allows. In early years, they are exposed to acquiring the habit of indulging the domineering and selfish passions towards those weaker than themselves. Great numbers of men, ashamed to work, spend much of their time in gambling and horse-racing, and in unending talks about street-fights and party politics. The profits of their plantations depend on the large amount of work which they can extract from the slave, and on the small amount of food and clothing on which he can be made to live. Thus, without those checks which exist between the free laborer and his employer, there is a perpetual temptation to harshness and cruelty; and there never yet was a continuous influence of this kind brought to bear on a man, which did not finally reveal itself in the character. In addition to this, so far as the white males are concerned, there is another evil which can never be passed over when slavery is spoken of,—the temptation to licentiousness. The word *marriage* among the slaves has no legal, and scarcely a moral meaning. And the result of their relations with the whites is seen written ineffaceably in the variable color of the slave population. The horror of amalgamation at the South must be a qualified one. There is far less of it than at the North. A single fact is sufficient to answer all opposing arguments or assertions. In passing through the streets of New Orleans, among the first ten children you meet, there will probably be five different colors. At the South the prejudice is not against color, but against the blacks ceasing to be a servile class.

In reading these narratives, we are forcibly struck with the peculiar hardships to which the female slave is subjected. All that should, in a civilized land, be her protection makes her lot doubly accursed. She suffers all that the male suffers, and in addition miseries peculiar to herself. Her condition is hopeless. There are few females who, even if they could resolve to leave their children behind them, can ever hope to escape from bondage. The bearing of children, except for a very brief period, dces not exempt them from labor in the fields, and this under the perpetual terror of the overseer's lash. If they possess any attractiveness of person, they are too often exposed to the danger of becoming doubly victims, first, to the corrupting urgencies of the white males around them, and then to the jealous dislike of the females. And in addition to all, the children whom they have borne in misery are liable to be taken from them, and sold away from their knowledge into hopeless bondage. Doubtless these evils do not appear on every plantation; but exposure to them is incident to slavery, is a part of the institution, and cannot be separated from it. And these narratives show how easily exposure passes into horrible reality.

In reading these little volumes, there is another evil of American slavery whose horrors are constantly brought before the mind. We refer to the internal slave trade. If we leave out of view the physical horrors of the Middle Passage, we believe that this internal slave trade is a system more accursed, more deserving of execration, the cause of more suffering, than the direct trade from Africa. It is a horrible phantom, making miserable the whole slave population of the South. They who are never made the victims of this traffic, who live and die on the same plantation, know that, at any moment,—sometimes from the selfishness of avaricious masters, sometimes from the misfortunes or death of the kind-hearted,—they are liable to be sold to the slave-dealer who will bid highest, and sent to some other region, under circumstances which, to their ignorant imaginations, seem worse than the reality proves. When added to all other deprivations and sufferings, this horrible fear, weighing incessantly on the thoughts of millions of men and women, is itself an evil of terrible magnitude.

But a still more important consideration is to be kept in mind. The blacks of the South are no longer such as their fathers were when brought from the shores of Africa. They have ceased to be savages. In its worse or better forms, all of them have caught some tincture of civilization. The better class of slaves are more civilized, have less of the brutal about them, than the lower class of whites. With increasing civilization, there is a development of the affections, of the moral sensibilities, and of that forethought also which makes men more apprehensive of future evil. They have learned to place the same estimate on kindred and domestic bonds as their masters; and they have intelligence enough to understand the nature of those advantages which they never must look on except as blessings, from whose enjoyment they are to be forever excluded. The very improvement, which is sometimes put forward as one of the compensations of their lot, has made them sensitive to forms of suffering from which their forefathers were protected by their more brutal condition. The coffle of slaves torn from their families, which the slave-driver conducts by slow and weary stages from Virginia to the sugar-houses of the South, is, to the eye of reason, a more mournful spectacle than the barracoons on the coast of Africa. The wretched beings subjected to this doom are not less dragged away from all to which they are most attached, and carried, powerless victims, to a region and a fate which they most of all dread, but they are capable of a more clinging and paralyzing fear, and feel with infinitely more keenness everything that tears and wounds the affections. Every truth of religion which has dawned on their minds, every domestic bond they have learned to value, every idea and sentiment of a better kind which they have insensibly derived from intercourse with a better instructed race around them, only makes them more sensitive to the lot to which they are doomed. Common humanity demands that, if this traffic—"without mercy and without natural affection"—is to go on, the slaves should be kept as near the condition of brutes as possible. Ignorance, brutality, and callousness to every claim of the affections, if suffering only is to be thought of, constitute a boon for the slave, by putting him into a state of moral insensibility, scarcely less blessed than the state induced by that medical discovery of the present time which promises so to alleviate the physical pains of man.

Is there exaggeration in this? We wish we could believe there was; but there is not. A perpetual fear haunts the slaves, as the fear of ghosts haunts superstitious children, with the mournful difference that the slaves' apprehensions are well founded. This dread of being torn from their families, of being sold to they know not whom, and of being sent to the cotton and sugar plantations of the Southwest, is seen running through and giving a dark coloring to all the narratives before us. In fact, the slaves are not merely liable to be thus sold, but the threat of it serves as an instrument of the police to make them submissive and industrious. It is held up constantly as a punishment for the refractory and disobedient; and that it may be more effective, every circumstance which can make it alarming to the slave's imagination is kept before him. But in trying to avoid this peril, it does not do for him to show too many of the qualities of a self-supporting manhood. The slave's path is a Mahomet's bridge. His virtues may be as dangerous to himself as his vices. If a slave is restless, intelligent, and enterprising, the master is tempted to sell him to the South, lest he should escape to freedom and the North. And no matter what the master's feelings or wishes, if he becomes poor, or dies, his slaves are always exposed, even if they be not actually subjected, to this doom.

The narrative of Douglass contains the life of a superior man. Since his escape from slavery, he has been employed as an antislavery lecturer, and is now the editor of a newspaper in Rochester, N.Y. He does not belong to the class, always small, of those who bring to light great principles, or who originate new methods of carrying them out. He has, however, the vividness of sensibility and of thought which we are accustomed to associate with a Southern climate. He has a natural and ready eloquence, a delicacy of taste, a quick perception of proprieties, a quick apprehension of ideas, and a felicity of expression, which are possessed by few among the more cultivated, and which are surprising when we consider that it is but a few years since he was a slave. In any popular assembly met for the discussion of subjects with which he has had the opportunity to become familiar, he is a man to command and hold attention. He is a natural orator, and his original endowments and the peculiarity of his position have given him a high place among antislavery speakers.

But while our sympathies go strongly with him, and because they go with him, we are disposed to make a criticism on a mode of address in which he sometimes indulges himself, which we believe is likely to diminish, not only his usefulness, but his real influence. We would not detract from his merits, and we can easily excuse in him a severity of judgment and a one-sidedness of view which might be inexcusable in another. We can hardly condemn one who has been a slave for seeing only the evils of slavery, and for thinking lightly of the difficulty of remedying them; but we have wished, when we have heard him speak, or read what he has written, that he might wholly avoid a fault from which a natural magnanimity does something towards saving him, but to which he is nevertheless exposed. His associates at the North have been among those who are apt to mistake violence and extravagance of expression and denunciation for eloquence;—men who, whatever their virtues otherwise, are not in the habit of using discrimination to their judgments of men or of measures which they do not approve. To him they have doubtless been true and faithful friends, and he naturally adopts their style of speech. But it is a mistaken one, if the speaker wishes to sway the judgment of his hearers and to accomplish any practical end. No matter what the vehemence of tone or expression, whenever a public speaker indulges himself in violent and unqualified statements and in sweeping denunciations, he not only makes it apparent that he is deficient in a sound and fair judgment, but what is worse, he creates in his hearers a secret distrust of his real earnestness,—a vague feeling that after all he is thinking more of his speech than of the end for which he professes to make it. When men are profoundly in earnest, they are not apt to be extravagant. The more earnest, the more rigidly true. A merchant, in discussing the politics of the day, about which he knows or cares little, freely indulges in loose, extravagant, and violent declarations. But follow him to his counting-room; let him be making inquiries or giving directions about some enterprise which he really has deeply at heart, and the extravagance is gone. Nothing will answer here but truth, and the exact truth. His earnestness makes him calm. It is seen in the moderated accuracy, as well as in the decision and strength, of his statements. Extravagance and passion and rhetorical flourishes might do when nothing which he greatly valued was at stake; but here is something too serious for trifling. Just so it is in other cases. A flippant, extravagant speaker, especially if he be gifted with the power of sarcasm, will probably be listened to and applauded, but nothing comes of it. They who applaud the most understand very well that this is not the kind of person whose judgment is to be relied on as a guide in action. His words are listened to with much the same sort of interest that is given to the personated passion of the theatre. A few sober words from a calm, wise, discriminating mind are, after all, the ones which are followed. Nothing is less effective, for any practical end, than the "withering and scorching" eloquence with which American speeches seem so to abound. It conciliates no opponent, and though it may light up the momentary passions, it gives no new strength of conviction to the friends of a cause. It is the last kind of eloquence to be cultivated by those who are heartily in earnest in their desire to promote any great reform.

We by no means think that these remarks apply peculiarly to Douglass. We make them, however, because we think that, more often than he is probably aware, he suffers himself to fall into this mode of speech. He has such ability to appeal to the higher and more generous sentiments, and such appeals do so much to win over enemies and to strengthen friends, he has such personal knowledge of slavery, and is so competent to make all he says effective, through candor and a just appreciation of the difficulties that beset the subject of emancipation, and is withal so much of a man, that we regret any mistake of judgment which tends to diminish his power as an advocate of the anti-slavery cause.*. . .

There are many passages in the narrative of Douglass which we should be pleased to quote, but it has been so long published and so widely circulated, that many of our readers have probably seen it. We would only say, in conclusion, that we feel a deep interest in his career. He is one of the living evidences that there is in the colored population of the South no natural incapacity for the enjoyment of freedom; and he occupies a position and possesses abilities which enable him, if he pursues a wise course, to be a most useful laborer in the cause of human rights.

The life of Henson has but just been published, and he has shown himself to be so remarkable a man, that we propose to give a more particular account of him. The narrative owes its existence to the interest which his judicious, far-seeing, and persevering efforts to improve the condition of the colored people who have found a home in Canada have excited in his behalf. It was written to his dictation by a gentleman of this city, who has done good service to humanity in preparing and publishing it. It is as simple, straightforward, and to the point, as the character which it describes, and cannot be read without suggesting many subjects for profitable thought.

Henson is one of those who, in any situation, among his associates would be a marked and leading man. Though an effective speaker, he is not one of the popular declaimers; he is a large-hearted, large-minded man, tolerant, calm, benevolent, and wise. He has not only shown himself to be competent to understand and portray the evils of slavery, but, what implies far higher qualities of mind and heart, that he possesses the wisdom to conceive, and the practical talent and energy to carry out, large and far-reaching schemes for the improvement of his brethren. . . .

---

* We have hesitated about making these remarks; and now, on reading them over, the sympathy which his narrative excites, and our respect for the force of character he has shown in rising from the depths of bondage to be equal associate of those who have possessed every opportunity of cultivation and refinement, almost make us erase what we have written. We would avoid giving pain to one who has suffered all that we should most dread ourselves, and who has risen above obstacles by which we should probably have been crushed. But still, whatever the past has been, he is now free. By his indisputable deserts, he has secured for himself an influential position. The course which he takes is important to others beside himself. Should he read this criticism, we hope that the internal evidence will be sufficient to show that it is written by one who rejoices in his usefulness. And in the faith that he may so read it, and that its suggestions may not be without value, we allow it to stand.

For his journey across Ohio, his escape to Canada, and for his subsesequent career, we must refer our readers to the volume before us. It is full of instructive suggestions respecting the highest question of social progress. The wisdom of his plans for the improvement of the colored race appears strikingly when contrasted with the multitude of fancies which prevail respecting the best methods of regenerating and elevating society. We have already given a brief account of his labors for the benefit of the fugitive slaves congregated in Canada, and of what he has proposed to accomplish. We are so accustomed to judge of men by the conspicuous positions which they occupy, that our estimate of what Henson has done may seem exaggerated. We think it will not, however, to those who feel sufficient interest in him to become acquainted with his course. It shows a very unusual elevation of mind and moral feeling, that one with his training should have conceived so clearly the importance of raising the general condition of the colored population, and should have been so self-impelled to seek the means of its improvement. But when we see one bred a slave, destitute, and obliged to labor steadily for the daily support of a large family, not learning to read till past middle life, and since then, probably, having read hardly any book but the Bible,—when we see such a one rousing the sluggish minds of his brethren to the idea of improvement, and, with no guide but his native good-sense and a benevolent heart, endeavouring to induce them to put into practice principles which such men as Adam Smith and Mill, and the best writers on political economy, have only slowly attained to,— we feel warranted in saying that under the slave's garb and this African skin there is no ordinary man. We think his history and his opinions quite as deserving of lengthened attention as those of a successful soldier or a mere party politician.

There are five things on which he has relied for the improvement of the blacks:—on religious instruction; on education; on withdrawing them from town and village life into the country, and, for the present, till new habits and ideas are established, away from the overshadowing presence of the whites; on inducing them to become the owners of the soil which they cultivate; and on habits of industry directed to the cultivation of those products most suitable to the region where they dwell. Through these means he hopes to promote, instead of the mental and moral childhood and imbecility of slavery, independence, forethought, intelligence, and a higher standard of character. If the founder of every little robber state of antiquity has been deemed worthy of eternal commemoration in history and song, we think that he is deserving of respect, whether he finally succeeds or not, who but heartily attempts, by wise methods, to convert these thousands of fugitive slaves into a commonwealth of free and Christian men and women. If any of our readers think our notice of him too long, they may take to themselves the satisfaction of believing that there will not speedily appear another man of a similar sort, engaged in a similar undertaking, to weary their attention. If we may trust history, such men come singly, and only at considerable intervals. At any rate, however common they may be, so peculiar an opportunity for trying an experiment in civilization cannot often occur. We have no fear, however, that an apology will be thought needful. We believe that our readers will be interested in the efforts of one who, without noise or pretension, without bitterness towards the whites, without extravagant claims in behalf of the blacks, has patiently, wisely, and devotedly given himself to the improvement of the large body of his wretched countrymen amongst whom his lot has been cast.

If death does not interrupt his exertions, we hope for important results from his labors. Even then, others who have learned to sympathize with him may be prepared to take his place. And if in this way a large and successful example can be given of the slave's capacity for freedom, we can hardly forebear hoping that it may ultimately have an important influence on the efforts made to relieve the whole South from the burden of slave institutions.

Christian Examiner, Vol. XLVII, No. 1 (July-September, 1849), 61-93.

Life of Henry Bibb.

Life and Adventures of Henry Bibb, an American Slave, Written by Himself.

ANONYMOUS

This fugitive slave literature is destined to be a powerful lever. We have the most profound conviction of its potency. We see in it the easy and infallible means of abolitionizing the free States. Argument provokes argument, reason is met by sophistry. But narratives of slaves go right to the hearts of men. We defy any man to think with any patience or tolerance of slavery after reading Bibb's narrative, unless he is one of those infidels to nature, who float on the race as monsters, from it, but not of it.

Henry Bibb is a bright, mild looking, gentlemanly sort of man, about 34 years of age, not more African than European in his lineage, and in fact, doubtless, having some of the finest Kentucky blood in his veins. He early began, while being used as the tool of Kentucky luxury, to educate himself in the science of running away. But falling in love with a damsel of his own condition, he married her and almost forgot his plans for freedom, till he found himself the *father of a slave,* and felt the full degradation of seeing wife and child brutally abused before his eyes without the power to protect them. He escaped to Canada. Returned with the design of bringing off his wife and child; was betrayed; imprisoned; escaped; was betrayed again, and finally he and his wife and child were taken to New Orleans by the slave-traders and sold to one "Deacon Whitfield," a Red River planter.

Life on that plantation is very particularly described. That Deacon flogged him most unmercifully for attending a prayer meeting. His various attempts to get away from the incarnate fiend are full of the most painfully romantic interest, full, too, of "human nature." His experience as the slave of a gang of blacklegs, to whom his pious master sold him, and their benevolent endeavor to purchase his wife and child that the family might not be separated, do credit to humanity. He at last became the property of an Indian, from whose heirs he escaped, journeying to Jefferson City on the Missouri River, whence steam and his own good wit transferred him to Cincinnati and final Liberty.

We believe this to be an unvarnished tale, giving a true picture of slavery, in all its features, good, bad and indifferent, if it has so many. The book is written with perfect artlessness, and the man who can read it unmoved must be fit for treasons, stratagems and spoils.

One conclusion forced upon the philosophical reader of such narratives of runaway slaves is this, that however tolerable chattel slavery may be as an institution for savage and barbarous life, when you bring it into the purlieus of civilization and Christianity, it becomes unspeakably iniquitous and intolerable. If Mr. Calhoun really means to uphold slavery, he *must*—there is no help for it—abolish Christianity, printing, art, science, and take his patriarchs back to the standard of Central Africa, or the days of Shem, Ham and Japhet—*Chronotype.*

The Anti-Slavery Bugle, Vol. 5, No. 85 (Nov. 3, 1849), 1.

The Life and Bondage of Frederick Douglass

My Bondage and My Freedom by Frederick Douglass

ANONYMOUS

A third biography before us furnishes a still further contrast—the *Life and Bondage* of Frederick Douglass, the well-known fugitive slave, who has come to occupy so conspicuous a position, both as a writer and speaker. It details the incidents of his experience on the slave plantation of Maryland, where he was born, of his subsequent escape, and of his public career in England and the northern States. We need hardly say that it abounds in interest. The mere fact that the member of an outcast and enslaved race should accomplish his freedom, and educate himself up to an equality of intellectual and moral vigor with the leaders of the race by which he was held in bondage, is, in itself, so remarkable, that the story of the change cannot be otherwise than exciting. For ourselves, we confess to have read it with the unbroken attention with which we absorbed Uncle Tom's Cabin. It has the advantage of the latter book in that it is no fiction. Of course, it is impossible to say how far the author's prejudices, and remembrances of wrong, may have deepened the color of his pictures, but the general tone of them is truthful. He writes bitterly, as we might expect of one who writes under a personal provocation, taking incidents of individual experience for essential characteristics, but not more bitterly than the circumstances seem to justify. His denunciations of slavery and slaveholders are not indiscriminate, while he wars upon the system rather than upon the persons whom that system has made. In the details of his early life upon the plantation, of his youthful thoughts on life and destiny, and of the means by which he gradually worked his way to freedom, there is much that is profoundly touching. Our English literature has recorded many an example of genius struggling against adversity,—of the poor Ferguson, for instance, making himself an astronomer, of Burns becoming a poet, of Hugh Miller finding his geology in a stone quarry, and a thousand similar cases—yet none of these are so impressive as the case of the solitary slave, in a remote district, surrounded by none but enemies, conceiving the project of his escape, teaching himself to read and write to facilitate it, accomplishing it at last, and subsequently raising himself to a leadership in a great movement in behalf of his brethren. Whatever may be our opinions of slavery, or of the best means of acting upon it, we cannot but admire the force and integrity of character which has enabled Frederick Douglass to attain his present unique position.

Putnam's Monthly Magazine, Vol. VI (Nov. 1855), 547.

Kidnapped and Ransomed

The Kidnapped and the Ransomed. Being the personal recollections of Peter Still and his wife "Vina," after forty years of slavery. By Mrs. Kate E.R. Pickard. With an Introduction, by Rev. Samuel J. May, and an Appendix by William H. Furness, D.D. Syracuse: William T. Hamilton. New York and Auburn: Miller, Orten & Mulligan.

ANONYMOUS

The literature of slavery is becoming a very considerable affair. We do not refer particularly to the anti-slavery societies' tracts, and argumentative volumes, nor to the Southside View and other works of that description. Mrs. Stowe's works, of world-wide fame, are awakening in all quarters a demand for authentic personal narratives of experience in slavery; and the demand is likely to be well supplied. The personal recollections of Peter Still and his wife, are the latest contribution to this most important department of the literature of slavery. The authenticity of the story is beyond the reach of cavil or skepticism. The style is, as it should be, simple and lucid, with no offensive attempt at fine writing. The story itself is full of incident and of character, and the lessons which it gives, need no philosophy to make them passable.

Peter Still was born free in the vicinity of Philadelphia. In his early childhood, he and his little brother Levin, were stolen, carried away, and sold for slaves. They remembered the home from which they had been kidnapped; they kept alive between themselves the memory of father and mother, and sisters, and the Christian names by which they had known them, but their own family name soon faded from their memory—their only names as slaves were Peter and Levin. They soon learned to breathe only to each other the fact that they were born free. They submitted to their dreadful lot; they were cheerful, obedient, honest; and a superficial observer—base enough to forget that of all wrongs—might have pronounced them happy. They formed such ties as are possible to slaves; each as he became a man learned to love with the affection of a husband a wife who may be torn from him at an owner's caprice or convenience. Children were born to them—children that were the property of other men. Levin died in the house of bondage. Peter at last—having passed into the ownership of a humane Jew, who had not the full benefit of that Christianity which we are urgently invited to "aid" at the South—was allowed to purchase his freedom. Returning to Philadelphia, after an absence of forty years, the good providence of God so guided his steps that he found his aged mother and the surviving members of his family. Then begging from door to door, he accumulated slowly the gifts of human sympathy which at last enabled him to buy his wife and children. And here in this volume, we have the whole story, with its marvelous and touching details.

New Englander, Vol. 14, No. LVI (Nov. 1856), 628-29.

Linda: Incidents in the Life of a Slave Girl Written by Herself

Edited by Lydia Maria Child. Boston: Published for the Author. 1861.

ANONYMOUS

We have read this book with no ordinary interest, for we are acquainted with the writer; we have heard many of the incidents from her own lips, and have great confidence in her truthfulness and integrity. Between two and three years ago, a coloured woman, about as dark as a southern Spaniard or a Portuguese, aged about five-and-forty, and with a kind and pleasing expression of countenance, called on us, bearing an introductory letter from one of the most honoured friends of the anti-slavery cause in the United States. This letter requested our friendly offices on behalf of Linda, who was desirous of publishing her narrative in England. It happened that the friends at whose house we were then staying were so much interested by this dusky stranger's conversation and demeanour, that they induced her to become their guest for some weeks. Thus we had an excellent opportunity of becoming acquainted with one of the truest heroines we have ever met with. Her manners were marked by refinement and sensibility, and by an utter absence of pretence or affectation; and we were deeply touched by the circumstances of her early life which she then communicated, and which exactly coincide with those of the volume now before us. A lady who was also enjoying the hospitality thus extended to Linda kindly undertook to peruse her manuscript, from the publication of which she hoped to raise a small fund for the benefit of her two children. We have this friend's testimony that the manuscript and the printed volume are substantially the same; whilst the narrative has been condensed and rendered more fluent and compact by the friendly assistance of Mrs. Child, than whom no one is better qualified to perform such a task with delicacy and discrimination. One of the mottoes is taken from the following testimony of a woman of North Carolina:—"Northerners know nothing at all about slavery. They think it is perpetual bondage only. They have no conception of the depth of degradation involved in that word, *slavery*. If they had, they would *never* cease their efforts until so horrible a system was overthrown." This declaration is amply justified by a perusal of Linda's narrative.

During her bondage she does not appear to have suffered any great amount of physical hardship. But the bitterness of mental suffering and enforced degradation which she was compelled to endure from her master's vices and the hatred of her mistress—and which she was utterly helpless to prevent—is fearful to contemplate. This book shows as forcibly as any story we have ever read the moral pollution and perversion inevitable in a community where slavery is a recognised institution. The narrative is chiefly devoted to the exhibition of this phase of slavery, and to an account of her sufferings whilst hidden for seven years in a small chamber, so narrow and so low that she could neither walk nor stand, into which she was stowed in the immediate neighbourhood of her master's residence, whilst on the look-out for a way of escape into the Free States. This at length was happily accomplished, and after some time she was so fortunate as to obtain a confidential situation in the family of one of the most eminent literateurs of the United States. Of their kindness we have often heard her speak with grateful enthusiasm. Amongst other substantial benefits, we may mention that her legal freedom was obtained by purchase from a son-in-law of the cruel and profligate wretch who had formerly claimed her as his property.

During Linda's stay on this side of the Atlantic, she was recommended to publish her book in America; and we think this has proved to be good advice, for she has thus secured the invaluable assistance of Mrs. Child in pruning some redundancies of matter and style. At the same time she will be sure to effect more good for her brethren and sisters still in bonds, by the diffusion of her story amongst the people of the Free States, whom it is above all others important to inform, since they alone are able, by withholding their support from it, to shake down the whole system of chattel slavery.

The Anti-Slavery Advocate, No. 53, Vol. 2 (1 May 1861), 1.

2. The Slave Narratives as History

One of the most significant research projects generated by the Depression was the Federal Writers Project's Slave Narrative Collection. Drawing upon precedents established by Lawrence Reddick and John McCade, the F.W.P. collected thousands of oral narratives during the nineteen thirties from black men and women who had once been enslaved. Used as sources of folklore by Benjamin Botkin in his collection *Lay My Burden Down* (1945), the worth of these narratives as historical data has remained in question until the last decade.

Sterling Brown's memorandum to that project's interviewers reveals the care encouraged by the project's directors to make those data collected of potential use to historians, linguists, and to literary scholars. One such literary scholar, John Wideman, compares the use of language in these narratives to that used by Charles Chesnutt in his fictions. Essays by historians are sustained responses to the published edition of these oral tales, edited by the historian, George P. Rawick, and published as a "composite history" in over forty-volumes entitled *The American Slave*. Scholars are only beginning to understand both the ironic limitations of and the splendid opportunities for research derived from these oral sources. It is apparent, however, that Rawick's collection is unparalleled in the history of slavery as a record of the ex-slave's conscious recountings of daily life in enslavement. Indeed, one can safely conclude that the written and oral accounts of slavery known collectively as "Afro-American Slave Narratives" have no parallel in the Western tradition in terms of sheer scope of testimony. This section of our collection is perhaps the most potentially meaningful to subsequent students of American history.

The historians and the sole economist collected here also argue forcefully for the use of the slave's narrative as historical data, against arguments epitomized by those of the historian Ulrich B. Phillips (*American Negro Slavery*, 1918) that these narratives are essentially false or mis-

leading. It is difficult for us to imagine upon what sound, scholarly presuppositions could the testimony *of the slave* be regarded as invalid
testimony. Clearly, such objections were rooted in essentially ideological
presuppositions, rather than in scholarly concerns.

Nevertheless, as these essays show, historians were forced to disprove
Phillips' charges by painstakingly researching the slave's texts themselves
to demonstrate their truth and accuracy of description. What had been
a polemical necessity for antebellum reviewers of the narratives, as
reprinted in Part One of this book, became in the twentieth-century an
academic necessity among historians: these scholars had to *establish* the
historical accuracy of their evidence before they could analyze it in
their recreation of the slave's experience. John W. Blassingame was a
central figure in this reconsideration of evidence. Robin W. Winks's
case study is one of the most salient examples of the complex textual
relation between fiction and history, while Gerald Jaynes's essay uses
the narratives as source material to recreate the economic relations implicit in the slave economy.

Perhaps a meaningful way by which to suggest the sheer irony of
the demand that the scholar *prove* the worth of these narratives as historical evidence is to imagine the uses scholars would put even *one*
newly-discovered narrative written by a Greek or Roman slave. There is
little doubt that such a text would be hailed as a great discovery, and
would generate scores of reconsiderations of classical slavery. Perhaps
the ultimate irony of American slavery is that the Afro-American bondsman, denied a "voice" in print by the *de jure* and *de facto* prohibition of
literary training, has had to continue his or her struggle to "testify," as
it were, into the twentieth-century through such surrogates as these historical scholars.

On Dialect Usage

Notes by an editor on dialect usage in accounts by interviews with ex-slaves.

STERLING A. BROWN

Simplicity in recording the dialect is to be desired in order to hold the interest and attention of the readers. It seems to me that readers are repelled by pages sprinkled with misspellings, commas and apostrophes. The value of exact phonetic transcription is, of course, a great one. But few artists attempt this completely. Thomas Nelson Page was meticulous in his dialect; Joel Chandler Harris less meticulous but in my opinion even more accurate. But the values they sought are different from the values that I believe this book of slave narratives should have. Present day readers are less ready for the overstress of phonetic spelling than in the days of local color. Authors realize this: Julia Peterkin uses a modified Gullah instead of Gonzales' carefully spelled out Gullah. Howard Odum has questioned the use of goin' for going since the g is seldom pronounced even by the educated.

Truth to idiom is more important, I believe, than truth to pronunciation. Erskine Caldwell in his stories of Georgia, Ruth Suckow in stories of Iowa, and Zora Neale Hurston in stories of Florida Negroes get a truth to the manner of speaking without excessive misspellings. In order to make this volume of slave narratives more appealing and less difficult for the average reader, I recommend that truth to idiom be paramount, and exact truth to pronunciation secondary.

I appreciate the fact that many of the writers have recorded sensitively. The writer who wrote "ret" for right is probably as accurate as the one who spelled it "raght." But in a single publication, not devoted to a study of local speech, the reader may conceivably be puzzled by different spellings of the same word. The words "whafolks," "whufolks," "whi'folks," etc., can all be heard in the South. But "white-folks" is easier for the reader, and the word itself is suggestive of the setting and the attitude.

Words that definitely have a notably different pronunciation from the usual should be recorded as heard. More important is the recording of words with a different local meaning. Most important, however, are the turns of phrase that have flavor and vividness. Examples occurring in the copy I read are:

> durin' of de war
> outman my daddy (good, but unnecessarily put into quotes)
> piddled in de fields
> skit of woods
> kinder chillish

There are, of course, questionable words, for which it may be hard to set up a single standard. Such words are:

paddyrollers, padrollers, pattyrollers	for patrollers
missis, mistess	for mistress
marsa, massa, maussa, mastuh	for master
ter, tuh, teh	for to

I believe that there should be, for this book, a uniform word for each of these.

The following list is composed of words which I think should not be used. These are merely samples of certain faults:

1.	ah	for	I
2.	bawn	for	born
3.	capper	for	caper
4.	com'	for	come
5.	do	for	dough
6.	ebry, ev'ry	for	every
7.	hawd	for	hard
8.	muh	for	my
9.	nakid	for	naked
10.	ole, ol'	for	old
11.	ret, raght	for	right
12.	snaik	for	snake
13.	sowd	for	sword
14.	sto'	for	store
15.	teh	for	tell
16.	twon't	for	twan't
17.	useter, useta	for	used to
18.	uv	for	of
19.	waggin	for	wagon
20.	whi'	for	white
21.	wuz	for	was

I should like to recommend that the stories be told in the language of the ex-slave, without excessive editorializing and "artistic" introductions on the part of the interviewer. The contrast between the directness of the ex-slave speech and the roundabout and at times pompous comments of the interviewer is frequently glaring. Care should be taken lest expressions such as the following creep in: "inflicting wounds from which he never fully recovered" (supposed to be spoken by an ex-slave).

Finally, I should like to recommend that the words darky and nigger and such expressions as "a comical little old black woman" be omitted from the editorial writing. Where the ex-slave himself uses these, they should be retained.

This material sent June 20 [1936] to states of: Ala., Ark., Fla., Ga., Ky., La., Md., Miss., Mo., N.C., Ohio, Okla., Tenn., Texas, Va., and S. Car.

Negro Dialect Suggestions
(Stories of Ex-Slaves)

Do not write:

Ah for I
Poe for po' (poor)
Hit for it
Tuh for to
Wuz for was
Baid for bed
Daid for dead
Ouh for our
Mah for my
Ovah for over
Othuh for other
Wha for whar (where)
Undah for under
Fuh for for
Yondah for yonder
Moster for marster or massa

Gwainter for gwineter (going to)
Oman for woman
Ifn for iffen (if)
Fiuh or *fiah* for fire
Uz or *uv* or *o'* for of
Poar for poor or po'
J'in for jine
Coase for cose
Utha for other
Yo' for you
Gi' for give
Cot for caught
Kin' for kind
Cose for 'cause
Tho't for thought

The Art and Science of Reading
WPA Slave Narratives

PAUL D. ESCOTT

For all who want to understand slavery in North America, the WPA slave narratives are an indispensable source.[1] Along with other types of slave narratives, they open a window on a side of slavery that was largely hidden from white observers. In 1863, when members of the American Freedmen's Inquiry Commission questioned Robert Smalls, a former slave and Union naval hero, they asked whether masters knew anything of the "secret life" of the slaves. "No, sir," was the forthright reply of Smalls. "One life they show their masters and another life they don't show."[2] The WPA narratives help to provide access to this "secret life." They are a unique cache of data and a rare guide to the slave's perception of his world. Fortunately, many historians have come to accept their value and expect their use in any study of slavery.

How to use these narratives properly is a sometimes debated question. Cliometricians have taken data from the WPA narratives and subjected them to rigorous mathematical analysis; other historians favor only a cautious, impressionistic use of these sources.[3] This difference in approach reflects an unfortunate divergence in the profession, a split that some at least perceive between quantifiers and non-quantifiers. The present author has made a careful study of approximately 2,500 of the WPA slave narratives.[4] Based on the experience of that study, it is evident that both methodologies can and should be used in examining the WPA narratives. Quantitative and non-quantitative methods encounter some common problems and others that are particular to the method, but, used together, they can make different and cumulative contributions to our understanding of slavery.

In any area of research, historians ask different kinds of questions of the past. At times their concern is with facts and numbers, as in the question: were slaves whipped, and how often? In other instances their focus must be on value-laden and perceptual matters, such as: how did slaves feel about their masters? Obviously some of these questions require a quantitative approach and others do not; each method should be used where appropriate. The author's experience has convinced him that in certain vital ways the historian's use of the narratives inevitably remains humanistic rather than scientific, but that experience also has convinced him that simple quantitative methods have a wide applicability and value in studying the WPA narratives.

What is the nature of the WPA slave narratives? What kind of source are these documents that offer a great deal to the historian of slavery? In simplest terms, each narrative is a written report of an interview, or several interviews, with a former slave, recorded in the 1930s by a field worker hired by the Works Progress Administration. These reports vary considerably in length and in quality. Some are barely a page, whereas others run to several pages or more; the "typical" narrative might be between two and four pages in length. Likewise some of these reports treat very important topics in great detail, whereas others are mainly fluff or evasion. Most offer to the careful reader a fair amount of material both on the ex-slave and on his interviewer.

The historian must start with the fact that these reports are not a direct presentation of the slave's views. They are not even a direct transcription of the interview itself. Although a few interview sessions were captured on an early version of the tape recorder, the vast majority of interviews probably involved no more than the former slave and his questioner, who took some notes. The report written from these notes might not present the former slave's statements in their original order or with full accuracy. Moreover, after a WPA field worker drafted a narrative, his or her writing was reviewed and sometimes edited or rewritten by higher officials in the project. Thus the WPA narratives are one or more stages removed from the original interview. Clearly, therefore, the form of these valuable sources is not optimal, but it is typical of the kind of material that historians often must use and of the problems they often face with sources.[5]

To use the narratives wisely, the researcher constantly must bear in mind the variety of factors that shaped the interview itself. All these factors had the potential to affect the interview, possibly to destroy its accuracy or lessen its value. Many commentators, particularly those who reject the narratives, have pointed to the advanced age of the respondents. Black men and women contacted in the 1930s had lived seventy or more years since their experience of slavery, and possibly time had dimmed their recollections. Then too, the critics argue, since many of these survivors were children in the days of the peculiar institution, their perceptions might not be representative and trustworthy because their experience differed from that of adults. The milieu of the 1930s itself constitutes a potential problem. Due to the Depression, most of the former slaves were destitute and dependent upon the aid of family, white people, or government officials. Perhaps poverty coerced people into saying what they thought the "government man" wanted to hear. Moreover, the South of that day was a tightly segregated society. Institutionalized racial discrimination dominated social life as pervasively and almost as harshly as slavery ever had. Black people were not free to speak their minds to whites, and some former slaves admitted that they did not tell the "white folks nuthin' 'case [they were] skeer'd to make enemies." According to one former slave named Martin Jackson, "Lots of old slaves closes the door before they tell the truth about their days of slavery. When the door is open, they tell how kind their masters was and how rosy it all was." Those who would talk to whites customarily followed the ritual of racial etiquette required at the time before they made any critical comments. Not infrequently an ex-slave described his master and family as "jus' as good to us as dey could be" at the start of a narrative, only to relate horrifying mistreatment near the end.[6] Such problems were especially severe when the interviewer was a descendant of the ex-slave's master, as sometimes happened. Even without these special circumstances, each interview could be affected by the kind of feeling and rapport that grew up between interviewer and respondent.

All these factors are problems; the historian cannot use the WPA narratives thoughtlessly and uncritically. But such problems do not vitiate the value of the narratives as a source. Examination reveals that some of these problems are not as serious as they initially appear, and others may be reduced or avoided through care on the part of the researcher. As C. Vann Woodward concluded, "These interviews with ex-slaves will have to be used with caution and discrimination. . . . The necessary precautions, however, are no more elaborate or burdensome than those required by many other types of sources [the historian] is accustomed to use."[7]

Consider, for example, the supposed difficulty stemming from the advanced age of the former slaves. It is, of course, true that human memory is fallible, but there is no reason to believe that the memories of the ex-slaves interviewed were worse than anyone else's. Modern psychological research demonstrates that loss of memory is associated with morbidity at any age. That is, when an individual's health declines in terminal illness, his memory deteriorates also. But healthy old people enjoy full mental function or even improved abilities, and the ex-slaves interviewed obviously had benefitted from sturdy constitutions in reaching their advanced ages.[8] Besides, many of the experiences about which the former slaves were questioned were pivotal moments in their lives. Just as people today remember their graduations, marriages, or other moments of signal achievement, the ex-slaves were likely to have clear memories of the day of jubilee when bondage ended or of the tragic selling of a relative. To deal with the possibility that those who were children in slavery gained a different perspective on the institution from that of adults, the researcher needs only to compare the stories of younger and older former slaves.

The basic solution to all the other contextual problems surrounding the interview is simply care. Through alertness to nuance, detail, consistency, forms of address, and such things as the content of the narrative compared to declarations of feelings made within it, it is possible to work through layers of distortion toward a truer understanding of the former slave's perspective. What follows is a brief description of some of the qualitative methods used to this end by the author.

Despite many variations, most of the interviews follow a suggested set of questions fairly closely. According to a memorandum sent to field workers by Henry G. Alsberg, interviewers were to "take the greatest care not to influence the point of view of the informant" and to prepare reports that were *"as nearly word-for-word as is possible."* Sample questions covered work, food, clothing, religion, resistance, care of the sick, and relations with owners in slavery, experiences during the Civil War and Reconstruction, and later patterns of life. Some questions in these areas were admirably specific and probing, such as, "Did the slaves have a church on your plantation? . . . What do you think of voodoo? . . . What happened on the day news came that you were free?"[9] These sample questions give a similarity of structure to many narratives and make it easier to discern variations in response or attitude.

One indicator of the tone of the original interview is the form of address used by the ex-slave. Extremely formal and respectful phrases suggest considerable distance between the respondent and the questioner, but more informal and relaxed phraseology often indicate a warmer atmosphere or reveal the presence of a black interviewer. Another nuance that can be very helpful is the degree of responsiveness of ex-slaves to the questions they were asked. If the interviewer betrayed the fact that he held traditional and racist views, he might obtain only a series of entertaining but irrelevant stories for his trouble. Story-telling was a skill used effectively by some former slaves to divert the conversation and avoid giving offense; it had reached a high level of development as a survival tactic. Evasion also is prominent in some interviews. The same ex-slaves who had spoken volubly about Abraham Lincoln might deny all knowledge of Jefferson Davis and refuse to express an opinion.

Due to the existence of such factors, the author tried constantly to separate the content of the interviews from declarations of feeling that were designed to satisfy the racial etiquette of the day. Shortly after praising her master, for example, Callie Elder related the whippings that occurred on her plantation and especially the sufferings of her father and grandfather.[10] In this case and others it seemed wiser to rely on described events as an indicator of feeling rather than on patterned and otherwise unsupported statements made at the beginning of the interview. Similarly the author decided to eliminate references to events that occurred on neighboring plantations. Only specifics arising from the slave's own experience were studied, in order to limit the influence of second- and third-hand testimony and to increase reliability. In general, recollections that were convincing were specific and fleshed out with individual circumstance or detail.

All these methods are the conventional tools and techniques of the historian. They represent the traditional skills of analyzing documents applied to a new material, the slave narratives. Such methods can take us far, and an additional means of assuring accuracy remains to be employed. Conclusions reached from analyzing slave narratives can be checked for consistency—with themselves and, more importantly, with white sources. In a number of ways the WPA narratives already have met this test. For example, many historical accounts of first contact between slaves and the liberating Union army have left an impression of joyous welcome on the part of slaves for the bluecoats and a mass departure of the plantation labor force. The narratives show that this happened occasionally but indicate that the more general reaction was a happy but cautious one by bondsmen who stayed on their plantations. Records of the Union army confirm that Federals encountered a wary and suspicious attitude among the slaves and that, even though many slaves followed generals such as Sherman, the majority of bondsmen in the affected area stayed home.[11] Likewise the shock felt by white slave owners when their human chattel behaved in "ungrateful" ways during 1865 testifies to the validity of the attitudes revealed by blacks in the narratives.

The techniques discussed so far are part of a method, but do not constitute a science. Working in this way with the data, the historian is a traditional humanistic scholar. Sensitivity and care facilitate the sifting of truth from misrepresentation. The scholar does his best, forms working hypotheses, and checks them as he or she proceeds. These steps add up to appropriate caution but not to mathematical precision, for a large number of factors that are not measurable have impinged on the final product, the narrative. Assessing the influence of each factor in each narrative is essentially an act of judgment. In the end, of course, any scholar must present evidence to support the generalizations offered, and this evidence can be examined and weighed. But in large collections of material there is generally something to cite in support of any position. Thus the accuracy of an historian's conclusions ultimately depend, at least to some extent, on the quality of that person's judgment. Professional skills enter into that judgment, but so also do personal traits and the insight gained from one's whole life experience.

If this is true, some would ask, why bother to supplement a method that is partially subjective with complicated "scientific" or quantitative methodology? The answer to this question is simply that quantitative methods add something; they do help in many ways. The scholar would be foolish to ignore techniques that can provide valuable assistance.

The first way in which quantitative methods prove to be extremely useful is simple: they help a scholar to check the accuracy of his or her impressions. It is easy for anyone researching a large and interesting body of material to mislead himself. Interesting theories or possibilities sometimes make part of the evidence appear larger than other parts. Facts that one has been looking for tend to shine with a special clarity in one's memory. Without a quantitative record of the data, the researcher has no way to confirm the validity of his conclusions. Through quantitative methods this author discovered areas in which his feelings had mislead him; how many other instances like this have gone undetected in historical scholarship?

It may be especially important to have a numerical check on one's impressions when the matters at issue concern perceptions. For example, scholars have speculated a great deal on the differences in slave life on large plantations as compared to small plantations. Small slaveholdings, they have argued, had a markedly different atmosphere. The master and slave shared a close and more personal relationship and may at times have worked side-by-side in the fields. As a result, according to this interpretation, slavery on small farms was far milder and less harsh. The WPA narratives both confirm this from the white perspective and refute it from the black viewpoint. There were differences, as described, in the two environments. Quantitative analysis reveals that only in small slaveholdings did any sizeable proportion of the slaves eat the same food as the master. Similarly, only on smaller units did a noticeable fraction of owners eschew whipping altogether. These are signs that there was an objective difference between large and small plantation environments. But such a difference does not ensure that slaves *perceived* their bondage in substantially different fashion on small farms. To the slaves, the basic fact of bondage may have been more significant than slight advantages in treatment. Indeed, a tabulation of slaves' attitudes toward their masters demonstrates that differences in these attitudes between large and small plantations were quite modest. Apparently most bondsmen tended to agree with Thomas Lewis, who explained, "There was no such thing as being good to slaves. Many people were better than others, but a slave belonged to his master and there was no way to get out of it."[12]

The most important advantage of quantitative methods is inherent in their nature. Quantitative methods allow the researcher to test for and examine the relationships that he suspects. Whether one relies on words or on numbers, the explanatory process of the historian remains the same. The historian essentially makes an argument that a relationship exists, that one factor influences another factor. Many arguments couched in qualitative terms can be put into quantitative form. When this is done, the result is a gain in precision that confirms or denies the relationship and allows one to see how strong the relationship is. Such a gain in precision is not just a matter of fastidiousness; it may have major interpretive consequences.

An important area that this author considered, for example, was the effect of occupation upon attitudes held by the slaves. Many scholars had previously suggested that the occupation of slaves exerted a great influence on their views toward bondage and their masters. To test this possibility, the author used data in the WPA narratives and some simple statistics that measure the degree of association between variables. This elementary quantitative analysis demonstrated that there was a relationship between occupation and attitude, but the degree of association proved to be modest. This last fact, coupled with a large body of qualitative evidence in the narratives, led the author to conclude that a sense of brotherhood with other slaves was widespread and overshadowed tendencies toward class division in the slave community.[13] Without the help of a statistic, which showed modest association, this author would have faced two conflicting masses of evidence—one suggesting differences based on occupation and the other pointing to strong community ties—with only guesswork to strike the balance between them.

Quantitative techniques are not foolproof. They have their limitations just as do other methods. Poor data can only produce poor results, and some information in the slave narratives, such as reference to rape, is so sketchy and subject to pressures in the interview that it should not be pushed too far.[14] Similarly on some subjects the slave narratives, rich as they are, provide too few cases to make quantitative summaries meaningful. Yet the scope of usefulness for quantitative methodologies is often much wider than scholars in the humanities have supposed. By availing themselves of these tools historians will gain in their power to analyze both numerical data and such documents as the WPA narratives.

Notes

1. These narratives are formally known as the Federal Writers' Project Slave Narratives of the Works Progress Administration. The best article on their provenance is Norman R. Yetman, "The Background of the Slave Narrative Collection," *American Quarterly,* Volume 19 (1967), pp. 534-53. The best source of the narratives is George P. Rawick, editor, *The American Slave: A Composite Autobiography,* 18 volumes (Westport, Conn.: Greenwood Press, 1972), volumes 2-16 and *The American Slave: A Composite Autobiography,* Supplement, Series I, 12 volumes (Westport, Conn.: Greenwood Press, 1977). See also the excellent edition of Virginia narratives by Charles L. Perdue, Jr., Thomas E. Barden, and Robert K. Phillips, editors, *Weevils in the Wheat* (Charlottesville: University Press of Virginia, 1976). Illuminating discussions by George Rawick of the background and nature of the narratives are in his book, *From Sundown to Sunup: The Making of the Black Community* (which is volume 1 of *The American Slave: A Composite Autobiography*) and in his general introduction to the Supplement, Series I.

2. John W. Blassingame, editor, *Slave Testimony: Two Centuries of Letters, Speeches, Interviews, and Autobiographies* (Baton Rouge: Louisiana State University Press, 1977) p. 377.

3. For example, see: Thomas L. Haskell, "The True and Tragical History of *Time on the Cross,*" *New York Review of Books* (October 2, 1975), pp. 33-39; John W. Blassingame, "Using the Testimony of Ex-Slaves: Approaches and Problems," *Journal of Southern History,* Vol. XLI (1975), pp. 473-92; Blassingame, *Slave Testimony,* p. lvi; and Eugene D. Genovese, "Getting to Know the Slaves," *New York Review of Books* (September 21, 1972), pp. 16-19.

4. Paul D. Escott, *Slavery Remembered: A Record of Twentieth-Century Slave Narratives* (Chapel Hill: The University of North Carolina Press, 1979).

5. For additional discussion of some of these matters, see Escott, *Slavery Remembered,* Introduction.

6. *Ibid.,* pp. 8, 186.

7. C. Vann Woodward, "History from Slave Sources," *American Historical Review* Vol. 79 (1974), p. 480.

8. K. Warner Schaie, "Translations in Gerontology—From Lab to Life: Intellectual Functioning," *American Psychologist,* Vol. 29 (1974), pp. 802-807; Lissy F. Jarvik and Arthur Falek, "Intellectual Stability and Survival in the Aged," *Journal of Gerontology,* Vol. 18 (1963), pp. 173-76; Robert L. Kahn, Steven H. Zarit, Nancy M. Hilbert, and George Niederehe, "Memory Complaint and Impairment in the Aged," *Archives of General Psychiatry,* Vol. 32 (1975), pp. 1569-73; June E. Blum, Edward T. Clark, and Lissy F. Jarvik, "The New York State Psychiatric Institute Study of Aging Twins," in *Intellectual Functioning in Adults,* edited by Lissy F. Jarvik, Carl Eisdorfer, and June E. Blum (New York: Springer Publishing Co., 1973).

9. See Rawick, *From Sundown to Sunup,* pp. 173-78.

10. Rawick, ed., *The American Slave,* vol. 12, part I, pp. 309-10.

11. Escott, *Slavery Remembered,* chapter 5 and Paul D. Escott, "The Context of Freedom: Georgia's Slaves during the Civil War," *The Georgia Historical Quarterly,* LVIII, No. 1 (Spring, 1974), pp. 79-104.

12. Escott, *Slavery Remembered,* pp. 53-57 and 27.
13. *Ibid.,* p. 63.
14. *Ibid.,* p. 45.

History from Slave Sources

C. VANN WOODWARD

George P. Rawick, general editor. *The American Slave: A Composite Autobiography.* Volume 1, *From Sundown to Sunup: The Making of the Black Community,* pp. xxi, 208; volume 2, *South Carolina Narratives,* parts 1 and 2, pp. 348, 346; volume 3, *South Carolina Narrative,* parts 3 and 4, pp. 286, 275; volume 4, *Texas Narratives,* parts 1 and 2, pp. 308, 295; volume 5, *Texas Narratives,* parts 3 and 4, pp. 279, 237; volume 6. *Alabama and Indiana Narratives,* pp. 436, 217; volume 7, *Oklahoma and Mississippi Narratives,* pp. 362, 174; volume 8, *Arkansas Narratives,* parts 1 and 2, pp. 351, 354; volume 9, *Arkansas Narratives,* parts 3 and 4, pp. 393, 310; volume 10, *Arkansas Narratives,* parts 5 and 6, pp. 368, 371; volume 11, *Arkansas Narratives,* part 7, *and Missouri Narratives,* pp. 257, 383; volume 12, *Georgia Narratives,* parts 1 and 2, pp. 352, 357; volume 13, *Georgia Narratives,* parts 3 and 4, pp. 346, 364; volume 14, *North Carolina Narratives,* part 1, pp. 460; volume 15, *North Carolina Narratives,* part 2, pp. 436; volume 16, *Kansas, Kentucky, Maryland, Ohio, Virginia, and Tennessee Narratives,* pp. 17, 123, 78, 116, 56, 81; volume 17, *Florida Narratives,* pp. 379; volume 18, *Unwritten History of Slavery (Fisk University),* pp. v, 322; volume 19, *God Struck Me Dead (Fisk University),* pp. xi, 218. (Contributions in Afro-American and African Studies, Series 2.) Westport, Conn.: Greenwood Publishing Company, 1972.

The interviews with ex-slaves contained in these recently published volumes have been available to scholars in one form or another for some thirty years. Sixteen of the volumes contain the interviews prepared by the Federal Writers' Project (FWP) in 1936-38. The typescript was assembled, bound, and deposited for the use of readers in the rare book room of the Library of Congress in 1941 and later microfilmed for distribution. The two volumes that originated at Fisk University in 1929-30 have been available in mimeograph form since 1945. In the latter year,

B.A. Botkin published a small book of excerpts from the FWP interviews consisting mainly of anecdotes and folklore, but containing quite enough material of historical value to alert the scholarly community to the character of the sources he sampled.[1]

In spite of this, historians have almost completely neglected these materials. Examining all works dealing primarily with slavery and the antebellum Negro that were reviewed in the *Journal of Negro History* during the years 1945-64, one investigator discovered that the FWP narratives had "gone virtually unexploited by serious scholars." About one-third of them cited Botkin's selection, but only one referred to the original collection and then only in a bibliography.[2] The neglect is all the more striking because it continued almost uninterrupted through the next decade and thus through the peak of activity in black history as well as the wave of productivity in the history of slavery. In this same period, one of the most frequent complaints was about the lack of existing evidence from the illiterate, inarticulate, voiceless mass of slaves. How was it that the historian could not escape his dependence on the testimony of the master class and the abolitionists about the experience of slavery—how it was to be a slave? The published narratives of former slaves were available, to be sure, but were they representative of the illiterate millions?

Why these questions did not stimulate extensive exploitation of the slave testimony under review is rather a puzzle. The existence of the material was widely known, and its comparative inaccessibility is not very helpful as an explanation of its neglect. It was more accessible than many manuscript and archive materials that were extensively used at the time. The questions Ulrich B. Phillips had raised about the authenticity and bias of old slave narratives published before and after the Civil War had inhibited their use for a generation.[3] But by the 1950s a neoabolitionist mood prevailed among historians of slavery and the views of the slaves were considered at least as important to an understanding of slavery as the views of the slave-owners. Yet while the published slave narratives were increasingly used, the unpublished testimony of slaves was scarcely touched. What appears to have been the main explanation for the neglect was a prevailing suspicion of the authenticity and quality of the material itself. Grounds for some of these suspicions certainly existed. It will be one of the purposes of this essay to explore and assess the basis for these suspicions. Before doing that, however, it would be well to indicate something of the scope and character of the enterprise.

The sixteen volumes of the FWP narratives, containing about 10,000 pages and roughly 3.5 million words, are based on interviews with more than twenty-two hundred people in seventeen states. Some three hundred interviewers took part in the government financed project. Preparation of the two remaining volumes, *Unwritten History of Slavery* and *God Struck Me Dead,* was privately financed and directed at Fisk University. They are the work of a small staff and represent the records of interviews with some one hundred people in two states, Tennessee and Kentucky. The writers and editors of both projects strove with widely varying success to record the narratives in the words and dialect of the persons interviewed. George P. Rawick, nominal editor of the present publication, says that he has "left the interviews exactly as they were recorded," merely reproducing the original typescripts by photocopy. His only editorial contribution, therefore, is a brief but helpful introduction. His own monograph, *From Sundown to Sunup: The Making of the Black Community,* is published as the first volume of the series.

Virtually all the significant types of slave occupations, skilled and unskilled, are represented among the people interviewed. So are all sizes of plantations and farms and all sizes of slave holdings, from one to a thousand slaves. With the exception of Louisiana, all the states and territories where slavery was still legal toward the end of the regime are represented by samples of some extent, in addition to small samples from Indiana, Kansas, and Ohio. To go beyond these few descriptive facts, however, is to begin a list of shortcomings and faults. Yet these must also be fully conceded and appreciated before any just appraisal of the merits and values of the collection can be attempted.

The claim of "a high degree of representativeness and inclusiveness"[4] that has been made in behalf of the FWP narratives is clouded by evidence of skewed sampling of several kinds. For example, the states included are very disproportionately represented. Arkansas, which never had more than 3.5 per cent of the slave population, furnished about 33 per cent of the ex-slaves interviewed, while Mississippi, which in 1860 contained more than 10 per cent of the slaves, is represented by little more than 1 per cent of those interviewed. The border states are skimpily sampled; Louisiana did not participate, and Virginia diverted all but a small portion of her collection to another publication.[5] While the number interviewed has been estimated to be approximately 2 per cent of the total ex-slave population surviving at the time the interviews were taken, it cannot be assumed that this was a random sample. There is too much evidence of chance or self-selection to assure randomness. Among categories of the population represented by larger than their proportional number are urban residents, males, and former house servants, with a consequent under-representation of rural population, females, and former field hands.

The very age of the former slaves at the time they were interviewed raises several serious questions—about two-thirds were eighty or more, and 15 per cent were over ninety-three, with numerous centenarians (especially in Texas for unknown reasons) among the group. Not only is the question of failing memory raised, but also the question of whether longevity may not be partly attributed to exceptionally good rather than typical treatment as slaves. Age raises other questions of typicality. The age of interviewees at the time of emancipation ranged from one to fifty. About 16 per cent were under six years of age at that time and their testimony about slavery has to be considered largely hearsay. The slave experience of the majority was, in fact, mainly that of childhood, a period before the full rigors and worst aspects of the slave discipline were typically felt and a period more likely than others to be favorably colored in the memory of the aged.[6]

Other distortions doubtless arise from skewed sampling and faulty memories, but in all probability, the most serious sources of distortion in the FWP narratives came not from the interviewees but from the interviewers—their biases, procedures, and methods—and the interracial circumstances of the interviews. The overwhelming majority of the interviewers were Southern whites. In several states they were almost exclusively so. While the direction and guiding spirit of the project in its formative stages was a white Southerner, John A. Lomax, the folklorist, his duties were editorial rather than administrative. Responsibility for drawing the color line in employment of interviewers lies elsewhere, but the line was drawn rather firmly. The typical circumstances, therefore, were those of a Southern white interviewing old-style blacks on their doorsteps in the Deep South in the late 1930s. Jim Crow etiquette and white supremacy attitudes prevailed virtually unchallenged in those years: segregation was at its fully developed height, lynchings were still numerous in spite of a decline, and peonage sustained by force and terror was still a way of life known to millions of blacks.[7]

In that climate of race relations, the white interrogators customarily adopted a patronizing or at best paternalistic tone and at worst an offensive condescension. They flouted very nearly every rule in the handbooks of interview procedure.[8] There were exceptions, to be sure, especially among the white interviewers in Arkansas and Georgia. But as a rule, the questions were leading and sometimes insulting, the answers routine or compliant, and the insensitivity of the interrogator and the evasiveness of the interrogated were flagrantly displayed. An occasional writer brought insight, tact, and inspired sensitivity to the task. The quality of the interview reports varied greatly, but too often they were mechanical or routine, "quaint" or "genial." The interrogator regularly got what he asked for: "Yes, sir, Boss Man, de niggers wuz treated good in slabery times en wuz trained up right, ter wuk, en obey, en ter hab good manners." Were they punished severely? "I'spects dat dey needed all de punishment what dey got."[9] The candor of Martin Jackson of Texas (age ninety) was rare: "Lots of old slaves closes the door before they tell the truth about their days of slavery. When the door is open, they tell how kind their masters was and how rosy it all was."[10]

In a few states, particularly Florida, Negro interviewers were numerous and the two volumes of Fisk narratives were entirely their work. The distinctiveness of interviews where the interviewer and the interviewed were of the same race is readily apparent. The whole atmosphere changes. The thick dialect diminishes and so do deference and evasiveness and tributes to planter benevolence. Candor and resentment surface more frequently. There is also a fuller sense of engagement and responsiveness in the joint enterprise of seeking truth about the past. The interview could become a challenge, as it did with Margaret Nickerson (age eighty-nine or ninety) of Florida:

> Now jes listen. I wanna tell you all I kin, but I wants to tell it right; wait now, I don' wanna make no mistakes and I don' wanna lie on nobody—I ain' mad now and I know how taint no use to lie, I takin' my time. I done prayed an' got all de malice out o' my heart and I ain' gonna tell no lie for um and I ain' gonna tell no lie on um.

She followed a chilling narrative with the statement, "Dis is what I know, not what somebody else say. I see dis myself."[11] It would be hard to find a better witness.

Even the black interviewers had their problems. "It was with difficulty," reported one of them in Florida, "that they were prevailed upon to relate some of the gruesome details recorded here."[12] On the other hand, black interviewers also reported a good deal of apparently unaffected nostalgia for "de good ole days." After all, these were old and helpless people, often living alone in the worst years of the Great Depression, sometimes admitting they were hungry and not knowing where the next meal was coming from. And they were recalling a remote childhood when few were put to field labor before the age of ten or twelve. It is not surprising that for many the memory of slavery that often returned was that of eating and eating regularly. Slavery times and depression times were frequently compared, sometimes at the expense of the latter. Or as an ex-slave of North Carolina put it, "It's all hard, slavery and freedom, both bad when you can't eat."[13] One can never be entirely sure, but some of the testimony of internalized values of master and mistress appear to ring true enough. Abram Harris (age ninety-three) of Arkansas, for example, "kin yit see Marse Hampton" in his dreams "en er heep er times in de day when I's by myself er hoein de cotton he talks ter me plain, so's I kin understand, en he ax me iffin I's yet en still er good nigger, en tell me ter not be disencouraged."[14] There *were* such people. Father figures as well as hate images were part of their heritage from slavery.

Given the mixture of sources and interpreters, interviewers and interviewees, the times and their "etiquette," the slave narratives can be mined for evidence to prove almost anything about slavery. Hester Hunter (age eighty-five) of Marion, South Carolina, actually pronounced it "a Paradise, be dat what I call it."[15] A paradise and a hell on earth, food in plenty and daily starvation, no punishment at all and brutal beatings for no reason at all, tender care and gruesome tortures, loving family ties and forced breedings, gentle masters and sadistic monsters.

That being the case, is the traditional suspicion of this material justified? Shall historians discard the slave interviews as worthless? Not unless they are prepared to be consistent and discard most of the other sources they habitually use. Not while they still use newspapers as sources, or, for that matter, diaries and letters and politicians' speeches and the *Congressional Record* and all those neatly printed official documents and the solemnly sworn testimony of high officials. Full of paradox and evasions, contrasts and contradictions, lies and exaggerations, pure truth and complete fabrication as they are, such sources still remain the daily bread on which historians feed. The slave narratives have their peculiarities, as all types of historical sources do, but they are not all that different from the norm. The norm for historical sources is a mess, a confusing mess, and the task of the historian is to make sense of it.

Sharing the normal shortcomings of historical sources, the slave interviews nevertheless have an unusual character. Confusing and contradictory as they are, they represent the voices of the normally voiceless, the inarticulate masses whose silence historians are forever lamenting. What would the colonial historians give for a comparable 2 per cent sampling of the views of the white indentured servants of the seventeenth and eighteenth centuries, or Southern historians for similar records of the poor whites of the nineteenth century, or Indian historians for such interviews with blanket-Indian tribesmen? Would there have been a comparable neglect of such sources by a whole generation of historians in those fields?

As full of pitfalls as the narratives are, they contain evidence and answers of some sort for almost any kind of question that can be asked about life under slavery—any kind, that is, save those requiring quantification. Our dauntless quantifiers will probably not be stopped by this warning. But to quantify data of this sort would be attempting to quantify the memories of childhood and the lamentations of old age. Most historians still hold, however, that not all admissible evidence has to be numerical and that there are still important historical questions that are not susceptible to quantification.

To suggest a few questions on which the narratives do shed light, there are those relating to childhood, a subject to which historians have been giving increasing attention of late. These include not only nursing and infant care, but prenatal care of the mother and responsibility for discipline and training. Who taught the child to be a "good" slave? On whom did the child look as an authority figure? Master or father, father or mother, mammy or mistress? How did father relate to family? Wife to husband? Within the slave community, what was the relative authority or status of the black overlooker compared with the white overseer? The slave preacher compared with the white minister? Voodoo and herb doctor with white pill doctor? The house slave as against the field slave? The mulatto compared with the black? How did the social structure of the slave community look from the inside? How much solidarity and how much cleavage? Were class lines emerging? Did status and privilege relate to degree of color and racial intermixture? Was the emergence of a West Indian or Jamaica-type brown class already foreshadowed in South Carolina? How did such lines of division relate to rebelliousness or accommodation in slave discipline?

The slave interview evidence requires re-examination of many old questions and assumptions. Abolitionists agreed with proslavery men about the work ethic of slaves—that they were lazy, indolent, incompetent, careless, and inefficient, and worked only under the whip. This abolitionist-slave-holder stereotype is challenged by slave testimony on the variety of crafts mastered by slave artisans, the skills developed in their practice, and the pride workers took in their work and productivity. The stereotype of laziness is challenged by the sheer amount of work they did and how much of it was devoted in off-hours to self-aggrandizement and self-purchase. The old model of planter-absolutism on and off the plantation is cracked by evidence of slave bargaining power. Especially in industrial slavery and slave hiring the lines between master-slave relations and employer-employee relations in free labor became increasingly blurred and indistinct as it becomes apparent that owners as well as employers are coping with common labor problems, sometimes in quite similar ways.

Old institutions and old assumptions about them require re-examination in light of the narratives. One instance is the old view of slave religion as an imitative parody of white evangelical Protestantism. Instead it emerges with a distinctive eschatology and theology as well as the more obviously distinctive styles of worship, preaching, hymns, and participation. A more totally religious culture is hard to imagine. Only one black atheist turned up among the twenty-three hundred interviewees and he was the son of a white atheist father.[16] "What else good for colored folks?" demanded Anne Bell of Winnsboro, South Carolina. "I ask you if dere ain't a heaven, what's colored folks got to look forward to? They can't get anywhere down here."[17] It was a curiously joyful religion. "There is joy on the inside and it wells up so strong that we can't keep still. It is fire in the bones. Any time fire touches a man, he will jump."[18]

The stock image of immobilized slaves chained to cabin, quarters, field, and plantation gives way to contrasting figures of mobility and restlessness. America was on the move and so were they, sometimes in chains and sometimes without them. Millie Evans tells of walking from North Carolina to Arkansas at a pace of fifteen or twenty miles a day and burying her master and three slaves on the way.[19] Rachel Fairley recounts a six-week walk from Charlottesville, Virginia, to Sardis, Mississippi.[20] "Uncle" Dave, born in Virginia, fled to Key West, Florida, was shanghaied on a naval vessel, sailed around the world, was shipwrecked twice, and returned to Florida.[21] Elias Mumford, after emancipation, took his family to Africa, prospered for eight years with his own construction business, and returned to America with capital for a new start.[22] Back and forth they wandered (more of them than whites) as helpless fugitives during the Civil War, sometimes making it on their own to federal lines and freedom, sometimes with their masters, who were seeking to keep them out of the reach of Union armies—from Alabama to Texas, from South Carolina to Oklahoma and back again. Some went as far as Antigua or St. Thomas, some to Canada and the Northern states, but few to stay, most to return to what they had learned to call "home," the South.

Any historian who attempts to make sense of emancipation and Reconstruction will have to bring his bucket to this well. It is one of the deepest reservoirs of ex-slave testimony on two of the most profound historical experiences of the race. Here are spelled out many of the meanings of freedom and how it was perceived. "I took my freedom by degrees," said Robert Glenn of Raleigh, and had trouble "taking myself into my own hands and getting out of feeling I was still under obligations to ask my master and mistress when I desired to leave the premises." He recalled vividly the first time he refused to obey an order of his former master, the first time he failed to touch his forelock on meeting him.[23] Freedom came not only by degrees, but also as cataclysm, like a storm in a time of troubles. Freedom came many ways and by no means all at one time. Sometimes it was years coming after the war, and to some it never seemed to have come at all. Testimony on that experience is often as revealing as testimony on slavery.

Reconstruction had as many meanings as perceivers. But the common and earthy meaning was aptly summed up by Ambus Gray of Biscoe, Arkansas:

> The Reconstruction time was like this. You go up to a man and tell him you and your family wants to hire for next year on his place. He say I'm broke, the war broke me. Move down there in the best empty house you find. You can get your provisions furnished at a certain little store in the closest town about. You say yesser. When the crop made bout all you got was a little money to take to give the man what run you and you have to stay on or starve or go get somebody else let you share crop wid them.[24]

And for the mass of ex-slaves, that spelled out the whole meaning of "Reconstruction."

The history of race relations should be enriched by slave testimony, especially the paradox of formal distance and physical intimacy between the races that slavery maximized. The evidence on intimacy is ample. "I nursed on one breast while that white child . . . pulled away at the other," recalled a former slave in Oklahoma.[25] "Grandma raised me on a bottle so mother could nurse Walter," the master's son. "Mother had good teeth and she chewed for us both," said another from Arkansas.[26] "Why wouldn't I love her," asked a third slave, referring to her owner, "when I sucked titty from her breast when my mammy was working in the field."[27] Love was not an invariable consequence of breast feeding. "I'm going to kill you," one slave told her master's son. "These black titties sucked you an then you come here to beat me." At the end of the encounter "he wasn't able to walk."[28]

The extended family of the planter patriarch included slaves of blood kin, and the interracial matings from which they sprang included not only casual couplings and rapes, but durable and affectionate unions. The degree of willingness partook of all the ambiguities traditionally associated with matings, and the initiative was the monopoly of neither of the races nor either of the sexes. Tempie James, white daughter of a large planter in North Carolina, was locked in her room and the head coachman sold in another state when her parents discovered she was in love with him. Tempie escaped, purchased the coachman, liberated him, married him, bore him fifteen children, and lived to bless many great grandchildren.[29] Harriet Ann Daves of the same state said her white father and owner "never denied me to anybody," and "would give me anything I asked for. He loved my mother and said if he could not marry [her] . . . he did not want to marry."[30] Another slave daughter spurned the affection of her father-master even though he supported her after her marriage, remembered her in his will, and enjoined his white son to visit her regularly after his death, which he did even after his half-sister moved to remote Oklahoma.[31]

Slave commentary on white society provides rich insights on antebellum social history. Black observers were capable of shrewd perceptions of lower class deference or subservience that punctured the myth of *Herrenvolk* democracy—the equality of all whites. One of them was amused by the conduct of a poor white overseer when visiting the quality at the big house and "use to laugh at de way he put grease on his hair, and de way he scraped one foot back'erds on de ground or de floor when they shake hands wid him. He never say much . . . [then, but] he speaks a whole lot though when he git down to de quarters where de slaves live. He wasn't like de same man then."[32] Ex-slaves tended to identify patrollers as well as overseers as poor whites and to remember relations with them as perpetual class warfare. Their attitude was similar to that of their descendants' toward white police. "The patrollers were for niggers just like the police and sheriffs were for white folks. They were just poor white folks," said an Arkansas survivor of slavery.[33] "We didn't think much of poor white men," said Sam Stuart of North Carolina. "He was down on us. He was driven to it by the rich slave owner."[34]

These volumes invite attention to a relatively unexplored field of race relations—those between Negroes and Indians. Black-red relations had most of the complications of black-white relations, plus peculiarities of their own. Indian masters enjoyed the reputation of being somewhat more indulgent than white masters toward the slaves. But there were cruel and brutal Indian slave owners as well. Recalling the beating of her uncle by one of them, Sarah Wilson of Oklahoma declared that "if I could hate that old Indian any more I guess I would, but I hated him all I could already I reckon."[35] The extent of black-red interbreeding and intermarriage needs serious research. The number of ex-slaves who claimed Indian blood is remarkable. One Arkansas interviewer went so far as to say he had "never talked to a Negro who did not claim to be part Indian." An exaggeration, to be sure, and the phenomenon is more prevalent in the Southwest than in the Southeast. There is probably also a psychological as well as a biological dimension to the claim of Indian blood or identity. At any rate, Indian blood is frequently invoked to account for cherished traits of rebelliousness, ferocity, and fortitude. "De Indian blood in me have held me up over a hundred years," said Louisa Daves of South Carolina, age 102.[36] White blood was never mentioned in such connections. If black-red interbreeding was anywhere as extensive as suggested by testimony of ex-slaves, then the monoracial concept of slavery in America requires revision. And if the amount of black-white interbreeding is realistically taken into account, the true description of American slavery would be multiracial rather than monoracial or biracial—white and red as well as black.

It should be clear that these interviews with ex-slaves will have to be used with caution and discrimination. The historian who does use them should be posted not only on the period with which they deal, but also familiar with the period in which they were taken down, especially with the nuances of race relations in the latter period. He should be sensitive to black speech patterns and to the marvelous ambiguities characteristic of them. And of course he should bring to bear all the skepticism his trade has taught him about the use of historical sources. The necessary precautions, however, are no more elaborate or burdensome than those required by many other types of sources he is accustomed to use. They are certainly not great enough to justify continued neglect of this valuable evidence on black history in America.

Notes

1. B.A. Botkin, ed., *Lay My Burden Down: A Folk History of Slavery* (Chicago, 1945). A more extensive and valuable selection of narratives appeared later. Norman R. Yetman, ed., *Voices From Slavery* (New York, 1970).

2. Norman R. Yetman, "The Background of the Slave Narrative Collection," *American Quarterly*, 19 (1967): 536n. This article provides a valuable history of the collection. One exception to the rule of neglecting these sources is Willie Lee Rose, *Rehearsal for Reconstruction: The Port Royal Experiment* (Indianapolis, 1964). Forthcoming books, one by Robert Fogel and Stanley Engerman and one by Eugene D. Genovese, will be exceptions.

3. Ulrich B. Phillips, *Life and Labor in the Old South* (Boston, 1929), 219.

4. Yetman, "The Background of the Slave Narrative Collection," 534-35.

5. Virginia Writers Project, *The Negro in Virginia* (New York, 1940).

6. The age estimates are in Yetman, "Background of the Slave Narrative Collection," 535.

7. Bertram W. Doyle, *The Etiquette of Race Relations in the South* (Chicago, 1937); John Dollard, *Caste and Class in a Southern Town* (New Haven, 1937); Arthur F. Rafer, *The Tragedy of Lynching* (Chapel Hill, 1933); Pete Daniel, *The Shadow of Slavery: Peonage in the South, 1901-1969* (Urbana, 1972); Charles S. Johnson, *Shadow of the Plantation* (Chicago, 1934).

8. See, for example, Stephen A. Richardson *et al.*, *Interviewing: Its Forms and Functions* (New York, 1965), especially 269-327.

9. Henry Green (age ninety), in Rawick, *The American Slave*, 9, *Arkansas*, pt. 2: 96, 100.

10. *Ibid.*, 4, *Texas*, 2: 189.

11. *Ibid.*, 17, *Florida*, 252, 254.
12. *Ibid.*, 131.
13. *Ibid.*, 14, *North Carolina*, 1: 137.
14. *Ibid.*, 9, *Arkansas*, 3: 7.
15. *Ibid.*, 2, *South Carolina*, 2: 340.
16. *Ibid.*, 18, *Unwritten History*, 82.
17. *Ibid.*, 2, *South Carolina*, 1: 53-54.
18. *Ibid.*, 19, *God Struck Me Dead*, 153.
19. *Ibid.*, 8, *Arkansas*, 2: 247.
20. Ibid., 260.
21. *Ibid.*, 17, *Florida*, 311-26.
22. *Ibid.*, 282-84.
23. *Ibid.*, 14, *North Carolina*, 1: 335-37.
24. *Ibid.*, 9, *Arkansas*, 3: 78-79.
25. *Ibid.*, 7, *Oklahoma and Mississippi*, 187.
26. *Ibid.*, 8, *Arkansas*, 2: 41.
27. *Ibid.*, 1: 113.
28. *Ibid.*, 2: 42.
29. *Ibid.*, 15, *North Carolina*, 2: 106-08. Tempie evaded the law against interracial marriage by drinking blood from her lover's veins and swearing she was of mixed blood.
30. *Ibid.*, 1: 233-35.
31. *Ibid.*, 7, *Oklahoma and Mississippi*, 18.
32. *Ibid.*, 2, *South Carolina*, 2: 235.
33. *Ibid.*, 9, *Arkansas*, 3: 293.
34. *Ibid.*, 15, *North Carolina*, 2: 319.
35. *Ibid.*, 7, *Oklahoma and Mississippi*, 347.
36. *Ibid.*, 2, *South Carolina*, 1: 302.

Charles Chesnutt and the WPA Narratives: The Oral and Literate Roots of Afro-American Literature

JOHN EDGAR WIDEMAN

I

Charles Waddell Chesnutt was a man who straddled two worlds. A rigorous program of self-education acquainted him with books. He studied Latin, German, French, and read the classic English writers. Like so many men of his time he sought to school himself in the Anglo-Saxon literary tradition; also, just as studiously, he absorbed the black folk culture of the rural South where he was raised and taught school. In his fiction Chesnutt drew from both worlds, the literate and oral, but what has endured as an original element in his work and as a model for other Afro-American writers in his use of the black oral tradition.

From the drama of the colonial period through the late nineteenth century when Chesnutt began to write, Negroes in American literature had been characterized in a special fashion by their speech. Negro dialect in drama, fiction and poetry was a way of pointing to the difference between blacks and whites; the form and function of black speech as it was represented was to indicate black inferiority. Black speech, the mirror of black people's mind and character, was codified by dialect into a deviant variety of good English. Negro dialect lacked proper grammar, its comic orthography suggested ignorance, its "dats" and "dems" and "possums" implied lazy, slovenly pronunciation if not the downright physical impossibility of getting thick lips around the King's English. Malapropisms, far-fetched words, the preoccupation with telling children's stories, with talk about eating, drinking and dancing, the rampant displays of superstition and fear of the supernatural expressed in black talk were all proof positive of the infantilism, carnality, instability and illogicality of black folk. *Difference* in the dialect tradition clearly signaled *deficiency*. Afro-American speech had been devalued, robbed of those mature aesthetic and functional dimensions it had developed in the New World.

One strategy for a black writer who wished to be taken seriously was to avoid altogether the incriminating dialect tradition. Phillis Wheatley is an early example of this tact. Chesnutt's contemporary Paul Laurence Dunbar experienced acutely the schizophrenia enforced upon the black writer. He lamented the neglect of his "straight" poetry and complained that he had no choice but to write in dialect if he wanted people to listen to him. Chesnutt chose another strategy, one for which he is seldom given credit as a major innovator. Employing a tale within a tale technique he "framed" black speech so that in his best stories Chesnutt blends the literary and oral traditions without implying that the black storyteller's mode of perceiving and recreating reality is any less valid than the written word. Black speech in the form of Negro dialect entered American literature as a curiosity, a comic interlude, a short-hand for perpetuating myths and prejudices about black people. Chesnutt's frame displays the written and spoken word on equal terms or at least as legitimate contenders for the reader's sympathy.

"As de storm tale come to me from my wife, who git it from her mammy, Nancy, it bout like this."

"Dat de blessed truth, too, cause dat exactly what I hear bout dem."

"Does I 'member much bout slavery times? Well, dere is no way for me to disremember, unless I die."

"I 'spects knowin' bout things is just 'bout good and true as seein' them."

These are the voices of ex-slaves recorded by Works Progress Administration workers during the late 1930's. They are from the South Carolina volumes, part of George P. Rawick's monumental collection of ex-slave narratives. Dozens of similar citations could be mustered from the narratives, testifying to the authority and tenacity of oral tradition in Afro-American culture. From 1866 to 1883, Chesnutt lived in the South. He was a contemporary of the former slaves who were interviewed during the 1930's. In his fiction he drew from the common stock of stories, memories and experiences which appear later in these reminiscences. The former slaves were young men and women when Chesnutt began writing; most of them could not read, they were bearers of an oral rather than literate tradition. In a sense Chesnutt wrote the stories they told thirty years later. The ramifications of this situation are fascinating. For historians Chesnutt's fiction and the WPA narratives offer a double focus on the period both attempt to reconstruct. Two views of slavery and reconstruction can be consulted for verification, contradiction, and for the light they shed on each other and upon the customs and facts of the times they reflect. Linguists have the rare opportunity to compare a fiction writer's stylization of a speech community with transcriptions of speech from that community. The literary scholar can look for points of confirmation, influence, continuity and synthesis between the oral and literate roots of Afro-American fiction.

Chesnutt's story "A Deep Sleeper" was first published in 1892, one of the *Two Tales* bound together and issued in a small printing by the Boston publisher Arthur Ware. "A Deep Sleeper" was included in the list of twenty stories Chesnutt hoped might make a book and submitted with that end in mind to Houghton Mifflin on Oct. 22, 1897. The story was not one of those eventually selected to be part of Chesnutt's first book *The Conjure Woman* (1899), and was not reprinted until the publication of *The Short Fiction of Charles W. Chesnutt* in 1974. It is safe to say the story has had few readers. However, it is Chesnutt at his best. Uncle Julius stands at the center of the story and its form embodies the tale within a tale structure of all the stories in *The Conjure Woman*.

Chesnutt frees the narrative of Uncle Julius so the old, ex-slave can stand as a witness, a source of truth about black life during slavery. The voice of Uncle Julius in "A Deep Sleeper" anticipates the voices of the thousands of former slaves who will be interviewed nearly half a century later. The remainder of this essay will examine (1) how Chesnutt altered the traditional frame which emasculated black speech; (2) how the art of the ex-slave narratives can be approached and defined; and (3) how Uncle Julius' narrative shares formal, stylistic features with the narratives of ex-slaves transcribed by the WPA workers.

II

"A Deep Sleeper" begins on a soporific, July afternoon in the rural south during Reconstruction. The first-person narrator, a transplanted northerner who owns the plantation upon which the action occurs, decides that the eating of a watermelon might break the monotony of the sultry July day so he commandeers the aid of Uncle Julius, a relic from the days of slavery inherited when the plantation was purchased. Julius complains of "rheumatiz" and instead of fetching the watermelon himself goes off to waken Tom and instruct him to bring a wheelbarrow to the piazza. When Julius returns to the whites sitting on the piazza he mentions that Tom is one of the "Seben Sleepers" and that the boy's grandfather had once slept a month. The curiosity of the whites is aroused and Julius complies with the women's clamor for a story. Julius' tale takes place during slavery days and concerns the deep sleeper Skundus, his courting of Cindy, their enforced separation, Skundus' "deep sleep" which caused him to disappear for a month and the eventual marriage of the slaves Cindy and Skundus. Julius' dialect narrative is the centerpiece of Chesnutt's story, taking up nearly five of its seven pages. When Tom finally arrives with the wheelbarrow, the group from the piazza stroll out to the watermelon patch and find the prize melon they intended to harvest is gone.

The title "A Deep Sleeper" is enigmatic, becoming more so after several readings of the text it commands. Does the title refer to a quality of the tale which follows? Is this story "a sleeper?" Are its form and message cunning, sly, crafty? Is the tale difficult to fathom or understand, is it obscure? Or do these meanings of the word "deep" describe Skundus, the sleeper whose tale Julius narrates? Or is it Uncle Julius himself who is deep-learned, understanding, wise? Who is sleeping? Skundus? His grandson Tom? All black people? All whites who continue to delude themselves about the depth, the humanity of the black folk over whom they wield lethal power? To whom is the title addressed? To a white audience which accepts the archetype of the sleepy, lethargic black and for whom Skundus and progeny would be humorous examples? Or instead of holding up the black clown (and watermelon thief) for derision, is the butt of the story's joke the self-enforced gullibility of the master-class, the masters who must accept the pilfering of their property, the tall tales of their slaves, accept "deep sleeps" which last for a month? However the title is construed, the words "deep" and "sleep" alert a reader to look below the surface and to be on the watch for someone asleep. The action of the story becomes a gloss on the multiple significations of these words.

"A Deep Sleeper" is composed of a number of movements, internal and external, and these movements can be understood as the result of exercises of power. The exercise of power is being dramatized in the tale. The movement of the words of the story, their linear progress from the title to last word, is a comment on the exercise of power. The first-person narrator (who for convenience will be called "John" as he is in subsequent stories) is compromised by the structure of the story he is relating; what he wishes to say is conditioned by how he must say it. A large part of his story is delivered by Uncle Julius' voice. The convention of labeling or titling a story allows another voice, not necessarily the first-person narrator's, to have the first word, or words, to set the scene and qualify all that comes after. The action of a story, the events portrayed, can have meaning which arises independent of the significance alleged by the narrator; so in fact "A Deep Sleeper" is bracketed by a first "word" (the title) and a last "word" (the disappearance of the popular watermelon), signifiers not controlled by the voice of the plantation-owner/narrator. What seems on the surface to be John's story is rather a demonstration of authorial control over the voice of a first-person narrator. The reader has no way of knowing how John would react to having his story called "A Deep Sleeper." The reader can only guess at the depth of John's understanding of the function or meaning of the story Julius tells. The reader's questions about such matters must be referred to someone outside the story, to an implied author as he is manifested in the weave of voices and events which constitute the story.

That we should be prepared to hear other voices and add their testimony to John's is emphasized by Uncle Julius' "tale within a tale." When the dialect voice of Julius takes over, the first-person narrator, John, disappears and is forgotten; he and the world he described in the opening "literary" paragraphs of "A Deep Sleeper" return only when Julius has finished his narration, only when, to put the matter another way, Julius permits him to speak again. An action has been completed that is a statement about power and authority. The literate narrator's role as proprietor of the story and owner of the watermelon, as master of words and property, has been undermined. The reader is left at the conclusion of the story to sort out his or her own conclusions rather than accept the words of the single, stable guide who seemed to be on hand in the story's first paragraphs.

If the movement of the story, its linear progression from beginning to end, expresses the tension between apparent power and power not so apparent, then one might expect to find parallel movements within the story illustrative of hidden versus apparent power. Like buckets to catch rain from a leaky roof, blacks are moved around in the story according to the needs, wills, and whims of whites. Cindy's removal to Kunnel Wash'n'ton McAdoo's place a hundred miles away from Skundus, her intended husband, is an obvious case. That black people had no control over such removals is made clear by Julius; "Skundus didn' lack ter hab Cindy go, but he couldn' do nuthin." Cindy "didn' hab no mo' ter say 'bout comin' dan she did 'bout goin!" The balance of power seems clear. The master class is absolutely in control. Promises made to blacks are not binding. When Marse Dugal's wife reminds him that niggers have no rights a white man need respect, he breaks his word to Cindy and Skundus, salving his conscience with a few little white lies, to them and to himself. John, Julius' employer, seems to have the same command over Julius' movements as masters had over their slaves. After all, the story occurs on a Sunday afternoon and Julius is on his way home from the church he serves as a deacon, but John does not hesitate to mobilize the old man into his watermelon-fetching scheme.

These apparent exercises of power describe only the surface of black-white relationships. Below the surface, other kinds of power affect other kinds of movement. Though the slaves Cindy and Skundus appear to be pawns, they make adjustments, and these *'justments* allow them to subvert the power of the master class over their lives. Skundus can "steal himself" by running away from the plantation to the swamp. Cindy can pretend her health is dependent on certain elusive roots which she must gather each day from the swamp, a dependency providing a daily excuse for being away from the Big House. Julius and his extended family work for the narrator and must follow his orders, yet Julius is a magician, a trickster, who enchants the whites lounging on the piazza, capturing them in his tale about other times and places so he controls their movements in the present. Julius contrives a fiction to entertain his listeners, to distract them from interfering with his plans. Marse Dugal' manufactures a fiction to smooth over Cindy's removal from Skundus. The parallel loses its symmetry when one recalls that at stake in one deception was a watermelon, while in the other are the lives, love and happiness of two human beings.

A series of confrontations between the powerful and powerless are enacted in the story and in each case an obvious kind of power is balanced by an unexpected force wielded by the supposed powerless. The pairs brought into opposition—Julius and the narrator, Skundus and Marse Dugal', Cindy and her Mistress on the McAdoo plantation—reflect a larger system of black-white power relationships in the South, the struggle to establish personal space and territorial rights. Because of its persistence over time, its pervasiveness in people's lives, this struggle has assumed the formal coherence, the stability and predictability of a ritual dance.

The elements of this dance provide a structural unity in "A Deep Sleeper" and are exhibited in the WPA narratives gathered in the 1930's. First the separation of black from white, a formal assumption paralleling the segregation of the sexes in many traditional African dances. The two groups regard each other over a broad, hard-packed dirt floor, a stage, arena, threshing ground where encounters will be choreographed. An individual dancer sallies out of each group of participants. The dancer's movements are strictly patterned. Facial expression, posture, tone of voice, all are predetermined by ancient canons of behavior. The object of the dance is complex. The whites, who have the advantage of establishing the outward forms of the dance, design the ritual to display their superiority, their dominance; the dance is a metaphor of their power. For the blacks who, like the whites, must perform for two audiences at once, the objective is to find room for maneuver within the rigid forms dictated by the whites, maneuver which allows space for private communication with the other black participants. This communication coded into the space disciplined by the whites becomes another version of the action in the exposed center of the floor. Like a good boxer, the white dancer crowds the black into a corner, cutting off the ring, systematically diminishing room for black display and maneuver, but of course such a strategy also defines the area in which the white must perform. Each pair that enacts the ritual embodies both individual norms of behavior and archetypal relationships. Though these confrontations occur within the framework sanctioned by white power, their inevitability can be turned to the advantage of blacks, can be incorporated into black routines. (Recall Muhamed Ali's "rope-a-dope" tactics vs. George Foreman.) An observer wishing to understand any movement of the dance must visualize it from the dual perspective of the two groups which are its audience.

The separation of black from white and the consequent rituals pro-

duce, among other things, two distinct types of speech which may be exemplified by the narrator, John's literary English, and Julius' dialect.
These varieties of speech describe two different worlds; each speech
form (speech community) represents a version of reality. At some levels
the languages of blacks and whites are mutually intelligible, or at least
seem to allow a variety of exchanges. Chesnutt explores the forms and
uses of language where the *seams* of mutual intelligibility burst. What
Chesnutt's characters are saying cannot be understood unless the reader
has an awareness of the total version of reality which a particular utterance signifies. Dell Hymes' discussion of the socio-linguistic concept *key*
is useful here. In speech acts, *key* provides the tone, manner, or spirit of
the words spoken. Speech acts, often the same as regards setting, participants, form of message, etc., may differ in *key*, that is, may be serious or mocking, painstaking or perfunctory depending on a signal (verbal or otherwise, i.e., wink, gesture) which is part of the speech act.
How something is said (the "how" being defined by the speech community of a speaker) is part of *what* is said. The more a way of speaking
has become shared and meaningful within a group, the more likely that
crucial cues will be efficient or small in scale. Chesnutt employs numerous subtle keys, often drawn from the repertoire of Afro-American oral
tradition, to achieve density of meaning in "A Deep Sleeper."

Manipulation of key can call attention to playful or artistic dimensions of speech. Satire, irony, ridicule, as Sylvia Render points out in her
introduction to *Chesnutt's Short Fiction*, are called into play by *signifying*, a traditional resource of black speech communities signalled by key.
Signifying is verbal art. Claudia Mitchell-Kernan has succinctly described
the dynamics of signifying: the apparent meaning of an utterance is can-
celled by the introduction of a key which signals to those who recognize
the key that the utterance should not be taken "straight." The speaker
who is signifying depends upon a body of experience he shares with the
audience to whom the signifying is addressed. The signifier expects his
audience to process his utterance metaphorically, because their shared
experience allows them to recognize the key and supplies the material
for re-interpreting the utterance. In the street a skillful signifier can talk
behind a victim's back while looking him in the face. Manipulation of
key, employed as a rhetorical device in fiction, permits the writer to address several audiences simultaneously by appealing to pools of knowledge only segments of his readers share with him. In effect, the writer
can profit from the diversity among his readers rather than be limited by
it. Chesnutt took full advantage of this possibility by playing to multiple
audiences, designing his "A Deep Sleeper" in layers, layers corresponding to the conflicting versions of reality perceived by blacks and whites.

"Tom's gran'daddy wuz name' Skundus," he began. "He had a brudder name' Tushus en' ernudder name' Cottus en' ernudder name' Squinchus." The old man paused a moment and gave his leg another hitch.

My sister-in-law was shaking with laughter. "What remarkable names!" she exclaimed. "Where in the world did they get them?"

Uncle Julius is speaking, *sho nuff*, like an old ignorant southern darky is supposed to speak in Negro dialect. And sho nuff he gets his laugh, the laughter Chesnutt could count on from the majority of his readers, the ones who enjoyed Joel Chandler Harris, Sidney Lanier and Irwin Russell, the ones who turned, as Mabel and Annie and John on the piazza, to Uncle Julius for an entertaining interlude. The laughter of such readers is encouraged, sanctioned by Mabel's. Julius' performance is that of a virtuoso dialect story-teller; he is rhyming "brudder" and "enudder" so they fall as syncopated beats in his narration. He is probably twisting his mouth in absurd ways to pronounce the strange names Skundus, Tushus, Squinchus. That his performance for the piazza is conscious and calculated is keyed by the "hitch" he gives his leg. One of the roles Julius is projecting for the whites is an old, feeble man whose ailments prevent him from fetching a watermelon. With sighs, grimaces, and explicit references, Julius sustains this role throughout the story. Given Julius' intentions and the successful working-out of his plan for appropriating the melon, his comments on his pain and the mannerisms by which he pantomimes its effects become a source of humor for those readers who appreciate the art of fooling master.

The source of the "remarkable names" turns out to be Marse Dugal' McAdoo, who named all the babies "wat wuz bawn on de plantation." The absolute power of the master licenced him to name his chattel. For some readers who share with Chesnutt a knowledge of Latin, the humor of the names is enriched because the slaves' names correspond to the Latin words for second, third, fourth and fifth. Recognizing the Latin key, certain readers have their classical learning rewarded, their vanity touched and their prejudice confirmed since Julius exhibits the Negro's darned comical funny habit of muddling words when he reaches above his proper sphere of ignorance. Within the small class that recognized the Latin key, a smaller grouping might respond with indignation towards the old Regime which allowed such abuses of power. Some of this group might even feel slightly ashamed that human beings were given numbers for names, numbers for the master's convenience, numbers which reverberate ironically since they are disguised in Latin, one of the classical languages and cultures which are the oft-exalted and extolled sources of Western Civilization. But some readers may be keyed to other kinds of

power at work here. Julius calls the names "Hebrew" suggesting that
their source, like the source of so many other mysterious indignities the
master class imposes on its slaves, is the Bible, the Bible Julius admits he
cannot read. Uncle Julius makes it clear that "Hit ain' my fault I ain't
able ter read," so his confession of illiteracy is also an indictment of the
ignorance enforced upon the slave by his master. In this light, the source
of the remarkable names might as well be Hebrew as Greek since, for
Julius, access to this kind of knowledge has been systematically with-
held. Chesnutt rightfully, ironically dismisses the question of origin and
points to another kind of meaning the names contain. When the Latin
words are translated into Blackspeech and given their unique pronunciation, an identity is created for the brothers apart from the dehumanizing
numerical designations. Skundus is "Skundus," not *Secundus*. He is baptised by the slave community and becomes a distinct individual. His
distinction, his individuality is defined and preserved in the tale Julius
narrates. Marse Dugal's joke (like so many kinds of humor, a sadistic exercise of power) is turned back on him and the culture he represents.
Originally named for the convenience of a white man, Secundus has
been transformed by Blackspeech and oral tradition into Skundus, a
legendary Deep Sleeper. The source of his name is as much of an enigma
for Mabel as his behavior is an embarrassment and thorn in the side of
Marse Dugal'. While Mabel laughs at the remarkable names, some readers are laughing at her. When Marse Dugal' threatens Skundus: "I'm
gwine ter hang yer up by yer thumbs en take ev'y bit er yer black hide
off'n yer," he is declaiming the literal power of the master over his slaves.
But Julius also states that "evey'body knowed Marse Dugal' bark uz
wuss'n his bite," and this knowledge shared by the slave community is
the key for interpreting Dugal's empty words, as well as the absurd actions he has no choice but to perform when Skundus returns from his
deep sleep.

In his fiction, Chesnutt is cleaning up Negro dialect, tinkering not so
much with its outward form, which he inherited and felt was hopelessly
artificial at best, but with its validity to carry a message apart from the
demeaning one with which it was traditionally burdened. Chesnutt's illiterate speakers from Uncle Julius to Mammy Jane are distinctive not
only because of the form (Negro dialect) of their speech, but because
what they say is true. Oral history in Chesnutt is a vehicle for recon-
structing the past so that the lies and misrepresentations of the master
class become part of the written record. Negro dialect has come full circle. Rather than being an instrument of power in the hands of the enemy
(Black speech framed in an inimical literary tradition), it is turned against
the oppressor.

Can I get a Witness! Chesnutt's answer is yes. He allows Julius to speak for himself. The point of view of the slave can be understood apart from and in spite of the voice of the white plantation owner. The Works Progress Administration oral history project nearly half a century later is another kind of attempt to record the black man's version of slavery and reconstruction. What Julius and the former slaves have to say is of crucial importance if one wishes a rounded view of the "peculiar institution," and scholars have begun to incorporate the slaves' view into the historiography of the period. But how the former slaves told their stories, the notions of style and form, the values embodied in the narratives have been neglected by scholars even though studying the narratives from this perspective perhaps could illuminate fundamental elements of Afro-American culture, the incredible inner sense of purpose and worth, the integrity and resiliency which enabled a people to survive their time on the cross.

III

In her study, *African Oral Literature,* Ruth Finnegan lists some elements to consider in the analysis of oral literature. She points out that any accurate analysis of oral poetry, epic, etc., must take into account non-verbal as well as verbal dimensions of oral performance. To ignore matters such as audience, occasion, details of performance in an oral work, is to "risk missing much of the subtlety, flexibility, and individual originality of its creator and, furthermore, to fail to give consideration to the aesthetic canons of those intimately concerned in the production and reception of this form of literature." Unfortunately, in the case of the WPA collection, we have minimal data on the actual conditions of oral performance, but some facts about the scenarios are retrievable. The speaker is most often performing for an audience of one, usually a white interviewer. The reader of the narratives is dependent on the skill of the interviewers in recording the interviewees' speech. The speaker cannot employ the full range of non-verbal effects, nor can he or she depend upon a responsiveness to the verbal interplay and overtones which would enrich his performance if his audience consisted of members of his speech community. The socio-economic context of the Jim Crow South, the expectations and role playing of blacks and whites obviously restrict the spontaneity of oral performance. The interviewers were often inexperienced and often armed with a list of questions and instructions tending to make all interviews structurally similar. These facts have the cumulative effect of making the interviews conservative in terms of represent-

ing the full range of Afro-American oral tradition. Obscenity, bitterness
and anger towards whites, sexual references (especially to miscegenation), the contribution of music or balletic elements to the narratives,
the audience's active, creative, participatory role are minimized by the
circumstances of the interviews. Just as Chesnutt was fenced in by
the dialect tradition, by the literary sensibilities, the morality, ethics, and
mores of his turn-of-the-century American audience, the ex-slaves who
told their tales to the WPA interviewers had to censure themselves, had to
talk between the lines, had to protect themselves and protect the corner
of truth they wished to preserve by being selective about what they
said and how they said it. This strategy is typical of Afro-American culture and is manifested in African religious practices, in the syncretism of
black churches in the New World, in the politics of Booker T. Washington. It is a survival technique, exemplifying an archetypal configuration,
the practical accommodation of the weak who must in some fashion give
in or seem to give in to the strong in order to shift the locus of com-
bat from external, physical tests of strength to internal, imaginative
competition.

In spite of the circumstances suggested above, the WPA narratives
are rich and exciting, more so in many ways than the more familiar
written narratives dating from the antebellum Battle of Books. Enough
of the style of Afro-American oral performance has survived in the
WPA narratives to allow us to analyze some of the aesthetic canons
underlying each speaker's story. Since the structure of the total interview
as it is printed was not controlled by the person being interviewed, one
must look at smaller segments within the interviews to gain a sense of
how the ex-slaves thought a story should be told. The ideal kind of seg-
ment for analysis is the self-contained story, or anecdote, which the
speaker initiates and shapes. The narratives abound in such set-pieces.
They are usually clearly delineated within the narratives and they possess distinct beginnings, middles, and ends. The economy, pungency,
and precision characteristic of so many of these tales within tales suggest that they have been told before, that given the age and experience
of the narrators, the set-pieces have had the benefit of numerous previous exposures to an audience. The unique interplay between performer
and audience, the fact that an audience actively participates in shaping
a song or story, means the form of an oft-told tale is a product of tradition and individual sensibility. When Frank Adamson begins telling
about his "tribulation," he brings to the telling a conception of what a
good story is and how it should be told. He shares these conceptions
with the other witnesses quoted in Rawick.

Because we have texts and only minimal, if any, descriptive material bearing on non-verbal elements of transmission, the analysis of the following set-piece within a narrative will treat the narrative primarily as one might treat a story or poem. This points to obvious limitations in the analysis, but has the advantage of placing the narratives in a relatively familiar evaluative frame. In spite of the interference of the interview format and the inherent limits of traditional literary analysis for describing oral performance, a strong case can be made for the distinctiveness and coherence of narrative segments.

1."I's been 'possum huntin' wid your pappy, when he lived on de Wateree, just after de war. 2.One night us got into tribulation, I tells you! 3."Twas 'bout midnight when de dogs make a tree. 4.Your pappy climb up de tree, git 'bout halfway up, heard sumpin' dat once you hears it you never forgits, and dats de rattlin' of de rattles on a rattle snake's tail. 5.Us both 'stinctly hear dat sound! 6.What us do? 7.Me on de ground, him up de tree, but where de snake? 8.Dat was de misery, us didn't know. 9.Dat snake give us fair warnin' though! 10.Marster Sam (dat your pa) 'low: 'Frank, ease down on de ground; I'll just stay up here for a while.' 11.I lay on them leaves, skeered to make a russle. 12.Your pa up de tree skeered to go up or down! 13.Broad daylight didn't move us. 14.Sun come up, he look all 'round from his vantage up de tree, then come down, not 'til then, do I gits on my foots.

15."Then I laugh and laugh and laugh, and ask Marster Sam how he felt. 16.Marster Sam kinda frown and say: 'Damn I feels like hell! 17.Git up dat tree! 18.Don't you see dat 'possum up dere?' 19.I say: 'But where de snake, Marster?' 20.He say: 'Dat rattler done gone home, where me and you and dat 'possum gonna be pretty soon!' "

Frank Adamson's narrative is strikingly immediate and affecting. He was 82 years old when interviewed, but age seems to have diminished neither the clarity of his memory nor the energy of his language. His story is vivid, concrete, actual. The speaker strikes out to involve his audience personally. *It's not just me I'm talking about, it's your Pappy.* The first sentence locates the time and place of the story. The next sentence states the subject of the story—tribulation—and encourages the listener's involvement with the collective pronoun *us.* The phatic *I tells you* establishes the narrator's voice as a kind of chorus. Here, as in the blues, the call and response pattern is embodied in a single voice; the teller or singer asserts his authority, his right to echo and *amen* his own pronouncements. The narrator/singer is both inside and outside his story, inside and outside of his experience. In sentence three, time is focused both more concretely—a precise hour is noted—and more abstractly—the hour, midnight, is the witching hour, a symbolic time of reversals, trial and tribulation, of darkness and mystery, a time like "once upon a time" that is the common property of countless stories. A specific event "when the dogs make a tree" limits the abstract, symbolic quality of midnight and returns the storyline to its actual, factual base. The idiomatic quality of the phrase is also a kind of self-description, identifying the speaker as one whose voice comes from the exact center of a specific speech community.

Sentence four is the longest in the narrative. It is balanced rhythmically by two short sentences preceding and two following it. It is musical in another sense. The tail of the sentence rattles with the repetition of *rattlin', rattles, rattle*. The phrase is difficult to say without a syncopated, cadenced, chanted inflection. The phrase is onomatopoeic, the words and the thing they describe become one. Logically, the "tribulation" of sentence one becomes identified with the snake's rattle. The word "tribulation" is onomatopoeic in a less obvious way than "rattling," but "tribulation's" quality as a sound image (echoing the tremor and shakiness of fear) is reinforced by the logical identity between trouble and snake. Sentence five once more asserts the involvement of the teller, his participation in the story and thus his authority. It is also the teller speaking in his own voice, a person (opposed to a disembodied voice of an "author") speaking to other people. Six emphasizes and sustains the unity (affectively heightens the identification) among speaker and audience and characters in the story since all are contained in the *us*. Tribulation affects everyone. The speaker is asking for help. The narrative device is a rhetorical question whose objective is closer listener identification and active involvement. Six is also the shortest sentence in the narrative and the one which conceivably was delivered in the most emotional tone of voice.

In the two balanced, symmetrical phrases which begin sentence seven, the narrator turns back to the objective facts of his story. The narration moves from aural (a question) to visual (a scene) imagery and back again as sentence seven ends with another rhetorical question demanding the reader's attention. The master and the slave are both in trouble, one up in a tree, the other on the ground, and the snake, invisible now, is a generalized tribulation. In sentence eight, the meaning of tribulation is defined, extended. It equals "misery," uncertainty. Uncertainty means loss of control; no decision can be made on rational grounds because the snake's location is a mystery. The story pauses, its narrative thrust slows in the next two sentences as the condition of being in tribulation is explored. The snake isn't to blame for tribulation. *Dat snake give us fair warnin'*. "Marster Sam (dat's your pa)" resigns himself to the situation. His words are as casual as possible; he speaks as master but is not in control and simply voices in the form of an order to his slave a course of action dictated by the mutual predicament of the two men. The story-teller uses dialogue in this sentence, giving himself an opportunity to impersonate his former Marster. Depending upon how Marster Sam's words are dramatized, the narrator can speak volumes about his character. Is the master afraid, pompous, humble, imperious, silly? The narrator has various masks to choose from and his impersonation of the master is limited only by consideration of audience, and his own mimetic abilities.

If we try to listen to Frank Adamson's story as we read it, we will hear the onomatopoeic word *russle* in sentence eleven and hear the alliteration of "lay" and "leaves." Words that sound like the thing they describe can be performed just as dialogue can be dramatized by an expert story-teller. We can share the fear of the story-teller when he whispers a hushed *russle* just as we are engaged by the syncopated rattling above. The word *skeered* is repeated in sentences eleven and twelve. The action of the story is recapitulated in these sentences; *skeered* links the men and the sentences, and the visual image of sentence seven, "Me on de ground, him up de tree" is restated. In this predicament, master and slave are equals. *Skeered* tells us so even though one man is down and the other up. "Broad daylight" of sentence thirteen doesn't change this equality; it doesn't illuminate two separate men, but *us*. The sun is personified, made a character in the story by sentence fourteen. Entering the story, the sun repeats the visual motif of up and down. The tribulation begins to be resolved, not by the voice of a master, but by a natural force to which the speaker cautiously attends. The sun dispells uncertainty, midnight, the fears at the heart of tribulation.

It's a new day. The final five sentences dramatize this new day, rounding the tale of tribulation with a moral. Dialogue is the dominant mode. The scene acted out at the foot of the tree gives the narrator maximum opportunity to play the role of Marster Sam and to use drama's inherent capacity for indirect, satirical comment on the players. Released by the sun, on his feet again, Frank can "laugh and laugh and laugh." The repetition of the word *laugh* gives the narrator ample chance to smile or chuckle as he utters sentence fifteen. But Marster Sam is frowning. He curses, then shouts, "Git up dat tree!" The period of enforced equality ends abruptly. Since both men have shared the same tribulation, the slave's laughter at himself and the situation is also laughter directed at the master. A master's powerlessness is never a laughing matter to the master, especially when a slave is witness, and Marster Sam reasserts his authority by ordering Frank up the tree for the possum. The narrator speaks *with* the lines (his manner of dramatizing the voices of his characters) and *between* the lines (talking about the players while the players are talking by making their behavior emblematic). The slave inquires after the master's health; the slave laughs at the silliness of the night tribulation. The master is disgruntled, coarse and imperious. When Frank asks "But where de snake, Marster?", even in his anxiety he uses a polite form of address. Marster Sam answers with a statement which re-orders the world into the familiar pattern of the Slavocracy. His resumption of the Bossman tone of voice would be immediately recognized by the Southern black and probably mimicked by the narrator. Tribulation is gone, and with it goes the "us," the pronoun uniting master and slave when both were threatened by the rattler. Now it's "you and me and dat 'possum," each creature in its proper sphere, each subject to the master's will. Everybody's going home.

The high density of "sound effects" in Adamson's narrative is striking. By "sound effects" in this context I mean narrative devices which lend themselves to performance as a tale is orally transmitted to an audience. Onomatopoeic words, dialogue, syncopation, phatic phrases, rhetorical questions, call and response patterns, repetitions of words and phrases, rhyme (the end-words of sentences eight and nine) are examples. The level of sound or aural imagery is complemented by both the rhythmic organization of the sentences and by the *percussive delivery* employed by the narrative voice.

There is, intriguingly, a correspondence between the number of words and the number of syllables in each sentence. (In the twenty sentences, four are exactly equal in number of syllables and words, eight differ only by one measure, four by only two.) What this suggests is a one-word, one-beat sentence rhythm, a pattern which allows maximum flexibility. Unencumbered by "correct" pronunciations which would determine the stress pattern in a multisyllabic word, the narrator can emphasize (tone, intensity, length) any word in a sentence; the words are unfettered notes he can arrange in patterns of his choice. Perhaps the close correspondence between number of words and number of syllables also suggests the words as things, a preference in the oral tradition for the concrete monosyllable over the less trustworthy (in terms of pronunciation, rhythm, meaning) polysyllable. An exception would be proper names, whose unique attraction to a teller of tales is their high potential as an aural image and their specificity in regard to a distinct person or place. The elision of syllables ('possum, 'stinctly,) may be partially accounted for as an accommodation to this percussive, striking-one-note-for-each-word style of delivery. If one discounts proper names as inevitable exceptions and grammatical inflections *'ed, 'ing, un'* as less inevitable but occasionally compelling exceptions which give a word more than one syllable (beat), then the correlation between number of words and number of syllables in the story-telling style of the narrative would be even higher.

The use of parallel phrases is also part of the aural imagery, or sound effects, in Adamson's story. They tie together ideas, repeat rhythms, balance contrasts. *Me on the ground, him up de tree.* Repetition of other kinds echo through the story: the same word repeated: *laugh, laugh, laugh;* the same word slightly inflected, with each repetition: *rattlin', rattles, rattle* (ringing the changes); a word repeated in different sentences in order to connect a thought or image the sentences share: *skeered;* visual patterns repeated (up and down) to sustain an idea. If monosyllables and repetition seem unpromisingly monotonous as basic elements in percussive story-telling style, one should recall Albert Murray's remarks on the story-telling of Jo Jones in *Stomping the Blues.* "Nothing is more down-to-earth or more obvious than the ever-steady but somehow also ever flexible Kansas City Four/Four dance beat. Nor is anything more subtle or less monotonous. Jo Jones, the most masterful, influential, and enduring of Kansas City percussionists, is as widely celebrated for the way he signifies with his sticks and wire brushes as for the way he testifies, bears witness, exhorts, annotates, approves or otherwise comments—not only with his sticks and his foot pedals, but also with his mallets and sometimes with his bare hands. Moreover, musicians and dancers alike almost always seem to respond as readily to his most offhand insinuations as to his most forthright declarations and most authorative decrees."

Little has been said about the form of the words in Adamson's narrative because the conventions used by interviewers for transcribing the speech of the ex-slaves are arbitrary. That the former slaves dropped some letters (sounds) and added others is a fact, but the WPA narratives share with the Dialect Tradition conventionalized approximations of standard written English that unfortunately suggest deficiency rather than the maturity and sophistication of Afro-American speech styles. For the student of linguistics, there is evidence in the narratives of enduring syntactical and grammatical habits such as the durative modes of *to be,* but evaluating the evidence of African cultural and linguistic continuities is beyond the scope of the present essay.

Though aural imagery dominates the set-piece quoted, just before launching into the story quoted, Frank reminisces with W.W. Dixon, his interviewer: "I 'members when you was barefoot at de bottom; now I see you a settin' dere, gittin' bare at de top, as bare as de palm of my hand." The language is powerful and evocative, "poetic" in the traditional sense; its simplicity, concreteness and immediacy are illustrative

of the kind of beauty usually attributed to the naturally poetic "folk."
Such linguistic creativity, common in the narratives, is best called Magic.
But if one is discussing stories which have been told and retold, sometimes for generations, one can also argue that the stories exhibit a high
degree of artistic self-consciousness, particularly because the audience of
the stories has participated in their shaping, exercising collectively perhaps greater demands on a piece and achieving a finer sense of when
it's right and finished than an individual author ever gains on his own
work. Eliot argues in "Tradition and the Individual talent" that "we
shall often find that not only the best, but the most individual parts of
[a poet's] work may be those in which the dead poets, his ancestors, assert their immortality most vigorously." The folk tradition reflects an ag-
gregate sensibility, a potential, a range of possibilities which manifest
themselves if and only if an individual embued with this sensibility per-
forms. The idiomatic fluency of the individual performer is a form of
consciousness, a consciousness brimming with ideas and ways of depicting those ideas. It is this consciousness, refined and critiqued by so
many, that the individual draws from. The paradoxical beauty of tradition is that it shapes but does not narrow consciousness; choices are
made by the artist at a level usually conceived of as preconscious, but
these choices enrich and complement rather than limit the choices he or
she "consciously" makes. Frank Adamson did not have to "think through"
every step of his story, but the depth and resonance of oral tradition inform his narrative with a sense of purpose usually attributed to conscious artistry.

IV

Turning again briefly to Chesnutt's "Deep Sleeper," we can locate a
set-piece parallel to Adamson's.

> [1.]"De only fault he had wuz his sleep'ness. [2.]He'd haf ter be woke up
> ev'y mawnin' ter go ter his wuk, en' w'enever he got a chance he'd fall
> ersleep. [3.]He wuz might'ly high gittin' inter trouble mo' d'n once for
> gwine ter sleep in de fiel'. [4.]I never seed his beat fer sleepin'. [5.]He could
> sleep in de sun er sleep in de shade. [6.]He could lean upon his hoe en'
> sleep. [7.]He went ter sleep walk'n 'long de road oncet, en' mighty nigh
> bust his head open 'gin a tree he run inter. [8.]I did heah he oncet went
> ter sleep while he wuz in swimmin'. [9.]He wuz floatin' at de time, en'
> come mighty nigh gittin' drowned befo' he work up. [10.]Ole Marse heared
> 'bout it, en' ferbid his gwine in swimmin' enny mo', fer he said he
> couldn't 'ford ter lose 'im."

The word "sleep'ness," like "tribulation" in Adamson's story, is the subject of this narrative. Instead of transformations of his subject word (tribulation-snake, tribulation-rattle), Chesnutt elaborates the concept of sleep'ness, giving his reader concrete examples of when, where and how sleep'ness effected (defined) Skundus. Chesnutt's narrator Julius is less involved than Adamson with the events of the story; Julius' voice engages the reader less directly than Frank's. The personal pronoun "I" appears only twice and "us" never. Most sentences (six) begin with *He* so that the narrator's energy is used in piling up descriptive details about Skundus. The elaborations of the word "sleep'ness" do not unravel a plot line but rather, attached to Skundus, release the word from its ordinary meaning. Sleep'ness is stretched until it becomes preposterous and comic. Julius blends realistic details into his special definition of sleep'ness, rendering the realistic touches in a plain matter-of-fact voice so that the reader is bounced from the fantastic to the commonplace and back again. The process is calculated. Julius' intent is to unsettle his audience, to humor them into suspending their disbelief so he can substitute for a moment his vision for theirs. If his listeners play his game, Julius will entertain them, he will transport them from the piazza to a much more interesting world where anything can happen.

Chesnutt's narrative, since it is written, is structured less by sound effects than it is by a theme and variations spinning out of humorous examples of sleep'ness. But Chesnutt does draw upon many devices employed by Adamson's oral narrative. Repetition of key words such as *sleep* to establish patterns of meaning and sound; rhythmic repetition in balanced phrases, "He could sleep in de sun er sleep in de shade"; the "I" voice as a chorus, as a witness to the facts of the story, "I never seed his beat fer sleepin'!" Chesnutt captures the one-syllable-per-word percussive beat in Uncle Julius' voice. The word count and syllable count highly correlate, especially if one discounts proper names and the necessary grammatical inflections. Chesnutt does not employ dialogue in this passage, but reports the master's speech in sentence ten. Though the quote is indirect, its form would allow Julius to imitate his master's voice: "he said he couldn't 'ford ter lose 'im." Like Adamson, Julius allows the master to have the last word, but both narrators are signifying, are rounding their tales with a moral. The master in "A Deep Sleeper" is concerned about Skundus the piece of property, not Skundus the human being. Julius reveals this fact, not by editorializing in his own voice, but by letting Marse Dugal speak for himself.

Julius' narrative about Skundus continues for approximately four pages after the passage quoted above. The entire story as discussed earlier functions in a fashion similar to Adamson's narrative, making its point through indirection, humor, satire. In the extended story, Chesnutt dramatizes the Afro-American propensity for word and image-making. *Fittified* and *catacornered fits* are two of Julius' coinages. The Latin names bestowed by Marse Dugal' (as well as Dugal's own name) are translated into the language of the black folk on the plantation. Chesnutt parallels the inventiveness of the oral tradition and illustrates the rich possibilities of this tradition when it is transmitted into written word. Newspapers advertising rewards for run-away slaves become *noospapers,* a punning, Joycean conflation of *news* and *noose,* evoking the lynch rope and the conspiracy of public institutions to keep the black man in bondage.

The oral tradition experienced first-hand during his youth in North Carolina is evidenced in Chesnutt's use of dialect, but it is dialect with roots in the black speech of ex-slaves like Frank Adamson rather than the Negro dialect tradition which by Chesnutt's time was mainly a literary convention for mocking black life.

Using the Testimony of Ex-Slaves: Approaches and Problems

JOHN W. BLASSINGAME

Historians of the South's Peculiar Institution have been engaged in a perennial debate about the reliability of various sources. Conceding the virtual impossibility of finding the completely objective observer, many of them insist that every class of sources should be investigated. Stanley M. Elkins presented the most convincing argument on this point in 1959 when he wrote that eyewitness accounts of slavery "were both hostile and sympathetic in nature. It is perhaps best that each kind be given equal weight, as evidence in the judicial sense must always be, and the best presumption probably is that none of these observers was lying about the facts as he saw them. Different facts impressed different people, of course. . . . Much is gained and not much is lost on the provisional operating principle that they were all telling the truth."[1]

Unfortunately, few historians have acted on the principles outlined by Elkins. While examining practically all kinds of accounts written by white eyewitnesses, they have largely rejected those accounts written by ex-slaves. Ulrich B. Phillips led the way in his *Life and Labor in the Old South* (1929) when he declared that "ex-slave narratives in general . . . were issued with so much abolitionist editing that as a class their authenticity is doubtful."[2] Most scholars have followed Phillips in refusing to read the accounts of former slaves. Only three of the sixteen state studies of plantation slavery published between 1902 and 1972 drew even moderately on slave testimony. Among the general studies of slavery, only Frederick Bancroft, in *Slave-Trading in the Old South* (1931), used the testimony of former slaves extensively.[3]

A number of scholars have challenged Phillips and contend that in order to understand slavery from the vantage point of blacks, one must carefully study black testimony and suggest ways it can be used.[4] Historians need to know, for example, how to analyze interviews that were conducted with former slaves in the twentieth century. Which of the published autobiographies can be verified by independent sources? Which of them are least reliable? What kinds of questions can and cannot be answered by resorting to the accounts of former slaves? How many of the stories were written by the blacks themselves? Who edited the published narratives?

The fundamental problem confronting anyone interested in studying black views of bondage is that the slaves had few opportunities to tell what it meant to be a chattel. Since the antebellum narratives were frequently dictated to and written by whites, any study of such sources must begin with an assessment of the editors. An editor's education, religious beliefs, literary skill, attitudes toward slavery, and occupation all affected how he recorded the account of the slave's life.

Generally, the editors of the antebellum narratives were an impressive group of people noted for their integrity. Most of those for whom biographical data were available were engaged in professions (lawyers, scientists, teachers, historians, journalists, ministers, and physicians) and businesses where they had gained a great deal of prior experience in separating truth from fiction, applying rules of evidence, and accurately portraying men and events. Many of them were either antagonistic to or had little or no connection with professional abolitionists. This was especially true of Samuel Atkins Eliot and David Wilson. Eliot, the editor of Josiah Henson's first narrative, was a musicologist and essayist who had served successively as state legislator, mayor of Boston, and congressman (1850-1851). When Eliot voted for the Fugitive Slave Law, he was denounced by abolitionists. Solomon Northup's editor, David Wilson, was a New York lawyer, state legislator, occasional poet, and former school superintendent. He had no relationship with abolitionists.[5]

Often, whites edited narratives because their interest in slavery was aroused by sensational trials involving kidnapped or fugitive blacks. For example, Harper Twelvetrees, a London manufacturer, copied John Anderson's story almost verbatim from the stenographic report of a Canadian extradition hearing. Similarly, when the New York free Negro Soloman Northup was rescued from slavery in Louisiana, he attracted the attention of one of his neighbors, David Wilson.[6]

Five of the editors, William George Hawkins, Joseph C. Lovejoy, James W.C. Pennington, Thomas Price, and William Greenleaf Eliot, were noted ministers in the United States and England. The most famous of them was William G. Eliot. Ubiquitous reformer and philanthropist, Eliot served a long tenure as pastor of a St. Louis congregational church, was president of the city's school board, and founded Washington University at St. Louis. During the antebellum period Eliot frequently castigated "fanatical abolitionists" and adhered rigidly to his belief in gradual emancipation.[7]

Many whites edited the narratives because of their interest in history. In fact, nine of the editors had published historical works before 1860. The editors who wrote one historical work during the antebellum period included Samuel A. Eliot, Pennington, and Price.[8] Other editors might properly be treated as amateur or professional historians and biographers. Numbered among them were James S. Loring, Henry Trumbull, David Wilson, Joseph C. Lovejoy, Charles E. Lester, and Charles Campbell.[9]

One of the most prolific was Charles E. Lester. A presbyterian minister, consul, and reporter, he published twenty-seven books during his lifetime and translated a number of French and Italian works into English. Lester's *The Life and Voyages of Americus Vespucius* went through several editions between 1846 and 1903.[10] Undoubtedly the most highly qualified of the historian-editors was a southerner, Virginia's Charles Campbell. School principal, newspaper editor, and essayist, Campbell edited the papers of Theodorick Bland, Jr., and the military records of the American Revolution and wrote a book on the colonial history of his state. One of Campbell's contemporaries characterized his work as "remarkable for its research and accuracy."[11]

Some of the abolitionist editors also had impressive credentials. This is especially true of those editors with considerable journalistic experience: Louis Alexis Chamerovzow, Isaac Tatem Hopper, and James W.C. Pennington. Chamerovzow had edited various journals and served as secretary of the British and Foreign Anti-Slavery Society before he edited the narrative of John Brown. Thomas Cooper's account was edited by Hopper, the implacable Quaker prison reformer who had served as coeditor of the *National Antislavery Standard* and was one of the foremost penologists of his time. Pennington, the editor of J.H. Banks's narrative, was a former Maryland slave who had spent sixteen years as an editor and investigative reporter for several black newspapers.[12]

Many of the procedures the editors adopted are now standard in any biographical study or oral-history project. Generally, the ex-slave lived in the same locale as the editor and had given oral accounts of his bondage. If the fugitive believed that the white man truly respected blacks, they discussed the advisability of publishing his account. Once the black was persuaded to record his experiences for posterity, the dictation might be completed in a few weeks or be spread over two or three years. Often, the editor read the story to the fugitive and asked for elaboration of certain points and clarification of confusing and contradictory details. When the dictation ended, the editor frequently compiled appendices to corroborate the ex-slave's narrative. The appendices consisted almost entirely of evidence obtained from southern sources: official reports of legislatures, courts, governors, churches, and agricultural societies, books written by southern whites, or newspapers edited by them. If any of those among the editor's friends who first heard the narrative doubted its authenticity, they sometimes interrogated the fugitive for hours.[13]

A comparison of the narratives with other works written by the editors reveals few essential differences between the techniques they employed. Charles Campbell approached Isaac Jefferson's narrative with the same detachment that he used in editing the papers of Theodorick Bland. The appendices, poems, and letters contained in Joseph C. Lovejoy's biographies of his brother and of the Reverend Charles T. Torrey are similar in character to those included in his edition of the narrative of Lewis G. and Milton Clarke. The same pattern prevails in various historical works and the narratives edited by Wilson, Lester, Loring, Price, and others.[14]

One indication of the general reliability of the edited narratives is that so few of them were challenged by antebellum southerners. The first exposé was of the narrative of James Williams, which Alabama whites proved was an outright fraud. The only other antebellum attack on a narrative involved the autobiography of Charles Ball. In Ball's case, however, the charges cannot be substantiated. A comparison of the narrative with antebellum gazetteers, travel accounts, manuscript census returns, and histories of South Carolina shows that Ball accurately described people, places, rivers, flora and fauna, and agricultural practices in the state. Since the only narrative included in U.B. Phillips's justly acclaimed *Plantation and Frontier Documents* was that of Charles Ball, it may have been more reliable than the antebellum critics were willing to concede.[15]

Of course, many of the more reliable narratives contain elements that cannot be attributed to the blacks. Certain literary devices that appear in the accounts were clearly beyond the ken of unlettered slaves. First, many of the narratives contain long dialogues that could only represent approximations of the truth. Sometimes it is obvious that the editors fleshed out the sparse details supplied by the fugitives to heighten the dramatic effect of the dialogues. Second, the abolitionist editors often included direct appeals to their white readers. Many of them also penned long digressions on the duplicity of northerners in maintaining slavery. Similarly, the most complicated philosophical, religious, and historical arguments were sometimes attributed to the slaves to show that bondage violated divine law and the natural rights of man.[16] On occasion a narrative contained so many of the editor's views that there was little room for the testimony of the fugitive. Sometimes the accounts were so romantic and focused so heavily on the flight from bondage that they were more akin to Indian-escape literature than slave autobiographies. These features are so prevalent in the narratives of Elleanor Eldridge, Sally Williams, Jane Blake, and others that they generally reveal few of the details of slave life.[17] There can be little doubt that the abolitionists interjected some of their own ideas into the narratives. Apparently, however, a majority of them faithfully recorded the factual details they received from the former slaves.

If it is conceded that many of the abolitionist editors were honest but biased men, the major task of the historian, then, is to find ways to separate their rhetoric from the sentiments of the slaves. The first step in this direction is to compare the antebellum narratives with some of the best autobiographies written by former slaves after the Civil War. Although they are sometimes rather romantic or devote few pages to their life on the plantation, the accounts published during the postbellum period are in many ways the most significant and reliable of the lot. The pain of the whip had generally faded enough for the former slaves to write about bondage with less passion than their antebellum predecessors.[18] Another way of identifying elements added by white editors is to compare the first edition of a narrative with each revised version. The first edition of most narratives is often the one with the fewest distortions.[19]

Even when one is able to identify and discount abolitionist rhetoric in the accounts of fugitive slaves, the "facts" supplied by the blacks may seem false. The only way such doubts can be removed is to try to verify the details of the account by examining independent sources. Fortunately, a plethora of antebellum sources enables historians to ascertain whether the abolitionist editors distorted the accounts of the fugitives. Several of the blacks, for example, made and wrote numerous speeches and letters antedating the publication of their narratives. When these records are compared with the published accounts, it is obvious that many of the editors tried to write the details of the fugitive's life as he dictated them. This is especially true of the narratives of Lewis G. and Milton Clarke,[20] Josiah Henson,[21] William and Ellen Craft,[22] and Henry Box Brown.[23] A number of scholars have investigated judicial proceedings, manuscript census returns, diaries and letters of whites, local records, newspapers, and city directories and have proven that the narratives of Solomon Northup, John Brown, Olaudah Equiano, and others were authentic.[24]

Many blacks who had purchased their freedom, been manumitted, or escaped from bondage wrote autobiographies without the aid of white editors. A comparison of the narratives of such well-known blacks as William Wells Brown, Frederick Douglass, Henry Bibb, James W.C. Pennington, Jermain Loguen, Austin Steward, and Richard Allen with their antebellum letters, speeches, sermons, and books reveals so many similarities in style that there can be no doubt about either the authorship or authenticity of their accounts. Even such obscure men as John Thompson, Noah Davis, Solomon Bayley, and G.W. Offley have left enough records to establish their authorship of their autobiographies.[25] Similarly, more than 90 percent of the sixty-seven narratives published after the Civil War were written by the blacks themselves.

Although most of them are authentic, the published narratives constitute a limited sample of the total slave population in a number of ways. First, there are many more accounts of slavery in the upper than the lower south (and practically none for Florida, Arkansas, and Texas). Second, and most important, black women wrote less than 12 percent of the narratives. Third, the percentage of fugitives among the narrators was much higher than the percentage of blacks who escaped from slavery. While less than 5 percent of the bondsmen successfully followed the North Star to freedom, fugitives wrote about 35 percent of all narratives. (The others were written by slaves who purchased their freedom, were manumitted, or were freed after the Civil War began.) Finally, an overwhelming majority of the narrators were among the most perceptive and gifted of the former slaves.

Because of the high proportion of exceptional slaves among the black autobiographers, many scholars insist that more of the average slaves should be heard and point to the 2,194 interviews with ex-slaves compiled by the Works Progress Administration between 1936 and 1938 as the chief source for such testimony. Deposited in the Library of Congress, the collection was rarely used until Greenwood Press published it in 1972. Even before the interviews were published, Benjamin A. Botkin and Norman R. Yetman had made a convincing case for their use. George P. Rawick and Eugene D. Genovese have added their own enthusiastic endorsement of Botkin's and Yetman's views. According to these scholars, the WPA interviews are much more representative of the total slave population, less biased, and less distorted than the published narratives of former slaves.[26] Since there are few systematic analyses of the interviews, it is difficult to assess the validity of their claims.

One obvious shortcoming of any study based on the WPA data, however, is that few American historians have been trained to use interviews. Because of his traditional fascination with the written word, the American historian, when confronted with the oral lore represented by the WPA interviews, has no methodological tools that are applicable to them.

Social scientists have pinpointed several problems in interpreting oral lore which are especially evident in the WPA interviews.[27] The first and most important question one must raise about these sources is whether the interview situation was conducive to the accurate communication and recording of what the informants remembered of slavery. In this regard, it should be noted that black interviewers were virtually excluded from the WPA staffs in all of the southern states except Virginia, Louisiana, and Florida. Discrimination in employment led to a distortion of information; during the 1930s caste etiquette generally impeded honest communication between southern blacks and whites.

John Dollard, Hortense Powdermaker, Allison Davis, and many other social scientists who studied the South during the 1930s give vivid pictures of the milieu in which the WPA data were collected. In the context of the 1930s the oft-repeated declaration of WPA officials that they were not interested in "taking sides" on contemporary racial problems seriously limited their ability to obtain accurate information from southern blacks.[28] Traditionally, any white man who is not "with" black folks is inevitably viewed as being "against" them. Anyone who doubts this should read the essay by William R. Ferris, Jr., on the problems he encountered while collecting oral lore in Mississippi in 1968. During his interviewing Ferris found:

> It was not possible to maintain rapport with both Whites and Blacks in the same community, for the confidence and cooperation of each was based on their belief that I was "with them" in my convictions about racial taboos of Delta society. Thus when I was "presented" to Blacks by a white member of the community, the informants regarded me as a

member of the white caste and therefore limited their lore to non-controversial topics.

Blacks rarely speak openly about their society with Whites because of their vulnerability as an oppressed minority. . . . As the group in power, Whites can afford to openly express their thoughts about Blacks, whereas the latter conceal their feelings toward Whites as a means of self-preservation.[29]

The black man's vulnerability to white oppression was painfully evident in the Depression South. From 1931 to 1935, for example, there were more than seventy lynchings in the South; nine blacks who had committed no crime were killed, and twenty-five were lynched for minor offenses. Many of the black informants lived in areas where labor contracts were negotiated in jails, debt was perpetual, travel was restricted, and the threat of violence made peonage a living hell. Historian Pete Daniel, after an exhaustive study of southern peonage, concluded: "The violence that attended peonage sent tentacles of dread throughout the entire black community."[30] Since many of the former slaves still resided in the same areas as their masters' descendants and were dependent on whites to help them obtain their old-age pensions, they were naturally guarded (and often misleading) in their responses to certain questions. Frequently the white interviewers were closely identified with the ancien régime; on occasion they were the grandsons of the blacks' former masters.

The answers to many of the questions on the WPA interview schedule could neither be divorced from the dependent position of the aged blacks nor the contemporary state of race relations in the South. Since attitudes toward the past were often so intertwined with the present in the minds of both informants and interviewers, there was a high premium placed on giving the "right" answers to such questions as: "Was your master kind to you?" "Now that slavery time is ended, what do you think of it?" "Was your master a good man?" "Which was best, slavery or freedom?"[31] Not content with these and other leading questions indicating the kinds of replies they wanted, many of the interviewers refused, initially, to accept the "wrong" answers. This was especially the case when the former slaves described their masters as cruel and said that life on the plantation was characterized by unusually hard work. A Georgia interviewer, for example, was disturbed by the responses of Nancy Boudry to her questions:

Nancy's recollections of plantation days were colored to a somber hue by overwork, childbearing, poor food and long working hours.

"Master was a hard taskmaster," said Nancy. . . . "I had to work hard, plow and go and split wood jus' like a man. Sometimes dey whup me. Dey whup me bad, pull de cloes off down to de wais'—my master did it, our folks didn' have overseer."

"Nancy, wasn't your mistress kind to you?"

"Mistis was sorta kin' to me, sometimes. But dey only give me meat and bread, didn' give me nothin' good—I ain' gwine tell no story. . . ."

"But the children had a good time, didn't they? They played games?"

"Maybe dey did play ring games, I never had no time to see what games my chillun play, I work so hard. . . ."[32]

The white staff of the WPA had mastered so little of the art and science of interviewing that many of them found it impossible to obtain trustworthy data from their informants. The whites disregarded a fundamental rule of interviewing that Ferris noted in 1968: "As a white collector, rapport with Blacks was particularly delicate and required constant sensitivity to the feelings of informants."[33] Many of the WPA interviewers consistently referred to their informants as darkeys, niggers, aunteys, mammies, and uncles. Reminiscent as these terms were of rigid plantation etiquette, they were not calculated to engender the trust of the blacks. Rather than being sensitive, the white interviewers failed to demonstrate respect for the Blacks, ignored cues indicating a tendency toward ingratiation, and repeatedly refused to correct the informants' belief that the interviewer was trying to help them obtain the coveted pension. Not only did most of the whites lack empathy with the former slaves, they often phrased their questions in ways that indicated the kinds of answers they wanted.

Every recorded interview had two authors, the person who asked the questions and the one who answered them.[34] Often the white interviewer-author's actions and demeanor led to distortions and limitations of what the black informant-author told him. Many of the blacks played it safe; they claimed that they remembered very little about slavery and gave one- or two-page interviews. Even the informants who gave the longest, most candid interviews refused to talk about certain things. One frustrated Kentuckian, for example, reported: "In interviewing the different negroes in this community I have not found a single negro that could admit [,] if I asked the direct question [,] that they are the least bit superstitious."[35] Sometimes it was impolitic, if not dangerous, for the ex-slave to tell all that he remembered. This is especially evident in the folk songs and tales. Although practically every intensive study of these cultural elements reveals much antiwhite sentiment, rarely does this attitude surface in the WPA collection. Many of the secular songs are lullabies or hunting songs; the white-hating trickster slave Jack almost never appears in the tales. The blacks were carefully editing what they told whites; generally, they told them only children's tales and songs. One indication of this is the difference between the tales recorded during the same period by the black folklorist J. Mason Brewer and those by the

WPA. Taken from the same class of informants, the tales Brewer recorded have a relatively high anti-white content and many Jack or John stories.[36]

A second weakness of the WPA interviews is that many of them are not verbatim accounts. The informants' stories were often edited or revised before they were typed and listed as official records. Even when the former slave's views are purportedly typed in his own words, the interview may have been "doctored," certain portions deleted without any indication in the typescript, and his language altered. Consequently, the interviews are not, as Norman R. Yetman claimed, "almost exclusively verbatim testimonies" in which blacks "describe in their own words what it felt like to be a slave." Indications of deliberate distortion and interpolation of the views of the WPA staffers pose a serious challenge to historians who rely on the interviews.[37]

The best evidence on the alteration of interviews appears in the records of Roscoe E. Lewis and a Georgia interviewer, J. Ralph Jones. In 1936 and 1937 Jones conducted five interviews that were returned to the state office of the WPA. Three of the five transcribed by the state office are virtually identical to the copies that Jones retained. The other two were significantly reduced in length and seriously distorted.[38]

Jones's interviews with Rias Body and Washington B. Allen were edited to delete references to cruel punishments, blacks serving in the Union Army, runaways, and blacks voting during Reconstruction. Jones had two interviews with W.B. Allen, and the second one is recorded in practically identical words in his record and the WPA typescript. The WPA typescript of the first interview, however, lists Allen's date and place of birth incorrectly and does not include 1,700 words that appear in Jones's record of the interview. About half of the section excluded from the WPA typescript referred to slave traders, the religious life of the slaves, the tricks they played on the patrollers, and the songs they sang. While the typescript refers to the kind treatment Allen received from his owners, Jones's records show that he spent a great deal of time talking about the hard work and cruel floggings characteristic of the plantation.[39] The WPA transcript gives the impression that Allen spoke in dialect, using such words as "fetched," "de," "dis," "chilluns," and "fokes." But in his records Jones observed that Allen "uses excellent English. . . ."[40]

J. Ralph Jones's experience was not unique. The same kinds of distortions appeared in the typescripts of the Virginia WPA. Nine of the Virginia informants included in the Library of Congress collection were also quoted in the 1940 publication, *The Negro in Virginia*. Roscoe E. Lewis, the editor, had the original report of the interviews in his possession, and seven of the nine informants he quoted presented views excluded from the typescripts of their accounts. According to the excerpts quoted by Lewis, between one and twelve hundred words of the original interviews were excluded from the typescripts of the accounts of Fanny Berry, Georgianna Gibbs, Charles Grandy, Della Harris, Mobile Hopson, Richard Slaughter, and Eliza[beth] Sparks. The typescripts are poor summaries of the ex-slaves' comments. Songs and religious sentiments were frequently left out of the WPA typescripts. Indications of cruel punishments, forced marriages, family separations, ridicule of whites, and the kindness of Union soldiers appeared in the records cited by Lewis but often do not appear in the WPA typescripts.[41]

Although the facts are not entirely clear, it is obvious that many of the WPA interviews were altered after the dictation ended. The national office of the WPA encouraged this in regard to the language patterns of the blacks when it urged state directors to record dialect uniformly. This may have accounted for dialect being ascribed to former slaves who spoke English perfectly. But how can one account for the discrepancies between the interviews Jones and others recorded and those the WPA staff typed? Were two out of every five interviews in Georgia and other southern states distorted in the same way? While there are no definitive answers to these intriguing questions, historians must ponder them when they try to use the WPA interviews.

A third factor that led to distortion of the WPA interviews was the average age of the informants; two-thirds of them were at least eighty years old when they were interviewed. And, since only 16 percent of the informants had been fifteen years or older when the Civil War began, an overwhelming majority of them could only describe how slavery appeared to a black child. Because all of the blacks were at least seventy-two years removed from slavery, there was no sense of immediacy in their responses; all too often they recalled very little of the cruelty of bondage. A good way of determining the impact of age on the responses of former slaves is to compare the WPA interviews with the hundreds conducted by northern journalists, soldiers, missionaries, and teachers during and immediately after the Civil War. These informants were still close to bondage, and consequently they remembered far more of the details of slavery than the WPA respondents.[42]

Were the WPA informants, as Yetman claimed, representative of the total antebellum slave population? Apparently not. Since the average life expectancy of a slave born in 1850 was less than fifty years, those who lived until the 1930s might have survived because they received better treatment than most slaves. Taken at face value, there seems to have been a bias in many states toward the inclusion of the most obsequious former slaves. This is especially true when most of the informants had spent all of their lives in the same locale as their former master's plantation. Since the least satisfied and most adventuresome of the former slaves might have migrated to northern states or cities after the Civil War, the WPA informants may have been atypical of antebellum slaves. Geographically, the WPA collection is also a biased sample. Although 920,266 of the South's 3,953,760 slaves (23 percent) lived in Virginia, Missouri, Maryland, Delaware, and Kentucky in 1860, only 155 Blacks from these states were included among the 2,194 published interviews (7 percent of the total). Consequently, the upper south (and especially the border states) is underrepresented. On the other hand, while Arkansas and Texas had only 293,681 or 7 percent of southern slaves in 1860, the 985 Black informants in these states constituted 45 percent of all former slaves interviewed by the WPA.[43]

Most of the interviews are so limited in focus or are so short that it requires considerable skill to extract reliable information from them. In the South Carolina volumes, which contain some of the longest interviews, only 18 percent of the accounts are more than five pages long. Because of the brevity of the interviews it is often impossible to resolve internal inconsistencies, reconcile tone with "facts," separate rumor from direct observations, fathom subtle nuances, verify uncertain chronology, or determine the extent of "structural amnesia" and the manipulation of data to conform to the conditions existing in the 1930s. Since the major objective of the WPA project was to record folklore, other topics relative to plantation slavery often received little attention.

Although there are probably other weaknesses and limitations of the interviews that could be noted, the historian's major concern must be with determining ways to utilize them. One of the cardinal principles in interpreting oral lore is that the investigator must have an intimate knowledge of the informant's group, tribe, or race. According to the Africanist Jan Vansina, "members steeped in the culture itself, and sometimes only the more sensitive among them" are in the best position to study oral lore; "it is preferable that study of traditions be entrusted to people who belong to the society itself."[44] But whether black or white scholars study the WPA interviews is not as important as the approaches they take. They should begin by mastering the skills of the linguist and then systematically examine the internal structure of the interviews, the recurrence of symbols and stereotypes, the sequence of episodes, and the functions they serve.

Given the staffing policies of the WPA, some effort must be made to determine the relationship between the sex and race of interviewers and the reliability of the accounts. Generally, the stories are most revealing when the informant and the interviewer were of the same sex; black interviewers obtained more reliable information than white ones; and white women received more honest responses than white men. Fortunately, a majority of the former slaves in most states were interviewed by white women: 60 percent in North Carolina; 80 percent in Arkansas; and 90 percent in Georgia. The reverse, however, was true in South Carolina, where 78 percent of the former slaves were interviewed by white men.

There are also other important variations in the collections. Although the Arkansas staff interviewed more blacks than any of the others, a larger percentage of them had never actually been slaves. For example, about 40 percent of the Arkansas informants were born during or after the Civil War. (Many of them were in their forties or fifties in 1938.) All things considered, the Georgia collection is one of the most reliable of the WPA volumes: Most of the informants had actually been slaves (though not as old as the South Carolina Blacks) and were interviewed by white women. The Georgia staff also made an effort to evaluate the interviews they collected. These evaluations were cautious and generally in accord with the data contained in the interviews. Louise Oliphant, for instance, asserted, "There are many ex-slaves . . . who have vivid recollections of the days when their lives were inseparably bound to those of their masters. . . . Mistreatment at the hands of their masters and the watchdog overseers is outstanding in the memory of most of them." On the other hand, Ruby Lorraine Radford discovered that "out of about thirty-five negroes contacted [,] only two seemed to feel bitter over memories of slave days. All the others spoke with much feeling and gratitude of good old days when they were so well cared for by their masters." Unlike most white interviewers, Radford did not accept such declarations as indicative of planter paternalism. Instead, she tried to correlate them with the average age of the informants and concluded that "most of the slaves interviewed were too young during the slavery period to have experienced any of the more cruel punishments, though some remembered hearing tales of brutal beatings."[45]

The interviewing skill of the Georgians differed greatly from that of many other white southerners. Consequently, it is mandatory to compare the stories collected by black interviewers with those collected by whites. The key questions in this comparison are those that involve life in the quarters and the treatment of slaves (frequency of floggings, adequacy of food, character of masters, etc.). The portrait given by South Carolina informants is a good example of those recorded by all-white interview staffs. According to South Carolina Blacks, most of them were well treated, bountifully fed and clothed, and rarely overworked by kind masters. Most of them longed for the old plantation days. Although a great deal of this can be attributed to the general propensity of man to view his childhood through rose-colored lenses, most of it was due to caste etiquette and the actions and attitudes of the white interviewers.

The former slaves who talked to black interviewers presented an entirely different portrait of their treatment from what they told white interviewers. Black scholars at Hampton Institute, Fisk University, and Southern University conducted approximately nine hundred interviews with ex-slaves between 1929 and 1938. The interviews they received run directly counter to the South Carolina image of planter paternalism. More important, none of the volumes of interviews conducted by whites reveal as much about the internal dynamics of slave life as these 882 accounts. The informants talked much more freely to black than white interviewers about miscegenation, hatred of whites, courtship, marriage and family customs, cruel punishments, separation of families, child labor, black resistance to whites, and their admiration of Nat Turner. If one begins with the testimony collected by the predominantly black WPA staff at Hampton, by John B. Cade in Louisiana, and by Ophelia Settles Egypt in Tennessee and uses them as the standard of accuracy, many of the general distortions in the WPA collection can be eliminated.[46]

In spite of the skewed sample, the distortions, and the biases, the WPA interviews reveal much about the nature of slavery. Given the average age of the informants when they were freed, for instance, their stories contain a great deal of information about the childhood experiences of slaves. And, given the interests of interviewers, they contain a large repository of folklore. Using only those slaves who were at least fifteen years old in 1860, it is possible to compile some limited statistics on the separation of families, the age at which children started work, the occupations of slaves, and the extent to which overseers and drivers were used. The most reliable information can be compiled by asking questions that differ from those asked by the white interviewers. In this way some of the distortions caused by the interview situation can be overcome. Since the memory of the harshness of the antebellum plantation was inversely related to the former slaves' geographical distance from it, it is necessary to compare the stories of informants still living on or near those plantations with those of blacks who had migrated and resided in other states. It is significant, for example, that former South Carolina slaves who were interviewed in Georgia had a far different view of bondage than those who were interviewed in South Carolina.[47] Such comparisons as this improve the accuracy of data compiled from the WPA interviews.

On certain topics the WPA interviews are incomparable sources. They probably contain, for example, more religious and secular songs than any other single source. Similarly, the interviews contain much genealogical data on black families not found anywhere else. The WPA collection is also a rich source of information on black speech patterns. There are, however, many problems involved in the use of such data.[48]

Uncritical use of the interviews will lead almost inevitably to a simplistic and distorted view of the plantation as a paternalistic institution where the chief feature of life was mutual love and respect between masters and slaves. A more sophisticated examination using the skills of the linguist, statistician, folklorist, behavioral scientist, anthropologist, and Africanist will uncover the complexity of life on the plantation. Such systematic studies of oral lore combined with critical examinations of published narratives will enable scholars to write more revealing and accurate portrayals of slavery.

Many scholars, while granting the desirability of studying both kinds of black testimony, still wonder which of them is the best kind of historical evidence. The WPA interviews are so numerous and now so much more accessible than the published narratives that at first glance they would appear to have the edge. On the other hand, the narratives, while part of the black oral tradition, are literary records and easier for most historians to study. Then, too, if all the narratives that have been published in newspapers, magazines, church minutes, and court records were collected, they would probably outnumber the WPA interviews. Actually, the two sources are complementary: the interviews include the women (50 percent of the total) and "average" slaves who did not publish their stories; the narratives include the blacks from the border states missing in the interviews; and the preponderance of WPA informants from Texas, Arkansas, and Florida makes up for the paucity of narrators from these states.

By and large, the topics covered in the interviews and the narratives are identical. Both kinds of testimony may be biased. The narrative has, however, three great advantages over the interview. First, the average narrator was twenty-eight years younger than the average WPA informant when their stories were recorded. Second, an overwhelming majority of the narrators were over twenty years of age when they obtained freedom and could thus tell what slavery was like for adults as well as for black children. Third, all of the book-length narratives were far longer than the WPA interviews. As a consequence of these differences, personality traits appear in sharp relief in the narratives, while often being obscured in the interviews.

Although there can be no definitive answer to the question, there is a way to demonstrate some of the advantages mentioned above. One former Kentucky slave, Peter Bruner, wrote a narrative (1918) and was interviewed by the WPA (1936). A careful reading of the two stories reveals many of their similarities. But there are so many contradictions in the two accounts that it is obvious that (1) Bruner concealed some things from the interviewers, (2) the transcription was inaccurate, or (3) Bruner by 1936 had forgotten many of the details he included in his 1918 narrative.

In both the 950-word interview and the 54-page narrative Bruner recalled his cruel master, the floggings he received, and his numerous attempts to escape. But in the interview he revealed nothing about his parents or the development of his attitudes, character, or personality. In the interview Bruner and his master have a one-dimensional quality; both have complex personalities in the narrative. Besides these elements, Bruner's narrative includes many other things that he did not reveal to the WPA interviewer: his addiction to alcohol; blacks who helped runaways and resisted floggings; the amusements (gambling, drinking, dueling) of the planters and their oppression of poor whites; introspective revelations about his feelings about being enslaved; the development of his attitudes toward work, slaveholders, and poor whites; and the Weltanschauung of the slave.[49]

In the final analysis, the methodological skills possessed by the historian and the questions he wants to answer will determine whether he uses the narratives or the interviews. Where skills and interests intersect, he will use both. In either case, the approach must be a critical one and take into account the following declaration of Solomon Northup:

> There may be humane masters, as there certainly are inhuman ones—there may be slaves well-clothed, well-fed, and happy, as there surely are those half-clad, half-starved and miserable. . . . Men may write fictions portraying lowly life as it is, or as it is not—may expatiate with owlish gravity upon the bliss of ignorance—discourse flippantly from arm chairs of the pleasures of slave life; but let them toil with him in the field—sleep with him in the cabin—feed with him on husks; let them behold him scourged, hunted, trampled on, and they will come back with another story in their mouths. Let them know the heart of the poor slave—learn his secret thoughts—thoughts he dare not utter in the hearing of the white man; let them sit by him in the silent watches of the night—converse with him in trustful confidence, of "life, liberty, and the pursuit of happiness," and they will find that ninety-nine out of every hundred are intelligent enough to understand their situation, and to cherish in their bosoms the love of freedom, as passionately as themselves.[50]

If scholars want to know the heart and secret thoughts of slaves, they must study the testimony of the blacks. But since the slave did not know the heart and secret thoughts of masters, they must also examine the testimony of whites. Neither the whites nor the blacks had a monopoly on truth, had rended the veil cloaking the life of the other, or had seen clearly the pain and the joy bounded by color and caste. The perceptions of neither can be accepted as encapsulating the totality of plantation life. Consequently, whether one focuses on the slaves or the master, one must systematically examine both black and white testimony. But, just as there are some topics on which only the masters can provide reliable information, there are some questions that only the slaves can answer. In this regard, scholars should always remember the perceptive observation of Frederick Douglass that a free man "cannot see things in the same light with the slave, because he does not, and cannot, look from the same point from which the slave does." Because of these differences in perceptions scholars who have studied a variety of sources have concluded that "there are questions about the slave system that can be answered only by one who has experienced slavery. How did it 'feel' to be owned? What were the pleasures and sufferings of a slave? What was the slave's attitude toward his owner, toward the white man's assumption of superiority, toward the white man's God? Did the slaves want to be free? Did they feel it was their right to be free?" The individual and collective mentality of the slaves, the ways they sought to fulfill their needs, the experiential context of life in the quarters and in the fields, and the Black man's personal perspective of bondage emerge only after an intensive examination of the testimony of ex-slaves.[51]

Notes

1. Stanley M. Elkins, *Slavery: A Problem in American Institutional and Intellectual Life*, 2nd. ed. (Chicago, 1968), 3.

2. Ulrich B. Phillips, *Life and Labor in the Old South* (Boston, 1929), 219.

3. Harrison A. Trexler, *Slavery in Missouri, 1804-1865* (Baltimore, 1914); Chase C. Mooney, *Slavery in Tennessee* (Bloomington, 1957); J. Winston Coleman, Jr., *Slavery Times in Kentucky* (Chapel Hill, 1940); and Frederick Bancroft, *Slave-Trading in the Old South* (Baltimore, 1931), cited many interviews and narratives in their studies.

4. Benjamin A. Botkin, "The Slave as His Own Interpreter," Library of Congress, *Quarterly Journal of Current Acquisitions* 2 (November 1944), 37;

Richard Hofstadter, "U.B. Phillips and the Plantation Legend," *Journal of Negro History* 29 (April 1944), 109-24.

5. Josiah Henson, *The Life of Josiah Henson, Formerly a Slave, Now an Inhabitant of Canada. Narrated by Himself* [to S.A. Eliot] (Boston, 1849); Solomon Northup, *Twelve Years a Slave*, edited by Sue Eakins and Joseph Logsdon (Baton Rouge, 1968), ix-xiv; Claude M. Fuess, "Samuel Atkins Eliott," *Dictionary of American Biography* (23 vols. and index, New York, 1928-1973; cited hereinafter as *DAB*) 6: 81-82.

6. Harper Twelvetrees, ed., *The Story of the Life of John Anderson, the Fugitive Slave* (London, 1863); Frederic Boase, ed., *Modern English Biography* (6 vols., London and Edinburgh, 1965) III, 1055; Northup, *Twelve Years a Slave*, ix-xiv.

7. Lunsford Lane, *The Narrative of Lunsford Lane* . . . [edited by William G. Hawkins] (Boston, 1848); William G. Eliot, *The Story of Archer Alexandre from Slavery to Freedom, March 30, 1863* (Boston, 1885); *Apleton's Cyclopaedia of American Biography* (6 vols., New York, 1886-1889) 3, 121; Charlotte C. Eliot, *William Greenleaf Eliot: Minister, Educator, Philanthropist* (Boston and New York, 1904), 126-51; Frank J. Bruno, "William Greenleaf Eliot," *DAB* 6, 82-83.

8. Thomas Price, *The History of Protestant Nonconformity in England from the Reformation Under Henry VIII* (2 vols., London, 1836-1838); Frank J. Bruno, "William Greenleaf Eliot," *DAB* 6, 82-83; A. Everett Peterson, "James W.C. Pennington," *DAB* 14, 441-42.

9. Henry Trumbull, *History of the Discovery of America* (Brooklyn, [1810]); Chloe Spear, *Memoir of Mrs. Chloe Spear, a Native of Africa,* [edited by James S. Loring] (Boston, 1832); Robert Voorhis, *Life and Adventures of Robert Voorhis,* [edited by Henry Trumbull] (Providence, 1829); James S. Loring, "The Franklin Manuscripts," *Historical Magazine* 3 (January 1859), 9-12; Israel R. Potter, *Life and Adventures of Israel Ralph Potter* (1744-1826), [edited by Henry Trumbull] (Providence, 1824); James S. Loring, *The Hundred Boston Orators Appointed by the Municipal Authorities and Other Public Bodies* . . . (Boston, 1852); Joseph C. Lovejoy, *Memoir of the Rev. Charles T. Torrey* . . . (Boston, 1847); Owen and Joseph C. Lovejoy, *Memoir of the Rev. Elijah P. Lovejoy* (New York, 1838).

10. Allan Westcott, "Charles Edwards Lester," *DAB* 11, 189-90.

11. Isaac Jefferson, *Memoirs of a Monticello Slave, as Dictated to Charles Campbell* . . . edited by Rayford W. Logan (Charlottesville, 1951), 3-8; Edward A. Wyatt, IV, *Charles Campbell, Virginia's "Old Mortality"* (Charlottesville, 1935).

12. James W.C. Pennington, *A Narrative of Events of the Life of J.H. Banks, an Escaped Slave* . . . (Liverpool, 1861); John Brown, *Slave Life in Georgia* . . . edited by Louis A. Chamerovzow (London, 1855); Isaac Tatem Hopper, *Narrative of the Life of Thomas Cooper* (New York, 1832); Rufus M. Jones, "Isaac Tatem Hopper," *DAB* 9, 224; A. Everett Peterson, "James W.C. Pennington," *DAB* 14, 441-42.

13. Lewis G. and Milton Clarke, *Narratives of the Sufferings of Lewis and Milton Clarke* . . . [edited by Joseph C. Lovejoy] (Boston, 1846), 192-241; Moses Roper, *A Narrative of the Adventures and Escape of Moses Roper* . . . edited by Thomas Price (London, 1840), 121-84.

14. See for example: Northup, *Twelve Years a Slave*, [edited by David

Wilson] (Auburn and Buffalo, 1853); Peter Wheeler, *Chains and Freedom: or, The Life and Adventures of Peter Wheeler* . . . , [edited by Charles E. Lester] (New York, 1839), v-20.

15. Charles Ball, *Slavery in the United States: A Narrative of the Life and Adventures of Charles Ball, a Black Man* . . . , [edited by Thomas Fisher] (New York, 1837); Edwin J. Scott, *Random Recollections of a Long Life, 1806 to 1876* (Columbia, S.C., 1884), 9-10, 31-32, 95-98; John M. Bateman, comp., *The Columbia Scrapbook, 1701-1842* (Columbia, S.C., 1915), 20, 31-34, 53; Helen K. Hennig, ed., *Columbia, Capital City of South Carolina, 1786-1936* (Columbia, S.C., 1936), 10, 67-70, 315, 374; Robert Mills, *Statistics of South Carolina* . . . (Charleston, 1826), 688, 713-14; John Drayton, *A View of South Carolina* . . . (Charleston, 1802), 104, 111, 116-49); William G. Simms, *The Geography of South Carolina* (Charleston, 1843), 122-27; Ulrich B. Phillips, ed., *Plantation and Frontier Documents: 1694-1863* (2 vols., Cleveland, 1909), 2, 59-67; James Williams, *Narrative of James Williams. An American Slave* . . . [edited by John G. Whittier] (Philadelphia, 1838).

16. Henry Box Brown, *Narrative of Henry Box Brown* . . . (Boston, 1849), 1-3.

17. Jane Blake, *Memoirs of Margaret Jane Blake* (Philadelphia, 1834); Elleanor Eldridge, *Memoirs of Elleanor Eldridge* (Providence, 1838); Sally Williams, *Aunt Sally; or, The Cross the Way to Freedom* (Cincinnati, 1858). Other unreliable narratives include Aaron, *The Light and Truth of Slavery* (Worcester, Mass., n.d.); Reginald Rowland, *An Ambitious Slave* (Buffalo, 1897); John H. Simpson, *Horrors of the Virginian Slave Trade* . . . *The True Story of Dinah* . . . (London, 1863); and Smith H. Platt, *The Martyrs, and the Fugitive* . . . (New York, 1859).

18. See: Henry C. Bruce, *The New Man. Twenty-nine Years a Slave. Twenty-nine Years a Free Man* (York, Pa., 1895); Louis Hughes, *Thirty Years a Slave* (Milwaukee, 1897); Jacob Stroyer, *My Life in the South* (Salem, 1889); Elizabeth H. Keckley, *Behind the Scenes* (New York, 1868).

19. Josiah Henson, *An Autobiography of the Reverend Josiah Henson*, edited by Robin W. Winks (Reading, Mass., and other cities, 1969), v-xxxiv.

20. Jean Vacheenos and Betty Volk, "Born in Bondage: History of a Slave Family," *Negro History Bulletin* 36 (May 1973), 161-66.

21. Robin W. Winks, *The Blacks in Canada: A History* (Montreal, New Haven, and London, 1971), 178-84, 195-204.

22. Mifflin W. Gibbs, *Shadow and Light: An Autobiography* (Washington, 1902), 12-13; *Chambers's Edinburgh Journal*, 2nd ser., 15 (March 15, 1851), 174-75; William Craft, *Running a Thousand Miles for Freedom* . . . (London, 1860).

23. *Liberator*, June 8, 1849; July 11, 1850; Gibbs, *Shadow and Light*, 13-14; *Non-slaveholder* 4 (May 1849), 107.

24. Northup, *Twelve Years a Slave*, edited by Eakins and Logsdon; John Brown, *Slave Life in Georgia*, edited by F. Nash Boney (Savannah, 1972); Philip D. Curtin, ed., *Africa Remembered: Narratives of West Africans from the Era of the Slave Trade* (Madison, Milwaukee, and London, 1967), 60-98.

25. See for example: Wilson Armistead, *A Tribute for the Negro* (Manchester, 1848), 519-22; Bayley, *Narrative of Some Remarkable Incidents in the Life of Solomon Bayley* . . . (London, 1825).

26. Eugene D. Genovese, "Getting to Know the Slaves," *New York Review*

of Books, September 21, 1972, pp. 16-19; Norman R. Yetman, "The Background of the Slave Narrative Collection," *American Quarterly* 19 (Fall 1967), 534-53. Unless otherwise indicated, all references to the WPA interviews are to George P. Rawick, ed., *The American Slave: A Composite Autobiography* (19 vols., Westport, Conn., 1972).

27. For suggestive critical essays see: Lewis A. Dexter, *Elite and Specialized Interviewing* (Evanston, 1970), 119-62; *American Journal of Sociology* 62 (September 1965), entire issue; Stephen A. Richardson, et al., *Interviewing: Its Form and Functions* (New York and London, 1965).

28. Yetman, "The Background of the Slave Narrative Collection," 534-53; Allison Davis, Burleigh B. Gardner, and Mary R. Gardner, *Deep South: A Social Anthropological Study of Caste and Class* (Chicago, 1941); Bertram W. Doyle, *The Etiquette of Race Relations in the South: A Study in Social Control* (Chicago, 1937); John Dollard, *Caste and Class in the Southern Town* (New Haven and London, 1937); Hortense Powdermaker, *After Freedom: A Cultural Study in the Deep South* (New York, 1939).

29. William R. Ferris, "The Collection of Racial Lore: Approaches and Problems," *New York Folklore Quarterly* 27 (September 1971), 261-62.

30. Pete Daniel, *The Shadow of Slavery: Peonage in the South 1901-1969* (Urbana, Chicago, and London, 1972), 29; Charles S. Johnson, Edwin R. Embree, and W.W. Alexander, *The Collapse of Cotton Tenancy* (Chapel Hill, 1935); Arthur F. Raper, *Preface to Peasantry: A Tale of Two Black Belt Counties* (Chapel Hill, 1936); Charles S. Johnson, *The Shadow of the Plantation* (Chicago, 1934); Commission on Interracial Cooperation, *The Mob Still Rides: A Review of the Lynching Record, 1931-1935* (Atlanta, 1936).

31. Rawick, ed., *The American Slave* 3, Pt. 3, 237, 253-54; Pt. 4, 82, 86; 17, 41, 303.

32. Ibid., 12, Pt. 1, 113-14.

33. Ferris, "The Collection of Racial Lore," 271.

34. On informant-interviewer interaction see Lewis A. Dexter, "Role Relationships and Conceptions of Neutrality in Interviewing," *American Journal of Sociology* 62 (September 1956), 153-57.

35. Rawick, ed., *The American Slave* 16 (Kentucky), 99.

36. J. Mason Brewer, "Juneteenth," Texas Folklore Society, *Publications* 10 (Austin, 1832), 9-54; Brewer, "John Tales," ibid., 21 (Austin, 1946), 81-104.

37. Norman R. Yetman, ed., *Voices from Slavery* (New York, Chicago, and San Francisco, 1970), 1; Rawick, ed., *The American Slave* 1, xvii-xviii.

38. J. Ralph Jones, "Portraits of Georgia Slaves," *Georgia Review* 21 (Spring-Winter 1967), 126-32, 268-73, 407-11, 521-25; 22 (Spring and Summer 1968), 125-27, 254-57; Rawick, ed., *The American Slave* 12. Pt. 1, 9-16, 86-90; Pt. 2, 17-27, 13; Pt. 3, 14-15; Pt. 4, 205-11.

39. Jones, "Portraits of Georgia Slaves," 21, 268-73, 407-11; Rawick, ed., *The American Slave* 12, Pt. 1, 9-16, 86-90.

40. Jones, "Portraits of Georgia Slaves," 21, 271.

41. Writers' Program, Virginia, *The Negro in Virginia* (New York, 1940), 31-33, 57, 65-71, 82, 92-95, 143-44, 154-55, 170-71, 201-202, 302; Rawick, ed., *The American Slave* 16 (Virginia), 1-6, 15-16, 21-26, 31-41, 46-54. Lewis contributed a preface to *The Negro in Virginia*, but he was not formally designated editor of the volume.

42. Yetman, "The Background of the Slave Narrative Collection," 534-53. For examples of interviews conducted by northerners during and immediately after the Civil War, see: Laura S. Haviland, *A Woman's Life-Work: Labors and Experiences of Laura S. Haviland* (Chicago, 1887), 439-49; and George H. Hepworth, *The Whip, Hoe and Sword; or, The Gulf-Department in '63* (Boston, 1864), 152-59.

43. U.S. Bureau of the Census, *Negro Population 1790-1915* (Washington, 1918), 57.

44. Jan Vansina, "Once upon a Time: Oral Traditions as History in Africa," *Daedalus* 100 (Spring 1971), 456. See also Vansina, *Oral Tradition: A Study in Historical Methodology* (Chicago, 1965).

45. Rawick, ed., *The American Slave* 13, Pt. 4, 291, 309, 326.

46. Ophelia Settles Egypt interviewed 100 former slaves; John B. Cade and his associates, 482; and Roscoe Lewis and Hampton Institute blacks, 300. Yetman, "The Background of the Slave Narrative Collection," 534-53.

47. Rawick, ed., *The American Slave* 13, Pt. 3, 233-35, 288-94.

48. Ibid., 1, 176.

49. Ibid., 16 (Kentucky), 88-90; Peter Bruner, *A Slave's Adventures Toward Freedom* (Oxford, Ohio [1918]).

50. Northup, *Twelve Years a Slave*, edited by David Wilson, 206-207.

51. Frederick Douglass, *My Bondage and My Freedom* (New York, 1855), 339; Writers' Program, Virginia, *The Negro in Virginia*, 27.

Plantation Factories and the Slave Work Ethic

GERALD JAYNES

Few images of the slave plantation have enjoyed a longer life than the analogy to a well ordered and disciplined factory. But factories that recruited an involuntary and pre-industrial workforce to an alien culture were not without disadvantages. Over two hundred years ago a French *philosophe*, the Abbé Raynal, penned a remarkable passage that even today contains most of the salient aspects of New World slavery with which modern scholars must grapple.

> In their common labours, the motion of their arms, or of their feet, is always in cadence. At all their employments they sing, and seem always

as if they were dancing. Music animates their courage, and rouzes them from their indolence. The marks of this extreme sensibility to harmony are visible in all the muscles of their bodies, which are always naked. Poets and musicians by nature, they make the words subservient to the music, by a license they arbitrarily assume of lengthening or shortening them, in order to accommodate them to an air that pleases them. *Whenever any object or incident strikes a negro, he instantly makes it the subject of a song.* In all ages, this has been the origin of poetry. Three or four words which are alternately repeated by the singer and the general chorus sometimes constitute the whole poem. Five or six bars of music compose the whole length of the song. A circumstance that appears singular, is, that the same air, though merely a continual repetition of the same tones, takes entire possession of them, *makes them work or dance for several hours:* neither they, nor even the white men, are disgusted with that tedious uniformity which these repetitions might naturally occasion. This particular attachment is owing to the warmth and expression which they introduce into their songs. *Their airs are generally double time.* None of them tend to inspire them with pride. Those intended to excite tenderness, promote rather a kind of langour. Even those which are most lively, carry in them a certain expression of melancholy. This is the highest entertainment to minds of great sensibility. So strong an inclination for music might become *a powerful motive of action under the direction of skillful hands.* Festivals, games and rewards might on this account be established among them. These amusements, conducted with judgment, would prevent that stupidity so common among slaves, ease their labors, and preserve them from that *constant melancholy* which consumes them, and shortens their days.[1]

To Raynal, the creation of an attitude to work among the slaves that would bring forth adequate quantities of labor without the debilitating effects of the whip was seen as a contest between the desire of masters to maximize production and the slaves' attempt to maintain some semblance of humanity.

Contemporary studies of American Negro slavery have recognized the need to assign fundamental importance to the meaning of work in the Negro slave's life. Two recent approaches, put forth virtually simultaneously, stress very different ideas, one arguing that the slaves were inculcated with a protestant work ethic and the other that the slaves possessed a preindustrial or noncapitalistic work ethic which recognized the need for some minimal work effort as their part of a social compact in a complex system of reciprocal obligations based upon a paternalistic relationship between master and slave.[2] Both of these theoretical constructs stem from ideas essentially identical to those put forth by the Abbé Raynal. Once it is realized that it would be to the master's advantage to devise some means of eliciting voluntary labor from his slaves it becomes almost obvious that much of the master-slave relationship must have revolved about that issue. Viewed from the perspective offered by

Raynal in the last paragraph of the above quotation a common thread joining the previously mentioned attempts to explicate the Negro slave's conception of the meaning of work is revealed by the recognition that each stems from the master's attempt to define the context within which the slave must structure any text of his own.

Two denotations of the words text and context are, respectively, "the actual structure of words in a piece of writing or printing" and "the whole situation, background, or environment relevant to some happening or personality."[3] To the student enmeshed in the attempt to understand the Atlantic slave system as a social institution there are perhaps no other two words which serve as a better warning and guideline to take care. The slave plantation was a business and a home, a system for mobilizing and directing labor and a prison, a residence and a community. To understand, when the slave or master spoke or acted, from which context the text should be analyzed is to cast into treacherous waters.

Textual interpretations of slave narratives present complexities that go far beyond the usual kinds of problems concerning context with which the scholar must be aware. Many of these problems have been admirably discussed by those scholars who have been most instrumental in demonstrating the historical and cultural value contained in this literature.[4] But an additional problem of great significance seems to me to have been neglected. The most blatant of the usual problems of context, the misrepresentation of the meaning of text by deletion or alteration of structure may be termed misuse of textual context. The problem we wish to focus upon may be illustrated by the following statement from the testimony of Mississippi freedman, Tines Kendrick.

> Boss, it was heap more better to be a slave nigger dan er free un. An' it was really er heavenly day when de freedom come for de race.[5]

The two sentences taken individually seem quite incompatible, and if we are to avoid assignment of the complete statement to the cemetery reserved for nonsensical language acts, it is clear that the complete statement must be viewed in a broader context than either of its constituent sentences.

An expert in the psychology of verbal interviewing and race relations in the early twentieth century South might argue that the key word in the statement is "Boss." Mr. Kendrick deferring to his perception of what the interviewer wanted to hear pacified that perception with the first sentence. Then unable to burden himself with the lie and realizing that the interviewer would dismiss the apparent incompatibility of the two sentences as the incoherent blathering of an old Negro, rectified his own self-concept by appending the second sentence. This makes for a plausible interpretation that seems to solve our problem. However, there exist some discrepancies which require closer attention.

This interpretation tells us much more about individual psychology and twentieth century race relations than it does about slavery. Furthermore, a quotation of the first sentence in isolation requires that we make the charge that Tines Kendrick's testimony had been victimized by severe misuse of textual context. But the scientific basis for such a charge, while not implausible, surely rests upon a very infirm scaffolding. Do we not need more information about Tines Kendrick's psychological makeup and the specific relationship between the interviewer and him? While the underlying assumptions regarding twentieth century race relations are generally safe they do not hold in every case. I am going to argue that quotation of the first sentence in isolation would not constitute a misuse of textual context. Tines Kendrick did in fact mean what the first sentence conveys in isolation.

The structure of these two sentences is much more complex than might be indicated by casual study. The key words are "was," "slave nigger," and "race." Kendrick's use of the past tense "was" in the first sentence and his transition from singular "slave nigger" and "free un" in the first sentence to a comprehensive plural "race" in the second indicates the full meaning. It was, when the overwhelming majority of blacks were slaves, better to be a slave in a social system which was based upon the enslavement of blacks. It was, however, quite different to be free when the entire race was also free. The broader context we seek is the hidden transition from a slave to a free social system, that which a Marxist would term a change in the "mode of production." The failure to recognize this particular problem of contextual transition is one of the most serious errors one can commit in the treatment of slave narratives as a source of evidence.

The problems of context and contextual transition, in the complete social and textual sense in which I have used them above, is of fundamental importance to any discussion of the slave work ethic. There is no better way to demonstrate this than with an analysis of some related issues in what seems to me to be our best study of this specific question. Eugene Genovese's masterful analysis of the "black work ethic," with its careful and well selected sampling of evidence from masters, nonslaveholders, and slave narrative presents a convincing argument that American slavery produced a laboring population whose ideas about the meaning of work was not embodied by a protestant work ethic, but was "precapitalistic." Despite this, his analysis makes some serious errors in failing to recognize subtle, but important distinctions in text and context. For example, Professor Genovese argues that the "slaveholders presided over a plantation system that constituted a halfway house between peasant and factory cultures," a situation presumably dictated by the rural setting, which as Genovese argues forced the rhythm of work to follow seasonal fluctuations and encouraged a task oriented or irregular work rhythm among the slaves.

> How could they (masters) instill factory-like discipline into a working population engaged in a rural system that, for all its tendencies toward modern discipline, remained bound to the rhythms of nature and to traditional ideas of work, time, and leisure?[6]

The error here is one of context, and it provides a particularly vivid example of the problem pointed out earlier.

It is historically true that peasant producers in agricultural societies have generally adopted irregular or task-oriented work patterns consonant with the length of the day and the turning of the seasons and crops. However, in societies where these producers were in principle free, the work-leisure decision and the rhythm of work were adapted to nature by the worker's choice. E.P. Thompson, upon whose work Genovese draws, points out that this task-oriented approach to labor and time presupposes "the independent peasant or craftsman as referent." "The farm servant, or the regular wage-earning field labourer," elaborates Thompson, "was undoubtedly subject to an intense labour discipline."[7] The slaves were bound in a class relationship in which their work-leisure decision was made by someone else. There is no logical connection between rural work patterns and nature and in the context of a master-slave relationship no social one either. The seasons and weather conditioned, not so much the rhythm of work, but the nature of the work performed. The free peasant's choice of an irregular work rhythm demonstrated that he valued leisure during the rainy season more highly than any output which could be produced inside his hut. Similarly, the value of alternative work to the slave was likely to be low, but the issue is whether that work had value to the master. Thus ex-slave Adrianna Kerns testified, "when we had to come out of the field on account of rain, we would go to the corn crib and shuck corn if we didn't have some weaving to do." Similarly Texan Andrew Goodman recalled his master's policy in regard to the effect of nature upon the slave's work pattern. "He didn't never put his niggers out in bad weather. He gave us something to do that we could do in out of the weather, like shelling corn and the womens could spin and knit."[8] This point should make us aware that the search for the causal roots of the slave's conceptualization of the meaning of work must also explain the master's failure to completely shape that conception. This failure is closely related to the slaves' own understanding of their relationship to a world order they seemingly could not alter. An understanding, while elusive, is not unattainable; for the slave narratives and testimony are replete with references to work and leisure.

To speak of a work ethic is to ask not how much work a people did, or even how much work they thought they should do, although the latter is getting tolerably close. It is to ask of a people what *meaning* did work have in their own conceptualization of their social existence. In this sense, the work ethic of a people is so securely bound to their collective Weltanschauung as to make meaningless any attempt to ask questions which transcend a given collective experience. Thus the alteration of the social relations embedded in slavery would precipitate a change in the very meaning of the concept of work itself. The frequently commented upon corn-shuckings is a case in point. Often a vehicle for performing what would be a large amount of tedious work, the corn-shucking was also an occasion for the gathering of friends and neighbors from many plantations. The corn-shucking was seen by many *slaves* as much more than work. In a typical example of *contextual transition* in slave testimony, freedman Cicero Finch reminisced about his days of thralldom in Georgia.

It was more fun to work in dem days than it is to play now.[9]

This statement reveals much about plantation life during the antebellum period, but any attempt to go outside the context of that experience is liable to become entrapped in serious errors. A time for festivities and rejoicing, corn-shucking was a communal experience, which although like the famous barn raisings and quilting bees of American pioneer days, was yet fundamentally different. Whether most slaves thought of the corn-shucking as leisure or work cannot be positively determined. What we may assert with confidence is that it was a communal experience, keeping in mind that it was the experience of a slave community; an experience that within its own context was voluntarily sought yet simultaneously one for which participation was not totally voluntary. Corn-shuckings were joyous activities for some slave communities, but for the freedpeople living under different class relations, corn-shuckings or other communal festivals could be scheduled at a time and place of their own choosing and we may suspect that such gatherings were joyful. As a free people even as soon after emancipation as 1870, when the planter's corn needed shucking, it was no longer an event which served a communal purpose. For the blacks, it had become simply work. The freedpeople, able to make self-determining choices along some lines, were attempting to define a clearer demarcation between work and leisure. How many planters were as perplexed with the change in the attitude of the freedpeople as the southerner who complained, "The corn has been gathered and housed, but not accompanied by those glorious corn-shuckings that once aroused all the mirth, melody, and merry-making qualities of the negro."[10]

That a revolutionary change in social status might require a rather subtle reconceptualization of what was and was not leisure, and therefore work, was understood by a freedman who reminisced about work during his days as a slave.

> The only good times I had was on Sundays. Of course, *I wouldn't call them good times now* for it wasn't nothing but a part day rest from work. You see a man's measure of a thing depends on what he can get. Where it is work, work all the time, a few hours rest may mean as much as two or three days if you know how to use it. It is just like a drowning man grabbing a straw. A little time to set around and talk on Sunday *seemed like a picnic* to us.[11]

This perceptive statement is of course much more than narrative or mere testimony. It contains two instances of contextual transition and uses them intelligently to construct a vivid image of the blurred distinction that existed between work and leisure in the mind of the slave.

Slaves, as a collective body, thought that they worked too intensely, too long, and perhaps most importantly, too often at times not of their own choosing. For the master class striving to overcome this apparently endemic feature of slavery, the slaves' idea of leisure could not be divorced from their attitude towards work. The planter's attempt to define the demarcation between leisure and work was seldom successful. For the slave, leisure came to mean any time period during which he was not under direct observation and control of the master. This is a theme which permeates the narratives in a variety of forms. Thus Frederick Douglass could speak authoritatively upon the reasons why the slaves on Colonel Lloyd's plantation coveted the privilege to do errands at the "great house farm," the home plantation. It was as much as anything else, perhaps more, the chance to "break the monotony of the field," "to be out of the field from under the driver's lash," and enjoy a state that was "*comparatively free*."[12] One former slave gave as good a definition of the slaves' demarcation between work and leisure as we are likely to find.

> There used to be some awful times during slavery days. Work! Work! Work! From dawn to dusk. But in spite of all the *work and strictness* some of the slaves used to slip from place to place after night and find a

little pleasure. But woe be unto you if the paddyrollers caught you out after dark without a pass.[13]

Leisure and its concomitant pleasures were precious commodities that the slave had to steal. The master, in his attempt to define the boundaries of the slave's existence, was all too successful in a way which could not have been further from his desires. When the slave thought of leisure, it was within the context of his bondage:

> Rabbit in the briar patch,
> Squirrel in the tree,
> Wish I could go hunting
> But I ain't free.
> Rooster's in the henhouse
> Hen's in the patch,
> Love to go shooting
> But I ain't free.[14]

This context, once having defined leisure, did not have to search very much for its antithesis. Slavery and work were inseparable concepts to the slave, so leisure and freedom came to be synonymous. Here is the basis for one of the more profound errors of context ever made about the "black work ethic." The planter class at the end of the Civil War was constantly complaining and congratulating itself that to the Negro, freedom and leisure were identical. Some outside observers such as General Wager Swayne, head of the Alabama Freedmen's Bureau, were in basic agreement, but more perceptive. Swayne commented at the end of 1866 that "slavery had been identified so thoroughly with work, that freedmen were not uncommon who believed that work was no part of freedom." Both observers were defining leisure outside its new and proper context. Once free, the blacks could no longer view work and leisure in the same way. Actually they were at this time not attempting to exist free of labor, but to become the independent peasants and craftsmen who could, according to E.P. Thompson, choose time and work rhythms that flowed naturally with nature. Asked why he and his family had left their former master for the coastal region of South Carolina, one ex-slave revealed his conception of freedom with a text that belied both his origins and his sense of changing context:

I heard there was a chance of we being our own driver here; thats why we come.[15]

The *planter's* own code of paternalism, an integral part of the defense of an institution increasingly under attack in the nineteenth century, owned that well treated and contented slaves performed their labors as voluntarily as possible for the sons and daughters of Africa. If the slaves worked out of a sense of obligation and contentment, it is difficult to corroborate by their testimony. One ex-slave explained what motivated her to work. "I didn't get many whippings because I always did what I was told, in a hurry. I hated to be whipped . . ." Slave narratives, especially the autobiographies, place great stress (too much according to some critics) upon the use of corporal punishment. Those who would dissent from harsh depictions of the slave system are forced to reject as atypical narratives such as Douglass', which launched an attack to expose the one-sidedness of the planter's code of paternalism. Douglass, in *My Bondage and My Freedom,* passing from the genre of the narrative to his role as an astute and special expert on the institution of slavery, captured the meaning of the previous quotation by transcending that which was merely personal and physical:

> The whip is all in all.

No single sentence in all the slave narratives I have read captures better the overwhelming presence of the whip in the minds of the slaves and their testimony. Freedman Austin Grant offers us a rare insight into the mechanics of family participation in the development of the slave child's Weltenschauung.

> My grandfather, . . . would tell us things! To keep the whip off your backs, you know . . . children, work, work, work, and work hard. You know how you hate to be whipped, so work hard.[16]

The extent of this attitude in slave culture is indicated by the ideas expressed by the actions of slave folk heroes. Heroes such as the powerful slave Randall on a Missouri plantation with William Wells Brown or the more apocryphal type such as one freedman's "old man jack" always appear as valuable hard workers who would not be whipped.[17] Figures like "Old Man Jack" and Randall, the slaves' ideal slave, tell us much about their attitudes to work. The powerful slave who refused to be whipped and was willing to die rather than submit to that ignominy was an ideal which few slaves could ever achieve. But its pervasive existence portrays a communal ideal. Such slaves had achieved in spirit that which most sought for the flesh. When Old Man Jack worked it was not from fear, but from a freely made choice not to die.

It is within the context of the "ideal slave" that we must look for the relationship among the planter's code of paternalism, the slave work ethic, and accommodation. We see in Old Man Jack a slave who is his own master. He must work if he is to live, for slaves exist to work. Yet it cannot be said that Jack has accepted the paternalist compact. He works not out of an obligation for being fed and cared for, but from a sense of his own being. Slaves such as Jack could take care of themselves. For instance, when his owner confronted the slaves with the fact of a missing pig, Jack supplies the following explanation:

> I killed that shoat and ate him up. I work hard for you everyday and you don't provide enough to eat for us. That is why I killed him.[18]

A lesser slave would have denied the fact for fear of punishment and in doing so would have accommodated, accepted the owner's authority. Jack has accommodated not to the owner's authority, but to physical reality. He will serve, but not be possessed. What accommodation means to "Old Man Jack" and therefore to slave culture has been said in far better terms than I could put it by Jose Craveirinha, a Negritude poet from Mozambique.

> I am coal!
> And you tear me brutally from the ground
> and you make me your source of wealth, boss.
> I am coal!
> And you ignite me, boss
> in order to serve you eternally as motive force
> but not eternally, boss.
> I am coal
> and I must blaze, yes
> and burn all with the force of my combustion.
> I am coal
> I must blaze in exploitation
> blaze into ashes of malediction
> blaze alive like tar brother
> until I am no longer your wealth, boss
> I am coal
> I must blaze
> burn all with the fire of my combustion
> Yes!
> I will be your coal, boss![19]

To those who did not have the inner strength of an "Old Man Jack," accommodation could be defined within the context of religion. One ex-slave recalled what role religion played in her life, while a slave. "I just gave up all earthly hopes and thought all the time about the next life." The slaves often sang about their acceptance of slavery.

> Our troubles will soon be over,
> I'm going to live with Jesus—
> After while;
> Praying time will soon be over,
> I'm going home to live with Jesus—
> After while
> All I want is Jesus; you may have
> all the world.
> Just give me Jesus.[20]

The many songs and spirituals similar to this one indicate a communal consciousness that utilized the power of religion in a way that differed broadly from the intentions of masters or the Abbé Raynal. If slaves could have accepted the world-view that masters offered there would have been far less need for the religion practiced in the quarters or deep in the woods.

Some slaves accepted the planter's model and code of behavior. But the slave's idea of the ideal slave must conform to the images created by the slave songs, the poetry of slavery which tell us so much about slave culture. Few of these lyrics are indicative of an acceptance of the planter's paternalistic compact. Frederick Douglass, in his attack upon this image of the slave system, offered one song as evidence of the slave's awareness of their unjust subjugation.

> We raise de wheat,
> Dey gib us de corn;
> We bake de bread,
> Dey gib us the cruss;
> We sif de meal,
> Dey gib us de huss;
> We peal de meat,
> Dey gib us de skin
> And dat's de way
> Dey takes us in.

That the last two lines of the song are evidence of an even deeper understanding and rejection of the planter's paternalism is made clear by a different version of this song.

> Old master eats beef and sucks
> on de bone
> And gives us de gristle
> To make, to make, to make,
> To make de nigger whistle.[21]

For many slave communities, corn-shucking was a time of singing and dancing, perhaps originally initiated at the surreptitious behest of a master who, unlike the planter who had "no objection to their whistling or singing some lively tune, but no *drawling* tunes are allowed in the field, for their motions are almost certain to keep time with the music," had discovered the full meaning of the Abbé Raynal's reflections.[22] This aspect of slavery, the fact that little of real significance could occur without the master's explicit or tacit permission, must surely have placed stringent boundaries upon the meaning of labor to the slaves. For even during the jubilee, "de big times," that accompanied a corn-shucking, the slaves might set the pace of their labors with songs of exploitation and class domination.

> Massa in the great house, counting out
> his money,
> Oh shuck that corn and throw it in the
> barn.
> Mistis in the parlor, eating bread and
> honey,
> Oh, shuck that corn and throw it in the
> barn.

But it is unlikely that the average fieldhand was endowed with even an unsophisticated class based understanding of his condition. Austin Grant remembered the basis for the distribution of wealth and work in more specific terms. "The boss man (overseer) had a nice rock house. The white women didn't do any work a-tall." Another version of the previous corn song is instructive.

> Missus in de big house,
> Mammy in de yard.
> Missus holdin her white hands,
> Mammy workin hard.
> Missus holdin her white hands,
> Mammy workin hard.[23]

The Negro slaves' sense of their exploitation was seen within the context of their color. Black slaves imprisoned in a white world were asked to accept their condition upon the basis of a natural inferiority. How some reacted is exemplified by the following song, which was supposed to have been popular among the South Carolina and Georgia Sea Island slaves.

> Oh, bruders, let us leave
> Dis buckra land for Hayti,

Dah we be receive
Grand as Lafayetty.
Make a mighty show
When we land from steamship,
You'll be like Monro,
Me like Lewis Philip.

O dat equal sod,
Who not want to go-y,
Dah we feel no rod,
Dah we hab no foe-y,
Dah we lib so fine,
Dah hab coach and horsey,
Ebbry day we dine,
We hab tree, four coursey.

No more our son cry sweep,
No more he play de lackey,
No more our daughters weep,
Kase dey call dem blacky.
No more dey servants be,
No more dey scrub and cook-y,
But ebbry day we'll see
Dem read de novel book-y.

Dah we sure to make
Our daughter de fine lady,
Dat dey husbands take
Bove de common grady;
And perhaps our son
He rise in glory splendour,
Be like Washington,
His country's brave defender.[24]

Frances Butler Leigh reported that this song was composed about 1840. She also, somewhat unwittingly, recognized one of the fundamental continuities in Afro-American culture. Replace Kansas for Hayti and 1789 for 1840 "and haven't we exactly the same story," asked Mrs. Leigh.

If the black slaves could have accepted their inferior status as natural, a status that need not have been maintained by the physical power of whites, then they may well have accepted the paternalist compact. But a system that relegated all blacks to a position below all whites regardless of obvious discrepancies of abilities in many individual cases was too flawed to escape the attention of those in bondage. As a result slavery was seen for what it was, an institution deriving its stability from the force of physical power. Slaves accommodated themselves to this superior force, an accommodation that was far from acceptance of the paternalist ideal. It was an accommodation which produced songs of exploitation and despair. It produced a labor force that developed concepts of work and leisure that were, from the context of our perspective, distorted by their very existence. Work after all, was the meaning of the slaves' existence. They were coal.

Notes

1. Abbé Raynal, *A Philosophical and Political History of the Settlements and Trade of the Europeans in the East and West Indies*, Vol. 11 (London, 1777), trans. J. Justamond, M.A., pp. 423-4.

2. Robert W. Fogel and Stanley Engermann, *Time on the Cross: The Economics of American Slavery* (New York, 1972). Eugene D. Genovese, *Roll Jordan Roll: The World the Slaves Made* (New York, 1972).

3. *Webster's New World Dictionary of the American Language* (New York, 1964), College edition.

4. John Blassingame, *The Slave Community* (New York, 1972), Eugene Genovese, ibid., George Rawick, *The American Slave: A Composite Autobiography* (Westport, Connecticut), and references therein.

5. George P. Rawick, ibid., Volume 9, Part 4, p. 182.

6. Genovese, ibid., pp. 286, 291.

7. E.P. Thompson, "Time, Work-Discipline, and Industrial Capitalism," *Past and Present*, No. 38, December 1967, pp. 61, 77.

8. Rawick, ibid., *Arkansas Narratives*, Vol. 9, Part 4, p. 193. *Texas Narratives*, Vol. 5, Part 4, p. 1523.

9. John W. Blassingame, *Slave Testimony* (Baton Rouge, 1977), p. 583.

10. *The Galaxy*, Vol. 12, No. 3, September 1871, p. 337.

11. Rawick, ibid., Vol. 19, p. 179.

12. Frederick Douglass, *Narrative of the Life of Frederick Douglass: An American Slave* (Cambridge, 1960), ed. Benjamin Quarles, pp. 35-37. *My Bondage and My Freedom*, p. 75.

13. Rawick, ibid., Vol. 19, p. 176.

14. Quoted in Julius Lester, *To Be a Slave* (New York, 1968), p. 107.

15. J.T. Trowbridge, *The South* (Hartford, Connecticut, 1865), p. 545.

16. Rawick, ibid., Vol. 19, p. 185. Douglass, ibid., p. 56. Rawick, ibid., *Texas Narratives*, Vol. 5, Part 4, p. 1537.

17. William Wells Brown, *Narrative of William Wells Brown*, in Gilbert Osofsky, *Puttin on Ole Massa* (New York, 1969), p. 181. Rawick, ibid., Vol. 19, p. 178.

18. Rawick, ibid., Vol. 19, p. 178.

19. Russell Hamilton, *Voices from an Empire: A History of Afro-Portuguese Literature* (Minneapolis, 1975), p. 204.

20. Rawick, ibid., Vol. 3, p. 6.

21. Douglass, *Bondage*, p. 253. Rawick, ibid., *Texas Narratives*, Vol. 5, Part 4, p. 1582.

22. *Southern Cultivator*, VIII (1850), p. 163. Quoted in Kenneth M. Stampp, *The Peculiar Institution* (New York, 1969), p. 78.

23. Genovese, ibid., p. 318. Rawick, ibid., Vol. 5, p. 1539. Howard W. Odum, *Negro Workaday Songs* (New York, 1969), p. 117.

24. Frances Butler Leigh, *Ten Years on a Georgia Plantation* (London, 1883), p. 229.

The Making of a Fugitive Slave Narrative: Josiah Henson and Uncle Tom—A Case Study

ROBIN W. WINKS

In recent years a number of historians have demonstrated that slave narratives are to be taken seriously as historical evidence. A sub-set of the genre, the narratives of fugitive slaves, has been subjected to even closer scrutiny than have the accounts of the slaves who remained in the Southern states, and again, the narratives have been found to contain much of great value to the historian and of emotional authenticity to the general reader. These accounts range from the *Narrative* of Frederick Douglass, first published in 1845, and submitted to the most intense study, ultimately to be shown to be largely trustworthy, to the *Memoirs* of Archy Moore, published in 1836, and shown to be almost wholly fabrication. In testing the authenticity of such accounts, the historian must define "authenticity," "accuracy," and "fabrication" both in terms of evidence and in the larger terms of meaning, intent, and impact. Obviously the memoirs of sometimes aged persons recalling a turbulent series of events from a distant past are always suspect, whatever the source; equally obviously historians of an earlier generation were right to doubt some of the narratives some of the time, simply because the authors of such narratives were bound at the least to be intent upon self-explanation if not self-serving. Those narratives written prior to the American Civil War suffered under the additional strain of being used, re-written, and both intentionally and unintentionally abused to support a case, usually (but not invariably) that of the abolitionists. Reprinted abroad, such narratives helped bolster received opinions about American institutions. To expect the narratives of fugitive slaves in particular to be free of error, or to deny such accounts both their truth and their fiction, would be as naive as were we to accept or dismiss all eye-witness reports on the War in Vietnam on the basis of some predetermined ideological position. Each account requires its own scrutiny, for each helped contribute to the perceptions North had of South, Britain had of America, white had of Black, free soiler had of slave owner, etc.: each was part of the mosaic which emerged as a series of stereotypes.

But stereotypes are not necessarily always false; indeed, for the person committed to certain goals, or choosing to perceive of humankind in certain ways, stereotypes may be "good" rather than "harmful," and in this sense "to stereotype" may not be a wholly negative act. In *The Good Earth* Pearl Buck provided millions of Western readers with a stereotype of the Chinese; yet, who would not agree that in many complex ways the favorable, or at least sympathetic, depiction of Chinese values presented in the work of Pearl Buck was "helpful" to international relations. The question, of course, when one discovers a stereotype at work, is not so much whether it is accurate (for almost by definition, a stereotype, like a cliché, has become what it is by virtue of being akin to a perceived truth) but how it came into being and whose ends, and to what purpose, did it serve.

In one sense a fugitive slave narrative falls into the category of autobiography. Yet many of the narratives were, in fact, ghost written, or taken from dictation, or were almost wholly the work of another person, and thus more nearly biography than autobiography. Even if the subject of a narrative did not share the Christian views of the time, the ghost writer might (and usually did) feel it appropriate, for a variety of reasons, to endow the putative author with the somewhat melancholic romanticisms of nineteenth century Christian piety. Thus the values of the age stand between our readings today and the original source, and doubly so in that one can seldom tell definitively whose values were being reflected. Where the act of self-confrontation is meant to serve a social vision, the self may frequently mis-remember. We know, from Ben Franklin, Henry Adams, and any number of others, that autobiography is meant to present the self for social immortality. But are slave narratives autobiography, or are they first-person novels? When they are clothed in the third person, what readings are we to take on the narratives? Clearly the narratives are not meant to be the private property of those who wrote or dictated them, for they were meant for publication. If one applies Roy Pascal's test of autobiography,[1] that it must reveal a conscious growth, a new self-awareness, on the part of the subject as a result of the self-analysis involved in the act of writing, almost none of the narratives can be judged "successful," for they are largely static in the sense that they rather breathlessly review the subject's life from a single unchanged perspective, that of a condition known as Freedom. The impersonality of language adds a further barrier, unless we can come to understand the actual structure of the language as used at the time for the specific intent at hand.[2]

Not all narratives present the same problem, of course, for some are more capable of external verification than others. In any event, not all are equally significant, for the question of influence is an important one: Sometimes the influence arises from the subsequent life of the author, sometimes from the use made of the narrative itself, sometimes from the impact the narrative has on others who employ it to their own purposes, sometimes from the justification the narrative offers for a course of action already decided upon, sometimes because the narrative is simply well-written, or passionately felt, a work of literature, of polemics, even of history in the fullest sense. One immediately thinks of the influence of the work of Douglass, William Wells Brown, Austin Steward, Lewis Clarke, Henry Box Brown, Moses Roper, William Craft, Samuel Ringgold Ward, and of course, Booker T. Washington. Each requires its own case study. Even so, none presents questions more clearly than does another influential narrative, that of Josiah Henson.[3]

Of the many narratives written for, and on occasion by, fugitive slaves who fled from the United States to the provinces of British North America before the Civil War, no single book has been so widely read, so frequently revised, and so influential as the autobiography of Josiah Henson. For Henson came to be identified with one of the best known figures in nineteenth century American literature, the venerable and self-sacrificing Uncle Tom of Harriet Beecher Stowe's most famous novel. To the popular mind then, and to many people now, Henson was undeniably Tom, the very figure from whom Mrs. Stowe borrowed large elements of plot and characterization, the figure who came to symbolize the succesful fugitive, the man who permanently settled in Canada and there won fame, if not fortune, and a permanent place in the history of the abolitionist struggle.

Indeed, Henson's fame is assured, for even he came in time to believe that he was the original Uncle Tom, and his neighbors accepted this evaluation. His cabin and grave, in rural Ontario, became tourist attractions, and Dresden, ironically the center of the province's most clearly practiced color bar in the 1950's, advertised itself as the Home of Uncle Tom. At first untended, but from 1930 looked after by the Independent Order of the Daughters of the Empire and later by the Dresden Horticultural Society, the grave became the scene of Negro Masonic pilgrimages. Henson's house was opened as a museum in 1948, and the cemetery of the colony of which the house was a part was restored by the National Historic Sites Board of Canada in 1965, with plans afoot to recreate a portion of the community itself, both to instill civic pride in black Canadians and as a tourist attraction. The Historic Sites Board gave the considerable force of its approval to the Henson saga when it placed a plaque near the restored home in honor of the man "whose life provided much of the material for . . . 'Uncle Tom's Cabin'."[4]

Henson became one of the best known of all fugitive slaves, the several editions of his narrative one of the most frequently consulted sources, his life thought to be the archetypical fugitive experience. The first version of his autobiography, published in 1849, is without guile, straight-forward, dramatic in its simplicity. But this fugitive from Kentucky, clearly intelligent and hard-working, also shared the normal desire to collect a few of the merit badges that life might offer, and when he found himself thrust into fame in a role that just might fit, he hugged his new role to himself until his death. To his credit, not until he was old and senile did Henson ever unequivocally claim to be Uncle Tom, but he did nothing to stop others from making the claim for him. Those versions of his autobiography which appeared after the publication of *Uncle Tom's Cabin* in 1852 showed substantial alterations, extensions, and fabrications, and the fullest of these accounts, ghost-written for Henson by an English clergyman-editor, John Lobb, was brought back into print in 1969 not only for what it tells us about Henson and the fugitive slaves, but for the fullness of detail it provides, most of it accurate, about fugitive life in Canada, and for the almost classic opportunity it afforded to study the ways in which texts might be altered to serve a cause.[5]

For the cause of the abolitionists was served well by Henson's narrative. In many ways his saga is illustrative of the problem of the intelligent fugitive slave of the time: Henson was seldom left free to be himself, to assimilate if he wished into the mainstream of Canadian life—even of black Canadian life—for he became the focus of abolitionist attention, a tool to be used in a propaganda campaign which was not above much juggling with the facts, however proper its ultimate goals may have been. For these reasons his life, and his autobiographical account of it, deserve examination in some detail. And that life, and narrative, must be seen against the background of the efforts made by and on behalf of the fugitive slaves to found all-black colonies in Canada West, or present-day Ontario. The most significant of these attempts was one initiated in 1842 under the promising name of Dawn, and it is with Dawn that we associate Henson's Canadian sojourn.[6]

Dawn represented one attempt to adjust to the presumed realities of a white America. No less than the European immigrants of the time, some blacks believed in the success ethic that lay behind one of the United States's chief messages to the world: hard work, clean living, education, and an eye for the main chance would bring a man, at least a free man, even if black—and unless flawed by character or caught by bad luck—to the top. However, the black was flawed, in the eyes of many, by character and certainly by luck, in terms of the hard truths of a white world, and enough realized that the demise of slavery alone (which surely was coming) was not sufficient to give the black American a place in the line inexorably marching toward success. Manual labor institutes, practical training, the fundamentals of a bookish education, and some understanding of how a capitalist economy actually worked were essential—or so Josiah Henson would argue later in his autobiography. A brief escape from the world was needed so that the black might master these tools, so that he might catch up with the white man, who had not been deprived of the necessary knowledge. A firm belief in education and the instant status it gave lay behind the many assumed titles, the Doctors, Professors, and Right Reverends who sprang so quickly from their soil. In a communal society, the black could train himself to use freedom, could come to follow the mores, to reflect the virtues, to accept the ethics of the dominant white society. In short, the virtues of the black community experiments were normative ones, most blacks accepted the social environment of the North much as it was, or as they saw it to be, and they did not intend to retreat from it permanently or to reform it. Rather than turning their backs upon white society, they sought a temporary refuge in which to prepare for a full place in that society.

Dawn began in Ohio. In 1834 the Board of Trustees of the Lane Seminary in Cincinnati told students and faculty that they were not to organize anti-slavery activities, and among the Lane Rebels, as they were named, who left for the more liberal atmosphere of Oberlin College, was Hiram Wilson.[7] In the late fall of 1836, with $25 given to him by Charles Grandison Finney, Wilson went to Upper Canada (as Ontario was then called) to see for himself how the fugitives were faring, and in the spring he returned to attend the annual meeting of the American Anti-Slavery Society as a delegate from the province. With the help of other Oberlin students, he began what he hoped would be a series of schools within the growing black communities, schools not restricted to blacks, and late in 1837 he addressed the newly-formed Upper Canada Anti-Slavery Society about the merits of educating fugitives. He also borrowed heavily, and although by the fall of 1839 his work in Amherst-

burg, across the river from Detroit, was well-known in Northern abolitionist circles, he confessed to the Peterboro anti-slavery leader, Gerrit
Smith, that he was trusting in the Lord to pay a debt of $10,000. In 1840
the American Anti-Slavery Society commended him to the "liberal patronage of every true-hearted abolitionist," and the next year Smith and
others organized a Rochester-based committee to help channel funds to
the several schools—ultimately fifteen in all—begun by or inspired through
Wilson's work. His efforts became the Canada Mission, and since he was
trusted, where itinerant black preachers often were not, funds, Bibles,
and clothing funnelled through Wilson to the fugitive slave encamp-
ment.[8]

Wilson attracted the attention of a Quaker philanthropist in Skane-
ateles, New York, James Cannines Fuller, who wished to help fugitives
but not to violate his principle that Americans must not interfere in
Canadian matters. Schools which were controlled from the United States
were not agreeable, therefore, but missions firmly rooted in Canadian
soil, although run according to Wilson's principles, were acceptable.
Fuller accordingly raised much of the initial money for The British-
American Institute, a school for the ". . . Education Mental Moral and
physical of the Coloured inhabitants of Canada not excluding white persons and Indians."[9] He sought money on a tour of England, contacted
Gerrit Smith, and agreed to serve on the new school's board, and in November of 1841 the sponsors purchased two hundred acres of land near
London, Canada West, for $800. Thirteen months later they opened the
doors of a manual-labor school to its first twelve students. The trustees
were three white men, Fuller, the Reverend John Roaf, a Congregational
Minister from Toronto who was active in the anti-slavery society there,[10]
and Frederick Stover of Norwich, Canada West, who had been associated with the British anti-slavery leader, William Wilberforce; and three
Blacks, Peter Smith, George Johnson, and James C. Brown, the last having moved to Dawn from Toronto in order to help.

Around the institute grew the community, and since the whites considered that the town was in charge of the school—as, in fact, it was
not—Dawn itself stood or fell on the school. The institute came to own
perhaps three hundred acres of land; the black settlers owned another
fifteen hundred, on which they raised tobacco, wheat, corn and oats. In
time, the population rose to five hundred or more, and the community
was served by its own saw and grist mills, a brick yard, and a rope walk.
Lumbering proved modestly rewarding, and in all, the settlers increased
the value of their land by over a dollar an acre within five years.

The man most responsible for Dawn's initial success was Josiah Henson, one of the few black leaders in Canada West who seems to have

won nearly universal white approval at first, both for his own activities and, later, for being taken as Mrs. Stowe's Uncle Tom. Born near Port Tobacco, in Charles County, Maryland, on June 15, 1789, Henson passed through the hands of three owners, became a Christian in his eighteenth year, and was maimed for life when one of his master's enemies beat him with a stake, breaking his arm and, perhaps, both of his shoulder blades. At twenty-two Henson married, and during the next forty years he fathered twelve children, eight of whom survived. Recognizing that, on the whole, he was owned by a fair man, he worked hard to ingratiate himself, toiling and inducing others to toil "many an extra hour, in order to show my master what an excellent day's work had been accomplished, and to win a kind word or a benevolent deed from his callous heart.[11] His sense of loyalty was so strong, he personally conducted eighteen of his owner's slaves to Kentucky, passing by the Ohio shores, yet resisting the temptation to run away. He remained in Kentucky for three years, became a preacher in the Methodist Episcopal Church, and was made an unofficial overseer, trusted with considerable freedom of movement. He then returned to his owner in Maryland, preaching in Ohio while on the way, thus collecting $275, a horse, and some clothes, with which he hoped to purchase his freedom. The owner agreed to sell for $450, and by disposing of horse and clothes, Henson raised $350 and signed a note for the rest. When he returned to Kentucky, he learned that his owner now said that the sale price was $1,000, and the slave was unable to disprove this. Henson still did not flee, however, although the Ohio River was nearby.

Henson's decision to escape arose from what he regarded as moral mistreatment in New Orleans. Asked to accompany his owner's nephew south, he realized that despite denials he was to be sold, and on the journey he took up an axe to kill his sleeping companions, only to realize that as a Christian he could not. He was saved from being sold, and parted from the wife he had left in Kentucky, only because his white companion fell seriously ill while in Louisiana and asked Henson to take him back to his home. Henson did so, but he resolved that the decision to sell him, together with his owner's "attempt to kidnap me again, after having pocketed three-fourths of my market value, absolved me from any obligation . . . to pay him any more, or to continue in a position which exposed me to his machinations."[12]

He decided to flee to Canada.

His escape showed foresight and considerable courage. By a ruse he drew out his son, who normally passed the night in the proprietor's house, and choosing a time when, because of the routine of the plantation, they would not be missed for three days, he crossed the Ohio River to the Indiana shore. He carried his two smallest children on his back in a large knapsack; two others walked, as did his wife. The family took a fortnight to reach Cincinnati; with the unexpected assistance of Indians, they pressed on to Sandusky, fell in with a sympathic Scots steamer captain and were taken to Buffalo. On October 28, 1830, about six weeks after crossing the Ohio, the Hensons threw themselves on Canadian soil, Josiah executing "sundry antics which excited the astonishment of those who were looking on."[13]

Josiah adjusted quickly to a life of freedom. On his second attempt he found employment. Home was an old shack, from which he expelled pigs, but in which, for the first time, his family could enjoy privacy and "some of the comforts of life, while the necessaries of food and fuel were abundant." Henson worked for both shares and wages, purchased some livestock, resumed preaching, and saw his boy Tom given two quarters' of schooling at the expense of his employer. Josiah had an excellent memory, and for some time he was able to give the impression that he could read the Bible by memorizing the passages he heard, but one day his son asked, "Why, father, can't you read?" and Josiah, a man of great and stubborn pride, confessed that he could not. The twelve-year-old lad then set out to teach him how, and in time Josiah learned "to read a little."[14] Soon after, he took employment with one Benjamin Riseley, who allowed him to call prayer meetings in his home.

At one of these meetings a small group of Blacks decided to invest their earnings collectively in land. "It was precisely the Yankee spirit which I wished to instil into my fellow slaves, if possible," Henson later wrote,[15] and in the fall of 1834 he set out to find a suitable area for them. He rented cleared lots near Colchester, where he and his followers sought to raise tobacco and wheat. According to Henson, he learned that the grantee had not complied with some of the conditions for his allotment, however, and he wrote to the Lieutenant-Governor, who advised the blacks to apply to the legislature for relief. Upon doing so they found themselves freed from rent, although now subject themselves to the usual improvement clauses. They had meant to leave the site quickly, but given this boon they remained for seven years.

Henson now was devoting most of his thought to the problems of how fugitives like himself might best adjust to Upper Canada. As he said, "The mere delight the slave took in his freedom, rendered him, at first, contented with a lot far inferior to that which he might have attained. Then his ignorance led him to make unprofitable bargains, and he would often hire wild land on short terms, and bind himself to clear a certain number of acres; and by the time they were cleared and fitted for cultivation his lease was out, and his landlord would come in, and

raise a splendid crop on the new land. . . ." Too, the blacks often raised
only tobacco, tempted by the high price it brought, and this created a
glut in an already depressed market, and the blacks who had not diversi-
fied with wheat consequently were driven to the wall. To correct this,
Henson "set seriously about the business of lecturing upon the subject
of crops, wages, and profits. . . ."[16]

While in Colchester, Henson met Hiram Wilson, and from 1836 the
two worked together. When Fuller returned from England with funds to
establish a manual labor institute, it was Henson and Wilson who called
a convention in June, 1838, to determine how and where the money
might best be spent. As Henson knew, with all the sensitivity of the self-
consciously unlettered who see universal education as a panacea, blacks
increasingly were excluded from the public schools of the province, and
upon his urging the delegates decided to found The British-American
Institute. In 1842 Henson moved to Dawn. "We look to the school, and
the possession of landed property by individuals, as two great means of
elevation of our oppressed and degraded race . . ." he later wrote in his
autobiography.[17]

This autobiography was first published by Arthur D. Phelps in Boston
early in 1849. Hoping to earn some small income for the British-American Institute, Henson spoke of his experiences to Samuel A. Eliot, a
former Mayor of Boston who was well-known for his moderate anti-
slavery views, and Eliot wrote *The Life of Josiah Henson, formerly a
Slave, Now an Inhabitant of Canada.*[18] In style, pace, and proportion the
account reflects the unembellished simplicity of Henson's life. Clearly,
he was an unusual man, alert and intelligent. Equally clearly, he emerged
as a natural leader to other Blacks, for he understood figures where they
did not, and he was imaginative and independent in his approach to
immediate problems. The narrative also showed that Henson was vain
behind his facade of humility, proud, possessive, and prone to seek out
quick approbation rather than long-range solutions. He needed to lead,
and often led well, but he rather enjoyed manipulating the lives of
others, if always for what he conceived to be their benefit. He seemed
immensely stable, given neither to recriminations nor to a paralyzing
fatalism, and in the main, he was an effective spokesman for the black
Canadians despite his deeply-felt need to please. If Dawn succeeded,
much would be due Henson; otherwise, he was unlikely to win recognition outside a limited circle.

But three years after the publication of Henson's life, there appeared
the book which was to enlarge this circle immeasurably. In 1851 a Washington weekly paper, *The National Era*, began the serial publication of
a long story written by Harriet Beecher Stowe, the wife of a Professor

at Bowdoin College in Maine. Originally to have carried the subtitle, "The Man that Was a Thing," Mrs. Stowe's narrative, renamed "Uncle Tom's Cabin; or, Life Among the Lowly," ran in the *Era* from June 1851, until April 1852. Uncle Tom quickly built a following, and ten days before the last installment appeared, the whole was issued in two volumes, to be sold for a dollar. The novel swept the Northern states, England—where in London alone twenty different pirated editions were published within the year—and the Continent.[19]

In British North America as well everyone seemed to be reading about Uncle Tom.[20] A Montreal monthly periodical, *The Maple Leaf*, serialized the book, with an abridged conclusion, from July 1852, until the following June. The influential Toronto *Globe*, edited by an ardent abolitionist, George Brown, printed extracts and the famous fifth chapter in its entirety. The Montreal *Gazette* noted it only less favorably. Within weeks there were separate Toronto and Montreal editions based upon the Boston printing.[21] In St. Thomas, Canada West, a diorama illustrative of Mrs. Stowe's more poignant scenes was widely viewed, in Toronto strolling players dramatized the novel in the streets, and the London Mechanic's Institute Library doubled its order for copies. In Montreal *La Case de l'Oncle Tom* was an immediate success, and Wilfrid Laurier, one day to be Canada's Prime Minister and then a boy of ten, borrowed a copy from a college friend and annoyed his landlady by burning his lamp through the night in order to finish it. Hundreds of young boys who, less than ten years later, would enter the Northern armies, devoured it in the one-volume edition. Soon incorporated into Erastus Beadle's Dime Novels, the book found an ever-expanding readership.[22] Only in Nova Scotia and Prince Edward Island did Mrs. Stowe receive a mixed press: in a lengthy review in *The Provincial*, a new Halifax monthly, an anonymous critic observed that *Uncle Tom's Cabin* had been discussed by everyone and that it justly condemned slavery, but he felt that its author had overdrawn her case, or that blacks in Nova Scotia were unusually inferior. "The insufferable arrogance and uncleanly habits of Colonial negroes make it almost impossible for us to hold association with them": "We are unwilling even to occupy the same conveyance, and disdain to sit at the same table"; "we have no hesitation in pronouncing them far inferior in morality, intelligence, and cleanliness, to the very lowest among the white population. . . ." The Charlottetown *Islander* also cautioned against romancers who described exceptional cases rather than the rule.[23]

But the hold taken by *Uncle Tom's Cabin* on the public imagination was secure and long-lasting—certainly longer in British North America than in the United States. In 1932 a report on reading habits among Canadian secondary school students showed that Tom still was the most popular American book, and in 1952 sales in Toronto, in particular, continued briskly.[24] In its several dramatized forms "Tom" became a perennial favorite for traveling troops, and with the addition of bloodhounds to pursue Eliza across the ice floes, Tom Shows played to appreciative audiences throughout English-speaking Canada. A touring group carried Tom and related minstrelsy into New Brunswick and Nova Scotia in the 1860's, and there were minstrel and Tom shows "galore" in Halifax in the '60's and '70's.[25] By the 1880's rural communities might be exposed to Tommers five or six times in the decade.[26] Ironically, similar groups performed in Dresden, Ontario, in 1919 and 1923, a mile from Josiah Henson's grave, to segregated audiences, and into the 1920's the almost lunatic jollity, the cringing piety, and the blackface distortions of the shows continued to attract crowds in the Maritime Provinces.[27]

This explosive and utterly unexpected effect of her work may have frightened Mrs. Stowe. Assuredly, the virulence of the Southern attack upon her novel, upon not only its sentiments, its plot, and its style, but also upon its allegedly factual base, disturbed her. Even friendly reviewers doubted her veracity: *The Times* of London found Tom too pure, too perfect to believe, and thought Mrs. Stowe's "honest zeal" had outrun her discretion.[28] As the London editions mounted toward forty, as the rage for Uncle Tom swept across the Continent, his creator felt obliged to justify what she had written.[29] In the novel she had claimed to be a close student of the slave states, and having lived in Cincinnati at the time of the Lane revolt, she was, in fact, tolerably well-informed. But she saw that the novel could not stand alone, undefended, and she went forth to her own defense, therefore, vigorously, massively—but not forthrightly.

Accordingly, she constructed *A Key to Uncle Tom's Cabin: Presenting the Original Facts and Documents upon which the Story is Founded* . . . , which was published in Boston, in 1853. The title was less than honest, for the documentation she brought together in the *Key*, while amply supporting much that she had put in her novel, had not all been in her possession at the time Uncle Tom was created; quite simply the *Key* was a *post hoc* attempt to buttress a thesis already expressed. Not unnaturally, she made the best case for herself in assembling her materials, and in an opening chapter she made clear her belief to have injected documentation into the novel would have been to clog its narrative drive.

To collect material for her *Key*, Mrs. Stowe consulted various books while in Boston. She drew in part from Theodore Dwight Weld's horrific compilation of atrocity stories, *American Slavery as It is: Testimony of a Thousand Witnesses,* published in 1839, and she also used Eliot's *Life* of Henson, from which she quoted at some length (with slight inaccuracies), identifying him correctly as "pastor of the missionary settlement at Dawn, in Canada." She clearly did not read Henson closely, however, for she was wrong about his purchase price and about the exact itinerary of his journey from Maryland to Kentucky on his first trip. She said that Henson's chief significance lay in his Christian decision not to kill his companions while travelling to New Orleans. Once she related Henson to one of the figures in her novel, George Harris, and once she found in Henson's narrative an "instance parallel" with Tom's Christian dedication.[30] Later she credited most of Uncle Tom to Weld's book, which she said she had kept in her workbasket by day and under her pillow at night.

At no time during the early years of her success, or of Henson's small fame arising from his narrative of 1849, did Mrs. Stowe identify Henson with Uncle Tom. To the contrary, she found as many "striking parallels" to her novel in the narrative of Solomon Northup as in Henson's. She never referred to having met Henson, and in the *Key* she cited his memoirs but not a conversation. On one occasion she said that the death scene of Uncle Tom was the first that she wrote, while living in Brunswick (in which case, no relationship to Henson was likely), but on another occasion she said that this scene was written after she had composed the death of Little Eva, and in Andover.[31] In 1878, apparently feeling that contradiction had gone too far, she said that once she had written letters for a former slave woman, who had become a servant in her own family, to a slave husband who remained in Kentucky, and that it was this "faithful slave" who was "a pattern of Uncle Tom." In the same essay she admitted that it was after her account began to appear in *The National Era* that she went to Boston to reinforce "her *repertoire* of facts" by consulting, among other books, those by Weld and Henson, particulars from which were "inwoven with the story."[32] Again, the sequence is not clear, and Mrs. Stowe seemed incapable of clarifying it, but nothing said publicly by the author of *Uncle Tom* gave real substance to any contention that Josiah Henson and Uncle Tom were one and the same.[33]

Nonetheless, they became so in the public mind, and some evidence was offered for this contention. Writing in 1911 Charles and Lyman Stowe, her son and grandson, said that she had met Henson in Boston in January of 1850, at the home of her brother, Lyman Beecher.[34] In the 1878, or fourth, revised edition of his life, Henson asserted that he had met her in Andover, Massachusetts, and that he had told her the story of his life, and indeed in 1876 in a private letter Mrs. Stowe said that

Henson had visited her there.[35] Upon this basis, as we shall see, Henson was able to imply and others who chose to use him for their own purposes were able to assert that he and Tom were the same man, that Tom yet lived, and that Eliza, Eva, and George were drawn from Henson's family and friends.

But none of these alleged facts will bear close scrutiny. Mrs. Stowe did not move to Andover until 1852, so if Henson visited her there, it was after she had completed all but a chapter or two of her novel. Henson was in Boston twice in 1850, but by his word both occasions were "after the Fugitive Slave Law was passed," which was in September, so he was not in Boston in January as Charles and Lyman Stowe wrote, and in any case Mrs. Stowe was in Cincinnati in January, not reaching Boston until May.[36] The first edition of his narrative, as published in 1849, appeared early in the year, while Mrs. Stowe was still in Cincinnati, and when she began writing furiously in February of 1851, she apparently mentioned neither Henson nor his book to anyone, although she normally shared her ideas freely with her husband. Had she communed with Henson before his book was written, as he later implied, surely he or Eliot would have mentioned it in his autobiography, for he was not slow to acquire prestige by dropping names; and if they met while Mrs. Stowe was writing her book she need not have journeyed to Boston to "re-enforce" her facts by reading his account. If Eva, Eliza, or George had any place in Henson's life, surely he would have mentioned that place before 1878—at least in his 1858 edition, published well after they were household names—but he did not.[37] Clearly, although he later hinted otherwise, he was not the "slave husband" to whom Mrs. Stowe wrote letters on behalf of her servant, for Josiah's wife was with him in Kentucky. Equally clearly, she did not meet him, as he also suggested, while in Kentucky, for he was a slave in Daviess County, well-removed from the Mason and Garrard county homes she did visit.

The books of Mrs. Stowe and Henson did morally reinforce each other, however, and she wrote an introduction to the second or 1858 edition of his book, in which he carried the story to 1852. But at this date—when association with Mrs. Stowe would bring a cachet to Henson's account—he made no mention of any meeting, nor did she in her introduction, which was bland and noncommittal. Moreover, the introduction was retained unaltered in Henson's 1878 edition, in which he claimed to have met her in Andover, but either she met Henson there after nearly all of *Uncle Tom's Cabin* was written or both unaccountably had forgotten their venue.[38]

Under the impact of abolitionist need, Henson's desire to please led to numerous changes in successive editions of his memoirs.[39] Perhaps spokesmen need be neither honest nor consistent but merely convincing, and Henson was at least this, and no one then had occasion to compare the various editions of his narrative. Such a comparison is revealing of his ability to weave his presence into almost any event that would provide a moral or add to his stature. He could exaggerate, transmuting the mundane into the dramatic (his broken shoulders became more crippling with each edition),[40] and he could move with the times, as he did when he excised the more obsequious passages from the original version of his life for later editions, when he struck entirely a passing reference to being arrested for debt, or when he added a chapter in 1858 on his exploits in returning to the South to help other fugitives to escape, a phase of his activities unaccountably forgotten in 1849.[41] He incorporated a pious refusal to participate in the Nat Turner rebellion into his local lectures, although the rebellion actually took place after he had reached Canada West. He claimed that he personally had written his books although in 1849, as we have seen, he recorded that he learned to read "a little" and one of his abolitionist supporters noted that he could "barely write and cannot read."[42] In the first post-Civil War edition of the autobiography he said he was a Captain in the Second Essex Company of Colored Volunteers—which he was not—and that his company captured the *Anne*, which he misspelled.

Perhaps the most important, and also the more subtle, of the changes lay in the title of the book itself. The second revised account was *Truth Stranger than Fiction: Father Henson's Story of His Own Life.* Thus he (or more properly, Eliot for him) invoked the spirit of Lord Byron, by then widely-known to be the center of one of Mrs. Stowe's spiritual obsessions, for it was Byron who had written in 1823, that "truth is always strange, / Stranger than fiction."[43] Throughout, he and his editors were consistent in seeing that his life was a great moral lesson, that original phraseology was embellished and twisted to make a homiletic statement clearer, and that his fellow fugitives fed upon the thought of his acceptance by Queen Victoria, Lord John Russell, or President Rutherford B. Hayes.[44] Still, Henson was true to his own lights, and while, by his own admission, he managed money badly, he appears not to have abused his positions of trust for personal gain. He also resisted becoming Uncle Tom, at first, even if in the end he fell to the pressures of financial need, the desire for prestige, and a fading memory.[45]

It was not Henson who first or most persistently insisted that he was the original Uncle Tom, and since he wrote none of the lives themselves, one must find his ghost writers as culpable as he in building the legend. In public lectures long after the Civil War, Henson repeatedly was introduced as Uncle Tom, but initially he appears to have been careful not to make the claim explicit himself: "It has been spread abroad that ' "Uncle Tom" is coming,' and that is what has brought you here. Now allow me to say that my name is not Tom, and never was Tom, and that I do not want to have any other name inserted in the newspapers for me than my own. My name is Josiah Henson, always was, and always will be. I never change my colors. (Loud laughter.) I would not if I could, and could not if I would. (Renewed laughter.) Well, inquiry in the minds of some has led to a deal of inquiry on the part of others. You have read and heard some persons says that, ' "Uncle Tom" was dead, and how can he be here? It is an imposition that is being practised on us.' . . . Very well, I do not blame you for saying that. . . . A great many have come to me in this country and asked me if I was not dead. (Laughter.) Says I, 'Dead?' Says he, 'Yes, I heard you were dead, and read you were.' 'Well,' says I; 'I heard so too, but I never believed it yet. (Laughter.) I thought in all probability I would have found it out as soon as anybody else.' " Thus did Henson skirt the edges of truth, adding that all should realize that Mrs. Stowe was writing a novel, and concluding—with a deft change of the subject—that if the audience would refer to chapters 34 through 57 of the *Key to Uncle Tom's Cabin*, ". . . I think you will there see me."[46] Yet, the *Key* ran to only forty-nine chapters.

Others were less clever at avoiding the central question, or chose not to. In 1851 there appeared a London and Edinburgh edition of Henson's narrative, slightly altered, and with the first appearance of the added section devoted to aiding fugitive slaves, together with a preface by Thomas Binney, Minister of the Weigh-House Chapel in London, where Henson made one of his most effective appeals for money. This edition was an abolitionist handbook, as the 1849 version had not been, for it included an appendix on runaways in Canada, on specific fugitive slave cases, and an appeal for £2,000. The edition of 1858, printed in Boston, with Mrs. Stowe's rather flat preface replacing Binney's more impassioned one, followed. A "revised and enlarged" London edition was next, in 1877; it retained Mrs. Stowe's preface, added an introduction by George Sturge and Samuel Morley, English abolitionists, and carried a title page specifying for the first time that Henson was Uncle Tom.[47]

The editions from 1877 were, in fact, almost entirely the work of John Lobb, the youthful managing editor of the weekly *Christian Age*. Lobb had been a religious journalist who knew how to attract an audience: when he took over the faltering *Age* in 1872, its circulation was five thousand, and in four years he raised the figure to eighty thousand. Morley and Sturge asked him to help solicit money for Henson, still in need of assistance at debt-ridden Dawn, and in seven months Lobb attracted £2,000.[48] Together with Henson, he went to Windsor Castle

where they were received by Queen Victoria, who asked all of her domestic staff to come to meet the real Uncle Tom. Adding an index,
drawing from Henson the promise that Lobb's would be the "only authorized edition" of his life, the editor soon had sales moving up to forty
thousand. The next year they reached ninety-six thousand, whereupon
Lobb made further modest revisions in the text and added extracts from
Henson's addresses and an account of his audience with the Queen. In
1877 Lobb also wrote, without Henson's assistance although from his
book, *The Young People's Illustrated Edition of "Uncle Tom's" Story of
His Life,* which contained a preface by the Earl of Shaftesbury and "Uncle Tom's Address to the Young People of Great Britain," which Henson
almost certainly did not dictate. The life was re-arranged and each chapter title, the illustrations, and even the index pointed moral lessons: "It
is noble to speak the truth."[49] Again, nowhere was Henson made to say
specifically that he was Uncle Tom, although Lobb, outside conve-
niently manipulated quotation marks, did so for him. Lobb's narrative of
his life sold a quarter of a million copies and became a Sunday School
favorite, although Henson seems to have received very little money from
the enterprise and his estate certainly received none.[50]

Lobb, on the other hand, left the *Christian Age* and set himself up as
a publisher. He wrote a similar life of Frederick Douglass, after Henson's death advertised the autobiography as dealing with "Legree, who
maimed Josiah Henson for Life," and with "Eva, who was saved from
Drowning by Josiah Henson, etc.,"[51] and declared that the narrative had
been translated into twelve languages.[52] At the end of the century, Lobb
turned to spiritualism; he communed with seven hundred dead over
three years, including Shakespeare, Lincoln, Gladstone, Shaftesbury, and
Henson, for the restless Josiah, still insinuating himself into all events,
was "a frequent visitor at the seances. . . ."[53]

For Mrs. Stowe, Henson would stay no more mute than he did for
Lobb, and she continued to be contradictory and evasive. In 1876 the
Reverend William H. Tilley, rector of the Cronyn Memorial Church in
London, Ontario, sought confirmation of Henson as Tom, possibly because of a brief association of Bishop Benjamin Cronyn with Henson earlier. Mrs. Stowe's reply of May 15 was made public, but it was seldom
quoted in full, and time and again her letter was cited to prove that she
had admitted the relationship. In fact, she was as unclear as usual, avoiding any direct identification: "I take pleasure in indorsing with all my
heart that noble man, Josiah Henson," she wrote, "to be worthy of all the
aid and help which any good man may be disposed to give. It is true
that a sketch of his life . . . furnished me many of the finest conceptions and incidents of 'Uncle Tom's' character, in particular the scene

where he refuses to free himself by the murder of a brutal master. He once visited me in Andover and personal intercourse confirmed my high esteem I had for him. . . ." But she did not say when the visit took place, and as we have seen, had the visit been before she wrote most of the novel, it could not have been to Andover.[54] In a special editorial note to the 1881 edition of Henson's *Life,* Lobb nonetheless asserted that Mrs. Stowe had "quite settle[d] the point," quoting a barely relevant extract from *The Times.*[55] Plagued by further inquiries, Mrs. Stowe wrote to the editor of the Indianapolis *News* in 1882 that Uncle Tom was "not the biography of any one man.[56]

The widely-read New York *Sun,* noting that this letter was going the rounds of the press, quoted her as saying that she had "introduced some" of "the most striking incidents" from Henson's *Autobiography* into her story, and that the "good people of England gave my simple good friend Josiah enthusiastic welcome as the Uncle Tom of the Story," which was true enough.[57] In 1883, writing to an inquirer from Florida, she declared that the "story as it stands is a work of fiction—a combination of circumstances," and that "several colored men" possessed "the excellencies of Uncle Tom. . . ."[58] She died in 1896 with the incubus of Josiah still firmly upon Tom's back.[59]

But of what matter is this problem of the linkage between Uncle Tom and Josiah Henson? Precisely this: as Canadians came increasingly to assign Henson's role to Tom and as the myth of the North Star, the Underground Railroad, and the Fugitives' haven "under the lion's paw"—a myth so well-explored by Larry Gara in his book, *The Liberty Line: The Legend of the Underground Railroad* (Lexington, Ky., 1961)—grew in the post-Civil War years, Canadians also came increasingly to congratulate themselves upon their lack of prejudice and to contrast themselves favorably with the immoral and once slave-ridden United States. The true contrast was favorable enough, indeed, but that the greatest, the best-known, the most pious and most Christian black fugitive of all time should have sought out Canadian soil for his resurrection bred a growing Canadian self-satisfaction with racial conditions above the forty-ninth parallel. If Uncle Tom came to Canada, could conditions merit improving? With every passing year since the late 1860's, at least until the 1890's, a stream of self-congratulatory Canadian newspaper accounts, editorials, and memoirs appeared in April or September, on the anniversaries of the outbreak of the Civil War or of the passage of the Fugitive Slave Act, in which Henson was cited as ample and sole evidence to prove that Canadians shared none of the American racial virus, that in this one area, at least, the pressures of continentalism had been resisted successfully.[60] That many Blacks agreed with Martin Delany in saying that Mrs. Stowe knew nothing about Black men;[61] that Henson himself apparently wrote that "in Canada, black children are despised";[62] that many black Canadians had concluded that Henson was self-serving and sly;[63] even that to blacks "Uncle Tom" had become a pejorative term— all were ignored in the recurrent annual flush of pleasure over the presence of "the real Uncle Tom's grave" on Canadian soil.[64]

Yet, while Henson was self-aggrandizing, having seen quickly enough that a popular identification with the decade's most rapidly-selling book could do him no harm, whatever little he gained financially he apparently did give to the community he died serving. The rest of his story we know from his own account, and although he added color to it and allowed Lobb to embroider events, the basic outline is quite accurate. Henson did pioneer a saw mill for Dawn, one which helped the community as well as himself, and he did exhibit his wares at the great London Exhibition, to the advantage of his colony, since he dramatically drew attention to the plight as well as to the resourcefulness of the fugitives in Canada West. He was deeply involved in litigation over his management at Dawn, and he broke sharply with members of the British and Foreign Anti-Slavery Society, developments at which he only hints in his narrative.

But for the most part the historian must conclude that Henson's motives were appropriate both to the needs of Dawn and to his own needs and that his opponents were mistaken. He also found himself in serious trouble, as he notes, for recruiting black Canadians to serve in the Northern armies during the Civil War, but charges that he kept their bounty money for himself seem to have been false. His trip to England and Scotland during the summer of 1876 was undertaken largely to raise funds to clear a mortgage he had been forced to accept in order to fight a law suit against him, and while the money he thus raised was for his personal use, one may argue—as he did—that the law suit itself arose from his efforts to help keep Dawn and its successor settlements active. He clearly was fractious, devious, and by the time he had worn the mantle of fame for some years, also paternalistic toward his less fortunate brethren. He lost valuable friends among the American abolitionist community before the war by not paying his debts, forcing them to cancel loans as a gift to the movement for which he was taken to be a spokesman, and he lost other friends among the black community by taking over functions of leadership which were not his to take.[65] As his once warm supporter turned cool, Amos A. Lawrence wrote to John Scoble, some of Henson's ability lay in being able to cajole people into doing what they knew to be financially unwise.[66] Edmund Quincy, who served several times as editor of *The Liberator* during William Lloyd Garrison's absence, concluded that Henson "was a time-serving sycophant."[67] But Henson's face continued to be an appealing one, and the money he earned on lecture tours continued to find its way into the diminished black community over which he served increasingly as patriarch. He was scorned by some but, it would appear, loved by more, and if he served himself, he also served others.

In the year before his death Henson lectured in the Park Street Baptist Church in Hamilton, Ontario; he was ninety-three and past caring, and for the first time he categorically, without the protective use of third-person and subjunctive phrases, assured his listeners that he was Uncle Tom, exhibiting a picture Queen Victoria had given to him, rambling on for two and a half hours, until led from the platform.[68] He had embraced the legend himself. In May of 1883, when he died, fifty wagons followed his hearse to the graveside, a black band from nearby Chatham played, nine black preachers prayed, and Josiah's body was frozen in ice. On the anniversary eighty years later, seven thousand Black Masons from Canada and the United States gathered at his graveside to honor him.[69]

In fairness to Henson, one must realize that the controversy that grew about him was not, in fact, over Henson so much as over that for which he stood. Those who disliked *Uncle Tom's Cabin*, either because it was thought to be anti-Christian, anti-Southern or, later, because of the servile Negro it depicted, cast much of their dislike toward Henson, while those who embraced the novel and its figures embraced him too. And among abolitionists, Henson could not hope to win universal approval, for the movement itself was split into warring camps. Henson attended a state convention of anti-slavery delegates in New Bedford, Massachusetts, in 1858, and there he strongly opposed the immediatist, violent approach of a portion of those present. When Charles L. Remond, a Garrisonian activist, recommended that a committee be appointed to prepare an address to the slaves in the Southern states suggesting that they resort to armed insurrection, Henson was on his feet with a powerful speech which was instrumental to the defeat of the motion. "As he didn't want to see three or four thousand men hung before this time," Henson remarked, "he should oppose any such action, head, neck and shoulders," now; the idea of armed insurrection was "ridiculous."[70] So it was, too, and Henson's influence undoubtedly was in the right direction, but there were those, such as Remond, who thought him cowardly. Ultimately Henson was to suffer the greatest irony of all: precisely through his successful self-identification with Uncle Tom, and because of his own moderate views on matters of race, he would become synonymous for many with the paths of moderation and even accommodation to the white community which the mid-twentieth century's Black Power advocates rejected.

The problems that Henson's life and his much-altered autobiography raise are important ones. Indeed, because of the many changes in his narrative, the events with which Henson may appropriately be associated—the arrival of the fugitive slaves, the rise and decline of the Negro community movement in nineteenth-century Canada, and the rôle in the abolitionist movement of those fugitives who elected to remain permanently resident in Canada—are more than ordinarily unclear. In *Tales of Unrest* Joseph Conrad wrote that, "The sustained invention of a really telling lie demands a talent which I do not possess," and Henson might well have said the same, for his story was substantially true, accurate enough to be accepted by many but not accurate enough to trust completely, especially where matters of nuance arise. Perhaps most of the problems that Henson's *Life* leaves for us are no more important than the question of how badly injured, and in precisely what way, he was. But as the quintessential Canadian Black, the successful fugitive, Henson's account remains important to the broader story of how the abolition of slavery itself took place.

In the end the final editions of Josiah Henson's *Life*, though still technically viewed as autobiography, and in 1878 once again called such, were less fugitive slave narratives and more nineteenth century success stories catering to a variety of subtle needs in both the Black and the white readerships. Popular history being what it is, Henson will probably remain inextricably linked to Mrs. Stowe's Uncle Tom, and to the extent that History is what people believe to be true, his rôle in history will continue to be defined by our changing perceptions of Mrs. Stowe's literary creation. Yet the several editions of the *Autobiography*—of which the 1881 edition is the fullest, containing all of the material added between 1851 and 1879 together with Lobb's own conclusion—are, taken collectively, a remarkable example of the way in which the fugitive slave narrative grew by accretion, by manipulation, and as a result of the demands of changing taste. Depending upon the questions we ask, Henson's autobiographical volumes—all of them—are valuable historical sources; equally, only one, the first, may be largely trustworthy in the simplest sense of lacking embroidery. Intelligently drawn upon, the 1849 *Autobiography* can tell us much about slave life in the old South, about the means of escape from that life, and about the initial reception in the North or in Canada.[71] Used more complexly, the editions that labored as *Truth Stranger than Fiction* provide us with a case study in the packaging of a nineteenth century body of literature that was as much a *genre* for its day as detective or science fiction are for ours. In the end,

Josiah Henson's volumes become once again *An Autobiography,* the title with which they began, not so much in order to veto the act of imagination that Lobb's additions, in particular, represented, as to put the house right, to bring the reader back to a moral order of things in which the moral tourist, seeking out renewal for old values, could once again invest Josiah Henson, through his presumed act of autobiography, with an assumption of having spoken, if not the literal, then the spiritual truth, not only about being a fugitive slave but—in the very manipulation of his narrative to serve the needs of others—about the condition of being black in nineteenth century North America.[72]

A note on the printing history of Henson's autobiography and a note on Henson's biographers follow.

A note on the printing history of Henson's autobiography.[73]
The first *Life of Josiah Henson, formerly a Slave, Now an Inhabitant of Canada. Narrated by Himself,* as ghost-written by Samuel A. Eliot, appeared in Boston in 1849. It has been reprinted twice, first with different pagination, by The Observer Press of Dresden, Ontario, for Uncle Tom's Cabin and Museum in Dresden. This edition, which appeared in 1965, includes a brief Foreword and the text of the plaque that demarks Henson's house. The 1849 edition appeared in London and Edinburgh in 1851 as *The Life of Josiah Henson, formerly a Slave: As Narrated by Himself.* The second edition, substantially revised, was retitled *Truth Stranger than Fiction: Father Henson's Story of His Own Life,* and was published in Boston in 1858 and in London in 1859. As noted in the text, all further revisions were in the hands of John Lobb, who usually listed himself on the title-pages as the editor. The third edition, "revised and enlarged," was Lobb's *"Uncle Tom's Story of His Life": An Autobiography of the Rev. Josiah Henson (Mrs. Harriet Beecher Stowe's "Uncle Tom"), From 1789 to 1876,* published in London in 1877. In the same year Lobb's *The Young People's Illustrated Edition of "Uncle Tom's" Story of His Life (From 1789 to 1877)* appeared, also in London, to be followed in 1878 with Lobb's London edition of *An Autobiography of the Rev. Josiah Henson (Mrs. Harriet Beecher Stowe's "Uncle Tom"): From 1789 to 1877,* with added material of a minor nature. In 1879 Lobb published, with the Henson portion of the text changed no further, *"Truth Stranger than Fiction": An Autobiography of the Rev. Josiah Henson (Mrs. Harriet Beecher Stowe's "Uncle Tom"), From 1789 to 1879,* on this occasion in Boston, and with a new preface by Mrs. Stowe, notes by Wendell Phillips and John Greenleaf Whittier, and an appendix by Gilbert Haven.

The fullest version of the Henson narrative to appear during his lifetime was Lobb's *An Autobiography of the Rev. Josiah Henson ("Uncle Tom") From 1789 to 1881*. This also was the first edition to be published in Canada, appearing in London, Ontario in 1881. It contained the Stowe, Phillips, Whittier, and Haven additions, but with the 1878 rather than the 1879 introduction, and a Conclusion written by Lobb, although not so attributed. This version was a "revised and enlarged" edition. Some slight additions were made to the final nineteenth-century edition, Lobb's *The Autobiography of the Rev. Josiah Henson ("Uncle Tom") From 1789 to 1883*, London, 1890, to include Henson's death, but some of the added matter was cut, so that the Ontario volume remains the fullest. There is also a disputed edition, normally ascribed to Halifax, Nova Scotia, in 1852, of the original Henson narrative of 1849, but (see footnote 21) I am convinced that this edition was published in England and that it, therefore, is merely a pirated edition of the London and Edinburgh printing of 1851. Of these original English-language editions, all save those of 1852, 1879, and 1881 are in the British Museum; the provenance of the others is discussed in the relevant footnotes, as is the question of editions in translation (see note 52). All but the 1849 edition have a picture of Henson as a frontispiece. The young people's edition includes a tipped-in tintype, usually missing (but present in the British Museum's copy), of Lobb and Henson and introduces an appendix on Henson's visit to the King Edward Industrial School and Girl's Refuge in 1877 that does not appear elsewhere. . . .

Although the first edition of Henson's memoir bears the imprint of Arthur D. Phelps, the original publishers were to have been Charles C. Little and James Brown, booksellers in Cambridge and Watertown respectively (*Boston Directory 1849*, p. 190). This is shown by the original manuscript copy of the narrative as taken down by Samuel Eliot. The manuscript, now in the Boston Public Library, was given by Miss Mary L. Bullard of Manchester-by-the-Sea in 1897, and it clearly states that Little and Brown were to publish the manuscript for the author, and that Eliot had written it.

I have made a line-by-line comparison between the manuscript and the first edition and find no changes of importance. There are numerous quite minor alterations—added commas, corrected spellings, the insertion of Roman numerals for the chapters of the Bible, and the substitution of *and* for *&*—and the original contains italicized words and insertions which have been regularized in the printed copy. The one omission of substance occurs at the end, where the final line of the manuscript was not printed; there are also changes of nuance by the substitution of other words on pages 17, 23, and 32 of the manuscript, and a garbled Biblical quotation is corrected. The manuscript apparently was read back to Henson when Eliot completed it.

A Note on Henson's Biographers.

Josiah Henson has been unfortunate in his biographers. The only acceptable statements on Henson are B[enjamin] B[rawley], "Josiah Henson," *D.A.B.*, VIII, 564-65, together with an obituary in the New York *Daily Tribune* for May 6, 1883. In addition to Jessie L. Beattie's *Black Moses* (see footnote 42) there is Brion Gysin's *To Master—A Long Good Night: The Story of Uncle Tom, A Historical Narrative* (New York, 1946), which is fictionalized and hostile. Gysin denounced Henson as "an appeaser" (New York *Times*, Feb. 2, 1947) even before "Uncle Tom" was a widely used synonym for a racial Quisling. W.B. Hartgrove, "The Story of Josiah Henson," *Journal of Negro History*, III (January, 1918), 1-21, is an utterly useless article taken directly from the 1858 edition of the autobiography, which Hartgrove frequently misreads. Margaret K. Zieman, "The Story Behind the Real Uncle Tom," in Canada's *Macleans Magazine*, LXVII (June, 1954), 20-21, 42-44, 46, helped renew the Canadian hagiography. Aileen Ward, "In Memory of Uncle Tom," *Dalhousie Review*, XX (October, 1940), 335-38, is quite without merit. Annie E. Duncan, "Josiah Henson," *The Negro History Bulletin* IV (April, 1941), 146-47, 163-64, is for children, while Lois M. Jones, "Josiah Henson's Lumbering Operations in Canada," *ibid.*, p. 157, is by a child. Elizabeth Ross Haynes, *Unsung Heroes* (New York, 1921), pp. 191-206; H.A. Tanser, "Josiah Henson, the Moses of His People," *Journal of Negro Education*, XII (Fall, 1943), 630-32; and Jean Tallach, "The Story of Rev. Josiah Henson," Kent Historical Society, *Papers & Records*, VII (1951), 43-52, uncritically accept all that Henson wrote. Herbert Hill, in "Uncle Tom: An Enduring American Myth," *The Crisis*, LXXII (May, 1965), 289-95, 325, also accepts Henson's own word but defends him as a black folk hero. *The American Bookseller*, X (October, 1880), 257, unqualifiedly identified Henson with Mrs. Stowe's Tom, as recent books continue to do. See, for example, Milton Meltzer, ed., *In Their Own Words: A History of the American Negro* (New York, 1964), p. 84, and William Chapple, *The Story of Uncle Tom* (Dresden, n.d.), which draws heavily upon Henson's 1858 edition. A bit more guardedly, *The Encyclopedia Americana* (New York, 1963), XIV, p. 109, concludes that Henson was "the basis for the character" of Tom. Richard Bardolph, *The Negro Vanguard* (Vintage ed., New York, 1961) accepts Henson's "chance meeting" with Mrs. Stowe but rightly concludes that "his peculiar place in history rests on the success with which he exploited his identification with Mrs. Stowe's hero" (p. 59). A brief, circumspect, summary of Henson's contributions appears in William Breyfogle, *Make Free: The Story of the Underground Railroad* (Philadelphia, 1958), pp. 184-89.

Notes

1. See Roy Pascal, *Design and Truth in Autobiography* (Cambridge, Mass., 1960).

2. Especially useful inquiries on these points appear as a series of articles in a special issue of *New Literary History: A Journal of Theory and Interpretation,* IX (Autumn, 1977). See also Jeffrey Mehlman, *A Structural Study of Autobiography* (Ithaca, 1974) which, though at times preposterous and restricted to the French, offers numerous fascinating insights.

3. One indication of contemporary influence for Josiah Henson may be taken from the fact that in 1979 no less than five editions of Henson's *Autobiography* (as it was called when first published in 1849) were in print: one of the 1849 version (from Irvington Books, New York), two of the 1858 version (one by Corinth Books, New Haven, Conn., and the other by Metro Books, Arlington Heights, Illinois), one of the 1855 version according to *Books in Print*, though actually also of the 1858 text (Corner House, Williamstown, Mass.), and one of the 1877 version (London: Frank Cass).

4. Toronto *Globe*, July 5, 1930, April 28, 1946; London, Ont. *Free Press*, Jan. 15, 1947; Huron *Church News*, Oct., 1959, 8-9; *Museum Directory of the United States and Canada*, 2nd ed. (Washington, 1965), p. 658. Efforts failed to interest the National Urban League of the United States, or the Association for the Study of Negro Life and History, in restoring the cemetery. See "Letters about 'Uncle Tom'," *The Negro History Bulletin*, 24 (Dec., 1960), 64-65. On Henson's Masonic connections, see Professor Fred Landon's private collection of letters, manuscripts, and clippings, at the University of Western Ontario in London, Ontario: Alvin McCurdy to Landon, Feb. 26, 1960, and exchanges of letters between Landon and Charles Foy.

5. The present essay, though substantially revised for publication here, first appeared in substance as an introduction to the 1969 reprint edition of the 1881 version of Henson's *Autobiography*, a title the narrative resumed after being called *Truth Stranger than Fiction*. The 1969 reprint was published by Addison-Wesley, of Reading, Massachusetts, and I wish to thank that company for permission to use my original essay as the basis for the present analysis.

6. Our concern here is with Henson's narrative, not with his biography as such. For a fuller account of Henson's work at Dawn, and on behalf of fugitive slaves (and himself) in Canada, see the present writer's book, *The Blacks in Canada: A History* (New Haven, 1971), and William H. and Jane H. Pease, *Black Utopia: Negro Communal Experiments in America* (Madison, 1963). K. Gordon MacLachlan, *A History of Dawn Township and Its Origin* (Oil Springs, Ont., 1971) contains only two paragraphs about the black community (p. 16).

7. For a recent inquiry on Wilson see Jane H. and William H. Pease, "The Clerical Do-Gooder: Hiram Wilson," in their *Bound with Them in Chains: A*

Biographical History of the Antislavery Movement (Westport, Conn., 1972), pp. 115-39.

8. *The Emancipator*, Dec. 22, 1836; *The Anti-Slavery Standard*, July 8, 1841; Toronto *Constitution*, Nov. 16, 1837; American Anti-Slavery Society, *Fourth Annual Report* (New York, 1837), p. 19; Boston Public Library, Weston Papers, 12: Maria F. Rice to Mrs. Maria W. Chapman, Oct. 23, 1839; Historical Records Survey, *Calendar of the Gerrit Smith Papers in the Syracuse University Library: General Correspondence*, Albany, 1941, 2, pp. 129, 255; Wilson to Smith, Dec. 18, 1839, Ray Potter to Smith, Jan. 25, 1846; Public Archives of Canada, Ottawa [hereafter, PAC], C series, 1, 803: Wilson to Governor General Lord Sydenham, June 18, 25, 1841; PAC, G 20, 310: Rice to Metcalfe, July 3, 24, 1844; Fred Landon, "The Canadian Anti-Slavery Group," *The University Magazine*, XXII (Dec., 1917), 542; Clayton S. Ellsworth, "Oberlin and the Anti-Slavery Movement Up to the Civil War," unpublished Ph.D. dissertation, Cornell University, 1930, pp. 47-48, 168; Marilyn Baily, "From Cincinnati, Ohio to Wilberforce, Canada: A Note on Antebellum Colonization," *Journal of Negro History*, LVIII (Oct., 1973), 427-40.

9. Quoted in Pease and Pease, *Black Utopia*, p. 64, from the Kent County Registry Office, Chatham, Ontario. Also valuable is Alexander L. Murray, "Canada and the Anglo-American Anti-Slavery Movement: A Study in International Philanthropy," unpublished Ph.D. dissertation, University of Pennsylvania, 1960, especially pp. 59-63. For Fuller's attitude on non-interference, see Historical Society of Pennsylvania, Philadelphia, Simon Gratz Autograph Collection: Fuller to William H. Seward, Dec. 31, 1837, Feb. 29, 1840; and *Calendar of the Gerrit Smith Papers*, p. 131; Fuller to Smith, Oct. 15, 1841. A recent study of value is Peter Carlesimo, "The Refugee Home Society: Its Origin, Operation and Results, 1851-1876," unpubl. M.A. thesis, University of Windsor, 1973. Carlesimo believes that the Society borrowed its ideas from Henson (p. 16).

10. On anti-slavery activity in Canada at this time, see Robin W. Winks, " 'A Sacred Animosity': Abolitionism in Canada," in Martin B. Duberman, ed., *The Antislavery Vanguard: New Essays on the Abolitionists* (Princeton, 1965), pp. 301-42.

11. *The Life of Josiah Henson, formerly a Slave, Now an Inhabitant of Canada. Narrated by Himself* (Boston, 1849), p. 8. This first edition is scarce: known copies are in the British Museum, the Yale University Library, the Boston Public Library, the Schomburg Collection of the New York Public Library, and Uncle Tom's Cabin and Museum, Dresden, Ontario. No doubt there are others, but since a reprint edition, issued by the Museum in 1965, is more readily available, page references to the edition of 1849 refer to the reprint. I cite the 1849 edition in preference to others for the pre-Canadian years since it has been embroidered less.

12. *Ibid.*, pp. 44-45.

13. *Ibid.*, p. 55.

14. *Ibid.*, pp. 59-61.

15. *Ibid.*, p. 63.

16. *Ibid.*, pp. 65-66; Boston *Recorder*, Jan. 7, 1848.

17. *Life of Josiah Henson*, p. 70; Lawson Memorial Library, University of Western Ontario, London: Henson's deed of property.

18. Massachusetts Historical Society, Amos A. Lawrence Papers: Lawrence

to Nathan Hale, Nov. 9, 1850, and to Samuel Morley, Nov. 30, 1852. On Eliot, see C[laude] M. F[uess], "Samuel Atkins Eliot," *Dictionary of American Biography* [hereafter, *D.A.B.*], VI (1931), pp. 81-82, which incorrectly dates Henson's book as 1842, and also Pease and Pease, *Black Utopia*, p. 75. Phelps was a printing agent with offices adjacent to the Boston Circulating Library. See *The Boston Directory: Containing the City Record, a General Directory of the Citizens . . . from July, 1849, to July, 1850* . . . (Boston, 1849), pp. 230, 336. In a life of Henson written for children, Frances Cavanah says that Eliot proposed the project to Henson after hearing him lecture, and that Henson dictated the autobiography (Cavanah, *The Truth about the Man Behind the Book that Sparked the War between the States* [Philadelphia, 1975], pp. 109-10). Others refer to the 1849 autobiography as having been "dictated" but there is no evidence to support the suggestion, if it is meant literally. More nearly correct, one suspects, is Ephraim Peabody's statement, in 1849, that the book was "written to [Henson's] dictation," which changes the nature of the collaboration subtly but importantly. See E.P., "Narratives of Fugitive Slaves," *The Christian Examiner and Religious Miscellany*, XLVII (July, 1849), 78.

19. Kenneth S. Lynn, ed., *Uncle Tom's Cabin: or, Life Among the Lowly*, (Cambridge, Mass.), 1962, p. xxviii. The best examination of the impact of *Uncle Tom's Cabin* on England is Frank J. Klingberg, "Harriet Beecher Stowe and Social Reform in England," *American Historical Review*, XLIII (April, 1938), 542-52, while Edith E. Lucas, *La littérature anti-esclavagiste au dix-neuvième siècle: étude sur Madame Beecher Stowe et son influence en France* (Paris 1930), and Grace Edith MacLean, " 'Uncle Tom's Cabin' in Germany," *Americana Germanica*, n.s., 10 (1910), whole no. (New York), are adequate. The Montreal edition was taken from the first Paris printing of *La Case de l'Oncle Tom*. The sequence of publishing in England, from which the Canadian sequence may be deduced, is described in William Talbot, "Uncle Tom's Cabin: First English Editions," *The American Book Collector*, III (June, 1933), 292.

20. See Fred Landon, "When *Uncle Tom's Cabin* Came to Canada," *Ontario History*, XLIV (Jan., 1952), 1-5.

21. *The Maple Leaf*, 1, July to Dec. 1852, 3-13, and variously, through 177-184, and 2, Jan.-June 1853; *Globe*, April 24, 27, 1852; *Gazette*, April 3, 17, 1852. Landon, "When *Uncle Tom's Cabin* Came to Canada," and other authors refer to a Halifax edition in the same year. I have examined a mint copy of this edition, held by the Yale University Library, and while the title page lists Halifax as the place of publication, I believe that Halifax, England, rather than Nova Scotia, is meant. The price is given as one shilling, but from 1858 the decimal system was used in Canada, and the Halifax merchants long before had taken up dollars and cents. The publishers, Milner and Sowerby, are unknown to the Public Archives of Nova Scotia (Miss Phyllis Blakeley to author, Oct. 7, 1966). The Yale copy is inscribed as a gift to Elizabeth Ann Langridge, and no such family name occurs in any Nova Scotian genealogies.

22. London Public Library, London, Ont., Minute Book, London Mechanics' Institute, 1851: entry for Aug. 9, 1852; Eleanor Shaw, "A History of the London Public Library," typescript, London Public Library, 1941, p. 15; Toronto *Weekly North American*, Feb. 2, 1852; St. Thomas *Weekly Dispatch*, June 21, 1853; New Glasgow, N.S., *Eastern Chronicle*, June 10, 1868; London, Ont., *Free Press*, Sept. 17, 1951; Toronto *Globe and Mail*, Dec. 2, 1952; Benjamin Sulte, "L'esclavage en Canada," *La revue Canadienne*, N.S., VIII (Oct.,

1911), 334; John I. Cooper, *Montreal, the Story of Three Hundred Years* (Montreal, 1942), p. 80.

23. "Literature of Slavery," *The Provincial*, 2, Jan., 1853, pp. 3-8; *Islander*, Nov. 28, 1856.

24. Arthur A. Hauck, *Some Educational Factors affecting the Relations between Canada and the United States* (Easton, Pa., 1932), p. 22; Albert R. Hassard, " 'Uncle Tom's Cabin' Recalled," *Onward*, XLI (July 18, 1931), 2; Toronto *Globe and Mail*, Dec. 2, 1952.

25. The first dramatization of *Uncle Tom's Cabin*, written by George L. Aiken and presented by Halifax-born George Howard in Troy, New York, in September 1852, includes a scene in which Eliza crossed the ice, but did not mention Canada (*French's Standard Drama: Uncle Tom's Cabin; or, Life Among the Lowly* [New York, 1858?]). Canada soon was moved to the nearside of the Ohio by Thomas Hailes Lacy in a version first performed at the Theatre Royal in Manchester, England, in February 1853 (*Lacy's Acting Edition of Plays . . .*, London, n.d., 12, entire), so that Eliza's "whirrleaps toward an outmost brightness" (in the words of E.E. Cummings, *Tom* [Santa Fe, 1935], p. 17) popularly reinforced the Underground Railroad myth by identifying Canada as that land of brightness. The continental French, in particular, seem to have believed that Canada was just across the Ohio from Kentucky: see J.C. Furnas, *Goodbye to Uncle Tom* (New York, 1956), p. 272.

26. See Carl Wittke, *Tambo and Bones: A History of the American Minstrel Stage* (Durham, N.C., 1930), pp. 98-103, 110, 222; J. Frank Davis, "Tom Shows," *Scribner's Magazine*, LXXVII (April, 1925), 350; Donald A. Smith, *At The Forks of the Grand: 20 Historical Essays on Paris, Ontario* (Paris, n.d.), pp. 182-84; Phyllis R. Blakeley, *Glimpses of Halifax, 1867-1900*, Public Archives of Nova Scotia publication, no. 9 (Halifax, 1949), pp. 77-78; F. Lauriston Bullard, "Uncle Tom on the Stage," *Lincoln Herald*, XLVIII (June, 1946), 19; Harry Birdoff, *The World's Greatest Hit: Uncle Tom's Cabin* (New York, 1947), p. 30.

27. W.A. Hewitt, *Down the Stretch: Recollections of a Pioneer Sportsman and Journalist* (Toronto, 1958), p. 114; Toronto Public Library [hereafter, TPL], Thomas H. Scott Collection: "Behind the Footlights," Mss. autobiography, with scrapbook of broadsides and playbills; TPL, Baldwin Room: broadsides, playbills, and clippings relating to the Negro theatre in Canada, New York Library for the Performing Arts, Lincoln Center: Saint John programme, April 29, 30, May 1, 1920; Uncle Tom's Cabin Museum: playbills; Harvard College Library, Theatre Collection: playbills for LaRue's Minstrels, The Harmonears, Halifax, and Sam Sharpley's Minstrels, Quebec; Toronto *Globe*, Oct. 15, 1861; Brantford *Review*, Nov. 4, 1880. The early Tom shows did not assert that Uncle Tom and Josiah Henson were the same person, though by 1878 playbills were explicit on this point. See, for example, the playbill for Booth's Theatre, New York, Feb. 23, 1878, in the Museum of the City of New York.

28. *Times*, Sept. 3, 1852.

29. See Charles Dudley Warner, "The Story of Uncle Tom's Cabin," *The Atlantic Monthly*, LXXVIII (Sept., 1896), 311-21, and reprinted as introduction to 1896 edition (Boston) of the novel, 1, xlii. The question of Mrs. Stowe's need for justification is, of course, a complex one, especially since she ultimately took refuge in the declaration that her book had been written by God. She will, as we shall see, equivocate over whether Henson's book was of central

importance to her, at one point wishing to identify with it for her own authentication, later trying to put distance between her book and her sources as God came to play the larger rôle. Although he mistakenly accepts Henson as "of course" Uncle Tom, the most sophisticated discussion of the psychological need still appears in Charles H. Foster, *The Rungless Ladder: Harriet Beecher Stowe and New England Puritanism* (Durham, N.C., 1954), pp. 18-33.

30. *Key*, pp. 19, 26, 174.

31. K[atherine] A[nthony], "Harriet Elizabeth Beecher Stowe," *D.A.B.*, XVIII (1943), 117. *The Anglo-American Magazine*, III (Aug. 1853), 212-15, published in Toronto, while not liking the *Key*, felt that it provided all necessary proof that the novel was accurate. See Raymond Weaver, introduction to *Limited Editions Club* issue of *Uncle Tom's Cabin* (New York, 1938), pp. vi-viii.

32. Introduction to 1878 edition, as reprinted as *Old South Leaflets*, no. 82 (Boston, n.d.), pp. 1, 5-6; and Florine Thayer McCray, *The Life-Work of the Author of Uncle Tom's Cabin* (New York, 1889), p. 72.

33. Mrs. Stowe became increasingly vague on matters relating to the sequence of composition of her work, and she clearly made herself believe her own myths to the point that she could not reconstruct her own writings. This is shown in a variety of studies. See in particular Barbara Rotundo, "Harriet Beecher Stowe and the Mythmakers," *American Notes & Queries*, XII (May, 1974), 131-33. To varying degrees, most biographies of Mrs. Stowe reflect an awareness of how she embroidered her historical record in order to enhance her novel. Particularly useful are John R. Adams, *Harriet Beecher Stowe* (New Haven, 1963), pp. 56-57, though he accepts Henson's two alleged visits to Mrs. Stowe uncritically; Alice Cooper Crozier, *The Novels of Harriet Beecher Stowe* (New York, 1969), which is strongest on works other than *Uncle Tom's Cabin* and full of good commonsense; and Donald E. Liedel, "The Antislavery Novel, 1836-1861," unpubl. Ph.D. diss., University of Michigan, 1961, which is especially good on the imitators of Uncle Tom.

34. Charles Edward and Lyman Beecher Stowe, *Harriet Beecher Stowe: The Story of Her Life* (Boston) p. 144; or "How Mrs. Stowe Wrote 'Uncle Tom's Cabin'," *McClure's Magazine* XXXVI (April, 1911), 613-14. Forrest Wilson, *Crusader in Crinoline: The Life of Harriet Beecher Stowe* (Philadelphia, 1941), pp. 249-50, and Chester E. Jorgenson, comp., *Uncle Tom's Cabin as Book and Legend* (Detroit, 1952), p. 10, accept the Stowes' statement, as does Edmund Wilson in *Patriotic Gore: Studies in the Literature of the American Civil War* (New York, 1962), pp. 31-32, but Edward Wagenknecht, *Harriet Beecher Stowe: The Known and the Unknown* (New York, 1965), stresses her inconsistency and adds that there have been rival Uncle Toms (p. 157). Lyman Stowe repeated his assertion that a meeting took place in Boston while the Fugitive Slave Law was being debated, in "Uncle Tom's Cabin," *Saturday Review of Literature* (Dec. 12, 1925).

35. On the alleged Andover meeting, see Charles Nichols, "The Origins of Uncle Tom's Cabin," *Phylon* XIX (Fall, 1958), 328-34.

36. Amos Lawrence Papers: Lawrence to Garrison, Feb. 16, 1851, on Henson; and Charles Edward Stowe, *Life of Harriet Beecher Stowe* (Boston, 1890), pp. 130-31.

37. The 1858 edition apparently was re-written by Samuel A. Eliot. The previous year Eliot, who had served in the House of Representatives in 1850-51,

and who refused to become an abolitionist although he continued to oppose slavery, had retired to Cambridge, his investments having gone sour, to live in genteel poverty. Abraham Chapman, in *Steal Away: Stories of the Runaway Slaves* (New York, 1971) p. 81, though apparently aware that earlier editions of Henson's life had been ghost-written, says that Henson actually wrote the 1858 version, but he provides no evidence or argument. John F. Bayliss, in *Black Slave Narratives* (New York, 1970), uses extracts from Henson's work (pp. 73-75, 101-107), and asserts that the *Christian Examiner and Religious Miscellany* for September, 1864, contains a "key document" supporting Henson as Uncle Tom (p. 10). Apparently this is a reference to Peabody's review published, in fact, in 1849 (see note 18, above), which does not relate to Uncle Tom but to the question of the degree of Henson's authorship in conjunction with Eliot.

38. Another possibility, though remote, is that Mrs. Stowe incorporated Henson into her work at some point between June 5, 1851, when the first chapter appeared in the *National Era,* and September 18, when her publisher, John P. Jewett, announced that he would issue the book, or even March 20, 1852, when the first run of the first edition came from the press. That she did revise her story, probably after Jewett agreed to publish it—that is, after September, 1851, and before March, 1852—and that she revised even the novel text during the course of publication, is shown by E. Bruce Kirkham in *The Building of Uncle Tom's Cabin* (Knoxville, 1977). However, only nine leaves from the original manuscript, in holograph or facsimile, are extant, so one can make only modest judgments on the matter. To the extent that one can judge, the revisions were entirely stylistic and did not touch upon Henson in any way. See Kirkham, "The First Editions of *Uncle Tom's Cabin:* A Bibliographical Study," *Papers of the Bibliographical Society of America,* LXV (iv/1971), 365-82.

39. On the various later editions, see the note following this essay.

40. His manumission papers, which he ultimately regained, refer only to his having stiff arms from an injury to the elbows. See Alvin McCurdy Collection, Amherstburg, Ontario: Brice Selby, March 9, 1829, copy.

41. See, from the 1849 (reprint) edition, pp. 8, 67 for suppressed sentences, and the 1858 edition, pp. 150-64, for an added chapter in which Henson says that he delivered one hundred and eighteen slaves to freedom.

42. On Henson's literacy, see Lawrence Papers: Lawrence to Hale, Nov. 7, 1850, in which Lawrence notes that Henson could "barely write and cannot read," and on Nat Turner see Jessie L. Beattie, *Black Moses, The Real Uncle Tom* (Toronto, 1957), p. 85. This unfortunate biography confuses more than it helps, for it mixes the several editions of Henson's narrative indiscriminately, accepts all that he says at face value, assumes that the 1849 account was not edited (p. ix) but later wrongly names an editor (p. 172), and at several points—notably pp. 1, 23, 36, 86, 90, 93, 107, and 110—misreads or manufactures evidence and conversation.

43. *Don Juan,* Canto XIV, stanza 101. She had published her accusation about Byron's incestuous relationship with his sister in 1869.

44. A good example of Henson's ability to enlarge his role in events is his description of his visit with President Hayes in 1878, in which he implies that

Hayes wished to see so famous a black as he. In fact, Frederick Douglass, the Washington-based black leader, gained Henson an audience by writing to the President's private secretary that the "aged preacher is anxious to see the face of President Hayes if but for a minute" (Rutherford B. Hayes Library, Fremont, Ohio, Hayes Papers: Douglass to William King Rogers, Feb. 26, 1878), and Hayes did not think the meeting significant enough to record in his diary (see T. Harry Williams, ed., *Hayes: The Diary of a President, 1875-1881* [New York, 1964], pp. 121-23). Other enlargements and inconsistencies appear in the various versions of Henson's ghosted works. For the 1878 edition he recalled "His Praying Mother" in a chapter not thought of before, and while in 1868 he mentioned John Scoble (misspelled Scobell) by name, a quarrel led to the English abolitionist's absence by the 1878 edition. The wording of a sign Henson placed on produce he exhibited at the London World's Fair changed slightly between the two editions, and in the latter he said he had corresponded with Lieutenant-Governor John Cockburn (meaning Colborne, further evidence that Henson spoke his account to someone else, since the two names are pronounced in approximately the same way). In 1849 he slipped his son away from his master without comment, but by 1858 he "could not refrain from an inward chuckle at the thought—how long a good night that will be!," thus giving Brian Gysin a title for his odd biography (see the end of this essay). Between 1849 and 1858 Henson quite forgot whether it was a man or woman who befriended him near Cincinnati (compare p. 48 of the former with p. 111 of the later edition). In 1849 he said there were twenty thousand Negroes in Canada, and he gave the same figure in 1858 although elsewhere he remarked upon how many had arrived in the interim. No one of these changes, errors, or contradictions is important, and some—such as removing his master's curse, "you black son of a bitch!," and his repetitive "damned nigger," from the later editions published by the editor of the *Christian Age*—are explicable enough, but collectively they are extremely damaging.

45. Mary Ann Shadd, editor of the best of the black Canadian fugitive newspapers, the *Provincial Freeman,* was convinced that Henson was a deliberate fraud and a charlatan, and she produced damaging evidence that he was collecting money in the United States without authorization and, she thought, for his personal gain. A close reading of the evidence may lead one to a more charitable conclusion on the second part of the charge. On this, and related, controversies concerning Henson's honesty within the black community, see Winks, *Blacks in Canada;* Jim Bearden and Linda Jean Butler, *Shadd: The Life and Times of Mary Shadd Cary* (Toronto, 1977); and more briefly, Marion Wilson Starling, "The Slave Narrative: Its Place in American Literary History," unpubl. Ph.D. diss., New York University, 1946, pp. 222, 339-40. Henson's feud with Scoble is taken up briefly in Howard Temperley, *British Antislavery, 1833-1870* (Columbia, S.C., 1972). Of course, Henson did not avoid being caught up in the struggle between contending anti-slavery groups. See the above works, and Benjamin Quarles, *Black Abolitionists* (New York, 1969); Betty Fladeland, *Men and Brothers: Anglo-American Antislavery Cooperation* (Urbana, 1972); and Jane H. and William H. Pease, *They Who Would be Free: Blacks' Search for Freedom, 1830-1861* (New York, 1974). Victor Ullman, *Martin R. Delany: The Beginnings of Black Nationalism* (Bos-

ton, 1971), also sheds light on Shadd's rôle in the dispute, as does Ian C. Pemberton, "The Anti-Slavery Society of Canada," unpubl. M.A. thesis, University of Toronto, 1967.

46. *Dumfries and Galloway Standard,* April 25, 1877, and first misprinted in Lobb, ed., 1878 edition, pp. 223-24. I should like to thank the Ewart Public Library in Dumfries, Scotland, for supplying a photostat of the original report. See also D. D. Buck, *The Progression of the Race in the United States and Canada, Treating of the Great Advancement of the Colored Race* (Chicago, 1907), pp. 136, 142-49, 159, 164, 171.

47. The 1858 edition was published by Mrs. Stowe's own publisher, John P. Jewett. Later, when queried on the relationship between the two books, Jewett appeared to be unaware that there had been an earlier edition than 1852, and he asserted that Mrs. Stowe could not have made use of Henson's work since it did not appear until 1858. Jewett apparently had his own reasons for confusing the earlier editions, though the central point he wished to make was correct enough. In c. 1882 he asserted that he had personally written about a quarter of the 1858 Henson book and that Gilbert Haven had written another quarter of it. Half of it was written by "a Unitarian clergyman of Springfield, Mass." Certainly the 1858 edition had been most substantially altered from the 1849 edition, and it is possible that Eliot was not involved in that his text was discarded, but this question of sequence and of authorship does not speak to the central point of whether Henson's first work directly influenced Mrs. Stowe's novel. It does, however, give further evidence of the extent to which anti-slavery writers manipulated texts.

48. On Lobb, see his (as editor) *Talks with the Dead: Illustrated with Spirit Photographs* (London, 1906), pp. xv-xx; Register of the Royal Geographical Society, London: certificate of Election as a Fellow; and appendices to the 1877, 1878, and young people's editions of Henson's autobiography. In 1972 Lobb's daughter gave her father's collection to The American Museum in Bath, England. Unhappily, the collection proves not to contain any additional information of substance, though it includes a gouache of the meeting at Windsor Castle and a bust of Henson, as well as an oil painting of Henson with Lobb, thus adding to our store of likenesses of Henson, which had been limited to a photograph in the hands of the Detroit Public Library and the various sketches used in the Henson edition. See Eileen Gonin, " 'Uncle Tom' in Fact and Fiction," *America in Britain,* XI (i/1973), 8-12. The Journal of Queen Victoria, in the Royal Archives, Round Tower, Windsor Castle, confirms that she received Henson, his second wife, and Lobb, on March 5, 1877, and in her entry of March 4 she refers to reading the book. Henson claimed to have dined with Lord John Russell, and with the Archbishop of Canterbury, with whom he had the following unlikely conversation: " 'At what university, Sir, did thee graduate?' 'I graduated, your grace,' said I in reply, 'at the university of adversity.' 'The university of adversity,' said he, looking up with astonishment; "where is that?' I saw his surprise, and explained. . . . 'But is it possible that you are not a scholar?' 'I am not,' said I. 'But I should never have suspected that you were not a liberally educated man. . . .' " (1858 ed., pp. 196-97). Archbishop Charles Sumner was not known as a wit, but he scarcely needed to have "adversity" explained to him. In any case, the official register, in Lambeth Palace Library, London, does not include Henson's name—although this is not conclusive evidence that the visit did not take place, of course.

49. Lobb, ed., 1878 edition, p. 176.

50. Henson left virtually nothing to his family, and his son Peter apparently sold the little landed property that he possessed. Two aged daughters who moved to Flint, Michigan, and a grandson, Beecher Stowe Henson, later said that nothing remained save his papers, which disappeared, and a few relics, which went to a friend in Ridgetown, Ontario. See Toronto *Star*, June 28, 1930; *The Crisis*, VI (June, 1913), 65; Fred Landon Correspondences: Jean Tallach and Landon exchange, July 7, 9, 15, 1935; and Library of Congress, Carter G. Woodson Collection of Negro Papers, V; sketch of Henson by Julia [*sic*] Tallach McKinley.

51. Lobb, ed., *Talks with the Dead*, p. 118, advertisement (which was dropped from the 1907 edition of this book). Copies in the British Museum.

52. Of the alleged twelve editions in translation, I have found but four, two in Swedish, and one in Dutch (all 1877). Lobb claimed there was a Welsh edition, for example, but a search by Mr. Meiner McDonald, Assistant Keeper of the Department of Printed Books, National Library of Wales, Aberystwyth, in August 1966, failed to produce one. (Possibly the Welsh translation was published in the United States, for in 1854 a publisher in Remsen, New York, published *Uncle Tom's Cabin* in a special Welsh edition for immigrants, and at least one each of the Swedish and German translations of *Uncle Tom* listed in bibliographies or referred to in introductory essays to reprint editions of Mrs. Stowe's work, turn out upon examination to have been published in the United States rather than abroad.) The Bowdoin College Library does hold a copy of the rare Bergen edition of 1877, translated into Norwegian by H. C. Knutfen.

53. Lobb, ed., *Talks with the Dead*, p. 32.

54. See London, Ont., *Free Press*, Aug. 20, 1932, and Windsor *Daily Record*, June 18, 1877, on the Stowe-Tilley exchange. Kirkham, *Building*, pp. 94-95, takes up the Tilley letter and notes that he surveyed Canadian libraries to find it. He is especially good on Brion Gysin's careless errors.

55. Lobb, ed., 1881 edition (1969 reprint), pp. 10-11.

56. *News*, July 27, 1882.

57. *Sun*, Aug. 7, 1882.

58. Quoted in Kenneth Allsop's essay, "Analyse de l'oeuvre," with photograph of letter, in Cercle du Bibliophile edition of *La Case de l'oncle Tom* (Geneva, 1970), p. 592. Philip van Doren Stern, on the other hand, asserted that Henson was "the main source" for Uncle Tom when he prepared *The Annotated Uncle Tom's Cabin* (New York, 1964), p. 567. Obviously we will never be quit of this story: even a legal scholar, John Anthony Scott, accepts the notion that Stowe and Henson met in Boston in 1850. See his *Woman Against Slavery: The Story of Harriet Beecher Stowe* (New York, 1978), p. 107.

59. Beattie, *Black Moses*, p. 206, says that Mrs. Stowe visited Henson at Dawn, while David P. Botsford, in *Amherstburg's Place in American History* (Amherstburg, 1959), pp. 14-15, asserts that she came to Amherstburg to gather information before she wrote of Uncle Tom. Both statements are nonsense, although she did visit Canada years later, in 1869, without touching upon western Ontario (Houghton Library, Harvard University, Stowe Papers: Rev. Edward Wood to Mrs. Stowe, Sept. 16, 1869). Walter Fisher, in his introduction to the 1962 reprint edition of Henson's narrative, p. v, says that Mrs. Stowe based her book "upon a fragment" of *Truth Stranger than Fiction: Father Henson's Story of His Own Life*, but this is impossible, for the edition

of this title appeared in 1858, six years after *Uncle Tom's Cabin.* Ironically, the Windsor *Daily Star* (Jan. 15, 1938, July 30, 1948) insisted that the real Eliza had lived in the old Matthew Elliott home, which had been owned by Upper Canada's largest slaver in the eighteenth century. See also R.C. Smedley, *History of the Underground Railroad in Chester and the Neighboring Counties of Pennsylvania* (Lancaster, Pa., 1883), p. 32, and Clare Taylor, "Notes on American Negro Reformers in Victorian Britain," British Association for American Studies *Bulletin*, N.S., no. 2, March 1961, 40-51.

60. For examples of the various forms the annual eulogies take, see the following, representative of dozens more: Montreal *Family Herald and Weekly Star,* Sept. 19, 1928; Toronto *Globe,* Jan. 19, 1935; Montreal *Star,* June 9, 1937; Detroit *Times,* May 1, 1938; Tannis Lee, "Uncle Tom's Cabin," *Imperial Oil Company Review,* XIII (April, 1952), 4-6; Hamilton *Review,* July 18, 1952; *The Canadian Woodman* (Oct., 1952), 2; *The Sentinel* (Dec., 1957), 6-7; Winifred Kincade, *The Torch: Ontario Monuments to Great Names* (Regina, 1962), 153-57.

61. *Frederick Douglass' Paper,* April 1, 1853, quoted in Howard H. Bell, "Negro Nationalism in the 1850s," *Journal of Negro Education,* XXXV (Winter, 1966), 101.

62. Lobb, *Young People's Illustrated Edition,* pp. 12-16.

63. Some of Henson's contemporaries doubted that he was Mrs. Stowe's Uncle Tom, although none appears to have been heard. Most scholarly works on black history, local histories of Ontario, and general accounts of abolitionism still accept the identification, but four scholars have questioned the association: In 1946 J. Winton Coleman, Jr., in "Mrs. Stowe, Kentucky, and Uncle Tom's Cabin," *Lincoln Herald,* XLVIII (June), 6, presented a better case for Lewis Clarke, who escaped in 1841 and who did talk with Mrs. Stowe; in 1937 Fred Landon challenged the association, Montreal *Star,* June 22, and in 1947 he somewhat harshly noted that Henson "made little practical contribution to the welfare of his people," *Canadian Historical Review,* XXVIII (Dec.), 440. In 1958 William H. and Jane H. Pease, in "Uncle Tom and Clayton: Fact, Fiction, and Mystery," *Ontario History,* L (Spring), 62, 68 found Henson "shrewdly devious" and a "Mystery." In 1907 William Harrison, in "Uncle Tom's Prototype," *Canadian Magazine,* XXVIII (April), 530-36, tried to substitute a fictitious Lemuel Page for Henson. But in 1964 Alex Haley still thought Henson to be the "majority candidate" for the role ("In 'Uncle Tom' are Our Guilt and Hope," *The New York Times Magazine,* March 1, 23).

64. Of course, despite ambivalence about "Uncle Tom," many blacks continued to find inspiration in the identification between Henson and Tom, James Baldwin and J.C. Furnas notwithstanding. Peter M. Bergman, *et al., The Chronological History of the Negro in America* (New York, 1969), pp. 67-68; Wade Baskin and Richard N. Runes, eds., *Dictionary of Black Culture* (New York, 1973), p. 210; and Harry A. Ploski and Warren Marr II, eds., *The Negro Almanac: A Reference Work on the Afro-American, 1776 Bicentennial Edition 1976* (New York, 1976), pp. 11, 168, are standard reference works that continue to accept the linkage, the last stating that Henson gave Mrs. Stowe an outline of his book in 1849. In Canada the 1970s brought a number of black histories written by black authors for general use. These books are more sensitive to the present connotations of "Uncle Tom" and deal more effectively

with the question of whether Henson was Mrs. Stowe's original, while finding ways to use Henson to instill a sense of pride in young readers. Two of the best are Headley Tulloch, *Black Canadians: A Long Line of Fighters* (Toronto, 1975), and Leo W. Bertley, *Canada and Its People of African Descent* (Pierrefonds, P.Q., 1977). The conventional treatment appears ironically enough, in the Centennial *Story of Dresden, 1825-1967*, by Alda L. Hyatt (Dresden, 1967), p. 5.

65. On these controversies, the most balanced account is Pease and Pease, *Black Utopia*, pp. 76-83, 176-77.

66. Henson borrowed $2,800 from J. Ingersoll Bowditch, Samuel Eliot, and Amos Lawrence (Rhodes House Library, Oxford University, Anti-Slavery Papers C 19/21: Lawrence to Scoble, March 30, 1851), a sum which Scoble finally liquidated for $1,500 (Lawrence Papers: Lawrence to Roaf, Dec. 22, 1852, June 30, 1853), by which time all three of the creditors had turned against Dawn (*ibid.*, Lawrence to Scoble, May 7, 1853).

67. Truman Nelson, ed., *Documents of Upheaval: Selections from William Lloyd Garrison's* The Liberator, *1831-1865* (New York, 1966), p. 239. Henson also lost the support of Mary Estlin and Maria Weston Chapman, partially because of his controversy with Scoble over the administration of the Dawn School, and partially because in 1851 he solicited funds on the basis of testimonials one of which, at least, was false (Weston Papers: John Bishop Estlin to Miss E. Wigham, May 3, and Fanny N. Tribe to Mary A. Estlin, June 12, 1851, and Mrs. Emma Michell to Maria W. Chapman, Aug. 30, 1852). The Rhodes House Anti-Slavery papers, as well as the Lawrence, Weston, and Samuel Gay Papers—the last at Columbia University—contain many letters about the feud between Henson and Scoble.

68. Hamilton *Times*, Jan. 13, 1882. On Victoria's picture, see the New York Public Library's Schomburg Collection, abolition materials, item 137: Henson Ms. [on visit to England], 1876.

69. See MacLachlan, *Dawn*, p. 16.

70. Herbert Aptheker, ed., *A Documentary History of the Negro People in the United States* (New York, 1951), pp. 406-08, drawing upon *The Liberator* for August 13, 1858.

71. See the use made in John W. Blassingame, *The Slave Community: Plantation Life in the Antebellum South* (New York, 1972), and Blassingame, "Using the Testimony of Ex-Slaves: Approaches and Problems," *Journal of Southern History*, XLI (Nov., 1975), 473-92; the intelligent use of extracts in Thomas L. Webber, *Deep Like the Rivers: Education in the Slave Quarter Community, 1831-1865* (New York, 1978); and the way in which three of the editions are drawn upon in Charles H. Nichols, *Many Thousand Gone: The Ex-Slaves' Account of Their Bondage and Freedom* (Leiden, 1963). See also the introductory essay to the 1971 Frank Cass reprint edition of the 1877 London version of Henson's narrative, written by C. Duncan Rice, which rightly finds *Uncle Tom's Story*, as the edition was called, "a splendid example of its type."

72. I wish to thank Mr. Dalton McBee, of Phillips Academy, Andover, for arranging for me to visit the Stowe house in Andover, and Mrs. Stowe's grave; James Ayres, for helping me during a visit to the American Museum, in Bath,

England; Roger Howell, for making possible a visit to the Stowe house in Brunswick, Maine; and the scholars who gave me the benefit of their criticisms on the original essay, of which this is an expansion: Professor and Mrs. William H. Pease of the University of Maine, Professor Edward Wagenknecht of Boston University; Professor C. Vann Woodward of Yale University; and Mr. Joseph S. Van Why, of the Stowe-Day Foundation in Hartford, Connecticut.

73. For the editions now in print, and not discussed here, see footnote 3.

Moses Roper

Henry Bibb

Archer Alexander

William Craft

Ellen Craft

A Ride for Liberty—The Fugitive Slaves, Eastman Johnson, circa 1862.
The Brooklyn Museum, Gift of Miss Gwendolyn O.L. Conkling.

Solomon Northup

John Anderson

Equiano

Frederick Douglass

Josiah Henson

William Wells Brown

3. The Slave Narratives as Literature

One of the most quickly expanding fields of contemporary literary history is narrative theory. Those principles upon which we define "autobiography" and "fiction," long thought to be self-evident and matters of common sense, have recently been recognized to be problematical. Moreover, the status of the black slave's texts have, only in the past two decades, received as much close analysis and practical criticism as have other sorts of written discourse. It was to collect these recent examples of literary criticism that the editors originally agreed to prepare this collection.

The essays collected here analyze the narratives as literary works. Some explicate the shared tropes and themes of the genre; others discuss their textual inter-relationships as literary history; still others are close readings of discrete texts. Jean Fagan Yellin's essay marshals evidence to prove that the richest female slave narrative, the veracity of which until recently disputed by historians as scrupulous as John Blassingame, is indeed the narrative written by the slave, Harriet Jacobs, "by herself." Charles Nichols compares the structural similarities of the genre to other genres, while Susan Willis's explication of Juan Manzano's little-known narrative of Cuban slavery is one of the first studies of that major text. Critics such as Houston A. Baker, Jr., James Olney, and Robert Burns Stepto read the narratives "against" contemporary narrative theory, while Paul Edwards explains in some detail the relatively-understudied eighteenth-century origins of the narratives. Melvin Dixon discusses the intertextuality of the narratives and recent black fictional forms.

Long after the historical and political issues addressed by the black slave's texts have lost their passion, these texts, the essays collected here argue, shall remain of interest to the students of literature and of criticism, both for what they can teach us of the nature of narrative and for what they reveal about the urge of the human will to transcend the very chaos of experience with imposed literary figures and structures.

"I Was Born":
Slave Narratives, Their Status
as Autobiography and as Literature

JAMES OLNEY

Anyone who sets about reading a single slave narrative, or even two or three slave narratives, might be forgiven the natural assumption that every such narrative will be, or ought to be, a unique production; for— so would go the unconscious argument—are not slave narratives autobiography, and is not every autobiography the unique tale, uniquely told, of a unique life? If such a reader should proceed to take up another half dozen narratives, however (and there is a great lot of them from which to choose the half dozen), a sense not of uniqueness but of overwhelming *sameness* is almost certain to be the result. And if our reader continues through two or three dozen more slave narratives, still having hardly begun to broach the whole body of material (one estimate puts the number of extant narratives at over six thousand), he is sure to come away dazed by the mere repetitiveness of it all: seldom will he discover anything new or different but only, always more and more of the same. This raises a number of difficult questions both for the student of autobiography and the student of Afro-American literature. Why should the narratives be so cumulative and so invariant, so repetitive and so much alike? Are the slave narratives classifiable under some larger grouping (are they history or literature or autobiography or polemical writing? and what relationship do these larger groupings bear to one another?); or do the narratives represent a mutant development really different in kind from any other mode of writing that might initially seem to relate to them as parent, as sibling, as cousin, or as some other formal relation? What narrative mode, what manner of story-telling, do we find in the slave narratives, and what is the place of memory both in this particular variety of narrative and in autobiography more generally? What is the relationship of the slave narratives to later narrative modes and later thematic complexes of Afro-American writing? The questions are multiple and manifold. I propose to come at them and to offer some tentative answers by first making some observations about autobiography and its special nature as a memorial, creative act; then outlining some of the common themes and nearly invariable conventions of slave narratives; and finally attempting to determine the place of the slave narrative 1) in the spectrum of autobiographical writing, 2) in the history of American literature, and 3) in the making of an Afro-American literary tradition.

I have argued elsewhere that there are many different ways that we can legitimately understand the word and the act of autobiography; here, however, I want to restrict myself to a fairly conventional and common-sense understanding of autobiography. I will not attempt to define autobiography but merely to describe a certain kind of autobiographical performance—not the only kind by any means but the one that will allow us to reflect most clearly on what goes on in slave narratives. For present purposes, then, autobiography may be understood as a recollective/narrative act in which the writer, from a certain point in his life—the present—, looks back over the events of that life and recounts them in such a way as to show how that past history has led to this present state of being. Exercising memory, in order that he may recollect and narrate, the autobiographer is not a neutral and passive recorder but rather a creative and active shaper. Recollection, or memory, in this way a most creative faculty, goes backward so that narrative, its twin and counterpart, may go forward: memory and narration move along the same line only in reverse directions. Or as in Heraclitus, the way up and the way down, the way back and the way forward, are one and the same. When I say that memory is immensely creative I do not mean that it creates for itself events that never occurred (of course this can happen too, but that is another matter). What I mean instead is that memory creates the *significance* of events in discovering the pattern into which those events fall. And such a pattern, in the kind of autobiography where memory rules, will be a teleological one bringing us, in and through narration, and as it were by an inevitable process, to the end of all past moments which is the present. It is in the interplay of past and present, of present memory reflecting over past experience on its way to becoming present being, that events are lifted out of time to be re-situated not in mere chronological sequence but in patterned significance.

Paul Ricoeur, in a paper on "Narrative and Hermeneutics," makes the point in a slightly different way but in a way that allows us to sort out the place of time and memory both in autobiography in general and in the Afro-American slave narrative in particular. *"Poiesis,"* according to

Ricoeur's analysis, "both reflects and resolves the paradox of time"; and he continues: "It reflects it to the extent that the act of emplotment combines in various proportions two temporal dimensions, one chronological and the other non-chronological. The first may be called the episodic dimension. It characterizes the story as made out of events. The second is the configurational dimension, thanks to which the plot construes significant wholes out of scattered events."[1] In autobiography it is memory that, in the recollecting and retelling of events, effects "emplotment"; it is memory that, shaping the past according to the configuration of the present, is responsible for "the configurational dimension" that "construes significant wholes out of scattered events." It is for this reason that in a classic of autobiographical literature like Augustine's *Confessions*, for example, memory is not only the mode but becomes the very subject of the writing. I should imagine, however, that any reader of slave narratives is most immediately struck by the almost complete dominance of "the episodic dimension," the nearly total lack of any "configurational dimension," and the virtual absence of any reference to memory or any sense that memory does anything but make the past facts and events of slavery immediately present to the writer and his reader. (Thus one often gets, "I can see even now. . . . I can still hear . . . ," etc.) There is a very good reason for this, but its being a very good reason does not alter the consequence that the slave narrative, with a very few exceptions, tends to exhibit a highly conventional, rigidly fixed form that bears much the same relationship to autobiography in a full sense as painting by numbers bears to painting as a creative act.

I say there is a good reason for this, and there is: The writer of a slave narrative finds himself in an irresolvably tight bind as a result of the very intention and premise of his narrative, which is to give a picture of "slavery *as it is*." Thus it is the writer's claim, it *must* be his claim, that he is not emplotting, he is not fictionalizing, and he is not performing any act of *poiesis* (= shaping, making). To give a true picture of slavery as it really is, he must maintain that he exercises a clear-glass, neutral memory that is neither creative nor faulty—indeed, if it were creative it would be *eo ipso* faulty for "creative" would be understood by skeptical readers as a synonym for "lying." Thus the ex-slave narrator is debarred from use of a memory that would make anything of his narrative beyond or other than the purely, merely episodic, and he is denied access, by the very nature and intent of his venture, to the configurational dimension of narrative.

Of the kind of memory central to the act of autobiography as I described it earlier, Ernst Cassirer has written: "Symbolic memory is the process by which man not only repeats his past experience but also reconstructs this experience. Imagination becomes a necessary element of true recollection." In that word "imagination," however, lies the joker for an ex-slave who would write the narrative of his life in slavery. What we find Augustine doing in Book X of the *Confessions*—offering up a disquisition on memory that makes both memory itself and the narrative that it surrounds fully symbolic—would be inconceivable in a slave narrative. Of course ex-slaves do exercise memory in their narratives, but they never talk about it as Augustine does, as Rousseau does, as Wordsworth does, as Thoreau does, as Henry James does, as a hundred other autobiographers (not to say novelists like Proust) do. Ex-slaves *cannot* talk about it because of the premises according to which they write, one of those premises being that there is nothing doubtful or mysterious about memory: on the contrary, it is assumed to be a clear, unfailing record of events sharp and distinct that need only be transformed into descriptive language to become the sequential narrative of a life in slavery. In the same way, the ex-slave writing his narrative cannot afford to put the present in conjunction with the past (again with very rare but significant exceptions to be mentioned later) for fear that in so doing he will appear, from the present, to be reshaping and so distorting and falsifying the past. As a result, the slave narrative is most often a non-memorial description fitted to a pre-formed mold, a mold with regular depressions here and equally regular prominences there—virtually obligatory figures, scenes, turns of phrase, observances, and authentications—that carry over from narrative to narrative and give to them as a group the species character that we designate by the phrase "slave narrative."

What is this species character by which we may recognize a slave narrative? The most obvious distinguishing mark is that it is an extremely mixed production typically including any or all of the following: an engraved portrait or photograph of the subject of the narrative; authenticating testimonials, prefixed or postfixed; poetic epigraphs, snatches of poetry in the text, poems appended; illustrations before, in the middle of, or after the narrative itself;[2] interruptions of the narrative proper by way of declamatory addresses to the reader and passages that as to style might well come from an adventure story, a romance, or a novel of sentiment; a bewildering variety of documents—letters to and from the narrator, bills of sale, newspaper clippings, notices of slave auctions and of escaped slaves, certificates of marriage, of manumission, of birth and death, wills, extracts from legal codes—that appear before the text, in the text itself, in footnotes, and in appendices; and sermons and anti-slavery speeches and essays tacked on at the end to demonstrate post-narrative activities of the narrator. In pointing out the extremely mixed nature of slave narratives one immediately has to acknowledge how mixed and impure classic autobiographies are or can be. The last three books of Augustine's *Confessions,* for example, are in a different mode from the rest of the volume, and Rousseau's *Confessions,* which begins as a novelistic romance and ends in a paranoid shambles, can hardly be considered modally consistent and all of a piece. Or if mention is made of the letters prefatory and appended to slave narratives, then one thinks quickly of the letters at the divide of Franklin's *Autobiography,* which have much the same extra-textual existence as letters at opposite ends of slave narratives. But all this said, we must recognize that the narrative letters or the appended sermons haven't the same intention as the Franklin letters or Augustine's exegesis of Genesis; and further, more important, all the mixed, heterogeneous, hetero*generic* elements in slave narratives come to be so regular, so constant, so indispensable to the mode that they finally establish a set of conventions—a series of observances that become virtually *de rigueur*—for slave narratives unto themselves.

The conventions for slave narratives were so early and so firmly established that one can imagine a sort of master outline drawn from the great narratives and guiding the lesser ones. Such an outline would look something like this:

A. An engraved portrait, signed by the narrator.

B. A title page that includes the claim, as an integral part of the title, "Written by Himself" (or some close variant: "Written from a statement of Facts Made by Himself"; or "Written by a Friend, as Related to Him by Brother Jones"; etc.).

C. A handful of testimonials and/or one or more prefaces or introductions written either by a white abolitionist friend of the narrator (William Lloyd Garrison, Wendell Phillips) or by a white amanuensis/editor/author actually responsible for the text (John Greenleaf Whittier, David Wilson, Louis Alexis Chamerovzow), in the course of which preface the reader is told that the narrative is a "plain, unvarnished tale" and that naught "has been set down in malice, nothing exaggerated, nothing drawn from the imagination"—indeed, the tale, it is claimed, understates the horrors of slavery.

D. A poetic epigraph, by preference from William Cowper.

E. The actual narrative:

1. a first sentence beginning, "I was born . . . ," then specifying a place but not a date of birth;

2. a sketchy account of parentage, often involving a white father;

3. description of a cruel master, mistress, or overseer, details of first observed whipping and numerous subsequent whippings, with women very frequently the victims;

4. an account of one extraordinarily strong, hardworking slave— often "pure African"—who, because there is no reason for it, refuses to be whipped;

5. record of the barriers raised against slave literacy and the overwhelming difficulties encountered in learning to read and write;

6. description of a "Christian" slaveholder (often of one such dying in terror) and the accompanying claim that "Christian" slave-holders are invariably worse than those professing no religion;

7. description of the amounts and kinds of food and clothing given to slaves, the work required of them, the pattern of a day, a week, a year;

8. account of a slave auction, of families being separated and de-stroyed, of distraught mothers clinging to their children as they are torn from them, of slave coffles being driven South;

9. description of patrols, of failed attempt(s) to escape, of pursuit by men and dogs;

10. description of successful attempt(s) to escape, lying by during the day, travelling by night guided by the North Star, reception in a free state by Quakers who offer a lavish breakfast and much genial thee/thou conversation;

11. taking of a new last name (frequently one suggested by a white abolitionist) to accord with new social identity as a free man, but retention of first name as a mark of continuity of individual identity;

12. reflections on slavery.

F. An appendix or appendices composed of documentary material— bills of sale, details of purchase from slavery, newspaper items—, further reflections on slavery, sermons, anti-slavery speeches, poems, appeals to the reader for funds and moral support in the battle against slavery.

About this "Master Plan for Slave Narratives" (the irony of the phras-ing being neither unintentional nor insignificant) two observations should be made: First, that it not only describes rather loosely a great many lesser narratives but that it also describes quite closely the greatest of them all, *Narrative of the Life of Frederick Douglass, An American Slave, Written by Himself,*[3] which paradoxically transcends the slave

narrative mode while being at the same time its fullest, most exact representative; second, that what is being recounted in the narratives is nearly
always the realities of the institution of slavery, almost never the intellectual, emotional, moral growth of the narrator (here, as often, Douglass
succeeds in being an exception without ceasing to be the best example:
he goes beyond the single intention of describing slavery, but he also
describes it more exactly and more convincingly than anyone else). The
lives in the narratives are never, or almost never, there for themselves and
for their own intrinsic, unique interest but nearly always in their capacity
as illustrations of what slavery is really like. Thus in one sense the narrative lives of the ex-slaves were as much possessed and used by the abolitionists as their actual lives had been by slaveholders. This is why John
Brown's story is titled *Slave Life in Georgia* and only subtitled "A Narrative of the Life, Sufferings, and Escape of John Brown, A Fugitive
Slave," and it is why Charles Ball's story (which reads like historical
fiction based on very extensive research) is called *Slavery in the United
States*, with the somewhat extended subtitle "A Narrative of the Life and
Adventures of Charles Ball, A Black Man, who lived forty years in Maryland, South Carolina and Georgia, as a slave, under various masters, and
was one year in the navy with Commodore Barney, during the late war.
Containing an account of the manners and usages of the planters and
slaveholders of the South—a description of the condition and treatment
of the slaves, with observations upon the state of morals amongst the
cotton planters, and the perils and sufferings of a fugitive slave, who
twice escaped from the cotton country." The central focus of these two,
as of nearly all the narratives, is slavery, an institution and an external
reality, rather than a particular and individual life as it is known inter-
nally and subjectively. This means that unlike autobiography in general
the narratives are all trained on one and the same objective reality, they
have a coherent and defined audience, they have behind them and guiding them an organized group of "sponsors," and they are possessed of
very specific motives, intentions, and uses understood by narrators, sponsors, and audience alike: to reveal the truth of slavery and so to bring
about its abolition. How, then, could the narratives be anything but very
much like one another?

Several of the conventions of slave-narrative writing established by
this triangular relationship of narrator, audience, and sponsors and the
logic that dictates development of those conventions will bear and will
reward closer scrutiny. The conventions I have in mind are both thematic
and formal and they tend to turn up as often in the paraphernalia surrounding the narratives as in the narratives themselves. I have already
remarked on the extra-textual letters so commonly associated with slave

narratives and have suggested that they have a different logic about
them from the logic that allows or impels Franklin to include similarly
alien documents in his autobiography; the same is true of the signed
engraved portraits or photographs so frequently to be found as frontis-
pieces in slave narratives. The portrait and the signature (which one
might well find in other nineteenth-century autobiographical documents
but with different motivation), like the prefatory and appended letters,
the titular tag "Written by Himself," and the standard opening "I was
born," are intended to attest to the real existence of a narrator, the sense
being that the status of the narrative will be continually called into
doubt, and so it cannot even begin, until the narrator's real existence is
firmly established. Of course the argument of the slave narratives is that
the events narrated are factual and truthful and that they all really happened to the narrator, but this is a second-stage argument; prior to the
claim of truthfulness is the simple, existential claim: "I exist." Photographs, portraits, signatures, authenticating letters all make the same
claim: "This man exists." Only then can the narrative begin. And how
do most of them actually begin? They begin with the existential claim
repeated. "I was born" are the first words of Moses Roper's *Narrative,*
and they are likewise the first words of the narratives of Henry Bibb
and Harriet Jacobs, of Henry Box Brown[4] and William Wells Brown, of
Frederick Douglass[5] and John Thompson, of Samuel Ringgold Ward and
James W.C. Pennington, of Austin Steward and James Roberts, of William Green and William Grimes, of Levin Tilmon and Peter Randolph,
of Louis Hughes and Lewis Clarke, of John Andrew Jackson and Thomas
H. Jones, of Lewis Charlton and Noah Davis, of James Williams and
William Parker and William and Ellen Craft (where the opening assertion is varied only to the extent of saying, "My wife and myself were
born").[6]

We can see the necessity for this first and most basic assertion on the
part of the ex-slave in the contrary situation of an autobiographer like
Benjamin Franklin. While any reader was free to doubt the motives of
Franklin's memoir, no one could doubt his existence, and so Franklin
begins not with any claims or proofs that he was born and now really
exists but with an explanation of why he has chosen to write such a
document as the one in hand. With the ex-slave, however, it was his
existence and his identity, not his reasons for writing, that were called
into question: if the former could be established the latter would be
obvious and the same from one narrative to another. Franklin cites four
motives for writing his book (to satisfy descendants' curiosity; to offer
an example to others; to provide himself the pleasure of reliving events
in the telling; to satisfy his own vanity), and while one can find narra-

tives by ex-slaves that might have in them something of each of these motives—James Mars, for example, displays in part the first of the motives, Douglass in part the second, Josiah Henson in part the third, and Samuel Ringgold Ward in part the fourth—the truth is that behind every slave narrative that is in any way characteristic or representative there is the one same persistent and dominant motivation, which is determined by the interplay of narrator, sponsors, and audience and which itself determines the narrative in theme, content, and form. The theme is the reality of slavery and the necessity of abolishing it; the content is a series of events and descriptions that will make the reader see and feel the realities of slavery; and the form is a chronological, episodic narrative beginning with an assertion of existence and surrounded by various testimonial evidences for that assertion.

In the title and subtitle of John Brown's narrative cited earlier—*Slave Life in Georgia: A Narrative of the Life, Sufferings, and Escape of John Brown, A Fugitive Slave*—we see that the theme promises to be treated on two levels, as it were titular and subtitular: the social or institutional and the personal or individual. What typically happens in the actual narratives, especially the best known and most reliable of them, is that the social theme, the reality of slavery and the necessity of abolishing it, trifurcates on the personal level to become subthemes of literacy, identity, and freedom which, though not obviously and at first sight closely related matters, nevertheless lead into one another in such a way that they end up being altogether interdependent and virtually indistinguishable as thematic strands. Here, as so often, Douglass' *Narrative* is at once the best example, the exceptional case, and the supreme achievement. The full title of Douglass' book is itself classic: *Narrative of the Life of Frederick Douglass, An American Slave, Written by Himself.*[7] There is much more to the phrase "written by himself," of course, than the mere laconic statement of a fact: it is literally a part of the narrative, becoming an important thematic element in the retelling of the life wherein literacy, identity, and a sense of freedom are all acquired simultaneously and without the first, according to Douglass, the latter two would never have been. The dual fact of literacy and identity ("written" and "himself") reflects back on the terrible irony of the phrase in apposition, "An American Slave": How can both of these—"American" and "Slave"—be true? And this in turn carries us back to the name, "Frederick Douglass," which is written all around the narrative: in the title, on the engraved portrait, and as the last words of the text:

> Sincerely and earnestly hoping that this little book may do something toward throwing light on the American slave system, and hastening the glad day of deliverance to the millions of my brethren in bonds—

faithfully relying upon the power of truth, love, and justice, for success in my humble efforts—and solemnly pledging myself anew to the sacred cause,—I subscribe myself,

Frederick Douglass

"I subscribe myself"— I write my self down in letters, I underwrite my identity and my very being, as indeed I have done in and all through the foregoing narrative that has brought me to this place, this moment, this state of being.

The ability to utter his name, and more significantly to utter it in the mysterious characters on a page where it will continue to sound in silence so long as readers continue to construe the characters, is what Douglass' *Narrative* is about, for in that lettered utterance is assertion of identity and in identity is freedom—freedom from slavery, freedom from ignorance, freedom from non-being, freedom even from time. When Wendell Phillips, in a standard letter prefatory to Douglass' *Narrative,* says that in the past he has always avoided knowing Douglass' "real name and birthplace" because it is "still dangerous, in Massachusetts, for honest men to tell their names," one understands well enough what he means by "your real name" and the danger of telling it—"Nobody knows my name," James Baldwin says. And yet in a very important way Phillips is profoundly wrong, for Douglass had been saying his "real name" ever since escaping from slavery in the way in which he went about creating and asserting his identity as a free man: *Frederick Douglass.* In the *Narrative* he says his real name not when he reveals that he "was born" Frederick Bailey but when he puts his signature below his portrait before the beginning and subscribes himself again after the end of the narrative. Douglass' name-changes and self-naming are highly revealing at each stage in his progress: "Frederick Augustus Washington Bailey," by the name given him by his mother, he was known as "Frederick Bailey" or simply "Fred" while growing up; he escaped from slavery under the name "Stanley," but when he reached New York took the name "Frederick Johnson." (He was married in New York under that name—and gives a copy of the marriage certificate in the text—by the Rev. J.W.C. Pennington who had himself escaped from slavery some ten years before Douglass and who would produce his own narrative some four years after Douglass.) Finally, in New Bedford, he found too many Johnsons and so gave to his black host (one of the too many—Nathan Johnson) the privilege of naming him, "but told him he must not take from me the name of 'Frederick.' I must hold on to that, to preserve a sense of my identity." Thus a new social identity but a continuity of personal identity.

In narrating the events that produced both change and continuity in his life, Douglass regularly reflects back and forth (and here he is very much the exception) from the person written about to the person writing, from a narrative of past events to a present narrator grown out of those events. In one marvellously revealing passage describing the cold he suffered from as a child, Douglass says, "My feet have been so cracked with the frost, that the pen with which I am writing might be laid in the gashes." One might be inclined to forget that it is a vastly different person writing from the person written about, but it is a very significant and immensely effective reminder to refer to the writing instrument as a way of realizing the distance between the literate, articulate writer and the illiterate, inarticulate subject of the writing. Douglass could have said that the cold caused lesions in his feet a quarter of an inch across, but in choosing the writing instrument held at the present moment—"the pen with which I am writing"—by one now known to the world as Frederick Douglass, he dramatizes how far removed he is from the boy once called Fred (and other, worse names, of course) with cracks in his feet and with no more use for a pen than for any of the other signs and appendages of the education that he had been denied and that he would finally acquire only with the greatest difficulty but also with the greatest, most telling success, as we feel in the quality of the narrative now flowing from the literal and symbolic pen he holds in his hand. Here we have literacy, identity, and freedom, the omnipresent thematic trio of the most important slave narratives, all conveyed in a single startling image.[8]

There is, however, only one Frederick Douglass among the ex-slaves who told their stories and the story of slavery in a single narrative, and in even the best known, most highly regarded of the other narratives—those, for example, by William Wells Brown, Charles Ball, Henry Bibb, Josiah Henson, Solomon Northup, J.W.C. Pennington, and Moses Roper[9]—all the conventions are observed—conventions of content, theme, form, and style—but they remain just that: conventions untransformed and unredeemed. The first three of these conventional aspects of the narratives are, as I have already suggested, pretty clearly determined by the relationship between the narrator himself and those I have termed the sponsors (as well as the audience) of the narrative. When the abolitionists invited an ex-slave to tell his story of experience in slavery to an anti-slavery convention, and when they subsequently sponsored the appearance of that story in print,[10] they had certain clear expectations, well understood by themselves and well understood by the ex-slave too, about the proper content to be observed, the proper theme to be developed, and the proper form to be followed. Moreover, content, theme, and form discovered early on an appropriate style and that appropriate style was also the personal style displayed by the sponsoring abolitionists in the letters and introductions they provided so generously for the narratives. It is not strange, of course, that the style of an introduction and the style of a narrative should be one and the same in those cases where introduction and narrative were written by the same person—Charles Stearns writing introduction and narrative of Box Brown, for example, or David Wilson writing preface and narrative of Solomon Northup. What is strange, perhaps, and a good deal more interesting, is the instance in which the style of the abolitionist introducer carries over into a narrative that is certified as "Written by Himself," and this latter instance is not nearly so isolated as one might initially suppose. I want to look somewhat closely at three variations on stylistic interchange that I take to represent more or less adequately the spectrum of possible relationships between prefatory style and narrative style, or more generally between sponsor and narrator: Henry Box Brown, where the preface and narrative are both clearly in the manner of Charles Stearns; Solomon Northup, where the enigmatical preface and narrative, although not so clearly as in the case of Box Brown, are nevertheless both in the manner of David Wilson; and Henry Bibb, where the introduction is signed by Lucius C. Matlack and the author's preface by Henry Bibb, and where the narrative is "Written by Himself"—but where also a single style is in control of introduction, author's preface, and narrative alike.

Henry Box Brown's *Narrative*, we are told on the title-page, was

WRITTEN FROM A
STATEMENT OF FACTS MADE BY HIMSELF.
WITH REMARKS UPON THE REMEDY FOR SLAVERY.

BY CHARLES STEARNS.

Whether it is intentional or not, the order of the elements and the punctuation of this subtitle (with full stops after lines two and three) make it very unclear just what is being claimed about authorship and stylistic responsibility for the narrative. Presumably the "remarks upon the remedy for slavery" are by Charles Stearns (who was also, at 25 Cornhill, Boston, the publisher of the *Narrative*), but this title-page could well leave a reader in doubt about the party responsible for the stylistic manner of the narration. Such doubt will soon be dispelled, however, if the reader proceeds from Charles Stearns' "preface" to Box Brown's "narrative" to Charles Stearns' "remarks upon the remedy for slavery." The preface is a most poetic, most high-flown, most grandiloquent peroration that, once cranked up, carries right over into and through the narrative to issue in the appended remarks which come to an end in a REPRE-SENTATION OF THE BOX in which Box Brown was transported from Richmond to Philadelphia. Thus from the preface: "Not for the purpose of administering to a prurient desire to 'hear and see some new thing,' nor to gratify any inclination on the part of the hero of the following story to be honored by man, is this simple and touching narrative of the perils of a seeker after the 'boon of liberty,' introduced to the public eye . . . ," etc.—the sentence goes on three times longer than this extract, describing as it proceeds "the horrid sufferings of one as, in a *portable prison,* shut out from the light of heaven, and nearly deprived of its balmy air, he pursued his fearful journey. . . ." As is usual in such prefaces, we are addressed directly by the author: "O reader, as you peruse this heart-rending tale, let the tear of sympathy roll freely from your eyes, and let the deep fountains of human feeling, which God has implanted in the breast of every son and daughter of Adam, burst forth from their enclosure, until a stream shall flow therefrom on to the surrounding world, of so invigorating and purifying a nature, as to arouse from the 'death of the sin' of slavery, and cleanse from the pollutions thereof, all with whom you may be connected." We may not be overwhelmed by the sense of this sentence but surely we must be by its rich rhetorical manner.

The narrative itself, which is all first person and "the plain narrative of our friend," as the preface says, begins in this manner:

> I am not about to harrow the feelings of my readers by a terrific representation of the untold horrors of that fearful system of oppression, which for thirty-three long years entwined its snaky folds about my soul, as the serpent of South America coils itself around the form of its unfortunate victim. It is not my purpose to descend deeply into the dark and noisome caverns of the hell of slavery, and drag from their frightful abode those lost spirits who haunt the souls of the poor slaves, daily and nightly with their frightful presence, and with the fearful sound of their terrific instruments of torture; for other pens far abler than mine have effectually performed that portion of the labor of an exposer of the enormities of slavery.

Suffice it to say of this piece of fine writing that the pen—than which there were others far abler—was held not by Box Brown but by Charles Stearns and that it could hardly be further removed than it is from the pen held by Frederick Douglass, that pen that could have been laid in the gashes in his feet made by the cold. At one point in his narrative Box Brown is made to say (after describing how his brother was turned away from a stream with the remark "We do not allow niggers to fish"), "Nothing daunted, however, by this rebuff, my brother went to another place, and was quite successful in his undertaking, obtaining a plentiful supply of the finny tribe."[11] It may be that Box Brown's story was told from "a statement of facts made by himself," but after those facts have been dressed up in the exotic rhetorical garments provided by Charles Stearns there is precious little of Box Brown (other than the representation of the box itself) that remains in the narrative. And indeed for every fact there are pages of self-conscious, self-gratifying, self-congratulatory philosophizing by Charles Stearns, so that if there is any life here at all it is the life of that man expressed in his very own overheated and foolish prose.[12]

David Wilson is a good deal more discreet than Charles Stearns, and the relationship of preface to narrative in *Twelve Years a Slave* is therefore a great deal more questionable, but also more interesting, than in the *Narrative of Henry Box Brown*. Wilson's preface is a page and a half long; Northup's narrative, with a song at the end and three or four appendices, is three hundred thirty pages long. In the preface Wilson says, "Many of the statements contained in the following pages are corroborated by abundant evidence—others rest entirely upon Solomon's assertion. That he has adhered strictly to the truth, the editor, at least, who has had an opportunity of detecting any contradiction or discrepancy in his statements, is well satisfied. He has invariably repeated the same story without deviating in the slightest particular. . . ."[13] Now Northup's narrative is not only a very long one but is filled with a vast amount of circumstantial detail, and hence it strains a reader's credulity somewhat to be told that he "invariably repeated the same story without deviating in the slightest particular." Moreover, since the style of the narrative (as I shall argue in a moment) is demonstrably not Northup's own, we might well suspect a filling in and fleshing out on the part of—perhaps not the "onlie begetter" but at least—the actual author of the narrative. But this is not the most interesting aspect of Wilson's performance in the preface nor the one that will repay closest examination. That comes with the conclusion of the preface which reads as follows:

> It is believed that the following account of his [Northup's] experience on Bayou Bœuf presents a correct picture of Slavery, in all its lights and shadows, as it now exists in that locality. Unbiased, as he conceives, by any prepossessions or prejudices, the only object of the editor has been to give a faithful history of Solomon Northup's life, as he received it from his lips.
> In the accomplishment of that object, he trusts he has succeeded, notwithstanding the numerous faults of style and of expression it may be found to contain.

To sort out, as far as possible, what is being asserted here we would do well to start with the final sentence, which is relatively easy to understand. To acknowledge faults in a publication and to assume responsibility for them is of course a commonplace gesture in prefaces, though why the question of style and expression should be so important in giving "a faithful history" of someone's life "as . . . received . . . from his lips" is not quite clear; presumably the virtues of style and expression are superadded to the faithful history to give it whatever literary merits it may lay claim to, and insofar as these fall short the author feels the need to acknowledge responsibility and apologize. Nevertheless, putting this ambiguity aside, there is no doubt about who is responsible for what in this sentence, which, if I might replace pronouns with names, would read thus: "In the accomplishment of that object, David Wilson trusts that he [David Wilson] has succeeded, notwithstanding the numerous faults of style and of expression [for which David Wilson assumes responsibility] it may be found by the reader to contain." The two preceding sentences, however, are altogether impenetrable both in syntax and in the assertion they are presumably designed to make. Casting the first statement as a passive one ("It is believed . . .") and dangling a participle in the second ("Unbiased . . ."), so that we cannot know in either case to whom the statement should be attached, Wilson succeeds in obscuring entirely the authority being claimed for the narrative.[14] It would take too much space to analyze the syntax, the psychology (one might, however, glance at the familiar use of Northup's given name), and the sense of these affirmations, but I would challenge anyone to diagram the second sentence ("Unbiased . . .") with any assurance at all.

As to the narrative to which these prefatory sentences refer: When we get a sentence like this on describing Northup's going into a swamp— "My midnight intrusion had awakened the feathered tribes [near relatives of the 'finny tribe' of Box Brown/Charles Stearns], which seemed to throng the morass in hundreds of thousands, and their garrulous throats poured forth such multitudinous sounds—there was such a fluttering of wings—such sullen plunges in the water all around me—that I was affrighted and appalled" (p. 141)—when we get such a sentence we may think it pretty fine writing and awfully literary, but the fine writer is clearly David Wilson rather than Solomon Northup. Perhaps a better instance of the white amanuensis/sentimental novelist laying his mannered style over the faithful history as received from Northup's lips is to be found in this description of a Christmas celebration where a huge meal was provided by one slaveholder for slaves from surrounding plantations: "They seat themselves at the rustic table—the males on one side, the females on the other. The two between whom there may have been an exchange of tenderness, invariably manage to sit opposite; for the omnipresent Cupid disdains not to hurl his arrows into the simple hearts of slaves" (p. 215). The entire passage should be consulted to get the full effect of Wilson's stylistic extravagances when he pulls the stops out, but any reader should be forgiven who declines to believe that this last clause, with its reference to "the simple hearts of slaves" and its self-conscious, inverted syntax ("disdains not"), was written by someone who had recently been in slavery for twelve years. "Red," we are told by Wilson's Northup, "is decidedly the favorite color among the enslaved damsels of my acquaintance. If a red ribbon does not encircle the neck, you will be certain to find all the hair of their woolly heads tied up with red strings of one sort or another" (p. 214). In the light of passages like these, David Wilson's apology for "numerous faults of style and of expression" takes on all sorts of interesting new meaning. The rustic table, the omnipresent Cupid, the simple hearts of slaves, and the woolly heads of enslaved damsels, like the finny and feathered tribes, might come from any sentimental novel of the nineteenth century—one, say, by Harriet Beecher Stowe; and so it comes as no great surprise to read on the dedication page the following: "To Harriet Beecher Stowe: Whose Name, Throughout the World, Is Identified with the Great Reform: This Narrative, Affording Another Key to Uncle Tom's Cabin, Is Respectfully Dedicated." While not surprising, given the style of the narrative, this dedication does little to clarify the authority that we are asked to discover in and behind the narrative, and the dedication, like the pervasive style, calls into serious question the status of *Twelve Years a Slave* as autobiography and/or literature.[15]

For Henry Bibb's narrative Lucius C. Matlack supplied an introduction in a mighty poetic vein in which he reflects on the paradox that out of the horrors of slavery have come some beautiful narrative productions. "Gushing fountains of poetic thought, have started from beneath the rod of violence, that will long continue to slake the feverish thirst of humanity outraged, until swelling to a flood it shall rush with wasting violence over the ill-gotten heritage of the oppressor. Startling incidents authenticated, far excelling fiction in their touching pathos, from the pen of self-emancipated slaves, do now exhibit slavery in such revolting aspects, as to secure the execrations of all good men, and become a monument more enduring than marble, in testimony strong as sacred writ against it."[16] The picture Matlack presents of an outraged humanity with a feverish thirst for gushing fountains started up by the rod of violence is a peculiar one and one that seems, psychologically speaking, not very healthy. At any rate, the narrative to which Matlack's observations have immediate reference was, as he says, from the pen of a self-emancipated

slave (self-emancipated several times), and it does indeed contain startling incidents with much touching pathos about them; but the really
curious thing about Bibb's narrative is that it displays much the same
florid, sentimental, declamatory rhetoric as we find in ghostwritten or
as-told-to narratives and also in prefaces such as those by Charles
Stearns, Louis Alexis Chamerovzow, and Lucius Matlack himself. Consider the account Bibb gives of his courtship and marriage. Having determined by a hundred signs that Malinda loved him even as he loved
her—"I could read it by her always giving me the preference of her company; by her pressing invitations to visit even in opposition to her
mother's will. I could read it in the language of her bright and sparkling
eye, penciled by the unchangable finger of nature, that spake but could
not lie" (pp. 34-35)—Bibb decided to speak and so, as he says, "broached
the subject of marriage":

> I said, "I never will give my heart nor hand to any girl in marriage,
> until I first know her sentiments upon the all-important subjects of
> Religion and Liberty. No matter how well I might love her, nor how
> great the sacrifice in carrying out these God-given principles. And I
> here pledge myself from this course never to be shaken while a single
> pulsation of my heart shall continue to throb for Liberty."

And did his "dear girl" flunk the challenge thus proposed by Bibb? Far
from it—if anything she proved more high-minded than Bibb himself.

> With this idea Malinda appeared to be well pleased, and with a smile
> she looked me in the face and said, "I have long entertained the same
> views, and this has been one of the greatest reasons why I have not felt
> inclined to enter the married state while a slave; I have always felt a
> desire to be free; I have long cherished a hope that I should yet be free,
> either by purchase or running away. In regard to the subject of Reli-
> gion, I have always felt that it was a good thing, and something that I
> would seek for at some future period."

It is all to the good, of course, that no one has ever spoken or could
ever speak as Bibb and his beloved are said to have done—no one, that
is, outside a bad, sentimental novel of date c. 1849.[17] Though actually
written by Bibb, the narrative, for style and tone, might as well have
been the product of the pen of Lucius Matlack. But the combination of
the sentimental rhetoric of white fiction and white preface-writing with
a realistic presentation of the facts of slavery, all parading under the
banner of an authentic—and authenticated—personal narrative, produces
something that is neither fish nor fowl. A text like Bibb's is committed
to two conventional forms, the slave narrative and the novel of senti-

ment, and caught by both it is unable to transcend either. Nor is the reason far to seek: the sensibility that produced *Uncle Tom's Cabin* was closely allied to the abolitionist sensibility that sponsored the slave narratives and largely determined the form they should take. The master-slave relationship might go underground or it might be turned inside out but it was not easily done away with.

Consider one small but recurrent and telling detail in the relationship of white sponsor to black narrator. John Brown's narrative, we are told by Louis Alexis Chamerovzow, the "Editor" (actually author) of *Slave Life in Georgia*, is "a plain, unvarnished tale of real Slave-life"; Edwin Scrantom, in his letter "recommendatory," writes to Austin Steward of his *Twenty-Two Years a Slave and Forty Years a Freeman*, "Let its plain, unvarnished tale be sent out, and the story of Slavery and its abominations, again be told by one who has felt in his own person its scorpion lash, and the weight of its grinding heel"; the preface writer ("W.M.S.") for *Experience of a Slave in South Carolina* calls it "the unvarnished, but ower true tale of John Andrew Jackson, the escaped Carolinian slave"; John Greenleaf Whittier, apparently the dupe of his "ex-slave," says of *The Narrative of James Williams*, "The following pages contain the simple and unvarnished story of an AMERICAN SLAVE"; Robert Hurnard tells us that he was determined to receive and transmit Solomon Bayley's *Narrative* "in his own simple, unvarnished style"; and Harriet Tubman too is given the "unvarnished" honorific by Sarah Bradford in her preface to *Scenes in the Life of Harriet Tubman:* "It is proposed in this little book to give a plain and unvarnished account of some scenes and adventures in the life of a woman who, though one of earth's lowly ones, and of dark-hued skin, has shown an amount of heroism in her character rarely possessed by those of any station in life." The fact that the varnish is laid on very thickly indeed in several of these (Brown, Jackson, and Williams, for example) is perhaps interesting, but it is not the essential point, which is to be found in the repeated use of just this word—"unvarnished"—to describe all these tales. The Oxford English Dictionary will tell us (which we should have surmised anyway) that Othello, another figure of "dark-hued skin" but vastly heroic character, first used the word "unvarnished"—"I will a round unvarnish'd tale deliver/ Of my whole course of love"; and that, at least so far as the OED record goes, the word does not turn up again until Burke used it in 1780, some 175 years later ("This is a true, unvarnished, undisguised state of the affair"). I doubt that anyone would imagine that white editors/amanuenses had an obscure passage from Burke in the back of their collective mind—or deep down in that mind—when they repeatedly used this word to characterize the narrative of their ex-slaves. No, it was certainly a Shakespearean hero they were unconsciously evoking, and not just any Shakespearean hero but always Othello, the Noble Moor.

Various narrators of documents "written by himself" apologize for their lack of grace or style or writing ability, and again various narrators say that theirs are simple, factual, realistic presentations; but no ex-slave that I have found who writes his own story calls it an "unvarnished" tale: the phrase is specific to white editors, amanuenses, writers, and authenticators. Moreover, to turn the matter around, when an ex-slave makes an allusion to Shakespeare (which is naturally a very infrequent occurrence) to suggest something about his situation or imply something of his character, the allusion is never to Othello. Frederick Douglass, for example, describing all the imagined horrors that might overtake him and his fellows should they try to escape, writes: "I say, this picture sometimes appalled us, and made us

> 'rather bear those ills we had,
> Than fly to others, that we knew not of.' "

Thus it was in the light of Hamlet's experience and character that Douglass saw his own, not in the light of Othello's experience and character. Not so William Lloyd Garrison, however, who says in the preface to Douglass' *Narrative,* "I am confident that it is essentially true in all its statements; that nothing has been set down in malice, nothing exaggerated, nothing drawn from the imagination. . . ."[18] We can be sure that it is entirely unconscious, this regular allusion to Othello, but it says much about the psychological relationship of white patron to black narrator that the former should invariably see the latter not as Hamlet, not as Lear, not as Antony, or any other Shakespearean hero but always and only as Othello.

> When you shall these unlucky deeds relate,
> Speak of them as they are. Nothing extenuate,
> Nor set down aught in malice. Then must you speak
> Of one that lov'd not wisely but too well;
> Of one not easily jealous, but, being wrought,
> Perplex'd in the extreme. . . .

The Moor, Shakespeare's or Garrison's, was noble, certainly, but he was also a creature of unreliable character and irrational passion—such, at least, seems to have been the logic of the abolitionists' attitude toward their ex-slave speakers and narrators—and it was just as well for the white sponsor to keep him, if possible, on a pretty short leash. Thus it was that the Garrisonians—though not Garrison himself—were opposed to the idea (and let their opposition be known) that Douglass and William Wells Brown should secure themselves against the Fugitive Slave Law by purchasing their freedom from ex-masters; and because it might harm their cause the Garrisonians attempted also to prevent William Wells Brown from dissolving his marriage. The reaction from the Garrisonians and from Garrison himself when Douglass insisted on going his own way anyhow was both excessive and revealing, suggesting that for them the Moor had ceased to be noble while still, unfortunately, remaining a Moor. *My Bondage and My Freedom*, Garrison wrote, "in its second portion, is reeking with the virus of personal malignity towards Wendell Phillips, myself, and the old organizationists generally, and *full of ingratitude and baseness towards as true and disinterested friends as any man ever yet had upon earth.*"[19] That this simply is not true of *My Bondage and My Freedom* is almost of secondary interest to what the words I have italicized reveal of Garrison's attitude toward his ex-slave and the unconscious psychology of betrayed, outraged proprietorship lying behind it. And when Garrison wrote to his wife that Douglass' conduct "has been impulsive, inconsiderate and highly inconsistent" and to Samuel J. May that Douglass himself was "destitute of every principle of honor, ungrateful to the last degree and malevolent in spirit,"[20] the picture is pretty clear: for Garrison, Douglass had become Othello gone wrong, Othello with all his dark-hued skin, his impulsiveness and passion but none of his nobility or heroism.

The relationship of sponsor to narrator did not much affect Douglass' own *Narrative:* he was capable of writing his story without asking the Garrisonians' leave or requiring their guidance. But Douglass was an extraordinary man and an altogether exceptional writer, and other narratives by ex-slaves, even those entirely "Written by Himself," scarcely rise above the level of the preformed, imposed and accepted conventional. Of the narratives that Charles Nichols judges to have been written without the help of an editor—those by "Frederick Douglass, William Wells Brown, James W.C. Pennington, Samuel Ringgold Ward, Austin Steward and perhaps Henry Bibb"[21]—none but Douglass' has any genuine appeal in itself, apart from the testimony it might provide about slavery, or any real claim to literary merit. And when we go beyond this bare handful of narratives to consider those written under immediate abolitionist guidance and control, we find, as we might well expect, even less of individual distinction or distinctiveness as the narrators show themselves more or less content to remain slaves to a prescribed, conventional, and imposed form; or perhaps it would be more precise to say that they were captive to the abolitionist intentions and so the question of their being content or otherwise hardly entered in. Just as the triangular relationship embracing sponsor, audience, and ex-slave made of the latter something other than an entirely free creator in the telling of his life story, so also it made of the narrative produced (always keeping the exceptional case in mind) something other than autobiography in any full sense and something other than literature in any reasonable understanding of that term as an act of creative imagination. An autobiography or a piece of imaginative literature may of course observe certain conventions, but it cannot be only, merely conventional without ceasing to be satisfactory as either autobiography or literature, and that is the case, I should say, with all the slave narratives except the great one by Frederick Douglass.

But here a most interesting paradox arises. While we may say that the slave narratives do not qualify as either autobiography or literature, and while we may argue, against John Bayliss and Gilbert Osofsky and others, and they have no real place in American Literature (just as we might argue, and on the same grounds, against Ellen Moers that *Uncle Tom's Cabin* is *not* a great American novel), yet the undeniable fact is that the Afro-American literary tradition takes its start, in theme certainly but also often in content and form, from the slave narratives. Richard Wright's *Black Boy*, which many readers (myself included) would take to be his supreme achievement as a creative writer, provides the perfect case in point, though a host of others could be adduced that would be nearly as exemplary (Du Bois' various autobiographical works; Johnson's *Autobiography of an Ex-Coloured Man;* Baldwin's autobiographical fiction and essays; Ellison's *Invisible Man;* Gaines' *Autobiography of Miss Jane Pittman;* Maya Angelou's writing; etc.). In effect, Wright looks back to slave narratives at the same time that he projects developments that would occur in Afro-American writing after *Black Boy* (published in 1945). Thematically, *Black Boy* reenacts both the general, objective portrayal of the realities of slavery as an institution (transmuted to what Wright calls "The Ethics of Living Jim Crow" in the little piece that lies behind *Black Boy*) and also the particular, individual complex of literacy-identity-freedom that we find at the thematic center of all of the most important slave narratives. In content and form as well *Black Boy* repeats, *mutatis mutandis,* much of the general plan given earlier in this essay describing the typical slave narrative: Wright, like the ex-slave, after a more or less chronological, episodic account of the conditions of slavery/Jim Crow, including a particularly vivid description of the difficulty or near impossibility—but also the inescapable necessity—of attaining full literacy, tells how he escaped from southern bondage, fleeing toward what he imagined would be freedom, a new identity, and the opportunity to exercise his hard-won literacy in a northern, free-state city. That he did not find exactly what he expected in Chicago and New York changes nothing about *Black Boy* itself: neither did Douglass find everything he anticipated or desired in the North, but that personally unhappy fact in no way affects his *Narrative*. Wright, impelled by a nascent sense of freedom that grew within him in direct proportion to his increasing literacy (particularly in the reading of realistic and naturalistic fiction), fled the world of the South, and abandoned the identity that world had imposed upon him ("I was what the white South called a 'nigger'"), in search of another identity, the identity of a writer, precisely that writer we know as "Richard Wright." "From where in this southern darkness had I caught a sense of freedom?"[22] Wright could discover only one answer to his question: "It had been only through books . . . that I had managed to keep myself alive in a negatively vital way" (p. 282). It was in his ability to construe letters and in the bare possibility of putting his life into writing that Wright "caught a sense of freedom" and knew that he must work out a new identity. "I could submit and live the life of a genial slave," Wright says, "but," he adds, "that was impossible" (p. 276). It was impossible because, like Douglass and other slaves, he had arrived at the crossroads where the three paths of literacy, identity, freedom met, and after such knowledge there was no turning back.

Black Boy resembles slave narratives in many ways but in other ways it is crucially different from its predecessors and ancestors. It is of more than trivial insignificance that Wright's narrative does not begin with "I was born," nor is it under the guidance of any intention or impulse other than its own, and while his book is largely episodic in structure, it is also—precisely by exercise of symbolic memory—"emplotted" and "configurational" in such a way as to construe "significant wholes out of scattered events." Ultimately, Wright freed himself from the South—at least this is what his narrative recounts—and he was also fortunately free, as the ex-slaves generally were not, from abolitionist control and free to exercise that creative memory that was peculiarly his. On the penultimate page of *Black Boy* Wright says, "I was leaving the South to fling myself into the unknown, to meet other situations that would perhaps elicit from me other responses. And if I could meet enough of a different life, then, perhaps, gradually and slowly I might learn who I was, what I might be. I was not leaving the South to forget the South, but so that some day I might understand it, might come to know what its rigors had done to me, to its children. I fled so that the numbness of my defensive living might thaw out and let me feel the pain—years later and far away—of what living in the South had meant." Here Wright not only exercises memory but also talks about it, reflecting on its creative, therapeutic, redemptive, and liberating capacities. In his conclusion Wright harks back to the themes and the form of the slave narratives, and at the same time he anticipates theme and form in a great deal of more recent Afro-American writing, perhaps most notably in *Invisible Man. Black Boy* is like a nexus joining slave narratives of the past to the most fully developed literary creations of the present: through the power of symbolic memory it transforms the earlier narrative mode into what everyone must recognize as imaginative, creative literature, both autobiography and fiction. In their narratives, we might say, the ex-slaves did that which, all unknowingly on their part and only when joined to capacities and possibilities not available to them, led right on to the tradition of Afro-American literature as we know it now.

Notes

1. Professor Ricoeur has generously given me permission to quote from this unpublished paper.
2. I have in mind such illustrations as the large drawing reproduced as frontispiece to John Andrew Jackson's *Experience of a Slave in South Carolina* (London: Passmore & Alabaster, 1862), described as a "Fac-simile of the gimlet which I used to bore a hole in the deck of the vessel"; the engraved drawing of a torture machine reproduced on p. 47 of *A Narrative of the Adventures and Escape of Moses Roper, from American Slavery* (Philadelphia: Merrihew & Gunn, 1838); and the "REPRESENTATION OF THE BOX, 3 feet 1 inch long, 2 feet wide, 2 feet 6 inches high," in which Henry Box Brown travelled by freight from Richmond to Philadelphia, reproduced following the text of the *Narrative of Henry Box Brown, Who Escaped from Slavery Enclosed in a Box 3 Feet Long and 2 Wide. Written from a Statement of Facts Made by Himself. With Remarks upon the Remedy for Slavery. By Charles Stearns.* (Boston: Brown & Stearns, 1849). The very title of Box Brown's *Narrative* demonstrates something of the mixed mode of slave narratives. On the question of the text of Brown's narrative see also notes 4 and 12 below.
3. Douglass' *Narrative* diverges from the master plan on E4 (he was himself the slave who refused to be whipped), E8 (slave auctions happened not to fall within his experience, but he does talk of the separation of mothers and children and the systematic destruction of slave families), and E10 (he refuses to tell how he escaped because to do so would close one escape route to those still in slavery; in the *Life and Times of Frederick Douglass* he reveals that his escape was different from the conventional one). For the purposes of the present essay—and also, I think, in general—the *Narrative* of 1845 is a much more interesting and a better book than Douglass' two later autobiographical

texts: *My Bondage and My Freedom* (1855) and *Life and Times of Frederick Douglass* (1881). These latter two are diffuse productions (*Bondage and Freedom* is three to four times longer than *Narrative, Life and Times* five to six times longer) that dissipate the focalized energy of the *Narrative* in lengthy accounts of post-slavery activities—abolitionist speeches, recollections of friends, trips abroad, etc. In interesting ways it seems to me that the relative weakness of these two later books is analogous to a similar weakness in the extended version of Richard Wright's autobiography published as *American Hunger* (originally conceived as part of the same text as *Black Boy*).

4. This is true of the version labelled "first English edition"—*Narrative of the Life of Henry Box Brown, Written by Himself* (Manchester: Lee & Glynn, 1851)—but not of the earlier American edition—*Narrative of Henry Box Brown, Who Escaped from Slavery Enclosed in a Box 3 Feet Long and 2 Wide. Written from a Statement of Facts Made by Himself. With Remarks upon the Remedy for Slavery. By Charles Stearns.* (Boston: Brown & Stearns, 1849). On the beginning of the American edition see the discussion later in this essay, and on the relationship between the two texts of Brown's narrative see note 12 below.

5. Douglass' *Narrative* begins this way. Neither *Bondage and Freedom* nor *Life and Times* starts with the existential assertion. This is one thing, though by no means the only or the most important one, that removes the latter two books from the category of slave narrative. It is as if by 1855 and even more by 1881 Frederick Douglass' existence and his identity were secure enough and sufficiently well known that he no longer felt the necessity of the first and basic assertion.

6. With the exception of William Parker's "The Freedman's Story" (published in the February and March 1866 issues of *Atlantic Monthly*) all the narratives listed were separate publications. There are many more brief "narratives"—so brief that they hardly warrant the title "narrative": from a single short paragraph to three or four pages in length—that begin with "I was born"; there are, for example, twenty-five or thirty such in the collection of Benjamin Drew published as *The Refugee: A North-Side View of Slavery*. I have not tried to multiply the instances by citing minor examples; those listed in the text include the most important of the narratives—Roper, Bibb, W.W. Brown, Douglass, Thompson, Ward, Pennington, Steward, Clarke, the Crafts—even James Williams, though it is generally agreed that his narrative is a fraud perpetrated on an unwitting amanuensis, John Greenleaf Whittier. In addition to those listed in the text, there are a number of other narratives that begin with only slight variations on the formulaic tag—William Hayden: "The subject of this narrative was born"; Moses Grandy: "My name is Moses Grandy; I was born"; Andrew Jackson: "I, Andrew Jackson, was born"; Elizabeth Keckley: "My life has been an eventful one. I was born"; Thomas L. Johnson: "According to information received from my mother, if the reckoning is correct, I was born. . . ." Perhaps more interesting than these is the variation played by Solomon Northup, who was born a free man in New York State and was kidnapped and sent into slavery for twelve years; thus he commences not with "I was born" but with "Having been born a freeman"—as it were the participial contingency that endows his narrative with a special poignancy and a marked difference from other narratives.

There is a nice and ironic turn on the "I was born" insistence in the rather foolish scene in *Uncle Tom's Cabin* (Chapter XX) when Topsy famously opines that she was not made but just "grow'd." Miss Ophelia catechizes her: " 'Where were you born?' 'Never was born!' persisted Topsy." Escaped slaves who hadn't Topsy's peculiar combination of Stowe-ic resignation and manic high spirits in the face of an imposed non-identity and non-existence were impelled to assert over and over, "I *was* born."

7. Douglass' title is classic to the degree that it is virtually repeated by Henry Bibb, changing only the name in the formula and inserting "Adventures," presumably to attract spectacle-loving readers: *Narrative of the Life and Adventures of Henry Bibb, An American Slave, Written by Himself.* Douglass' *Narrative* was published in 1845, Bibb's in 1849. I suspect that Bibb derived his title directly from Douglass. That ex-slaves writing their narratives were aware of earlier productions by fellow ex-slaves (and thus were impelled to sameness in narrative by outright imitation as well as by the conditions of narration adduced in the text above) is made clear in the preface to *The Life of John Thompson, A Fugitive Slave; Containing His History of 25 Years in Bondage, and His Providential Escape. Written by Himself* (Worcester: Published by John Thompson, 1856), p. v: "It was suggested to me about two years since, after relating to many the main facts relative to my bondage and escape to the land of freedom, that it would be a desirable thing to put these facts into permanent form. I first sought to discover what had been said by other partners in bondage once, but in freedom now. . . ." With this forewarning the reader should not be surprised to discover that Thompson's narrative follows the conventions of the form very closely indeed.

8. However much Douglass changed his narrative in successive incarnations—the opening paragraph, for example, underwent considerable transformation—he chose to retain this sentence intact. It occurs on p. 52 of the *Narrative of the Life of Frederick Douglass* . . . , ed. Benjamin Quarles (Cambridge, Mass., 1960); on p. 132 of *My Bondage and My Freedom,* intro. Philip S. Foner (New York, 1969); and on p. 72 of *Life and Times of Frederick Douglass,* intro. Rayford W. Logan (New York, 1962).

9. For convenience I have adopted this list from John F. Bayliss' introduction to *Black Slave Narratives* (New York, 1970), p. 18. As will be apparent, however, I do not agree with the point Bayliss wishes to make with his list. Having quoted from Marion Wilson Starling's unpublished dissertation, "The Black Slave Narrative: Its Place in American Literary History," to the effect that the slave narratives, except those from Equiano and Douglass, are not generally very distinguished as literature, Bayliss continues: "Starling is being unfair here since the narratives do show a diversity of interesting styles. . . . The leading narratives, such as those of Douglass, William Wells Brown, Ball, Bibb, Henson, Northup, Pennington, and Roper deserve to be considered for a place in American literature, a place beyond the merely historical." Since Ball's narrative was written by one "Mr. Fisher" and Northup's by David Wilson, and since Henson's narrative shows a good deal of the charlatanry one might expect from a man who billed himself as "The Original Uncle Tom," it seems at best a strategic error for Bayliss to include them among those slave narratives said to show the greatest literary distinction. To put it another way, it would be neither surprising nor specially meritorious if Mr. Fisher (a white man),

David Wilson (a white man), and Josiah Henson (The Original Uncle Tom) were to display "a diversity of interesting styles" when their narratives are put alongside those by Douglass, W.W. Brown, Bibb, Pennington, and Roper. But the really interesting fact, as I shall argue in the text, is that they do *not* show a diversity of interesting styles.

10. Here we discover another minor but revealing detail of the convention establishing itself. Just as it became conventional to have a signed portrait and authenticating letters/prefaces, so it became at least semi-conventional to have an imprint reading more or less like this: "Boston: Anti-Slavery Office, 25 Cornhill." A Cornhill address is given for, among others, the narratives of Douglass, William Wells Brown, Box Brown, Thomas Jones, Josiah Henson, Moses Grandy, and James Williams. The last of these is especially interesting for, although it seems that his narrative is at least semi-fraudulent, Williams is on this point, as on so many others, altogether representative.

11. *Narrative of Henry Box Brown.* . . . (Boston: Brown & Stearns, 1849), p. 25.

12. The question of the text of Brown's *Narrative* is a good deal more complicated than I have space to show, but that complication rather strengthens than invalidates my argument above. The text I analyze above was published in Boston in 1849. In 1851 a "first English edition" was published in Manchester with the specification "Written by Himself." It would appear that in preparing the American edition Stearns worked from a ms. copy of what would be published two years later as the first English edition—or from some ur-text lying behind both. In any case, Stearns has laid on the True Abolitionist Style very heavily, but there is already, in the version "Written by Himself," a good deal of the abolitionist manner present in diction, syntax, and tone. If the first English edition was really written by Brown this would make his case parallel to the case of Henry Bibb, discussed below, where the abolitionist style insinuates itself into the text and takes over the style of the writing even when that is actually done by an ex-slave. This is not the place for it, but the relationship between the two texts, the variations that occur in them, and the explanation for those variations would provide the subject for an immensely interesting study.

13. *Twelve Years a Slave: Narrative of Solomon Northup, a Citizen of New-York, Kidnapped in Washington City in 1841, and Rescued in 1853, from a Cotton Plantation Near the Red River, in Louisiana* (Auburn: Derby & Miller, 1853), p. xv. References in the text are to this first edition.

14. I am surprised that Robert Stepto, in his excellent analysis of the internal workings of the Wilson/Northup book, doesn't make more of this question of where to locate the real authorial authority of the book. See *From Behind the Veil: A Study of Afro-American Narrative* (Urbana, Ill., 1979), pp. 11-16.

Whether intentionally or not, Gilbert Osofsky badly misleads readers of the book unfortunately called *Puttin' On Ole Massa* when he fails to include the "Editor's Preface" by David Wilson with his printing of *Twelve Years a Slave: Narrative of Solomon Northup.* There is nothing in Osofsky's text to suggest that David Wilson or anyone else but Northup had anything to do with the narrative—on the contrary: "Northup, Brown, and Bibb, as their autobiographies demonstrate, were men of creativity, wisdom and talent. Each was capable of writing his life story with sophistication" (*Puttin' On Ole Massa* [New York, 1969], p. 44). Northup precisely does *not* write his life story, either with or without sophistication, and Osofsky is guilty of badly obscuring this fact. Osofsky's literary judgment, with two-thirds of which I do not agree, is that "The autobiographies of Frederick Douglass, Henry Bibb, and Solomon Northup fuse imaginative style with keenness of insight. They are penetrating and self-critical, superior autobiography by any standards" (p. 10).

15. To anticipate one possible objection, I would argue that the case is essentially different with *The Autobiography of Malcolm X*, written by Alex Haley. To put it simply, there were many things in common between Haley and Malcolm X; between white amanuenses/editors/authors and ex-slaves, on the other hand, almost nothing was shared.

16. *Narrative of the Life and Adventures of Henry Bibb, An American Slave, Written by Himself. With an Introduction by Lucius C. Matlack* (New York: Published by the Author; 5 Spruce Street, 1849), p. i. Page citations in the text are from this first edition.

It is a great pity that in modern reprintings of slave narratives—the three in Osofsky's *Puttin' On Ole Massa*, for example—the illustrations in the originals are omitted. A modern reader misses much of the flavor of a narrative like Bibb's when the illustrations, so full of pathos and tender sentiment, not to mention some exquisite cruelty and violence, are not with the text. The two illustrations on p. 45 (captions: "Can a mother forget her suckling child?" and "The tender mercies of the wicked are cruel"), the one on p. 53 ("Never mind the money"), and the one on p. 81 ("My heart is almost broken") can be taken as typical. An interesting psychological fact about the illustrations in Bibb's narrative is that of the twenty-one total, eighteen involve some form of physical cruelty, torture, or brutality. The uncaptioned illustration on p. 133 of two naked slaves on whom some infernal punishment is being practised says much about (in Matlack's phrase) the reader's feverish thirst for gushing beautiful fountains "started from beneath the rod of violence."

17. Or 1852, the date of *Uncle Tom's Cabin*. Harriet Beecher Stowe recognized a kindred novelistic spirit when she read one (just as David Wilson/Solomon Northup did). In 1851, when she was writing *Uncle Tom's Cabin*, Stowe wrote to Frederick Douglass saying that she was seeking information about life on a cotton plantation for her novel: "I have before me an able paper written by a southern planter in which the details & modus operandi are given from his point of sight—I am anxious to have some more from another standpoint—I wish to be able to make a picture that shall be graphic & true to nature in its details—Such a person as *Henry Bibb*, if in this country, might give me just the kind of information I desire." This letter is dated July 9, 1851 and has been transcribed from a photographic copy reproduced in Ellen Moers, *Harriet Beecher Stowe and American Literature* (Hartford, Conn.: Stowe-Day Foundation, 1978), p. 14.

18. Since writing the above, I discover that in his *Life and Times* Douglass says of the conclusion of his abolitionist work, "Othello's occupation was gone" (New York: Collier-Macmillan, 1962, p. 373), but this still seems to me rather a different matter from the white sponsor's invariant allusion to Othello in attesting to the truthfulness of the black narrator's account.

A contemporary reviewer of *The Interesting Narrative of the Life of*

Olaudah Equiano, or Gustavus Vassa, the African wrote, in *The General Magazine and Impartial Review* (July 1789), "This is 'a round unvarnished tale' of the chequered adventures of an African . . . ." (see appendix to vol. I of *The Life of Olaudah Equiano,* ed. Paul Edwards [London: Dawsons of Pall Mall, 1969].

John Greenleaf Whittier, though stung once in his sponsorship of James Williams' *Narrative,* did not shrink from a second, similar venture, writing, in his "introductory note" to the *Autobiography of the Rev. Josiah Henson (Mrs. Harriet Beecher Stowe's "Uncle Tom")*—also known as *Uncle Tom's Story of His Life From 1789 to 1879*—"The early life of the author, as a slave, . . . proves that in the terrible pictures of 'Uncle Tom's Cabin' there is 'nothing extenuate or aught set down in malice' " (Boston: B. B. Russell & Co., 1879, p. viii).

19. Quoted by Philip S. Foner in the introduction to *My Bondage and My Freedom,* pp. xi-xii.

20. Both quotations from Benjamin Quarles, "The Breach Between Douglass and Garrison," *Journal of Negro History,* XXIII (April 1938), p. 147, note 19, and p. 154.

21. The list is from Nichols' unpublished doctoral dissertation (Brown University, 1948), "A Study of the Slave Narrative," p. 9.

22. *Black Boy: A Record of Childhood and Youth* (New York, 1966), p. 282.

Three West African Writers of the 1780s

PAUL EDWARDS

During the eighteenth century a considerable number of Africans in Britain became literate in English. In some cases they had come to Britain to receive special training, but they were usually household servants, and most of them either were, or had been, slaves. Some competence in written and spoken English was needed to enable them to carry out their household duties, and occasional teaching was sometimes provided, as recorded in this item from a contemporary book of accounts:

> By paid James McKenzie, Schoolmaster of Huntly for Teaching the Black Boy Harry per Receipt Nine shillings sterling Due from the 5th of November 1760 to the first of February 1761, and from the 11th of May 1761 to the 27th of July 1762.[1]

But teaching was sometimes more than occasional: Samuel Johnson sent his servant, Francis Barber, to Bishops Stortford Grammar School for four or five years;[2] and Soubise, the favourite of the Duchess of Queensberry, was trained in fencing and horsemanship, as well as in polite conversation.[3] His one surviving letter gives support to the view that he was a man of style, for its message is delivered with a flourish:

> Dear Miss,
>
>   I have often beheld you in public with rapture; indeed it is impossible to view you without such emotions as must animate every man of sentiment. In a word, Madam, you have seized my heart, and I dare tell you that I am your *Negro Slave*. . .[4]

Some were given formal training for a profession. Philip Quaque, who lived in England from 1754 to 1766, married an Englishwoman (as did a good many of the Africans living in England), received an education at the expense of the Society for the Propagation of the Gospel, and returned to West Africa as Chaplain of Cape Coast Castle. After the death of his first wife he twice married African women, but his children were educated in England "in order to secure their tender minds from receiving the bad impression of the country, the vile customs and practices, and above all the losing of their mother's vile jargon."[5] Francis Williams was provided by his patron, the Duke of Montagu, with a place at Cambridge, where he studied Mathematics and returned to teach in Jamaica;[6] and by the early nineteenth century John Baptist Philip, a Trinidadian descendant of slaves, had graduated with the M.D. at Edinburgh University with a doctoral thesis, *De Hysteria*.[7] By this time, numbers of West African children and young men and women were being sent to Britain for schooling, either by their parents, such as the son of King Naimbanna of Sierra Leone,[8] or by the administrators of the Freetown settlement, from which the ex-Governor, Zachary Macaulay, brought twenty boys and four girls to Britain in 1799, to be educated privately in Clapham.[9]

Some African visitors were embraced by high society. Job ben Solomon, the enslaved son of a Muslim High Priest of Bondou, was rescued from slavery in the Americas by James Oglethorpe. On the discovery that Job was literate in Arabic, he was elected to the scholarly Spalding Society (whose members included Isaac Newton and Alexander Pope), was presented to the Queen (who gave him a gold watch), and became yet another protégé of the Duke of Montagu, before returning to West Africa as agent for the Royal African Company.[10] The black poet Phillis Wheatley travelled to London with the son of her Bostonian master in 1773, and was taken up by the Countess of Huntingdon. Brook Watson, a future Lord Mayor of London presented her with the 1770 Glasgow folio edition of *Paradise Lost,* and the Earl of Dartmouth with Smollett's translation of *Don Quixote.*[11] Yet for many, it continues to come as a surprise that the beginnings of an African literature in English should be found as early as the eighteenth century.

The words of the black people of this period come down to us in several ways. There are letters, some in manuscript, some printed, and there are quotations of the spoken word, such as the striking speech by John Frederick Henry Naimbanna recorded in Prince Hoare's *Memoirs of Granville Sharp* and elsewhere.[12] There are books acknowledged to have been written with assistance, such as the autobiography of James Albert Ukawsaw Gronniosaw (c.1770);[13] and there are the three books discussed here: the *Letters* of Ignatius Sancho (1782) and the autobiography of Olaudah Equiano (1789), of whose authenticity there is little, if any, doubt; and the *Thoughts and Sentiments on the Evil of Slavery* (1787) by Ottobah Cugoano, about which there must be reservations.[14]

Sancho's *Letters* might not at first glance appear to have much bearing upon a volume of essays on the slave-narrative. Though he was born in 1729 of enslaved parents, aboard the slave ship carrying them to the West Indies, by the age of two or three he was in England, virtually without memory of Africa or of the slave trade. His youth was marred by threats to return him to West Indian slavery, but by the time he was in his teens he had been taken up by the Duke and Duchess of Montagu, who did much to further his education, and most of his life was spent as the senior and respected servant of a distinguished household. He eventually acquired a grocery business in Mayfair, keeping such literary company as that of Sterne, Garrick and possibly Samuel Johnson. His letters consist largely of private correspondence about daily domestic business, or opinions on the conduct of public affairs. Nevertheless, these letters constitute a unique record of one kind of black experience, and can be shown to have a bearing on what is revealed in the slave autobiographies.

Sancho was about twenty-five years old, with no distinct memories of the slave trade, and settled into a comfortable London career, when Equiano, an eleven-year-old Ibo boy, was being carried off from his home somewhere in the region to the south of modern Onitsha, Nigeria. The comparative security of Sancho can be contrasted with Equiano's years of enslavement, but there are other factors to be born in mind. According to the introductory biography to Sancho's *Letters* written by Joseph Jekyll, his first London owners, three fierce ladies, "even threatened on angry occasions to return [him] to his African slavery." The legal position of the black servant in London at this time offered little opportunity or encouragement for protest. In 1729, the year of Sancho's birth, the

Attorney-General, Yorke, and the Solicitor-General, Talbot, had given their decision that a slave, baptised or not, even though resident in Britain, remained in enslavement and the property of his master. There was conflict between the Act of Habeas Corpus and the Navigation Acts which reduced black slaves to the status of commodity, but during the early part of the century little was done about it. A letter from a Welsh-man dated March 4, 1739, indicates the spirit of the age towards many black servants:

> I've a black lad about 16 years old to sell for a friend and I can't get any body to buy him. I wish I had him at London, I'd sell him under £30, ay, a little above £25.[15]

Black personal servants have been described as a privileged group, pampered in comparison with the American plantation slaves, but they remained commodities under British law—"they are like stock on a farm," declared Hardwicke in 1745.[16] And in 1749, Hardwicke reaffirmed that an escaped slave could be legally recovered in Britain and returned to the American plantations. Even those servants who, like Sancho, worked in liberal households under generous conditions of service, would have lacked any center of protest such as developed later in the century under the leadership of Granville Sharp.

The life of Equiano was another matter. Born around 1745, he bought back his freedom in 1766, shortly after an incident which was to be a turning point in the history of abolition. In 1765, Granville Sharp had taken up the case of a runaway slave, Jonathan Strong, who had been recaptured and was being reclaimed by his master. Sharp gained Strong's release, though only on a legal technicality. He was to go further. In 1771 he took up the case of Thomas Lewis, and in the following year James Somerset. Lord Chief Justice Mansfield declared, not without some misgivings about the status of property, that once a slave had set foot in England, he could not be returned to slavery in the Americas. This rather shuffling decision was repeated much less ambiguously in Scotland three years later, slavery itself being declared unacceptable under Scottish law.[17]

Thus it was not until the last decade of Sancho's life that there was any active, coherent antislavery movement in Britain. The 1770s, however, saw Equiano and Cugoano settled in Britain, free from their West Indian slavery, and by the end of the decade Equiano was well enough known to Granville Sharp to be given the present of a book by "that truly pious and benevolent man," as Equiano called him.[18] During the 1780s, both Equiano and Cugoano were active on behalf of the slaves who were still being trepanned and resold in Britain despite Lord Mansfield's ruling. By 1783, the considerable numbers of black people in Britain had been swelled by the arrival of freed slaves and freemen who had fought on the British side in the American War of Independence, as well as the servants of Americans displaced by the war. The problem of the numbers of "Black Poor," as they were called, was considered to be particularly serious in London, and during and after the 1780s there was a growing volume of discussion of their place in society and the consequences of slavery. The increasing effectiveness and popularity of the abolitionist movement and the social prominence of many of its supporters encouraged the black population to speak for itself, Equiano and Cugoano being two of an active group, the Sons of Africa, who at this time addressed a number of letters to leading abolitionists.[19] By the time these two published their books, however, Sancho had been dead many years. While Sancho's personality and viewpoint had been shaped largely by the life he had led as an Englishman of a moderately prosperous kind, Equiano had spent the first eleven or so years of his life in Ibo, knowing nothing of the world beyond his own; he had endured the terrors of the Middle Passage, had been bought and sold, and had gained laboriously a freedom not always easily preserved.

Much of Sancho's correspondence is devoted to the details of his domestic life: the illnesses of his children (the "six brats" or "Sanchonets"), greetings to their favourite dog Nutts, a spaniel belonging to the Crew family whose daughter edited the letters, and the ups and downs of trade in the Sancho shop. His son, Billy, who was to become a librarian in the employ of Sir Joseph Banks,[20] is well represented:

> You cannot imagine what hold little Billy gets of me—he grows—prattles—every day learns something new—and by his good will would ever be in the shop with me. The monkey! he clings round my legs—and if I chide him or look sour—he holds up his little mouth to kiss me;—I know I am the fool—for parent's weakness is child's strength:—truth orthodox—which will hold good between lover and lovee . . . (113)

The sentimental tone points to the features these letters share with Sancho's literary model: "If I am enthusiast in any thing it is in favour of my Sterne," (146) he writes, and on the Shandean theme of haircuts he begins, characteristically wide of the ultimate mark in Sterne's comic-melancholic manner:

> Lord! what is man?—and what business have such lazy, lousy, paltry beings of a day to form friendships, or to make connections? Man is an absurd animal—yea, I will ever maintain it—in his vices, dreadful—in his few virtues, silly—he has religion without devotion—philosophy without wisdom—the divine passion (as it is called) love too oft without affec-

tion—and anger without cause—friendship without reason—hate without reflection—knowledge (like Ashley's punch in small quantities) without judgment—and wit without discretion.—Look into old age, and you will see avarice joined to poverty—letchery, gout, impotency, like three monkeys or London bucks, in a one-horse whisky, driving to the Devil. (6)

Presenting a more sober front, there are, for example, in the *General Advertiser,* his proposals for establishing a naval reserve in order to reduce the need for impressment (81), and for the reduction of the national debt by a kind of voluntary tax on property (128). There is also his "Britishness," though this is usually mixed with an ironic sense of his own detachment—very strikingly so in his letter on the Gordon Riots (269 foll.) where he combines a distinctly middle-class concern for the *status quo,* and sympathy for the guards ("the poor fellows are just worn out for want of rest"), with irritable cries of "This—this—is liberty! Genuine British liberty!—This instant about two thousand liberty boys are swearing and swaggering by with large sticks," and in exasperation, "I am not sorry I was born in Afric." A good example of this detachment from British values in the very process of lamenting their decline can be found in a letter on the defeats of the navy:

> L(or)d S(andwic)h has gone to Portsmouth, to be a witness of England's disgrace—and his own shame.—In faith, my friend, the present time is rather *comique*—Ireland almost in as true a state of rebellion as America—Admirals quarrelling in the West-Indies—and at home Admirals that do not chuse to fight—The British Empire mouldering away in the West, annihilated in the North—Gibraltar going—and England fast asleep. What says Mr. B—— to all this?—he is a ministerialist:—for my part, it's nothing to me, as I am only a lodger, and hardly that. (213)

Reading letters like this, one begins to wonder if Sancho had been assimilated so fully into eighteenth-century English life after all. As the last phrase of the previous quotation shows, he was aware of himself as an African in England, and felt some of the tensions between two possible identities. While he can refer jocularly or sentimentally to his color—"blessed times for a poor Blacky grocer to hang or drown in!" (231) or "Figure to yourself, my dear Sir, a man of a convexity of belly exceeding Falstaff—and a black face into the bargain" (238)—yet the sentimentality and the jocularity may have a cutting edge:

> ". . . my hearty wishes . . . to all who have charity enough to admit dark faces into the fellowship of Christians." (143)
> ". . . our best respects to Miss A—s, and to every one who delighteth in Blackamoor greetings." (155)

Writing to a fellow-African, Soubise, Sancho reveals aspects of his experience which remain muted in his other letters:

> Look round upon the miserable fate of almost all of our unfortunate colour—superadded to ignorance,—see slavery, and the contempt of those very wretches who roll in affluence from our labours. Superadded to this woeful catalogue—hear the ill-bred and heart-racking abuse of the foolish vulgar. (31-2)

Soubise, however, is a favourite of the Duchess of Queensberry, and so in the same letter Sancho urges him to "look up to thy more than parents—look up to thy almost divine benefactors." The tensions working in Sancho emerge in a letter written shortly before the one to Soubise, addressed to a young protégé of Garrick:

> I thank you for your kindness to my poor black brethren—I flatter myself you will find them not ungrateful—they act commonly from their feelings:—I have observed a dog will love those who use him kindly—and surely, if so, negroes, in their state of ignorance and bondage, will not act less generously, if I may judge them by myself—I should suppose kindness would do any thing with them;—my soul melts at kindness—but the contrary—I own with shame—makes me almost a savage. (30)

Beneath the fashionable glow of the "Man of Feeling" there smoulders something of the rage that the Christian African had been earnestly exhorted to suppress.[21] The same strain is to be revealed at a deeper level by Equiano, but in Sancho the note of anger is invariably rapidly qualified. He comments, for example, on the Bostonian gentlemen who confirmed the authenticity and praised the quality of Phillis Wheatley's verse:

> These good great folks—all know—and perhaps admired—nay, praised Genius in bondage—and then, like the Priests and the Levites in sacred writ, passed by—not one good Samaritan amongst them. (127)

But in the same letter, having read some books upon "the unchristian and diabolical usage of my brother Negroes,"

> The perusal affected me more than I can express;—indeed I felt a double or mixt sensation—for while my heart was torn for the sufferings—which, for aught I know—some of my nearest kin might have undergone—my bosom, at the same time, glowed with gratitude—and praise toward the humane—the Christian—the friendly and learned Author of that most valuable book. (125-6)

Sancho's most famous letter, to Sterne applauding his sentiments on slavery and encouraging him to write more on the subject, spills over into emotional self-indulgence:

> Of all my favourite authors, not one has drawn a tear in favor of my miserable black brethren—excepting yourself, and the humane author of

Sir George Ellison.—I think you will forgive me;—I am sure you will applaud me for beseeching you to give one half-hour's attention to slavery, as it is at this day practised in our West Indies.—That subject, handled in your striking manner, would ease the yoke (perhaps) of many—but if of only one—Gracious God!—what a feast to a benevolent heart!—and, sure I am, you are an epicurean in acts of charity.—You, who are universally read, and as universally admired—you could not fail—Dear Sir, think in me you behold the uplifted hands of thousands of my brother Moors.—Grief (you pathetically observe) is eloquent;—figure to yourself the attitudes;—hear their supplicating addresses!—alas! —you cannot refuse.—Humanity must comply . . . (71-2)

More interesting, I think, is one of Sancho's letters to a young English-man who had gone out to India and had written home about "the treach-ery and chicanery of the Natives." Sancho replies:

I am sorry to observe that the practice of your country (which as a resident I love—and for its freedom, and for the many blessings I enjoy in it, shall ever have my warmest wishes—prayers—and blessings); I say, it is with reluctance that I must observe your country's conduct has been uniformly wicked in the East—West Indies—and even on the coast of Guinea.—The grand object of English navigators—indeed of all Chris-tian navigators—is money—money—money—for which I do not pretend to blame them.—Commerce was meant by the goodness of the Deity to diffuse the various goods of the earth into every part—to unite mankind in the blessed chains of brotherly love—society—and mutual depen-dence:—and the enlightened Christian should diffuse the riches of the Gospel of peace—with the commodities of his respective land.—Com-merce, attended with strict honesty—and with Religion for its com-panion—would be a blessing to every shore it touched at.— (148)

More than one voice can be discerned here. Sancho the ex-slave sounds a note of indignation and ironic anger at the greed of the "Christian navigators" whose "grand object" has been nothing but "money—money—money." The repetition itself seems a mark of accumulating rage, yet it is at this juncture that the voices of Sancho the peacemaker and Sancho the Mayfair shopkeeper break in, blending to sing the praises of com-merce and religion. The argument is decent and respectable in its min-gling of sense with sensibility, but sorts oddly with the earlier attack on "Christian navigators," seeming to turn its back on the issue.

Ten years later, the spirit of the writings of Equiano and Cugoano is more overtly aggressive, and as has been said above, both men were ac-tively involved in giving help to the black poor of Britain, and in the larger issue of abolition. Both men volunteered to go exploring for the African Association,[22] and Equiano was corresponding with Cugoano at the time of the resettlement expedition of freed slaves, which sailed for

Sierra Leone in 1787 with Equiano aboard as Commissary for Stores.[23] Equiano left the expedition at Plymouth after quarrelling with its white leaders, and wrote to Cugoano in London:

> I am sorry you and some more are not here with us. I am sure Irwin, and Fraser the Parson, are great villains, and Dr. Currie. I am exceedingly much aggrieved at the conduct of those who call themselves gentlemen. They now mean to serve (or use) the blacks the same as they do in the West Indies. . .[24]

Equiano and Cugoano were cosignatories of a number of letters to Granville Sharp, Sir William Dolben, William Pitt, Charles James Fox and others,[25] and both are known to have been acting as informants to Granville Sharp, Equiano having first drawn Sharp's attention to the murder of 130 slaves aboard the *Zong* in 1783,[26] and Cugoano to the "trepanning and carrying aboard ship for transportation back to the West Indies of a negro servant called Harry Demane" in 1786.[27]

So, as one of the leaders of opinion amongst the free Africans in London, Cugoano published his *Thoughts and Sentiments* on the slave trade in 1787. However, a holograph letter to Sharp from Cugoano[28] which can be proved to have been written in 1791 offers clear evidence that Cugoano could not have written *Thoughts and Sentiments* without very considerable assistance. Nevertheless, despite its errors of grammar and spelling, the letter demonstrates that Cugoano was able to use English with fluency and confidence. Here are some of the opening sentences, the subject being the repatriation to Africa of a group of black freemen in Nova Scotia:

> Honoured Sir, Pardon the liberty taken in troubling you with this few lines but as there is several ships now going to new Brunswick I could wish to have your answer that I might be able to gived the black settlers there some kind of an answer to their request, the generality of them are mediately the natives of Africa who Join the british forces Last war, they are consisting of different Macanicks such as Carpenters, Smiths, Masons and farmers, this are the people we have imediate use for in the Province of freedom. Most of them are people of property and able to pay their own passages, and the familly, as well as the country been by far the cheapest market for victualling vessels, I am of opinion that connections with them will be immediate service—should think it proper to make lest interest for me I shall go over with Cap. Younghusband who will sale for that province in a few days my motive is this, I should endeavour to know who is able to pay their ways, and they that might be thought useful to the free african settlers.

Turning to the book, the reader will see that its frequently elevated rhetorical manner must reflect the work of a writer having greater control of the language than Cugoano. All the same, we must allow for the difference between writing a casual letter and settling down to produce a book. One feature of the book which would support the case for its authenticity is the occurrence of a number of grammatical errors similar to those of the letter, but in concealed positions where they might be more likely to be missed by an editor or reviser. The most persistent of these is the failure of agreement, particularly when subject and verb are some distance apart. Thus on p. 2, we find *exertions . . . has* and *class . . . are,* and between pages 112 and 121 there is a whole cluster: *the blood of millions . . . do* (112), *Every slave holder . . . are, estates . . . is,* (113), *those . . . is,* (114), *the iniquity rise* (118), *afflictions . . . has* (119), *produce . . . bring* (121). In addition, there are many sentences which are more than simply clumsy:

> But amongst those who get their liberty, like all other ignorant men, are generally more corrupt in their morals, than they possibly could have been amongst their own people in Africa. (22)

Other sentences start well but get out of control, though the element of incoherence in the example below actually helps convey something of the author's indignation:

> But let their ignorance in some things (in which the Europeans have greatly the advantage of them) be what it will, it is not the intention of those who bring them away to make them better by it; nor is the design of the slave-holders of any other intention, but that they may serve them as a kind of engines and beasts of burden; that their own ease and profit may be advanced, by a set of poor helpless men and women, whom they despise and rank with brutes, and keep them in perpetual slavery, both themselves and children, and merciful death is the only release from their toil. (21-2)

The dramatic effect of this sentence is somewhat different from the more controlled but still energetic platform rhetoric also found in the book:

> For as we have been robbed of our natural right as men, and treated as beasts, those who have injured us are like to them who have robbed the widow, the orphans, the poor and the needy of their rights, and whose children are rioting on the spoils of those who are begging at their doors for bread. (119-120)

Yet along with this goes the "naive" sentence, characteristic of the section of the book dealing with Cugoano's early years and his capture and enslavement. Typical of this style are simple, co-ordinate sentences linked by "and" or "but," and a certain awkwardness in handling more complex sentences:

> Some of us attempted in vain to run away, but pistols and cutlasses were soon introduced, threatening, that if we offered to stir we should all lie dead on the spot. One of them pretended to be more friendly than the rest, and said, that he would speak to their lord to get us clear, and desired that we should follow him; we were then immediately divided into different parties, and drove after him. We were soon led out of the way which we knew, and towards the evening, as we came in sight of a town, they told us that this great man of theirs lived there, but pretended it was too late to go and see him that night. Next morning there came three other men whose language differed from ours, and spoke to some of those who watched us all the night, but he that pretended to be our friend with the great man, and some others, were gone away. We asked our keepers what these men had been saying to them, and they answered, that they had been asking them, and us together, to go and feast with them that day, and that we must put off seeing the great man till after; little thinking that our doom was so nigh, or that these villains meant to feast on us as their prey. We went with them again about half a day's journey, and came to a great multitude of people, having different music playing; and all the day after we got there, we were very merry with the music, dancing and singing. Towards the evening, we were again persuaded that we could not get back to where the great man lived till next day; and when bedtime came, we were separated into different houses with different people. When the next morning came, I asked for the men that brought me there, and for the rest of my companions; and I was told that they were gone to the sea side to bring home some rum, guns and powder, and that some of my companions were gone with them, and that some were gone to the fields to do something or other. This gave me strong suspicion that there was some treachery in the case, and I began to think that my hopes of returning home again were all over. (7-8)

This passage, similar to several in Equiano's autobiography in its simplicity and directness, seems to me very effective, and likely to come close to what Cugoano himself wrote. In view of the evidence of the holograph letter, it has to be acknowledged that a considerable part of the book must have been at least partly the work of a reviser, and probably an expander of the text. On the other hand, it is surprising that a reviser should have left so many characteristic grammatical errors uncorrected, though this might be explained were the reviser, whilst having better control of English, not to have been a native speaker of the language. Now, amongst Cugoano's African friends, co-signatories of the letters mentioned above, was Equiano. It is possible, even likely, that he was the one to assist Cugoano with *Thoughts and Sentiments*. We know that the two men were in close touch with one another during its year of publication, and Cugoano would surely have sought Equiano's advice on the draft of his book. Further evidence is to be found in the occurrence, at certain points in the book, of expressions which recur in letters written by Equiano:

> But, to return to my subject, I begin with the Cursory Remarker. This man stiles himself a friend to the West-India colonies and their inhabitants, like Demetrius, the silversmith, a man of some considerable abilities, seeing their craft in danger, a craft, however, not so innocent and justifiable as the making of shrines for Diana, though that was base and wicked enough to enslave the minds of men with superstition and idolatry. (Cugoano, *Thoughts and Sentiments*, 14)

> You and your friend, J. Tobin, the Cursory Remarker, resemble Demetrius, the Silversmith, seeing your craft in danger, a craft, however, not so innocent or justifiable as the making of shrines for Diana, for that though wicked enough, left the persons of men at liberty, but yours enslaves both body and soul . . . (Equiano in *The Public Advertiser*, Feb. 5th, 1788)[29]

Again, an editorial report in *The Public Advertiser*, April 6th, 1787, records the complaints of the black people on the Sierra Leone expedition. Equiano had just been relieved of the post of Commissary for Stores, and had come up to London to report as follows:

> They cannot conceive, say they, that Government would establish a free colony for them, while it supports its forts and factories to wrong and ensnare, and to carry others of their colour and country into slavery and bondage—They are afraid that their doom would be to drink of the bitter water, and observe that it will their prudence and safety to take warning from the cautious in Scripture: 'Doth a fountain send forth at the same place sweet water and bitter?'

Virtually the same point is made in the same words in Cugoano's book:

> For as it seemed prudent and obvious to many of them taking heed of that sacred enquiry, *Doth a fountain send forth at the same place sweet water and bitter?* They were afraid that their doom would be to drink of the bitter water. For can it be readily conceived that government would establish a free colony for them nearly on the spot, while it supports its forts and garrisons, to ensnare, merchandize, and to carry others into captivity and slavery. (*Thoughts and Sentiments*, 141-142)

It seems more than likely, in fact, that *Thoughts and Sentiments*, while possibly begun on Cugoano's initiative, developed into a collaboration between him and Equiano, as a contribution to the growing demand amongst black Londoners for self-expression and self-help. Equiano's book followed two years later, and then, in 1791, Cugoano published a shortened version of *Thoughts and Sentiments,* adding the following conclusion:

> The *Author* begs Leave to inform his Friends and the Public in general, particularly those humane and charitable Gentlemen, who Supported his original Thoughts and Sentiments on the *Evil of Slavery,* that he has only printed this Abstract, merely to convey Instructions to his *oppressed Countrymen,* and as much as possible to excite their Attention to the religious Observance of the *Laws* of God.
>
> He further proposes to open a *School,* for all such of his *Complexion* as are desirous of being acquainted with the Knowledge of the *Christian Religion* and the *Laws* of *Civilization.* His sole Motive for these Undertakings, are, that he finds several of his Countrymen, here in England, who have not only been in an unlawful Manner brought away from their peaceable Habitations, but also deprived of every Blessing of the Christian Knowledge, by their various Masters and Mistresses, either through the motives of Avarice, or the want of the Knowledge of their own Religion, which must be a great Dishonor to Christianity.
>
> Nothing engages my desire so much as the Descendants of my Countrymen, so as to have them educated in the Duties and Knowledge of that Religion which all good Christian People enjoy; these Blessings cannot be well conveyed without *Learning,* and as most of my Countrymen are Poor and cannot afford it, and others are so much engaged in Servitude, that they have little Time to attend to it; my Design, therefore, is to open a Place for the Instruction of such as can attend; but to accomplish it, I must wholly depend on the humane and charitable *Contributions* of those *Ladies* and *Gentlemen* who are inclinable to Support this Undertaking. I am not excluding some other young Persons, who need to be taught *Reading,* etc. but my Design is chiefly intended for my Countrymen.

Whether or not the school was founded I cannot say—one such "African Academy" had been founded at Clapham before the end of the century by Zachary Macaulay for Sierra Leonians—but what this passage reveals is the anger and aggression which lay beneath the pliant Christian surface. Independence was to be achieved by way of education, yet the means to that education was commonly denied, or provided only by the charity of a society that also proceeded to dishonor its Christian principles. The establishment of the Freetown settlement in Sierra Leone, however, had diverted a number of the potential black spokesmen away from Britain, and it was in Freetown that black education was to root itself. Equiano appears to have had this in mind when, in preparing his will, he left half the residue of his estate, should his daughters not survive him, for the foundation of schools in Sierra Leone.[30]

However, one of Equiano's two daughters lived to inherit; on her

twenty-first birthday, April 8, 1816, Joanna Vassa was given nine hundred and fifty pounds by her father's executor, John Audley, the sum
remaining after the cost of "board, maintenance and education" for nineteen years had been paid. Equiano did not die a poor man; in his will,
he speaks of the "Estates and property I have dearly earned by the sweat
of my Brow in some of the most remote and adverse corners of the whole
world to solace those I leave behind,"[31] and in his sole known holograph
letter he gives as his reason for visiting London ("this wick.ᵈ town") "to
save if I can, £232 I Lent to a man, who [is] now Dying."[32] In the same
letter, wishing on behalf of friends in Nottingham that "the Good Lord
may make all of that family rich in faith," he feels it necessary to inter-
polate a postscript, "as in the things of this World," and the letter gives
us a glimpse of the keen eye of the man of business that we catch too
in his *Narrative:*

> Sir, I went to Ireland & was there 8½ months & sold 1900 copies of my
> narrative. I came here on the 10th inst. & I now mean as it seem Pleasing
> to my Good God! to leave London in about 8 or 10 Days more, & take
> me a Wife (one Miss Cullen) of Soham in Cambridge shire & when I
> have given her about 8 or 10 Days comfort I mean Directly to go to
> Scotland & sell my 5th. Editions.

He lived from 1745 to 1797, and during those years worked as a slave, a
seaman, a surgeon's mate, a valet, a quartermaster, even as manager of
a slave estate. His years were mostly spent in Africa, North America, the
West Indies and Britain, but he stayed for a time with Turks in Smyrna
and with Miskito Indians in Central America. He travelled on an expedition to the Arctic, fought with Wolfe's fleet at Quebec and Boscawen's
in the Mediterranean, he learned how to navigate with the quadrant,
and to play the French horn, captained a merchant ship when its master
died at sea, and gave evidence before a parliamentary committee on the
slave trade. In 1789, Equiano published his autobiography, combining
a remarkable account of personal economic and moral survival with a
unique attack on slavery and the slave trade—unique because he was the
only African of his age to record in detail what it was like to undergo
the experience.

Equiano never forgot his African childhood. His account of the isolated Ibo community in which he spent the first ten or so years of his
life draws a picture which is strikingly similar in almost all respects to
descriptions of Ibo village life in the first half of the present century,[33]
and it is to the values underlying Ibo custom that his mind continues to
return:

I hope the reader will not think I have trespassed on his patience in introducing myself to him with some account of the manners and customs of my country. They had been implanted in me with great care, and made an impression on my mind, which time could not erase, and which all the adversity and variety of fortune I have since experienced served only to rivet and record; for, whether the love of one's country be real or imaginary, or a lesson of reason, or an instinct of nature, I still look back with pleasure on the first scenes of my life, though that pleasure has been for the most part mingled with sorrow. (I.45-46)

Thus at several points in the *Narrative* Equiano draws comparisons between non-Christian and Christian societies to the disadvantage of the latter. He likes the Amerindians because their customs and conduct remind him of "Eboe"—plurality of wives combined with propriety of married life, joint labour "exactly like the Africans," modesty of diet, the absence of swearing, their fondness for body-painting:

I never saw any mode of worship among them; but in this they are not worse than their European brethren or neighbours: for I am sorry to say that there was not one white person in our dwelling, nor any where else that I saw in different places I was at on the shore, that was better or more pious than those unenlightened Indians. (II.181-3)

Parallels also occur in Equiano's account of his experiences with the Turks; he constantly finds on his visits to Smyrna echoes of his homeland, and his general conclusion is that he believed "those who in general termed themselves Christians not so honest or so good in their morals as the Turks," with the result that "I really thought the Turks were in a safer way of salvation than my neighbours." (II.118-9)[34]

But there are pressures working in other directions. His first impression of white men was that they were monsters and he questioned "if we were not to be eaten by those white men with horrible looks, red faces, and loose hair." (I.72) But after the Atlantic crossing he was bought by a British naval officer, and befriended on the journey to England by a white boy named Dick Baker, who looked after him and gave him his earliest English lessons. He and Dick were at first lodged with a family at Falmouth where the woman of the house "behaved to me with great kindness and attention; and taught me every thing in the same manner as she did her own child, and indeed in every respect treated me as such." (I.109) The growth of personal affections coincided with the excitement of learning:

I have often reflected with surprise that I never felt half the alarm at any of the numerous dangers I have been in, that I was filled with at the first sight of the Europeans, and at every act of theirs, even the most trifling, when I first came among them, and for some time afterwards. That fear, however, which was the effect of my ignorance, wore away as I began to know them. I could now speak English tolerably well, and I perfectly understood every thing that was said. I now not only felt myself quite easy with these new countrymen, but relished their society and manners. I no longer looked upon them as spirits, but as men superior to us; and therefore I had the stronger desire to resemble them; to imbibe their spirit, and imitate their manners; I therefore embraced every occasion of improvement; and every new thing that I observed I treasured up in my memory. I had long wished to be able to read and write; and for this purpose I took every opportunity to gain instruction, but had made as yet very little progress. However, when I went to London with my master, I had soon an opportunity of improving myself, which I gladly embraced. Shortly after my arrival, he sent me to wait upon the Miss Guerins, who had treated me with much kindness when I was there before; and they sent me to school. (I.132-3)

Even aboard British men-of-war, he continued to get an education. By the age of fourteen he could read, and had begun to learn to write:

I had leisure [on the *Ætna*] to improve myself in reading and writing. The latter I had learned a little of before I left the *Namur,* as there was a school on board. (I.151-2)

The period on the *Ætna* was a happy one, leading to great expectations, but again we find that in the very process of discovering his new world, he turns to his origins, "wonderfully surprised to see the laws and rules of my country written almost exactly here" (i.e. in the Bible):

I thought now of nothing but being freed, and working for myself, and thereby getting money to enable me to get a good education; for I always had a great desire to be able at least to read and write; and while I was on ship-board I had endeavoured to improve myself in both. While I was in the Ætna particularly, the captain's clerk taught me to write, and gave me a smattering of arithmetic as far as the rule of three. There was also one Daniel Queen, about forty years of age, a man very well educated, who messed with me on board this ship, and he likewise dressed and attended the captain. Fortunately this man soon became very much attached to me, and took very great pains to instruct me in many things. He taught me to shave and dress hair a little, and also to read in the Bible, explaining many passages to me, which I did not comprehend. I was wonderfully surprised to see the laws and rules of my country written almost exactly here; a circumstance which I believe tended to impress our manners and customs more deeply on my memory. I used to tell him of this resemblance; and many a time we have sat up the whole night together at this employment. In short, he was like a father to me; and some even used to call me after his name;

they also styled me the black Christian. Indeed I almost loved him with the affection of a son. (I.171-2)

Had Equiano endured only the cruelty and barbarism of the slave trade he might have lived out his life in a state of inarticulate hatred, or sullen, unrelieved despair. But consequent upon the very nature of his experience of slavery, ambivalent feelings towards white people and white society were established which emerge in his attitudes towards authority even when it might seem benevolent, in conflicts more intense than those we have seen in Sancho.

In the passage just quoted, Equiano is hoping to buy back his freedom with the prize money being shared among the crew as a result of their capture of a French ship. It is at this very moment of hope, excitement, and emotional release that the blow falls. Not only does Equiano's owner, Captain Pascal, whom he had begun to see as a benefactor, refuse him any share in the prize money, he resells Equiano back to American slavery. Refusing him permission to take even his books and chest of clothes, Pascal has Equiano carried aboard a waiting ship:

> . . . just as we had got a little below Gravesend, we came alongside of a ship which was going away the next tide for the West Indies; her name was the Charming Sally, Captain James Doran; and my master went on board and agreed with him for me; and in a little time I was sent for into the cabin. When I came there Captain Doran asked me if I knew him; I answered that I did not; 'Then,' said he 'you are now my slave.' I told him my master could not sell me to him, nor to any one else. 'Why,' said he, 'did not your master buy you?' I confessed he did. 'But I have served him,' said I, 'many years, and he has taken all my wages and prize-money, for I only got one sixpence during the war; besides this I have been baptized; and by the laws of the land no man has a right to sell me:' And I added, that I had heard a lawyer and others at different times tell my master so. They both then said that those people who told me so were not my friends; but I replied—it was very extraordinary that other people did not know the law as well as they. Upon this Captain Doran said I talked too much English; and if I did not behave myself well, and be quiet, he had a method on board to make me. I was too well convinced of his power over me to doubt what he said; and my former sufferings in the slave ship presenting themselves to my mind, the recollection of them made me shudder. However, before I retired I told them that as I could not get any right among men here I hoped I should hereafter in Heaven; and I immediately left the cabin, filled with resentment and sorrow. The only coat I had with me my master took away with him, and said if my prize-money had been £10,000 he had a right to it all, and would have taken it. (I.176-8)

During Equiano's subsequent years as slave to a Quaker, Mr. King, England offers him a recurring vision of safety and security—his constant wish, he tells us, was "to return to old England" (I.250); or again, "I was determined that the year following, if it pleased God, I would see old England once more." (II.20) At the same time, he never ceases to be aware of himself (nor does the world allow it) as a Negro, a former slave, a member of a despised and maltreated race. His voyages in the West Indies and on the American coast, even after he had his freedom, show him to be profoundly vulnerable in a society where the white man's word was always taken against the black man's and where the black man's property, even his life, was subject to the whims and arbitrary violence of a white slave-owning society. The crucial ambivalence lies perhaps in the idea of a *good* slave-owner. If slavery is evil—and Equiano knows well enough that it is—how should he respond to what the world would call a *good* master? The very white men who aid and befriend him, in fact, are also playing their part in the appalling system which has enslaved and brutalized him and his people. Without the power to act for himself, he is forced to seek the aid of slave-owners, such as Robert King, in order to get his rights against the white barbarians. The trouble is that, in his situation, he has little choice but to make the best of things and think himself lucky not to be a plantation slave. All the same, the rage he has to crush emerges in unexpected ways, in ironies and contradictions which may or may not be conscious. Equiano's response to "generous" treatment is ambivalent:

> Many . . . used to find fault with my master for feeding his slaves so well as he did; although I often went hungry, and an Englishman might think my fare very indifferent; but he used to tell them that he always would do it, because the slaves thereby looked better and did more work. (I.205)

What begins as a compliment to King's humaneness is suddenly qualified by a rather bitter comparison with English diet, and then virtually reversed as Equiano redirects attention to the underlying self-interest of his owner. He writes of his transports of gratitude and delight when King grants him his freedom, but at the same time enables the reader to see the mean and grudging side of King's behaviour: first, King tries to go back on his promise to release Equiano and has to be persuaded by Captain Farmer; then King insists on full repayment even though as Captain Farmer says, "Gustavus has earned you more than a hundred a year." Equiano continued throughout his life to use the name Gustavus Vassa given him by Pascal, along with his African name. He stresses in this episode that had it not been for the support of Captain Farmer, King might well not have released him at all. And the reader must judge for himself the significance of this comment by Equiano on King:

I have often seen slaves, particularly those who were meagre, in different islands, put into scales and weighed, and then sold from three pence
to six pence or nine pence a pound. My master, however, whose humanity was shocked at this mode, used to sell such by the lump. (I. 220)

When Equiano, a few pages later, declares his wish to return to England
and see Captain Pascal—the man who had arbitrarily resold him at the
very moment Equiano was anticipating his freedom—from motives of
affection, it is clear that his real motive is to show Pascal that he has
survived in spite of Pascal's callous treatment of him. As it turns out,
their meeting is comically acrimonious:

When he saw me he appeared a good deal surprised, and asked me how
I came back? I answered, 'In a ship'. To which he replied drily 'I suppose you did not walk back to London on the water.' (II. 82)

But perhaps the most striking example of Equiano's ambivalent relationships with whites is with Captain Farmer, the very man who helped him
get his freedom, and consequently the man to whom he feels morally
indebted. Significantly, Equiano signs up for a voyage with Captain
Farmer only to repay this debt, and is burdened by it:

Here gratitude bowed me down; and none but the generous mind can
judge of my feelings, struggling between inclination and duty. (II. 20)

It is in this frame of mind that he begins his last voyage with Farmer,
and immediately they quarrel over whether or not he is to be allowed to
transport some bullocks of his own—the ship is carrying a cargo of bullocks. Farmer will only let him take turkeys, but the journey is rough, the
bullocks all die, the turkeys survive, and Equiano remarks, "I could not
help looking on this, otherwise trifling circumstance, as a particular
providence of God." (II.34) Farmer is butted by a bullock, falls mortally
ill, and asks on his deathbed for reassurance that he has never harmed
Equiano. Equiano pays lip-service to pious convention on Farmer's death,
but his real feelings are more complex, as the final paragraph indicates.
Equiano takes over the ship and steers it into port at Antigua:

Many were surprised when they heard of my conducting the sloop into
the port, and I now obtained a new appellation, and was called Captain.
This elated me not a little, and it was quite flattering to my vanity to be
thus styled by as high a title as any free man in this place possessed.
When the death of the captain became known, he was much regretted
by all who knew him; for he was universally respected. At the same
time, the sable captain lost no fame; for the success I had met with increased the affection of my friends in no small measure. (II. 35)

What is apparent is that Equiano needs release not simply from subjection to his enemies, but from indebtedness to his friends. This whole section is a revealing demonstration of the effects of paternalism and subordination, as regret for Farmer's death is assimlated into the pleasure Equiano feels—and seems prepared to reveal as having its touch of vanity—that Farmer's death has given him a way to display his own skills as a navigator and leader.

The very next section of his book describes yet another sea journey, this time aboard, of all vessels, a slave ship, which he takes over from a white captain. The former slave who has been "saved" by the paternalistic kindness of others, dreams that his master's ship "was wrecked amidst the surfs and rocks, and I was the means of saving every one on board." (II.38) The dream comes true and Equiano takes over from the cowardly and incompetent white captain. The captain orders the hatches to be nailed down on the slaves in the hold. Equiano countermands the order and the hatches are not nailed down. (II.44) The slaves, however, are still delivered to their destination.

Clearly the emancipation of the slave Equiano is not to be brought about by the mere payment of forty pounds sterling; he has also to act out roles of dominance through which he can shed his slave past. Yet it may seem ironical, though not consciously so perhaps, that the new role involves him in assuming the title of Captain (the rank of the man who first bought him as a slave, as well as of the man who helped to free him) and acting out that role as master of a slave ship.

After gaining his freedom, Equiano worked as surgeon's mate to Dr. Irving on expeditions to the Arctic in 1772 and to the Indians of Central America in 1775, and as gentleman's valet on a grand tour of the Mediterranean. In 1786 his status among the black people of Britain was acknowledged in his appointment as Commissary for Stores to the Sierra Leone expedition. But even in this he found his authority undermined not only by the enemies of abolition, who continued to attack him in the press, but also by men who should have been his friends and colleagues. Shortly after taking up his appointment, he was at loggerheads with several of the leaders of the expedition, notably the Agent in charge, Irwin, and the Chaplain, the Rev. Fraser. Equiano accused Irwin of misappropriating equipment and foodstuffs and gained himself a reputation of troublemaker. Captain Thompson, who commanded the expedition, acknowledged, "I do not find Mr. Irwin the least calculated to conduct this business: as I have never observed any wish of his to facilitate the sailing of the ships, or any steps taken by him which might indicate that he had the welfare of the people the least at heart." But he writes in the same letter criticizing "the conduct of Mr. Gustavus Vasa, which has been, since he held the Commissary, turbulent and discontented, taking every means to actuate the minds of the Blacks to discord."[35] Fraser complained that the black members of the expedition had, under Equiano's influence, absented themselves from divine service and public prayers "for no other reason whatever than that I am *white*,"[36] and even Granville Sharp was to write to his brother that "all the jealousies and animosities between the Whites and the Blacks had subsided, and that they had been very orderly since Mr. Vasa and two or three other discontented persons had been left on shore at Plymouth."[37] Whatever rift there might have been between Equiano and Sharp seems to have been healed, however; Equiano continues to have nothing but praise for him, and Sharp was at Equiano's deathbed. "He was a sober, honest man—and I went to see him when he lay upon his death bed, and had lost his voice so that he could only whisper," wrote Sharp to his niece many years later.[38]

The evidence indicates that Equiano was doing no more than his duty in drawing attention to the neglect of his fellows. Those in charge appear to have been often complacent or condescending, at worst downright dishonest, but as a black man, Equiano was virtually bound to experience conflicts, both within himself and outwardly, in his relations with even a benevolent white authority. Black people were expected to be acted upon rather than take the lead themselves, and for some of the supporters of abolition, charity could be an act of self-gratification, the pleasures of which were not so palatable when seasoned with the aggressive, uncompromising, and no doubt irritating rectitude of Equiano and his like. Even from his abolitionist friends, then, Equiano might sometimes experience wounding behavior, and one such slight is the subject of a letter written to him by a Susannah Atkinson in March 1791. "Suffer yourself not to be hurt with triffles (*sic*) since you must in this transitory and deceitful world meet with many unpleasing changes," she writes; "I was sorry we should be so unfortunate as to recommend you to any who would in the least slight you . . ."[39] That the activities of Equiano on behalf of his fellow Africans could arouse racist feelings even in the heart of an abolitionist can be seen in a letter to the *Public Advertiser* responding to his criticisms of the Sierra Leone preparations. He is accused of "advancing falsehoods as deeply black as his jetty face," and the author of the letter adds a cluster of puns on Equiano's "black reports" and "dark transactions of a Black."[40] So Equiano never returned to Africa, but left the expedition at Plymouth and came back to London, where he wrote his autobiography during the next two years. Perhaps we should be glad of his dismissal from his post of Commissary, for it left him free to carry out a task which many would consider more important, the writing of his autobiography. Equiano's *Interesting Narrative* is not only a unique document for the modern reader; in its own day, it was distributed so widely by its itinerant author and sold so many copies[41] that he was said by one of his contemporaries to be "a principal instrument in bringing about the motion for a repeal of the Slave-act."[42]

Notes

1. In the accounts of William Bell, Factor to the Duke of Gordon, July 27, 1762; Scottish R.O. GD44/51/80.

2. A.L. Reade, *Johnsonian Gleanings Part II: Francis Barber* (London, 1912). A useful account of Francis Barber is to be found in Folarin Shyllon, *Black People in Britain 1555-1833* (London, 1977), pp. 179-186.

3. For a summary, see Shyllon, op. cit., pp. 41-3.

4. Anon., *Nocturnal Reveals, or the History of Kings Place* (London, 1779), I. pp. 210-232 for a lively account of one or two of Soubise's adventures.

5. Margaret Priestley, 'Philip Quaque of Cape Coast,' in Philip Curtin (ed.), *Africa Remembered* (Madison, 1967), pp. 99-139.

6. Shyllon, op. cit., pp. 61-2.

7. Anon., *An Oration Pronounced On the 29th of July, 1829, After the Funeral Dirge of Doctor John Baptiste Philip Who died on the 16th of June, 1829, In Trinidad* (London 1829). The doctoral dissertation dated 1815 is in Edinburgh University Library.

8. Anon. [Zachary Macaulay], *The African Prince, A Sketch of the Life of John Henry Naimbanna* (London n.d. [1796]); Prince Hoare, *Memoirs of Granville Sharp* (London, 1820), pp. 364-371.

9. Christopher Fyfe, *History of Sierra Leone* (London, 1962), p. 77.

10. Douglas Grant, *The Fortunate Slave* (London, 1968).

11. Julian D. Mason (ed.), *The Poems of Phillis Wheatley* (Chapel Hill, 1966).

12. See below, footnote 21, for this speech.

13. *A Narrative of the Most remarkable Particulars in the Life of James Albert Ukawsaw Gronniosaw, an African Prince, As related by Himself* (London n.d. [c.1770]). There were several subsequent editions.

14. *Letters of the Late Ignatius Sancho* (London, 1782); *The Interesting Narrative of the Life of Olaudah Equiano, or Gustavus Vassa the African, Written by Himself* (London, 1789); *Thoughts and Sentiments on the Evil and Wicked Traffic of the Slavery and Commerce of the Human Species Humbly Submitted to The Inhabitants of Great-Britain, by Ottobah Cugoano, A Native of Africa* (London, 1787). All three volumes have been reissued in facsimile, with an introduction and notes by Paul Edwards, by Dawson of Pall Mall, 1968, 1969, 1969 respectively, and all quotations below are from these editions. Pages are indicated in brackets.

15. John Humphreys Davies (ed.), *The Morris Letters* (Aberystwyth, 1907-9), I p. 21.

16. H.T. Caterall, *Judicial Cases Concerning American Slavery and the Negro* (Washington, 1926), I pp. 9-11.

17. For a useful recent summary of these cases, see Shyllon, op. cit., pp. 10-38.

18. Edwards, *Equiano*, p. xvi.

19. Collected in Appendix II of Shyllon, op. cit., pp. 267-272.

20. One of William Sancho's letters survives in ms. See Edwards, *Sancho*, p. vi.

21. A very striking instance of this is found in a speech made by John Henry Naimbanna, quoted here in the version to be found in Zachary Macaulay's pamphlet on him, but also, in a slightly different version, in Prince Hoare's *Memoirs of Granville Sharp* (see footnote 8):

He was present once at the House of Commons during a debate on the Slave Trade. He there heard a gentleman who spoke in favor of the trade, say some things very degrading to the characters of his country-men. He was so enraged at this, that on coming out of the House, he cried out with great vehemence, "I will kill that fellow where ever I meet him, for he has told lies of my country;" he was put in mind of the christian duty of forgiving his enemies; on which he answered nearly in the following words:—"If a man should rob me of my money, I can for-give him; if a man should shoot at me, I can forgive him; if a man should sell me and all my family to a slave ship, so that we should pass all the rest of our lives in slavery in the West Indies, I can forgive him; but, (added he with much emotion) if a man takes away the character of the people of my country, I never can forgive him." Being asked why he would not extend his forgiveness to one who took away the character of the people of his country, he answered.—"If a man should try to kill me, or should sell my family for slaves, he would do an injury to as many as he might kill or sell, but if any one takes away the character of black people, that man injures black people all over the world; and when he has once taken away their character, there is nothing which he may not do to black people ever after. That man, for instance, will beat black men, and say, 'O, it is only a black man, why should I not beat him?' That man will make slaves of black people; for when he has taken away their character, he will say, 'O, they are only black people, why should not I make them slaves?' That man will take away all the people of Africa, if he can catch them, and if you ask him, 'Why do you take away those people' he will say, 'O, they are only black people, they are not like white people, why should I not take them?' That is the rea-son why I cannot forgive the man who takes away the character of the people of my country."

He was then told that it would be very wicked to kill this gentleman, or even not to forgive him, seeing the Scriptures said, "Forgive your enemies."—"Vengence is mine, I will repay, saith the Lord." This im-mediately quieted his rage, and he became as calm as a lamb, nor was used afterwards to express the least anger against the gentleman who had so much offended him.

22. Edwards, *Equiano*, lvii, f.2.

23. For an account of Equiano's appointment to and dismissal from the post of Commissary for Stores, see Edwards, *Equiano*, xxx-xlv.

24. Edwards, *Equiano*, xxxiii.

25. See footnote 19.

26. Hoare, op. cit., p. 236; Edwards, *Equiano*, pp. lvi-lvii.

27. Hoare, op. cit., p. 247; Edwards, *Cugoano*, p. vii.

28. The full text of the letter is in Edwards, *Cugoano*, pp. xxi-xxiii.

29. Shyllon, op. cit., pp. 251-3 gives the letter in full, in his very valuable Appendix I on the letters of Equiano.

30. Cambridge R.O., Papers of John Audley (executor of Equiano's will).

31. The quotations from Equiano's will are taken from a transcript in the John Audley Papers, in which Joanna's letter of receipt of her inheritance is also to be found.

32. The letter is in the Hornby Collection of the City of Liverpool Library. Its text is printed in Edwards, *Equiano*, pp. xiv-xv and its authenticity discussed in Paul Edwards, '. . . *written by himself:* A Manuscript Letter of Olaudah Equiano', *Notes and Queries* (N.S.) Vol. 15, No. 6 (June 1968), 222-225.

33. For a discussion of Equiano's description of 'Eboe', see Edwards, *Equiano*, pp. xviii-xxx.

34. See Ian Duffield and Paul Edwards, 'Equiano's Turks and Christians: An Eighteenth-Century African View of Islam,' in *Journal of African Studies* Vol. 2, No. 4 (Winter 1975-76), 433-444.

35. P.R.O. London: T.i./643. See Edwards, *Equiano*, pp. xlii-xliii.

36. *Public Advertiser* July 2, 1787. See Edwards, *Equiano*, p. xli.

37. Prince Hoare, *Memoirs of Granville Sharpe* (London, 1820), p. 313.

38. Granville Sharp Papers, Hardwicke Court, Glos., Sharp to his niece Jemima, February 22, 1811.

39. Cambridge R.O., Papers of John Audley.

40. *Public Advertiser*, April 14, 1787. See Edwards, *Equiano*, pp. xxvii-xxxix.

41. At least eight editions were published in Britain during Equiano's lifetime, as well as an American edition and translations into Dutch and German. Many more appeared after his death: see Edwards, *Equiano*, pp. vii-viii.

42. Thomas Digges, December 25, 1791. See Edwards, *Equiano*, Appendix B.

Crushed Geraniums:
Juan Francisco Manzano
and the Language of Slavery

SUSAN WILLIS

Malo es ser esclavo, pero mil veces peor es ser esclavo despierto;
un esclavo que piensa es una protesta viva, es un juez mudo y
terrible que esta estudiando el crimen social.

Francisco Calcagno

The scene is a slave compound on the island of Barbados in the eighteenth century. The narrator is seated beside a young girl named Gow
and her six year old brother, Thry, who lies curled in her lap. They have
been in Barbados about a week; have been fed very little; and, while
they await being sold, have been set to work picking oakum. Thry is
hungry and begs his sister to get him something to eat, which of course
is impossible.

> They both burst into a flood of tears, which continued for some time.
> After their lamentation ceased, she spoke to me, saying, I should not
> feel so bad if the white people had not taken from me the bracelet of
> gold, which was on my right arm, as my grand-father, when my grand-
> mother died, took it from her arm and gave it to me (on account of my
> bearing her name) as a token of remembrance and affection, which was
> always expressed; and now I have nothing in this foreign land to re-
> member her by, it makes me feel as if it would break my heart; but
> what's worse than all, I fear, if they don't kill me, they will take away
> my little brother; and if they don't starve him, he will mourn himself to
> death. . . . At this instant the driver came in with a long whip under his
> arm, and placed himself in the center of the circle in which we were
> chained, he stood about four minutes, cast his eyes upon the slaves, a
> dead silence prevailed through the whole house except the re-echoing
> of sobs and sighs. He fixed his eyes upon us, stepped up to the bunch of
> oakum which Gow had been picking, took it up in his hand with some
> vehemence, threw it down instantly, struck her upon the side of her
> head with the butt end of the whip, which laid her quivering upon the
> ground for one or two minutes. When she began to recover and to get
> upon her hands and feet, during which time he continued whipping her.

Her little brother began to scream and cry, begging in his artless manner and unintelligible dialect for her relief. She at length regained her former situation, when he again turned the butt of his whip and struck her on the other temple, which levelled her with the ground; she seemed frantic, and instantly rose upon her feet, the driver with a terrible grin and countenance, that bespoke his brutality, struck her with a drawing blow over the left shoulder, which came round under her right arm, near the pit of her stomach, and cut a hole through, out of which the blood gushed every breath. The wretch continued whipping until he had satiated his unprovoked vengeance, then he sat her up and handed her a rope to pick, he composedly walked round to see some of the rest of the slaves. She sat reeling backwards and forwards for about two or three minutes, the blood gushing from her wounds every breath, then fell down and expired. Thry, her little brother, went and laid his head upon her neck and said, Come Gow, don't cry any more, come get up, don't go to sleep and leave me awake, because I am so lonesome I cannot bear it, do wake up.[1]

The plight of the kidnapped children, torn from a loving family; the sorrow of the young girl whose own anguish is heightened by her need to care for her little brother; and finally her merciless beating, from which there is no escape and no one to comfort her dying moments, make this a most profoundly horrible scene of human victimization and suffering. The powerful emotions stirred by this passage are largely due to the narrator's sympathetic understanding of the young girl's situation, expressed in the care with which he describes her background and her tender regard for her younger brother. Because the reader perceives the episode from the narrator's point of view, he cannot help but experience its deep emotional impact.

What I would propose is that understanding the position of the narrator is the key to understanding the slave narrative as a whole. What this passage clearly demonstrates is the narrator's limited comprehension of his new situation as a slave. While he has full access to his own past experience and that of his people, he is unable to grasp the motives behind the overseer's actions. This bestows a deeply human quality to his description of the young girl, whom he identifies with and understands; and at the same time renders the overseer's actions all the more brutal because they are given as raw information.

The striking horror of the scene is largely produced by its apparent spontaneity. It seems the overseer, for no reason at all, has chosen to torture and kill a totally innocent girl, whom he falls upon at random. This, however is not the case; and if we look at the raw information supplied by the narrator, interpreting it with a basic knowledge of Caribbean slavery, which the narrator, himself, lacked, we gain a fuller understanding of the episode, which while it diminishes the brute spontaneity of the overseer's actions by supplying the missing motives, in no way lessens the guilt of his extreme cruelty.

First of all it is important to note that the slaves are recent arrivals. They have not yet been sold and in the meantime have been set to work picking oakum, which, by comparison to the extreme economic importance of their future toil in the cane fields, is a somewhat insignificant task. This, then, is a transitional period; and the slaves, half famished and lamenting their lost homelands, pass the uncertain hours with meaningless toil. So as not to let them experience the moment as one of relaxation or indecision on the part of the overlords, an example must be made. To introduce them to the full meaning of slavery—the absolute and unquestionable authority of the white man over the black—someone must be killed.

The choice of victim is not as spontaneous as the narrator seems to suggest. This is clear even in the way he has described the scene; the overseerer "stood about four minutes, cast his eyes upon the slaves, a dead silence prevailed through the whole house except the re-echoing of sobs and sighs. He fixed his eyes upon us." Obviously surveying the group, the overseer selects his victim. What gives the narration a sense of spontaneity, even though the process of selection takes four minutes, is the narrator's inability to know what is happening and for what purpose.

Then, too, the choice is not random. That the overseer singles out the young girl, as the narrator senses but cannot explain, is directly related to the bunch of oakum she had been working on which the overseer seizes and disdainfully casts aside. This is an important bit of information which the narrator cannot interpret from his limited point of view. Quite possibly the young girl had done the least work on her pile of oakum; most probably, out of the group of slaves, she is the least productive and offers the least potential for future production. What the narrator doesn't know is that Caribbean slavery, based on an intensive, one-crop economy, needed a steady supply of young adult male slaves. Women were less important, for as long as the slave trade continued, there was no need to tolerate less productive field laborers solely for the purpose of reproducing the labor force. A young girl not yet big enough or strong enough to be a fully productive field laborer, and not yet mature enough to function sexually was the least valuable property. Her younger brother escapes murder solely on the promise of his future productivity.

Moreover, the overseer's actions were premeditated, intended for their pedagogical effect. This is evident as he "composedly walked round to see some of the rest of the slaves" while the young girl agonizes in the throws of death. Parading his authority and surveying his defenseless chattels, he has made sure everyone gets the message by placing the oakum once more in the dying girl's hand—for the slave there is only work and death.

To varying degrees all slave narratives are conditioned by the narrator's partial understanding of his situation. While the narrator can report on his condition, giving a full, often tactile, account of physical and emotional experiences, he has no access to the realm of causality. He is a blind receiver whose perspective on the motives behind all the demands and actions which govern his life has been short circuited. This then places the narrator in a very different relationship to the reader than what normally obtains in the tradition of prose literature; for the narrator often cannot supply his reader with meaning.

Perspectival limitations are particularly strong in the slave narratives from the Caribbean, where the influence of abolitionists, either as editors or instigators of the narrative, is not a strong factor. By comparison, the fugitive North American slave, once in the free states and in contact with abolitionists, could, with broadened perspective, look back over the events of his life and understand them in a more meaningful way. Essentially, the first hand experience of the difference in mode of production between the slave-based agricultural South and the wage-labor North, took the fugitive out of the microcosmic master/slave relationship and supplied the logic necessary to write, not raw data, but a meaningful narrative. Then, at a secondary level, the strong influence of Christian religion so often voiced in the American slave narrative, functions as a means to further interpret and evaluate past experience.

In comparison with other slave narratives published in North America, the Boyrereau Brinch text is atypical. After escaping from the Caribbean, he wound up in Vermont where the abolitionist, Benjamin Prentiss, transcribed his memoirs. However, his narration occurred at a time prior to the great interest in slave literature (1810) and so is less influenced by abolition as a cause and the American slave narrative as a genre. The narrator, not fully aware of an audience and the purpose to which his narrative might be put, is not constrained to supply meaning. Brinch, in the process of relating the past, re-experiences the lack of perspective which conditioned his life as a slave and narrates the raw unevaluated material of experience as an assemblage of undigested bits and pieces. Even his appeals to Scripture, which occur unexpectedly throughout the text, are given as data, juxtaposed, rather than integrated in the narration.

A few decades after Brinch's narration, in Havana, Cuba, Juan Francisco Manzano, a recently liberated mulatto, wrote a narrative where the lack of perspective and the distance from an audience produced an extremely disordered narration. To understand Manzano's narrative it is first of all necessary to define his relationship to literature. While he was not writing in a total void, his access to literary texts, tradition and audience was limited by the two-fold influence of slavery and colonialism. The early nineteenth century Cuban reading public was comprised basically of sugarocrats and urban professionals, whose class interests were tied to sugar production—neither of which could have been an audience for Manzano's narrative text. Furthermore, those who could read were often more interested in cards and dice and only a few enlightened individuals actually sought out literary and scientific reading material.[2]

Nevertheless, nineteenth century Cuba did possess a strong center of literary interest, organized and defined by Domingo del Monte and his circle of writers and critics.[3] While its influence was highly localized, it had close contact with European critical debates, sponsored indigenous literary production, and published more than one literary journal. The critique of neo-classicism and the general espousal of romanticism was one of the group's central concerns. The strong interest in Rousseau, Goethe and Chateaubriand provided an atmosphere favorable to autobiography and confessional literature, which suggests a possible generic background for Manzano's narration.

While many of our observations will suggest the confessional[4] nature of Manzano's text (the way in which it becomes a vehicle for self observation through monological discourse and the re-living of past experience in the process of narrating), the direct influence of the del Monte group and its critical concerns ought not to be taken too seriously. While Manzano was a participant in the literary circle, he was not one of its central members. Moreover, the group saw him as a poet rather than a prose essayist and thus would have had only minimal influence on his prose writing.

Another possible area of literary influence is the slave narrative itself and its relationship to abolition as a movement. While Manzano's narrative was probably prompted by his contact with the English abolitionist, Richard R. Madden,[5] the slave narrative as a genre had no real presence in Cuba. Rather, anti-slavery was the literary concern of the novel; notably, Suarez y Romero's *Francisco*.

While the influence of literary models on Manzano's text was at best partial, the lack of tangible audience was perhaps the most significant factor. Just as Manzano was not writing for the reading public of sugarocrats and professionals, so too the small group of anti-slavery writers and critics could not have been his intended audience. To some extent he wrote his fragmented and incoherent remembrances as confessions directed to himself with no real audience in mind. But this is only a partial explanation; for Manzano's text (much like many contemporary texts from the third world) is a text written for export—entrusted with Madden on the eve of his departure from Cuba and destined for the English abolitionist audience. If this was Manzano's ultimate audience, it (being foreign and unknowable) could have had no concrete presence or function for the writer. In this way, all of Manzano's possible audiences—the indigenous, the self, and the foreign—are partialities, which, as the text demonstrates, are incapable of fulfilling the demands of narrative communication.

What one notices first about the Manzano text is its total ignorance of form. Paragraphs begin and end at random, sometimes encompassing only a few sentences, sometimes stretching over pages. Indeed, the Soviet linguist, Volosinov, has observed that the ability to formulate orderly paragraphs representing whole conceptual units is directly related to the narrator's awareness of his audience. A paragraph is "a vitiated dialogue worked into the body of a monologic utterance." And "if we could imagine speech that absolutely ignored the addressee (an impossible kind of speech, of course), we would have a case of speech with organic partition reduced to the minimum."[6] In Manzano's narration the impossible becomes reality. Rather than a "speech" directed to an audience, his is an interiorized monologue entrusted to Madden and sent like a message in a bottle to London and an unknown readership.

Directly related to the text's breakdown at the level of the paragraph is its flagrant disregard for sentence punctuation. As is generally agreed among stylistic critics,[7] the sentence is the basic unit of meaning in prose writing. As such, it functions to "direct" the reader's apprehension of the material in a particular and meaningful way. However, Manzano, recording his own interior voice and writing with only partial awareness of literary models, is not constrained to supply sentence punctuation. Consequently, the reader can follow the text only by suspending learned habits of reading and allowing the text to speak. Only then does the narration become logical. Otherwise, sentences run on and subjects get lost or attached to the wrong verbs. However the experience of reading in the context of speech patterns is not unrewarding, for it suggests a wholly different direction prose literature might have taken had it not been for the invention of punctuation which eliminates textual variety and readerly sport.

Obviously the narration has a strong oral orientation; however it exhibits a very special form of orality. Manzano, whose punishments occasionally included field labor, was primarily a houseslave, a *falderillo*, or personal page, who from the age of ten had to wait upon a cruel and pretentious woman of the provincial landed elite. His was the world of operas, *tertulias* and gambling halls. His language was never that of the field workers; consequently his access to oral culture, in the traditional sense, was certainly limited.

The oral influence on his narration derives instead from poetry and the circumstances under which he learned to write. While his first mistress, something of a benevolent aristocrat, sent him to school as she had his mother before him, Manzano's education was early ended by the death of this mistress. From then on, he received no formal training, was discouraged from learning to read and write on his own, and only sporadically came in contact with people, basically professionals and artists, who gave him assistance. However, with only the rudiments of reading and writing, Manzano was able to become an accomplished poet. This he achieved by cultivating his innate ability to listen, memorize, and, when allowed, recite. As a houseslave, he was exposed to (or could overhear) prodigious sermons (sometimes two hours long) and poetry readings by local artists or devotees—all of which he memorized, mumbling and musing over them through the long hours of his daily and nightly toil. It was not long before his inner voice was able to compose and record for memory his own *décimas*. That his poetry, particularly one unpublished poem which we will examine, transcends the lifeless, second-rate provincial models he had to work with gives all the more credit to his remarkable achievement and poetic insight.

Born in 1797, Manzano divides his life in two phases: a prehistory of childhood plenitude, during which his first mistress gave him every advantage; and his "real history" which began after her death in 1809. While the narrative follows a linear sequentiality and there are no digressions, it is nevertheless disorderly. On close analysis, while the lack of punctuation contributes to the confusion, narrative disorder is more profoundly linked to the fragmentation of the episodes described and the seemingly arbitrary selection of material for narration. Because the overall text is extremely short, it is obvious that some process of selecting certain events out of the flow of life experience has occurred. However, there appears to be no meaningful logic behind the selection.

Here is where the Brinch narrative, with its perspectival limitations and partial access to meaning, supplies the key. Manzano's text is incomprehensible only if we try to make meaning a criterion for narration. By trying to force his narration into conventional categories of prose, we overlook and exclude the possibility of other organizational features.

Once we suspend the need for meaning, a very different narrative framework is revealed. Essentially, the narrative is based on a series of discontinuous events, each of which is a crystalized moment of torture.

For Manzano, the child of twelve, the first of these memorable moments is of dark and dank solitary confinement, where tormented by thirst, hunger and cold, and liable for a whipping if he should cry out, his active mind played host to nightmare visions.

> I suffered for the slightest act of boyish mischief, shut up in a coal pit with not even a plank for a bed nor anything to wrap myself up in for more than twenty four hours I was extremely frightened and wanted to eat my jail as can still be seen needs in the brightest noontime light a strong candle for one to see anything inside it here after suffering a severe whipping I was shut up under orders and the threat of a severe punishment for anyone who might give me even a drop of water, what I suffered there afflicted with hunger, and well I know it, tormented with fear, in such a deep and isolated place separated from the house, in a backyard next to a stable, and a pestilent, foul-smelling trash heap, along side a wet, infested and noxious outhouse which was only separated by a wall full of holes, a den for huge rats that walked over me without even stopping, so afraid was everyone in the house that absolutely no one dared even if they had the opportunity to give me even a bite my head was full of stories about evil things from long ago, of apparitions from beyond the grave and of spells cast by the dead so that when a troop of rats rushed out making a lot of noise I imagined the cave was full of ghosts and cried out asking for pity they then took me out and tormented me with so many lashes that I couldn't take any more and they shut me up again keeping the key in my mistress's own room.[8]

The words tumbling out in a rush, these lines, while written some twenty years later, bear the stamp of fresh experience as if they were spoken by the young Manzano only moments after being removed from the pit and allowed to seek comfort in his mother's waiting arms. The lack of sentence divisions gives the narrative a hurried and unreflected appearance as if the narrator wanted to say everything at once—the rats, the ghosts, the damp, the darkness, the stench, the people who might have helped him, and those who intensified his suffering—all are given in the form of narrative raw material, which another, more literary hand, might have transformed into a coherent narration. It is this disregard for literary convention, the result of the narrator's separation from an audience, which differentiates Manzano's narration from the North American slave narratives.

Although Manzano openly expresses the desire for readerly contact—someone to verify that his cell really was as dark as he claims—his writing shows that he has no sense of a reader or how to direct the reader's apprehension of his story. This is particularly evident in the unintended—and consequently ridiculous—juxtaposition within the phrase, "I was extremely frightened and wanted to eat my jail. . . ."

While the rush of words that the passage evokes is visibly related to its lack of sentence markers, it is a direct consequence of extreme parataxis. Substantive phrase follows upon substantive phrase with no more than a comma, a reiteration of the subject or some new piece of descriptive detail to bind the phrases together. Rendering a strong sense of immediacy, the passage records sensory data but cannot account for causal relationships. It is significant that the only hypotactic construction introduces a troop of rats—of a lower order than the condemned slave and therefore belonging to a system of causality to which he has access. "Paratactic bluntness" is the phrase used by Auerbach to describe Roland's inescapable doom and it equally applies here. In parataxis "everything must happen as it does happen, it could not be otherwise and there is no need for explanatory connectives."[9]

While Manzano informs us that he was often punished in the coal pit (sometimes two or three times a week) he describes the event only once. Significantly, all the episodes of torture described in the narration are given as single, isolated events, each different from the others and therefore all the more horrifying for its novelty. These form the nodal points of the narrative, and at the same time suggest the sadistic nature of his mistress whose agile mind had but one task, and that to conceive ever new ways of torturing her young slave.

While the organization of Manzano's narration is based on a series of isolated anecdotes of torture, other Caribbean slave narratives demonstrate the same importance of the nodal moment, where novelty and singularity are not necessarily related to torture. The most interesting example is the adventure filled narration of Olaudah Equiano,[10] who for very good reasons has been called the Caribbean Robinson Crusoe. Not a field slave, but a ship's steward, who served under a variety of Caribbean traders and Mediterranean military commanders, Equiano's narrative has as its basic structuring unit the moment of discovery. Each nodal moment is marked by the confrontation with some new object, cultural practice, situation, scientific discovery, religious revelation, personality or geographic terrain. His long term achievements, such as learning to read and write, mastering the art of navigation, and earning enough money through petty trade to eventually buy his own freedom, are secondary to the narrative emphasis on the moment of discovery. With each episode the narrative renews itself, and in each discovery creates something of the vivid shock experienced by the Aztecs when they first beheld their mounted Spanish conquerors. In this way, the narrative is a continual expression of the collision between two very different worlds, in which the slave, ignorant of the new situation, is made to feel inferior. Then too, in a deeper sense, Equiano's discoveries express the same uncertainty about the future and inability to attach meaning to the events which mark his life as a slave that inform the more brutal slave narrations.

For Manzano, the second nodal moment occurs when he, accompanying his mistress home late one night, as he had done on many a previous night, is lulled to sleep by the motion of the carriage. He wakes to see, glimmering behind, the lantern which he is supposed to carry. Leaping down from the carriage, he is able to retrieve the lantern but it is impossible to regain the disappearing carriage. Numb with fear, he knows he must return on foot. Once at the hacienda he is seized and taken away to be punished. His mother intercedes but is struck down by the angered *mayoral*. This so maddens the young Manzano that he strikes back at the mayoral, biting and scratching like "a lion." For this impudence, both Manzano and his mother are to be whipped.

> they led us out my mother brought to the place of sacrifice for the first time in her life even though she was a part of the hacienda she was exempt from work being the wife of a respected slave [a carpenter who probably bought the privilege to work his own jobs]; seeing my mother in this state I couldn't cry, move, or flee I was shaking all over the four Negroes took hold of her and threw her on the ground to whip her I asked God to help her I restrained myself but on hearing the first whip lash, transformed into a lion or tiger or the wildest beast I was ready to lose my life [for her] at the hands of don Silvestre [the mayoral] but let's leave to silence the rest of this painful scene.[11]

The novel feature of this episode is the punishment of the mother, who, because she had never been whipped before, had been Manzano's one source of emotional strength. The fact that she too is subject to punishment for the slightest affront to authority demonstrates that she is really nothing more than a slave. The episode has a pedagogical purpose similar to the beating of the young girl in the Brinch narrative. However, while the mother's punishment is intended totally to demoralize her son, and it does have this overall effect, Manzano's immediate response is to fight back. This rebellious outburst is a significant opposition to the narrator's admitted sense of martyrdom which he expresses when he refers to the place of punishment as the place of "sacrifice." It is important to understand that the slave's deep desire for freedom can manifest itself spontaneously and often in apparent contradiction to his overall attitude of excessive passivity and timidity. While Manzano presents himself as long-suffering and totally defenseless, he is nevertheless capable of flying at four powerful adults armed with whips and the tremendous weight of authority. Many years later, the same submerged desire for freedom causes the poet to flee his mistress and undertake a hazardous night-time ride to Havana. As is the case in numerous slave narratives,[12] Manzano's determination to be free comes as a result of some new threat which brings with it a tightening of the bonds of slavery. For Manzano, this occurs on his coming of age, a time when his first mistress had intimated that he would be freed. However, seeing that the new mistress has no such intentions, and instead plans to condemn him to the rural hacienda, Manzano decides his only recourse is to seek his own freedom. This decision radically changes the organization of the narrative for it supplies the sense of a long range goal, which Manzano, living from moment to moment, had previously lacked. However, because the impetus to freedom comes toward the end of the first part of Manzano's narration, and because the second part was never published[13] the narrative effects of this decision cannot be fully known, and manifest themselves only in the persistently stated longing for the metropolis of Havana, which by comparison to the country hacienda, becomes charged with the illusion of freedom.

There is, however, one very false note in the above passage and that is its melodramatic closing. The narrator's veil of silence smacks of literary convention,[14] which seems out of place by comparison with the full, vivid detail and immediate nature of the rest of the narration. Moreover, this sort of artificial lapse in the narration occurs more than once and always at an extreme moment of torture. The following is a good example:

The mistress is strolling in her garden and Manzano, her page, must follow her every footstep. He is rather bored, and in a detached state, passes the time mentally composing poems. While wandering about the garden, he has picked a leaf from a fragrant geranium, which he absent-mindedly crumples between his fingers. Upon leaving the garden and entering the closed atmosphere of the house, the mistress passes very close to her slave, notices the fragrance about his body and is thrown into a horrible rage.

What do you have in your hands; I was as still as death my body suddenly frozen and without being able to keep my two legs from shaking, I dropped the remaining pieces [of leaf] on the floor she took my hands and smelled them and taking hold of the pieces as if it were a great pile, a whole bush, the most audacious act, my nose was broken and immediately in came the administrator, don Lucas Rodriguez an emigrant from Santo Domingo to whom she turned me over, it must have been six o'clock in the evening and in the depths of winter the carriage was

ready to leave for town and I was to have gone but how fragile luck is
for the one who is subject to its vicissitudes, I never had a moment of
certainty as can be seen in this case and in many others, I was taken to
the place of punishment, a former infirmary where fifty beds fit along
two walls since the field laborers from the hacienda and those from the
San Miguel plantation were taken there but at that time it was empty
and not used for anything the stocks were there and only an occasional
cadaver was left there until the time to carry it to town for burial left
standing there in the freezing cold without a single blanket I was shut
up scarsely did I find myself alone in that place when I seemed to see
the dead rise up and wander about the room there was a broken window
which gave on a river near a steep place which made a waterfall cas-
cading without stopping and with every cascade I seemed to see a dead
man entering from beyond the tomb imagine how the night passed it
had hardly begun to grow light when I heard the door bolt slide a
contra mayoral enters followed by the administrator they take out a
plank intended for me which was attached to a gibbet from which hung
a bunch of hooks, about fifty of them at the foot of the plank I see the
administrator wrapped in his cape from under his scarf he tells the
others in a rough voice to gag me they bind my hands tie them up like
Christ's they pick me up and put my feet in the two openings [of the
stocks] and also tie my feet Oh God! let us draw a veil over the rest of
this scene my blood has poured out I lost consciousness[15]

What makes this episode of torture so poignant is the way in which
novelty is used to re-create well established fears. Knowing that Manzano is terrified by solitary confinement, the administrator (who we must
assume acts under the direction of the mistress) shuts him in the cold,
empty infirmary rather than the coal pit, where Manzano is again
haunted by night-long visions of the dead.

It is not gratuitous that such an extreme form of physical punishment
should follow what appears to be so trivial an act. What the slave learns
in this, another instance of pedagogical torture, is that damage done to
private property is the greatest crime. The reason why property is so
highly significant is a direct expression of capitalism. That slavery was a
mode of capitalist production has been demonstrated by Eric Williams,[16]
whose central thesis is that colonial slavery provided the terrific increase
in accumulation needed to transform European capitalism from the commercial to the industrial form. Later, as an extension of this process, the
influx of European finance capital and the large scale importation of
industrial machinery then made slavery unprofitable and brought an end
to this mode of production.

Williams's work is important in its attempt to define a necessary relationship between slavery and capitalism, which according to traditional
economics are separate historical modes which come into simultaneous
existence only because of unequal development. However, it is not until

Immanuel Wallerstein's[17] elaboration of dependency theory that slavery can be understood as a mode of production within capitalism. Whereas Williams sees the relationship between capitalism and slavery solely in terms of accumulation, Wallerstein defines it as one of three forms of labor control in a global capitalist system, where the resulting modes of production define three dialectically related economic areas: the periphery, semipheriphery and core. From this point of view, once capitalism comes into existence it governs all modes of production from the third world periphery, where a single crop economy and slave based production are determined by the demands of a global market; to the Eastern European semiperiphery, where the dominant mode is coerced serf labor; and finally, the European core, which gives birth to the form wage labor.

It is significant that theorists not trained in dependency economics have also sensed the global nature of capitalism.[18] Certainly C.L.R. James's description of slave labor captures the essence of Wallerstein's theory:

> When three centuries ago the slaves came to the West Indies, they entered directly into the large-scale agriculture of the sugar plantation, which was a modern system. It further required that the slaves live together in a social relation far closer than any proletariat of the time. The cane when reaped had to be rapidly transported to what was a factory production. The product was shipped abroad for sale. Even the cloth the slaves wore and the food they ate was imported. The Negroes, therefore, from the very start lived a life that was in its essence a modern life.[19]

Essentially, Manzano's crushed geranium is not a part of nature, nor did it ever belong to the natural order. Nature exists only for tribal economy; as such, it is a part of the slave's cultural past. In the Caribbean periphery all that might be seen as nature—the freshly turned soil, the orderly cane rows, the vast fields of green—belong instead to the order of production. The plantation is a nature factory where the mode of production—the tools and the laborers themselves—are owned by the capitalist, who in this case appears in the guise of an agrarian rather than an industrialist. The geranium growing in the garden is thus not a natural phenomenon to be shared, enjoyed or destroyed, but a piece of capital.

Moreover, slavery and a money economy are not antagonistic. It is not gratuitous that another of Manzano's severest tortures is occasioned by the suspicion that he stole a coin. We are not dealing here with a form of feudalism (an interpretation of plantation economy often raised in Latin American economics which has no real basis in fact but seems to derive purely from the agrarian nature of production). The relationship between master and slave is not based on the feudal exchange of protection for production, governed by mutual loyalty, but on coerced bondage and the extraction of surplus value. Money becomes the universal equivalent of human lives, and the moment of torture represents the renewal and reconfirmation of the terms of the laborer's relationship to the owner of the means of production.

The logic of the system which makes torture its most significant movement confirms its place and organizational function in Manzano's narration. That the moments are so vividly described is largely due to narrative discontinuities which a more practiced writer of prose might have avoided. For example, in the passage which describes the consequences of the crushed geranium, there is a marked rupture in the narration which occurs when Manzano, confined in the infirmary, hears the door bolt slide open. Up to this point he has described everything in the past tense. However, the moment the administrator enters and the instruments of torture are revealed to him, Manzano begins to relive the horrible event, noting each detail as he re-sees it in the present tense. Here, what literary minds might criticize as a lapse in temporal form makes the scene all the more real and demonstrates how deeply these moments of torture are etched in the poet's memory. Later, the shift to the past perfect followed by the simple past ("my blood has poured out" and "I lost consciousness") expresses a total temporal disorientation which coincides with the moment of extreme physical pain. What these shifts suggest is that while Manzano relives the moment up to the commencement of torture, the remembrance of the first sensation of pain drives his narration into an empty phrase "Oh God! let us draw a veil over the rest of this scene," through which he is able to repress the memory of pain. The past perfect initiates the process of distancing the event and finally, Manzano, something of a detached bystander notes that his blood "has poured out." Distancing is fully achieved with the simple past "I lost consciousness," a moment which the author could not have felt, but only realized later upon regaining consciousness.

Here, Manzano's use of the veil of silence, which we previously criticized as lending a false note to the narration, serves an extremely meaningful function. What better means than this hollow sounding phrase to repress severe pain and agony and, at the same time and by the fact that its hollowness contrasts so sharply with the rest of the narration, suggest to the reader the inexpressible magnitude of torture. This interpretation, then, sheds light on Manzano's earlier inability to describe his mother's whipping. Rather than a genteel cover up for his mother's disgrace and pain, the veil of silence here represses Manzano's deep investment in his mother's semi-privileged position, which had become the reservoir of his own hopes and aspirations for the future, and which were then shattered the instant her beating began. By refusing to describe his mother's beating, Manzano avoids having to come to grips with the essential contradictions of slavery which manifest themselves in unlimited, unquestionable and perpetual authority. However, Manzano is not a revolutionary, nor is his moment one of radical polarization, which in the Caribbean was only achieved in Haiti.

Nevertheless, one of the most striking demystifications of Cuba as a third world colony and slavery as its appropriate mode of production is found in one of Manzano's poems. As we shall see, the poem focuses on a number of third worldisms (the mythic supports and rationalizations for peripherality), then demystifies them by demonstrating their ideological nature. Manzano's ability to see through the veil of myth suggests that the Caribbean, as the locus for the convergence of the accumulation of European capital, is the place where the contradictions of the system, expressed in the most inflated myths, are most readily exploded and reduced to their basic contradictory nature. The poem also demonstrates how Manzano, as a slave and therefore the most highly exploited link in the chain of accumulation, while limited in his ability to confront the contradictions of slavery manifested in his personal life (as the narrative voids suggest), is capable of understanding the broad system of contradictions which define the Caribbean as a whole.

Simply titled, "To Cuba" the poem was for obvious reasons not published in Cuba at the time it was written. Rather, it was presented to the abolitionist, Madden, at the time of his departure from Cuba and later translated by him and included with Manzano's narration and other of his poems in a book which Madden published in London.[20] The text I will use here is Madden's translation, whose authenticity I accept based on his able translations of other poems by Manzano which I have compared to the original Spanish versions.

TO CUBA

Cuba, of what avail that thou art fair!
Pearl of the seas, the pride of the Antilles!
If thy poor sons, have still to see thee share
The pangs of bondage, and its thousand ills;
Of what avail the verdure of thy hills?
The purple bloom the coffee plain displays
Thy canes luxuriant growth; whose culture fills
More graves than famine, or the swords find ways
To glut with victims calmly as it slays.

Of what avail that sweet streams abound
With precious ore: if wealth there's none to buy,
Thy children's rights, and not one grain is found
For learning's shrine, or for the altar nigh,
Of poor forsaken, downcast liberty!
Of what avail the riches of thy port,
Forests of masts, and ships from every sea,
If trade alone is free, and man the sport,
The spoil of trade, bears wrongs of ev'ry sort?

Oh, if the name of Cuban! makes my breast
Thrill with a moment's pride, that soon is o'er,
Or throb with joy to dream that thou art blest!
Thy sons were free—thy soil unstained with gore.
Reproach awakes me, to assail once more,
And taint that name, as if the loathsome pest
That spreads from slavery had seized the core,
Polluting both th' oppressor and the oppressed:—
Yet God be thanked, it has not reached my breast.

'Tis not alone the wretched negro's fate
That calls for pity, sad as it may be;
There's more to weep for in that hapless state
Of men who proudly boast that they are free,
Whose moral sense is warped to that degree,
That self-debasement seems to them unknown,
And life's sole object, is for means to play,
To roll a carriage, or to seek renown
In all the futile follies of the town.

Cuba! canst thou, my own beloved land,
Counsel thy children to withhold a curse,
And call to mind the deeds of that fell band
Who's boasted conquests, mark one frightful course
Of spoil and plunder, wrung by fraud or force;
Of human carnage in religious gear,
Of peace destroyed—defenceless people worse
Than rudely outraged, nay, reserved to wear
Their lives away in bondage and despair.

To think unmoved of millions of our race,
Swept from thy soil by cruelties prolonged,
Another clime then ravaged to replace
The wretched Indians; Africa then wronged
To fill the void where myriads lately thronged,
And add new guilt to that long list of crimes,

> That cries aloud, in accents trumpet-tongued,
> And shakes the cloud that gathers o'er these climes,
> Portending evil and disastrous times.
>
> Cuba, oh, Cuba, when they call thee fair!
> And rich and beautiful, the Queen of isles!
> Star of the West, and ocean's gem most rare!
> Oh, say to them who mock thee with such wiles
> Take of these flowers, and view these lifeless spoils
> That wait the worm; behold the hues beneath
> The pale cold cheek, and seek for living smiles,
> Where beauty lies not in the arms of death,
> And bondage taints not with its poisoned breath.

The poem opens with the myth of exotic third world beauty, conjuring an image of shimmering seas and jewel-like islands. It is not gratuitous that the first important literary movement to emerge from Latin America and find acceptance in the European metropolis is one based on an orgy of *exotismos.* Coming some fifty years after Manzano's poem, the Modernist movement brought to Europe a full cargo of rich clothes, rare jewels, exotic princesses; and in a highly exaggerated manner, made of the third world just what the first world had always imagined it to be; namely, the source of unlimited wealth. However, in the Manzano poem, Cuba's exotic beauty is undermined by its cliché-like formulation, something which the later Modernist poetry, convinced of its own exoticism, never achieves. In this way, the poem recognizes the ideology behind the myth, whose function is to inhibit the possibility for historical change. Essentially, the hard perfection of the pearl defines Cuba as impenetrable and unchanging; its setting in the boundless sea serves to isolate the island making it inaccessible to change.

Here, cliché works two ways. On the one hand, it expresses the durability of the myth, which takes on the well-worn acceptability of a slogan; and on the other, it manifests its own hollow nature. That mythic clichés are exceptionally durable is evident in the contemporary reiteration of the same myth in George Lamming's autobiographical novel, *In the Castle of My Skin:*

"An where's England?" Boy Blue asked.

Bob smiled and to our utter astonishment spoke with a kind of religious conviction: "Barbados or Little England, an island of coral formation set like a jewel in the Caribbean Sea."

We heard the words, and we know they weren't Bob's. "That ain't in no Michael John hist'ry book," Trumper said. " 'Cause 'tis no joke," Bob answered. " 'Tis facts. Facts."[21]

While the historical moment is pre-World War II, the island Barbados rather than Cuba, and the colonial heritage English rather than Spanish, the ideology behind the myth has the same function. "Little England" is made the hard and fast bastion of colonial integrity, indoctrinated by rote learning, and endowed with the mystique of "fact," which Lamming's novel, then, confronts and demystifies by examining the social and cultural institutions which support the ideology.

Manzano never allows the reader to believe in the Caribbean pearl, making its beauty problematical even in the opening line, "of what avail that thou art fair." Then, to totally explode the image, he names the real source of Cuba's wealth and beauty: slavery. In like manner, the lush and abundant landscape is removed from the realm of nature (which as we shall see throughout is the common source of many third world exoticisms) and rightly defined as the products of cultivation and human toil.

The second stanza continues the demystification of the natural order by redefining it in terms of the early history of the colonies. The promise of gold, or spontaneous natural wealth, which brought the Spaniards and condemned Cuba's Indian population to slavery and extinction in the mines, is devalued by comparison to the vast sums needed to buy the freedom of Cuba's black slaves. With this notion, wealth too is transformed into a capitalist category, suggesting the profits reaped in the buying and selling of human slaves.

An historical understanding of slavery as it evolved through various stages is evident throughout the poem. Manzano posits a period of pre-historical plenitude when "Thy sons [the Indians] were free—they soil unstained with gore," which was transformed into real history, defined by the wholesale acquisition of a labor force: first Indian, then African,—and finally Chinese. (The latter lies outside the historical scope of Manzano's poem, since the importation of coolies became common practice after the slave trade was abolished and at a time when the heavy use of British machinery increased the demand for production in the field. Nevertheless, the voracious production machine, which the poem describes, defines the need for ever new sources of labor supply.)

Just as the category of wealth is defined in historical terms, so too is economic accumulation. The development of the second stanza is from the early mercantile economics of exploration and conquest to the more advanced form, of commerce. In the colonial periphery, trade or commerce, is a polite term for trafficking in human lives.

The third stanza brings out a theme often encountered in the slave narrative: that slavery corrupts master and slave alike. This is clearly the case in Frederick Douglass's account of his gentle young mistress who became a fierce tiger once aware of her unlimited power over her young slave. In similar fashion, Harriet Jacobs (alias, Linda Brent) sees beyond the cruelty of slave owners and the remorseless jealousy of their wives to condemn slavery as a whole for its degradation of the oppressed and the oppressor.

The importance of Manzano's similar critique is the way in which he understands the debasement of the master class in terms of a uniquely third world phenomenon: the boredom of daily life. The essence of the third world is its distance from the European metropolis, which is the center, not only of economic accumulation, but of recognized cultural production. The colony, dependent on the importation of culture along with manufactured goods, is made to feel incapable of generating a viable indigenous culture. However, this does not imply that the inability to create culture informs all classes of the third world. As Manzano's poem clearly shows, only that class which defines itself in terms of the European center is bereft of culture and wastes itself in futile amusements and gambling.

By comparison, and this is the recurring image of daily life in another Cuban slave narrative—*Autobiografía de un Cimarron* by Esteban Montejo—the cultural life of the deprived class is extremely rich. Montejo, who at the age of 105 was discovered and interviewed by the Cuban anthropologist, Miguel Barnet, gives an account of slavery which focuses, not on work or even the master/slave relationship, but on the slaves' cultural production. He describes in detail the dances, the mode of dress, the hair styles, the types of food and their preparation, the music, religious beliefs, witchcraft and the art of curing. While his reminiscence raises a question common to all slave narratives—that is their dialogical[22] nature, wherein the selection of material and the mode of its narration is influenced by an invisible interlocutor, be it the anthropologist interviewer with a pre-determined list of questions, or the nineteenth century abolitionist who solicits the slave's life story with the tacit understanding that the narrative will be used for a specific purpose—we should not discount Montejo's narration purely on the grounds of its contrived origin. The strength of his memory of daily life, the rich detail of his account, as well as the freely loquacious mode of his narration speak for the prominence and durability of cultural production. Moreover, while Montejo was for many years a solitary cimarron, who of necessity cut himself off from human society, his understanding of culture is strictly communal in nature. The celebrations marking the día de San Juan, the contests and games in the local tavern, the practice of witchcraft—all are defined as group praxis.

From a novelistic point of view, Cuba's great contemporary writer,

Alejo Carpentier, depicts a similar contrast between the vitality of slave culture and the degradation of colonial society in his *El Reino de Este Mundo*. Set in Haiti, the novel traces the history of early slave revolt, linking the leaders, Mackandal and Boukman, to a process of political consciousness-raising realized within *vaudou* culture. Political revolt aimed at the extermination of the white overlords is understood in terms of group cultural practice and preached to the rhythm of drum beats and chants. On the other hand, *colono* culture is presented as a festering wasteland of imported European commodities—wigs, engravings and second rate operas performed by third rate artists. What's more, those *colonos* who manage to escape the fire and poison of slave revolution by fleeing to Cuba—a more secure preserve of slavery—find themselves doubly exiled from their European cultural center. To the French colonists, Spanish provincials appear uncouth, their culture barbaric. Carpentier's ultimate condemnation of the *colono* class dooms them to spend the remainder of their days in exile, living off the remnants of their hollow, commodified culture.

While the boredom of the third world is experienced as a breakdown of culture, it has its roots in concrete physical and historical factors. C.L.R. James, writing in *Black Jacobins*, attributes the "monotony" of the third world to the orderly, unchanging landscape, the result of large-scale, single crop cultivation, and to the absence of seasons which had so conditioned the European emigrant that their lack left him in a state of limbo. But the most profound cause of boredom was slavery itself. As James sees it, "The ignorance inherent in rural life prior to the industrial revolution was reinforced by the irascibility and conceit of isolation allied to undisputed dominion over hundreds of human beings."[23] The colonists, surfeited with leisure time, their every wish indulged by a ready slave, wallowed in "food, drink, dice and black women."[24]

The importance of Manzano's poem is its ability to comprehend the degradation of colonial life which defined his own historical period, then to place this colonial present in a larger historical perspective which encompasses both the past and the future. The fifth stanza records the past, which, in the Spanish empire, was defined by the two-pronged intervention of conquistadors ("the fell band Who's boasted conquests, mark one frightful course of spoil and plunder,") and priests ("Of human carnage in religious gear,").

Once more the critical understanding which Manzano brings to bear in his poems transcends his historical moment and finds continued relevancy in contemporary Spanish American texts. One in particular is Mario Vargas Llosa's *La Casa Verde*, where soldier and nun join forces to capture and enslave young Indian girls, condemning them to the contemporary servitude of mission schools and the future of a *criada*. The significance of the union of political and religious power, both during the conquest and throughout the process of acculturation, cannot be over-stated. One has only to remember that Padre Bartolome de las Casas, recognized savior of the Indians, was one of the official spokesmen responsible for the importation of Negro slaves. That the Indian population, particularly on the islands, was at that time already decimated suggests to what extent his priestly concerns were motivated by economic priorities.

However, the end of Manzano's fifth stanza gives rise to a new and gathering presence which by the end of the sixth cannot be denied. Here the cumulative history of outrage, torture and wholesale genocide gives shape and voice to the enslaved masses. Their centuries-long agony swells to produce the poem's only optimistic "trumpet-tongued" outcry, heralding the growing storm of rebellion. The direct historical influence is of course the Haitian revolution, whose image of blood and poison continues to haunt the Cuban slaveowners thirty years later. Then too, the period of the late 1830's, during which Manzano wrote this poem, saw an increase in rural slave rebellion particularly in Matanzas, the poet's home province, and the savage reaction of General O'Donnell, who by the 1840s had single-handedly set out to destroy Cuba's urban black bourgeoisie. The moment was thus one of political ferment countered by heightened repression. Manzano himself was thrown in jail and only narrowly escaped death, while other black poets and professionals were murdered.[25] These grim realities make a mockery of the poem's closing epithets, Cuba "rich and beautiful, the Queen of isles! Star of the West, and ocean's gem most rare!." By coming full circle to the already debunked myth of gem-like Caribbean beauty, the poem strikes a hollow note, which, by contrast, makes all the more meaningful the historical realities it has defined and all the more resonant the voice of the oppressed.

Significantly these epithets don't end the poem, rather they frame an imperative directing the reader to tell those who perpetuate the falsehoods of the third world, those who refuse to see the reality behind its beauty, those who profit by its myths to "Take of these flowers." Here Manzano deflowers the poetic image, showing it to be a worldly beauty, doomed to decay. But the poem goes much further than this, for the closing lines are based on a complicated set of reversals whereby false beauty is transformed into real beauty, and death into life. In the first phrase ("Take of these flowers, and view these lifeless spoils That wait the worm"), the products of cultivation which define false beauty are shown to be a part of death. The second phrase is transitional ("behold the hues beneath The pale cold cheek"). It asks the reader to merge antithetical notions and look for life in death. Here, color, which we associate with beauty and the flower, is still related to death, but beginning to be separate from it. The final phrase ("and seek for living smiles, Where beauty lies not in the arms of death, And bondage taints not with its poisoned breath") accomplishes the separation of beauty and death, which can only come about with the end of slavery.

The flower image is pivotal because it maintains the whole death/ beauty transformation. And as we noted it functions in a command, throwing its empty falsehood in the face of those who do pick Cuba's wealth. In a sense, Manzano is throwing the geranium, for which he suffered and bled as a child, back into his mistress's face. With his words, he acknowledges the right of the first world to harvest the wealth of the third world—an activity which he early learned could not be his. However, by his act of appropriating traditional poetic form and making it the vehicle for critical discourse, he has in fact picked and profited by a European flower. This then is the poem's final and most profound transformation—the ode is written not to praise, but to condemn; and the most marginal of poets, separated from the center by his racial and colonial heritage, seizes the hegemonic form and turns it back on the metropolis.

Essentially, the flower image can function in these many ways and be so highly charged with meaning because it partakes of established poetic form. On the other hand, the geranium in Manzano's narration is not much more than an important piece of narrative detail. The fact that in one mode of writing the author can speak with a high degree of comprehension and frames his words with a sophisticated rhetorical style, while in another mode he recounts raw, received information and has very little recourse to literary form suggests something about the influence of slavery on the writer. Essentially, Manzano is incapable of perspectivizing the lived experience of slavery. Those things which touch his life personally and form the basis of his narration escape evaluation. On the other hand, when slavery is understood with a degree of abstraction, as it is in the poem, then everything falls into place and critical discourse is possible.

The fact that Manzano has two very different languages—one immanent and monological, the other abstract and directed to a reader— demonstrates the fragmentation of the slave's relationship to language. For Manzano, struggling within the dominant language, one mode is more personally his own voice, but not a very apt means of communication; while the other is more communicative, but an appropriation and therefore less personal. The historical significance of these discontinuities becomes evident only when Manzano's fragmented language is compared to that of later black Caribbean poets, particularly Nicolás Guillen and Aimé Césaire. Manzano's is the lone and frustrated voice of the black slave who will not in his life time see the end of slavery nor experience the tremendous surge of cultural revolution and its implications for black language wrought by the Négritude movement. Within his historical frame, Manzano's narrative truly is a message found in a bottle; his poem, a stolen flower.

Notes

1. Benjamin F. Prentiss, *The Blind African Slave or Memoirs of Boyrereau Brinch* (St. Albans, Vt.: Harry Whitney, 1810), pp. 97-100.

2. One of the most enlightened sugarocrats was Francisco de Arango y Parreno who published a book on sugar production, studied its cultivation on the other sugar islands, and traveled extensively in Europe seeking out industrial innovations applicable to sugar refining. Arango's endeavors as well as those of the small group of progressive sugarocrats are described in Moreno Fraginals, Manuel, *The Sugarmill* (New York: Monthly Review Press, 1976). See the chapter "The Sugarmill as Intellectual Adventure."

3. For a sample of the kind of work done by the del Monte group, see Cintio Vitier, *La Critica Literaria y Estética en el Siglo XIX Cubano* (Havana, 1968).

4. Robert Scholes and Robert Kellogg, *The Nature of Narrative* (New York: Oxford University Press, 1966), p. 179.

5. Madden was in Cuba serving on the Comision Mixta, a committee set up to observe anti-slave trade agreements between England and Spain.

6. V.N. Volosinov, *Marxism and the Philosophy of Language* (New York: Seminar Press, 1973), p. 111.

7. As an example, see Richard Ohmann's article, "Literature as Sentences" in *Essays in Stylistic Analysis,* Howard S. Babb, ed. (New York: Harcourt Brace, 1972).

8. Jose L. Franco, *Autogiografía, Cartas y Versos de Juan Francisco Manzano* (Havana, 1937), p. 38. In this and subsequent translations, I have tried to render Manzano's incoherencies while at the same time substituting certain English words and phrases for the sake of understanding.

Sufria p^r. la mas leve maldad propia de muchacho, enserrado en una carbonera sin mas tabla ni con q^e. taparme mas de beinte y cuatro oras yo era en estremo medroso y me gustaba comer mi carsel como se puede ber todavia en lo mas claro de medio dia se necesita una buena bela p^a. distinguir en ella algun objeto aqui despues de sufrir resios azotes era enserrado con orden y pena de gran castigo al q^e. me diese ni una gota de agua, lo q^e. alli sufria aquejado de la ambre, y la se, atormentado del miedo, en un lugar tan soturno como apartado de la casa, en un traspatio junto a una caballeriza, y un apestoso y ebaporante basurero, contigua a un lugar comun infesto umedo y siempre pestifero q^e. solo estaba separado p^r. unas paredes todas agujereadas, guarida de diformes ratas q^e. sin sesar me passaban p^r. en sima tanto se temia en esta casa a tal orden q^e. nadie nadie se atrebia a un q^e. ubiera collontura a darme ni un comino y tenia la cabeza llena de los cuentos de cosa mala de otros tiempos, de las almas aparesidas en este de la otra vida y de los encantamientos de los muertos, q^e. cuando salian un tropel de ratas asiendo ruido me paresia ber aquel sotano lleno de fantasmas y daba tantos gritos pidiendo a boses misericordia entonses se me sacaba me atormentaban con tanto fuete hasta mas no poder y se me enserraba otra vez guardandose la llabe en el curato mismo de la Sra.

9. Erich Auerbach, *Mimesis* (Princeton: Princeton University Press, 1968), p. 101.

10. Olaudah Equiano (alias Gustavas Vassa), *The Life of Olaudah Equiano* (Boston: Isaac Knapp, 1837).

11. Franco, *op. cit.*, pp. 44-45.

nos codugeron puesta mi madre en el lugar del sacrifisio p^r. primera vez en su vida pues aunq^e. estaba en la asienda estaba esenta del trabajo como muger de un esclavo q^e. se supo condusir y aserse considerar de todos; viendo yo a mi madre en este estado suspenso no podia ni yorar ni discurrir ni huir temblaba inter sin pudor lo cuatro negros se apoderaron de ella la arrojaron en ticrra p^a. azotarla pedia p^r. Dios p . ella todo lo resisti pero al oir estallar el primmer fuetazo, combertido en leon en tigre o en la fiera mas animosa estube a pique de perder la vida a manos de el sitado Silvestre pero pasemos en silencio el resto de esta exena dolorosa.

12. For Harriet Jacobs (alias Linda Brent), the decision to flee her master came only after she had been transferred from household service to the more exacting and degrading slavery of the plantation. While her life as a household slave was one of daily torment, caught between the leachery of her master and jealousy of her mistress, her yearning for freedom was unfocused until she reached the plantation. Here, her actual flight was triggered by her master's decision to bring her children as well to the plantation, thus condemning them to the grim toil of field labor. See Linda Brent, *Incidents in the Life of a Slave Girl* (New York: Harcourt Brace, 1973).

13. While some accounts hold that Manzano never wrote a second part, Jose L. Franco's explanation that the second half of the narration fell into the hands of various supporters of Manzano's master seems plausible given the political unrest at the time Manzano wrote the first part and entrusted it to Madden.

14. The veil of silence may be attributed to two very different literary modes: the confessional, and the realism of Walter Scott—both of which were available in Cuba at the time.

15. Franco, *op. cit.*, pp. 51-52.

q^e. traes en las manos; yo me quedé muerto mi cuerpo se eló de improviso y sin poder apenas tenerme del temblor q^e. me dió en ambas piernas, dejé caer la porsión de pedasitos en el suelo tomóseme las manos se me olio y tomandose los pedasitos fue un monton una mata

y un atrevimiento de marca mis narises se rompieron y en seguida
vino el arministrador Dn. Lucas Rodriguez emigrado de S^{to}. Domingo
aquien se me entregó, serian las seis de tarde y era en el rigor del
ivierno la volante estaba puesta p^a. partir al pueblo yo debia seguirlos
pero cuan frajil es la suerte del q^e. esta sujeto a continuas visisi-
tudes, yo nunca tenia ora segura y en esta vez se berifico como en otras
muchas como beremos, yo fui p^a. el cepo en este lugar antes enfermeria
de hombres cabran si esiste sincuenta camas en cada lado pues en ella
se resibian los en fermos de la finca y a mas los del ingenio S^n. Miguel
pero ya estaba basia y no se le daba ningun empleo alli estaba el cepo y
solo se depositaba en el algun cadaber hasta la ora de llebar al pueblo a
darle sepultura alli puesto de dos pies con un frio q^e. elaba sin ninguna
cuvierta se me enserro apenas me vi solo en aquel lugar cuando todos
los muertos me paresia q^e. se le levantaban y q^e. vagavan p^r. todo lo
largo de el salon una bentana media derrumbada q^e. caia al rio o sanja
serca de un despenadero ruidoso q^r. asia un torrente de agua golpeaba
sin sesar y cada golpe me paresia un muerto q^e. entraba p^r. alli de la
otra vida considerar ahora q^e. noche pasaria no bien avia empesado a
aclarar cuando senti correr el serrojo entra un contra mayoral seguido
del arministrador me sacan una tabla parada a un orcon q^e. sostiene el
colgadiso un maso de cujes con sincuenta de ellos beo al pie de la tabla
el arministrador embuelto en su capote dise debajo del panuel q^e. lo
tapaba la boca con una voz ronca amarra mis manos se atan como las
de Jesueristo se me carga y meto los pies en las dos aberturas q^e. tiene
tambien mis pies se atan Oh Dios! corramos un belo p^r. el resto de esta
exena mi sangre se ha derramado yo perdi el sentido.

16. Eric Williams, *Capitalism and Slavery* (New York: Capricorn Books,
1966).

17. Immanuel Wallerstein, *The Modern World System* (New York: Academic Press, 1974).

18. While my own work is strongly influenced by dependency theory and
the desire to apply this economic model to literary criticism, it should be noted
that Wallerstein's work is highly controversial, particularly among Latin
American economists; and a number of alternative explanations for dependency
have been formulated. In terms of Cuba and slave labor, the work of the
Cuban Marxist, Moreno Fraginals, is the most important. In his book, *The
Sugarmill*, Fraginals gives a detailed account of sugar production from cultivation to refinement. However, his central thesis includes a number of contradictions. First of all, Fraginals sees the class of Cuban sugarocrats as an
independent bourgeoisie, and therefore, not determined by developments in
global capitalism. While it is true that Cuba's sugarocrats, unlike their French
and English counterparts in the Caribbean, were basically free of colonial controls and that the influence of Spain had greatly diminished in relation to the
rise of European capital, Cuban sugar production was clearly for the global
market (even if labelled contraband). The function of the sugarocrats as
a class was determined, not by national politics, but by their relationship to
the demands of world-wide production. Finally, Fraginals defines slave labor
outside of capitalism. This produces a somewhat tragic view of the sugarocrats,
who, as capitalists, were essentially bound and limited by their relationship to

a non-capitalist mode of production. Here, Fraginal's definition of slavery is based on the impossibility of innovation under slave labor and the fact that changes in production can only be quantitative rather than qualitative. The problem is that Fraginals is looking at the internal dynamic of slavery rather than seeing it as a complete mode of production. It is inconceivable that the owners of the means of production can be defined in terms of capitalism while the labor force is not.

19. C.L.R. James, *The Black Jacobins* (New York: Random House, 1963), p. 392.

20. Richard R. Madden, *Poems by a Slave in the Island of Cuba, Recently Liberated* (London: Thomas Ward and Co., 1840), p. 112.

21. George Lamming, *In the Castle of My Skin* (New York: Macmillan Publishing Co., 1975), p. 172.

22. Bakhtin defines the pure Socratic form of the dialogical discourse as one in which the truth is not known or possessed, but born out of the discussion between two people. This, he sees eroded by monological forms until the dialogue becomes nothing more than an uncovering of pre-existing truths. In this context, the vested interests of the abolitionist or anthropologist define the slave narrative somewhere between the pure dialogical and monological. Mikhail Bakhtin, *La Poetique de Dostoievski* (Paris: de Sevil, 1970), pp. 151-169.

23. James, *op. cit.*, p. 29.

24. *Ibid.*

25. During the early part of the 19th century, Cuba's black bourgeoisie became a strong social factor, concentrated in certain professions: dentistry, teaching, music, writing, the military and dock work. However, in 1844, the class of free black professionals was all but exterminated. As a reaction against violent uprisings throughout the rural plantations, urban blacks were unmercifully persecuted. The culmination was the Escalera Conspiracy during which 98 Negroes were executed, 600 imprisoned, and 400 exiled. For an understanding of the situation of the blacks in 19th century Cuba, see: Pedro Deschamps Chapeaux and Juan Perez de la Riva, *Contribucion a la historia de la Gente sin Historia* (Havana: Editorial de Ciencias Sociales, 1974).

I Rose and Found My Voice:
Narration, Authentication, and Authorial
Control in Four Slave Narratives

ROBERT BURNS STEPTO

The strident, moral voice of the former slave recounting, exposing, appealing, apostrophizing, and above all *remembering* his ordeal in bondage is the single most impressive feature of a slave narrative. This voice is striking because of what it relates, but even more so because the slave's acquisition of that voice is quite possibly his only permanent achievement once he escapes and casts himself upon a new and larger landscape. In their most elementary form, slave narratives are full of other voices which are frequently just as responsible for articulating a narrative's tale and strategy. These other voices may belong to various "characters" in the "story," but mainly they appear in the appended documents written by slaveholders and abolitionists alike. These documents—and voices—may not always be smoothly integrated with the former slave's tale, but they are nevertheless parts of the narrative. Their primary function is, of course, to authenticate the former slave's account; in doing so, they are at least partially responsible for the narrative's acceptance as historical evidence. However, in literary terms, the documents collectively create something close to a dialogue—of forms as well as voices—which suggests that, in its primal state or first phase, the slave narrative is an *eclectic narrative* form. A "first phase" slave narrative that illustrates these points rather well is Henry Bibb's *Narrative of the Life and Adventures of Henry Bibb, an American Slave* (1849).

When the various forms (letters, prefaces, guarantees, tales) and their accompanying voices become integrated in the slave narrative text, we are presented with another type of basic narrative which I call an *integrated narrative*. This type of narrative represents the second phase of slave narrative narration; it usually yields a more sophisticated text, wherein most of the literary and rhetorical functions previously performed by several texts and voices (the appended prefaces, letters, and documents as well as the tale) are now rendered by a loosely unified single text and voice. In this second phase, the authenticating documents "come alive" in the former slave's tale as speech and even action; and the former slave—often while assuming a deferential posture toward his white friends, editors, and guarantors—carries much of the burden of introducing and authenticating his own tale. In short, as my remarks on Solomon Northup's *Twelve Years a Slave* (1854) will suggest, a "second phase" narrative is a more sophisticated narrative because the former slave's voice is responsible for much more than recounting the tale.

Because an integrated or second-phase narrative is less a collection of texts and more a unified narrative, we may say that, in terms of narration, the integrated narrative is in the process of becoming—irrespective of authorial intent—a generic narrative, by which I mean a narrative of discernible genre such as history, fiction, essay, or autobiography. This process is no simple "gourd vine" activity: an integrated narrative does not become a generic narrative overnight, and indeed, there are no assurances that in becoming a new type of narrative it is transformed automatically into a distinctive generic text. What we discover, then, is a third phase to slave narration wherein two developments may occur: the integrated narrative (phase II) may be dominated either by its tale or by its authenticating strategies. In the first instance, as we see in Frederick Douglass's *Narrative of the Life of Frederick Douglass, an American Slave, Written by Himself* (1845), the narrative and moral energies of the former slave's voice and tale so resolutely dominate the narrative's authenticating machinery (voices, documents, rhetorical strategies) that the narrative becomes, in thrust and purpose, far more metaphorical than rhetorical. When the integrated narrative becomes, in this way, a figurative account of action, landscape, and heroic self-transformation, it is so close generally to history, fiction, and autobiography that I term it a *generic narrative*.

In the second instance, as we see in William Wells Brown's *Narrative of the Life and Escape of William Wells Brown* (1852; appended to his novel, *Clotel, or The President's Daughter*), the authenticating machinery either remains as important as the tale or actually becomes, usually for some purpose residing outside the text, the dominant and motivating feature of the narrative. Since this is also a sophisticated narrative phase, figurative presentations of action, landscape, and self may also occur; however, such developments are rare and always ancillary to the central thrust of the text. When the authenticating machinery dominates in this fashion, the integrated narrative becomes an *authenticating narrative*.

As these remarks suggest, one reason for investigating the phases of slave narrative narration is to gain a clearer view of how some slave narrative types become generic narratives, and how, in turn, *generic narratives—once formed, shaped, and set in motion by certain distinctly Afro-American cultural imperatives—have roots in the slave narratives.*

The Three Phases of Narration

PHASE I: Basic Narrative (a): "Eclectic Narrative"—authenticating documents and strategies (sometimes including one by the author of the tale) are *appended* to the tale

PHASE II: Basic Narrative (b): "Integrated Narrative"—authenticating documents and strategies are *integrated* into the tale and formally become voices and/or characters in the tale

PHASE III:

(a) "Generic Narrative"—authenticating documents and strategies are totally *subsumed by the tale;* the slave narrative becomes an identifiable generic text, e.g., autobiography

(b) "Authenticating Narrative"—the tale is *subsumed by the authenticating strategy;* the slave narrative becomes an authenticating document for other, usually generic, texts, e.g., novels, histories

All this is, of course, central to our understanding of Washington's *Up from Slavery,* Du Bois's *The Souls of Black Folk,* Johnson's *The Autobiography of an Ex-Coloured Man,* Wright's *Black Boy,* and Ellison's *Invisible Man.* Moreover, it bears on our ability to distinguish between narrative modes and forms, and to describe what we see. When a historian or literary critic calls a slave narrative an autobiography, for example, what he or she sees most likely is a first-person narrative that possesses literary features to distinguish it from ordinary documents providing historical and sociological data. But a slave narrative is *not* necessarily an autobiography. We need to observe the finer shades between the more easily discernible categories of narration, and we must discover whether these stops arrange themselves in progressive, contrapuntal, or dialectic fashion—or if they possess any arrangement at all. As the scheme described above and diagrammed above suggests, I believe there are at least four identifiable modes of narration within the slave narratives, and that all four have a direct bearing on the development of subsequent Afro-American narrative forms.

PHASE I: ECLECTIC NARRATIVE

Henry Bibb's *Narrative of the Life and Adventures of Henry Bibb, an American Slave,* begins with several introductory documents offering, collectively, what may be the most elaborate guarantee of authenticity found in the slave narrative canon. What is most revealing—in terms of eclectic narrative form, authenticating strategy, and race rituals along the color line—is the segregation of Bibb's own "Author's Preface" from the white-authored texts of the "Introduction." Bibb's "Author's Preface" is further removed from the preceding introductory texts by the fact that he does not address or acknowledge what has gone before. There is no exchange, no verbal bond, between the two major units of introductory material; this reflects not only the quality of Bibb's relations with his benefactors, but also his relatively modest degree of control over the text and event of the narrative itself.

The "Introduction" is basically a frame created by Bibb's publisher, Lucius Matlack, for the presentation of guarantees composed mostly by abolitionists in Detroit (where, in freedom, Bibb chose to reside). Yet Matlack, as the publisher, also has his own authenticating duties to perform. He assures the reader that while he did indeed "examine" and "prepare" Bibb's manuscript, "The work of preparation . . . was that of orthography and punctuation merely, an arrangement of the chapters, and a table of contents—little more than falls to the lot of publishers generally." When Matlack tackles the issue of the tale's veracity, he mutes his own voice and offers instead those of various "authentic" documents gathered by the abolitionists. These gentlemen, all members of the Detroit Liberty Association, appear most sympathetic to Bibb, especially since he has spoken before their assemblies and lived an exemplary Christian life in their midst. To aid him—and their cause—they have interrogated Bibb (to which he submitted with "praiseworthy spirit") and have solicited letters from slaveholders, jailors, and Bibb's acquaintances, so that the truth of his tale might be established. No fewer than six of these letters plus the conclusion of the Association's report, all substantiating Bibb's story, appear in the "Introduction"; and, as if to "guarantee the guarantee," a note certifying the "friendly recommendation" of the abolitionists and verifying Bibb's "correct deportment" (composed, quite significantly, by a Detroit *judge*) is appended as well.

The elaborate authenticating strategy contained in Matlack's "Introduction" is typical of those found in the first-phase or eclectic narrative. The publisher or editor, far more than the former slave, assembles and manipulates the authenticating machinery, and seems to act on the premise that there is a direct correlation between the quantity of documents or texts assembled and the readership's acceptance of the narrative as a whole. I would like to suggest that Matlack's "Introduction" also constitutes a literary presentation of race rituals and cultural conditions, and that, as such, it functions as a kind of metaphor in the narrative.

To be sure, Matlack displays typical nineteenth-century American enthusiasm and superficiality when he writes of the literary merits of slave narratives: "Gushing fountains of poetic thought have started from beneath the rod of violence, that will long continue to slake the feverish thirst of humanity outraged, until swelling to a flood it shall rush with wasting violence over the ill-gotten heritage of the oppressor." However, the thrust of his "Introduction" is to guarantee the truth of a tale and, by extension, the *existence* of a man calling himself Henry Bibb. In his own aforementiond remarks regarding the preparation of Bibb's text for publication, Matlack appears to address the issue of the author's—Bibb's—credibility. However, the issue is really the audience's—white America's—credulity: their acceptance not so much of the former slave's escape and newfound freedom, but of his literacy. Many race rituals are enacted here, not the least of which is Matlack's "conversation" with white America across the text and figurative body of a silent former slave. The point we may glean from them all is that, insofar as Bibb must depend on his publisher to be an intermediary between his text and his audience, he relinquishes control of the narrative—which is, after all, the vehicle for the account of how he obtained his voice in freedom.

While we are impressed by the efforts of the Detroit Liberty Association's members to conduct an investigation of Bibb's tale, issue a report, and lend their names to the guarantee, we are still far more overwhelmed by the examples of the cultural disease with which they wrestle than by their desire to find a cure. That disease is, of course, cultural myopia, the badge and sore bestowed upon every nation mindlessly heedful of race ritual instead of morality: Henry Bibb is alive and well in Detroit, but by what miraculous stroke will he, as a man, be able to cast his shadow on this soil? The effort in the narrative's "Introduction" to prove that Bibb exists, and hence has a tale, goes far to explain why a prevailing metaphor in Afro-American letters is, in varying configurations, one of invisibility and translucence. Indirectly, and undoubtedly on a subconscious level, Matlack and the abolitionists confront the issue of Bibb's inability "to cast his shadow." But even in their case we may ask: Are they bolstering a cause, comforting a former slave, or recognizing a man?

The letters from the slaveholders and jailors Bibb knew while in bondage must not be overlooked here, for they help illuminate the history of the disease we are diagnosing. The letter from Silas Gatewood, whose father once owned Bibb, is designed solely to portray Bibb as "a notorious liar . . . and a rogue." Placed within the compendium of documents assembled by the abolitionists, the letter completes, through its nearly hysterical denunciation of Bibb, the "Introduction's" portrait of America at war with itself. The debate over Bibb's character, and, by extension, his right to a personal history bound to that of white Americans, is really nothing less than a literary omen of the Civil War. In this regard, the segregation of Bibb's "Author's Preface" from the introductory compendium of documents is, even more than his silence within the compendium, indicative of how the former slave's voice was kept muted and distant while the nation debated questions of slavery and the Negro's humanity.

Bibb's "Preface" reveals two features to his thinking, each of which helps us see how the former slave approached the task of composing a narrative. In answer to his own rhetorical question as to why he wrote the narrative, he replies, "in no place have I given orally the detail of my narrative; and some of the most interesting events of my life have never reached the public ear." This is not extraordinary except in that it reminds us of the oral techniques and traditions that lay behind most of the written narratives. The former slave's accomplishment of a written narrative should by no means be minimized, but we must also recognize the extent to which the abolitionist lecture circuit, whether in Michigan, Maine, or New York, gave former slaves an opportunity to structure, to embellish, and above all to polish an oral version of their tale—and to do so before the very audiences who would soon purchase hundreds, if not thousands, of copies of the written account. The former slave, not altogether unlike the semi-literate Black preacher whose sermons were (and are) masterpieces of oral composition and rhetorical strategy, often had a fairly well developed version of his or her tale either memorized or (more likely) sufficiently *patterned* for effective presentation, even before the question of written composition was entertained. Certainly such was the case for Bibb, and this reminds us not to be too narrow when we call the basic slave narrative an eclectic narrative form. Oral as well as written forms are part of the eclectic whole.

The second revealing feature of Bibb's "Preface" returns us to a point on which his publisher, Matlack, began. Bibb appears extremely aware of the issue of his authorship when he writes:

> The reader will remember that I make no pretension to literature; for
> I can truly say, that I have been educated in the school of adversity,
> whips, and chains. Experience and observation have been my principal

teachers, with the exception of three weeks schooling which I have had the good fortune to receive since my escape from the "grave yard of the mind," or the dark prison of human bondage.

That Bibb had only three weeks of formal schooling is astonishing; however, I am intrigued even more by the two metaphors for slavery with which he concludes. While both obviously suggest confinement—one of the mind, the other of his body—it seems significant that Bibb did not choose between the two (for reasons of style, if no other). Both images are offered *after* the act of writing his tale, possibly because Bibb is so terribly aware of both. His body is now free, his mind limber, his voice resonant; together they and his tale, if not his narrative, are his own.

On a certain level, we must study Matlack's "Introduction," with all its documents and guarantees, and Bibb's "Author's Preface" as a medley of voices, rather than as a loose conglomerate of discrete and even segregated texts. Together, both in what they do and do not say, these statements reflect the passions, politics, interpersonal relations, race rituals, and uses of language of a cross-section of America in the 1840's. But on another level, we must hold fast to what we have discovered regarding how Bibb's removal from the primary authenticating documents and strategy (that is, from the "Introduction") weakens his control of the narrative and, in my view, relegates him to a posture of partial literacy. Bibb's tale proves that he has acquired a voice, but his narrative shows that his voice does not yet control the imaginative forms which his personal history assumes in print.

In the Bibb narrative, the various texts within the "Introduction" guarantee Bibb and his tale; Bibb sustains this strategy of guarantee late in his tale by quoting letters and proclamations by many of the same figures who provided documents for the "Introduction." As we will discover in Solomon Northup's narrative, this use of authenticating documents within the text of the tale indicates the direction of more sophisticated slave narrative texts. Indeed, the question of whether the authenticating documents and strategies have been integrated into the central text (usually the tale) of the slave narrative is a major criterion by which we may judge author and narrative alike. The inclusion and manipulation of peripheral documents and voices suggests a remarkable level of literacy and self-assurance on the part of the former slave, and the reduction of many texts and strategies into one reflects a search, irrespective of authorial intent, for a more sophisticated written narrative form. Here, then, is a point of departure from which we may study the development of pregeneric narratives into generic and other sophisticated narrative types.

PHASE II: INTEGRATED NARRATIVE

While I am not prepared to classify Solomon Northup's *Twelve Years a Slave* (1854) as an autobiography, it is certainly a more sophisticated text than Henry Bibb's, principally because its most important authenticating document is integrated into the tale as a voice and character. *Twelve Years a Slave* is, however, an integrated narrative unsure of itself. Ultimately, its authenticating strategy depends as much upon an appended set of authenticating texts as upon integrated documents and voices.

In comparison to the Bibb "Introduction," the Northup introductory materials appear purposely short and undeveloped. Northup's editor and amanuensis, a Mr. David Wilson, offers a one-page "Preface," not a full-blown "Introduction," and Northup's own introductory words are placed in the first chapter of his tale, rather than in a discrete entry written expressly for that purpose. Wilson's "Preface" is, predictably, an authenticating document, formulaically acknowledging whatever "faults of style and of expression" the narrative may contain while assuring the reader that he, the editor and a white man, is convinced of Northup's strict adherence to the truth. Northup's own contributions, like Bibb's, are not so much authenticating as they are reflective of what a slave may have been forced to consider while committing his tale to print.

Northup's first entry is simply and profoundly his signature—his proof of literacy writ large, with a bold, clear hand. It appears beneath a pen-and-ink frontispiece portrait entitled "Solomon in His Plantation Suit." His subsequent entries quite self-consciously place his narrative amid the antislavery literature of the era, in particular, with Harriet Beecher Stowe's *Uncle Tom's Cabin* (1852) and *Key to Uncle Tom's Cabin* (1853). If one wonders why Northup neither establishes his experience among those of other kidnapped and enslaved blacks nor positions his narrative with other narratives, the answer is provided in part by his dedicatory page. There, after quoting a passage from *Key to Uncle Tom's Cabin* which, in effect, verifies his account of slavery because it is said to "form a striking parallel" to Uncle Tom's, Northup respectfully dedicates his narrative to Miss Stowe, remarking that his tale affords "another *Key to Uncle Tom's Cabin.*"

This is no conventional dedication; it tells us much about the requisite act of authentication. While the Bibb narrative is authenticated by documents provided by the Detroit Liberty Association, the Northup narrative begins the process of authentication by assuming kinship with a popular antislavery novel. Audience, and the former slave's relationship to that audience, are the key issues here: authentication is, apparently, a rhetorical strategy designed not only for verification purposes, but also for the task of initiating and insuring a readership. No matter how efficacious it undoubtedly was for Northup (or his editor) to ride Miss Stowe's coattails and share in her immense notoriety, one cannot help wondering about the profound implications involved in authenticating personal history by binding it to historical fiction. In its way, this strategy says as much about a former slave's inability to confirm his existence and "cast his shadow" as does the more conventional strategy observed in the Bibb narrative. Apparently, a novel may authenticate a personal history, especially when the personal history is that of a former slave.

While not expressing the issue in these terms, Northup seems to have thought about the dilemma of authentication and that of slave narratives competing with fictions of both the pro- and antislavery variety. He writes:

> Since my return to liberty, I have not failed to perceive the increasing interest throughout the Northern states, in regard to the subject of Slavery. Works of fiction, professing to portray its features in their more pleasing as well as more repugnant aspects, have been circulated to an extent unprecedented, and, as I understand, have created a fruitful topic of comment and discussion.
>
> I can speak of Slavery only so far as it came under my own observation—only so far as I have known and experienced it in my own person. My object is, to give a candid and truthful statement of facts: to repeat the story of my life, without exaggeration, leaving it for others to determine, whether even the pages of fiction present a picture of more cruel wrong or a severer bondage.

Clearly, Northup felt that the authenticity of his tale would not be taken for granted, and that, on a certain peculiar but familiar level enforced by rituals along the color line, his narrative would be viewed as a fiction competing with other fictions. However, in this passage Northup also inaugurates a counter-strategy. His reference to his own observation of slavery may be a just and subtle dig at the "armchair sociologists" of North and South alike, who wrote of the slavery question amid the comforts of their libraries and verandas. But more important, in terms of plot as well as point of view, the remark establishes Northup's authorial posture as a "participant-observer" in the truest and (given his bondage) most regrettable sense of the phrase. In these terms, then, Northup contributes personally to the authentication of *Twelve Years a Slave:* he challenges the authenticity of the popular slavery fictions and their power of authenticating his own personal history by first exploiting the bond between them and his tale and then assuming the posture of an authenticator. One needn't delve far into the annals of American race relations for proof that Northup's rhetorical strategy is but a paradigm for the classic manipulation of the master by the slave.

As the first chapter of *Twelve Years a Slave* unfolds, Northup tells of his family's history and circumstances. His father, Mintus Northup, was a slave in Rhode Island and in Rensselaer County, New York, before gaining his freedom in 1803 upon the death of his master. Mintus quickly amassed property and gained suffrage; he came to expect the freedoms that accompany self-willed mobility and self-initiated employment, and gave his son, Solomon, the extraordinary advantage of being born a free man. As a result, Solomon writes of gaining "an education surpassing that ordinarily bestowed upon children in our condition," and he recollects leisure hours "employed over my books, or playing the violin." Solomon describes employment (such as lumber-rafting on Lake Champlain) that was not only profitable but also, in a way associated with the romance of the frontier, adventurous and even manly. When Solomon Northup married Anne Hampton on Christmas Day of 1829, they did not jump over a broomstick, as was the (reported) lot of most enslaved black Americans; rather, the two were married by a magistrate of the neighborhood, Timothy Eddy, Esq. Furthermore, their first home was neither a hovel nor a hut but the "Fort House," a residence "lately occupied by Captain Lathrop" and used in 1777 by General Burgoyne.

This saga of Solomon's heritage is full of interest, and it has its rhetorical and strategical properties as well. Northup has begun to establish his authorial posture removed from the condition of the black masses in slavery—a move which, as we have indicated, is as integral to the authenticating strategy as to the plot of his tale. In addition to portraying circumstances far more pleasant and fulfilling than those which he suffers in slavery, Northup's family history also yields some indication of his relations with whites in the district, especially the white Northups. Of course, these indications also advance both the plot and the authenticating strategy. One notes, for example, that while Mintus Northup did indeed migrate from the site of his enslavement once he was free, he retained the Northup surname and labored for a relative of his former master. Amid his new prosperity and mobility, Mintus maintained fairly amicable ties with his past; apparently this set the tone for relations between Northups, black and white. One should be wary of depicting New York north of Albany as an ideal or integrated area in the early 1800's, but the black Northups had bonds with whites—perhaps blood ties. To the end Solomon depends on these bonds for his escape from slavery and for the implicit verification of his tale.

In the first chapter of *Twelve Years a Slave*, Henry B. Northup, Esq., is mentioned only briefly as a relative of Mintus Northup's former master; in the context of Solomon's family history, he is but a looming branch of the (white) Northup family tree. However, as the tale concludes, Henry Northup becomes a voice and character in the narrative. He requests various legal documents essential to nullifying Solomon's sale into bondage; he inquires into Solomon's whereabouts in Bayou Boeuf, Louisiana; he presents the facts before lawyers, sheriffs, and Solomon's master, Edwin Epps; he pleads Solomon's case against his abductors before a District of Columbia court of law; and, most important, after the twelve years of assault on Solomon's sense of identity, Henry Northup utters, to Solomon's profound thanksgiving, Solomon's given name—not his slave name. In this way Henry Northup enters the narrative, and whatever linguistic authentication of the tale Solomon inaugurated by assuming the rather objective posture of the participant-observer-authenticator is concluded and confirmed, not by appended letter, but by Henry Northup's presence.

This strategy of authentication functions hand in hand with the narrative's strategy of reform. Like the carpenter, Bass, who jeopardizes his own safety by personally mailing Solomon's appeals for help to New York, Henry Northup embodies the spirit of reform in the narrative. In terms of reform strategy, Henry Northup and Bass—who, as a Canadian, represents a variation on the archetype of deliverance in Canada—are not only saviors but also models whose example might enlist other whites in the reform cause. Certainly abolitionists near and far could identify with these men, and that was important. Slave narratives were often most successful when they were as subtly pro-abolition as they were overtly antislavery—a consideration which could only have exacerbated the former slave's already sizable problems with telling his tale in such a way that he, and not his editors or guarantors, controlled it.

But Henry Northup is a different kind of savior from Bass: he is an American descended from slaveowners, and he shares his surname with the kidnapped Solomon. Furthermore, his posture as a family friend is inextricably bound to his position in the tale as a lawyer. At the end of *Twelve Years a Slave*, Henry Northup appears in Louisiana as an embodiment of the law, as well as of Solomon Northup's past (in all its racial complexity) come to reclaim him. In this way, Solomon's *tale* assumes the properties of an integrated narrative—the authenticating texts (here, the words and actions of Henry Northup) are integrated into the former slave's tale. But in what follows after the tale, we see that Solomon's *narrative* ultimately retrogresses to the old strategies of a phase-one eclectic narrative. Whereas the Bibb narrative begins with a discrete set of authenticating texts, the Northup narrative ends with such a set—an "Appendix."

The Northup Appendix contains three types of documents. First comes the New York state law, passed May 14, 1840, employed by Henry Northup and others to reclaim Solomon Northup from bondage in Louisiana. There follows a petition to the Governor of New York from Solomon's wife, Ann Northup, replete with legal language that persists in terming her a "memorialist." The remaining documents are letters, mostly from the black Northups' white neighbors, authenticating Solomon's claim that he is a free Negro. Despite our initial disappointment upon finding such an orthodox authenticating strategy appended to what had heretofore been a refreshingly sophisticated slave narrative (the narrative does not need the Appendix to fulfill its form), the Appendix does have its points of interest. Taken as a whole, it portrays the unfolding of a law; the New York law with which it begins precipitates the texts that follow, notably, in chronological order. On one level, then, Northup's Appendix is, far more than Bibb's Introduction, a story in epistolary form that authenticates not only his tale but also those voices within the tale, such as Henry Northup's. On another level, however, the Appendix becomes a further dimension to the reform strategy subsumed within the narrative. Just as Bass and Henry Northup posture as model reformers, the narrative's Appendix functions as a primer, complete with illustrative documents, on how to use the law to retrieve kidnapped free Negroes. Thus, the Appendix, as much as the tale itself, can be seen (quite correctly) as an elaborate rhetorical strategy against the Fugitive Slave Law of 1850.

In the end, the Northup narrative reverts to primitive authenticating techniques, but that does not diminish the sophistication and achievement of the tale within the narrative. We must now ask: To what end does the immersion of authenticating documents and strategies within the texture of Northup's tale occur? Furthermore, is this goal literary or extraliterary? In answering these questions we come a little closer, I think, to an opinion on whether narratives like Northup's may be autobiographies.

Northup's conscious or unconscious integration and subsequent manipulation of authenticating voices advances his tale's plot and most certainly advances his narrative's validation and reform strategies. However, it does little to develop what Albert Stone has called a literary strategy of self-presentation. The narrative renders an extraordinary experience, but not a remarkable self. The two need not be exclusive, as Frederick Douglass's 1845 *Narrative* illustrates, but in the Northup book they appear to be distinct entities, principally because of the eye or "I" shaping and controlling the narration. Northup's eye and "I" are not so much introspective as they are inquisitive; even while in the pit of slavery in Louisiana, Northup takes time to inform us of various farming methods and of how they differ from practices in the North. Of course, this remarkable objective posture results directly from Northup assuming the role of a participant-observer for authentication purposes. But it all has a terrible price. Northup's tale is neither the history nor a metaphor for the history of his life; and because this is so, his tale cannot be called autobiographical.

PHASE IIIa: GENERIC NARRATIVE

In the first two phases of slave narrative narration we observe the former slave's ultimate lack of control over his own narrative, occasioned primarily by the demands of audience and authentication. This dilemma is not unique to the authors of these narratives; indeed, many modern black writers still do not control their personal history once it assumes literary form. For this reason, Frederick Douglass's *Narrative of the Life of Frederick Douglass, an American Slave, Written by Himself* (1845) seems all the more a remarkable literary achievement. Because it contains several segregated narrative texts—a preface, a prefatory letter, the tale, an appendix—it appears to be, in terms of the narrative phases, a rather primitive slave narrative. But each ancillary text is drawn to the tale by some sort of extraordinary gravitational pull or magnetic attraction. There is, in short, a dynamic energy between the tale and each supporting text that we do not discover in the Bibb or Northup narratives, save perhaps in the relationship between Solomon Northup and his guarantor-become-character, Henry Northup. The Douglass narrative is an integrated narrative of a very special order. The integrating process does, in a small way, pursue the conventional path found in Northup's narrative, creating characters out of authenticating texts (William Lloyd Garrison silently enters Douglass's tale at the very end); however, its new and major thrust is the creation of that aforementioned energy which binds the supporting texts to the tale, while at the same time removing them from participation in the narrative's rhetorical and authenticating strategies. Douglass's tale dominates the narrative because it alone authenticates the narrative. . . .

PHASE IIIb: AUTHENTICATING NARRATIVE

In an authenticating narrative, represented here by William Wells Brown's *Narrative of the Life and Escape of William Wells Brown* (not to be confused with Brown's 1847 volume, *Narrative of William Wells*

Brown, a Fugitive Slave, Written by Himself), the narrator exhibits considerable control of his narrative by becoming an editor of disparate texts for authentication purposes, far more than for the goal of recounting personal history. The texts Brown displays include passages from his speeches and other writings, but for the most part they are testimonials from antislavery groups in both America and England, excerpts from reviews of his travel book, *Three Years in Europe* (1852), selections from antislavery verse, and, quite significantly, letters to Brown's benefactors from his last master in slavery, Mr. Enoch Price of St. Louis. Brown's control of his narrative is comparable to Douglass's, but while Douglass gains control by improving upon the narrative failures of authors like Henry Bibb, Brown's control represents a refinement of the authenticating strategies used by publishers like Bibb's Lucius Matlack, who edited and deployed authenticating documents very much like those gathered by Brown. In this way, Brown's narrative is not so much a tale of personal history as it is a conceit upon the authorial mode of the white guarantor. Control and authentication are achieved, but at the enormous price of abandoning the quest to present personal history in and as literary form.

Brown's "Preface," written notably by himself and not by a white guarantor, is peculiar in that it introduces both his narrative and the text authenticated by the narrative, *Clotel; or, The President's Daughter*. By and large, the tone of the "Preface" is sophisticated and generally that of a self-assured writer. Unlike Bibb or Northup, Brown does not skirmish with other authenticators for authorial control of the text, nor is he anxious about competition from other literary quarters of the antislavery ranks. He scans briefly the history of slavery in North America and reasons, with the British (with whom he resides after passage of the 1850 Fugitive Slave Law), that they who controlled the American colonies when slavery was introduced should feel "a lively interest in its abolition." All this is done without resort to conventional apologia or the confession of verbal deficiencies; Brown is humble not so much in his rhetoric as in his goal: "If the incidents set forth in the following pages should add anything new to the information already given to the public through similar publications, and should thereby aid in bringing British influence to bear upon American slavery, the main object for which this work was written will have been accomplished." That Brown introduces a personal narrative and a somewhat fictive narrative (*Clotel*) with language and intentions commonly reserved for works of history and journalism constitutes his first admission of being motivated by extraliterary concerns. His second admission emerges from his persistent use of the term "memoir." In contrast to a confession or autobiography, a memoir refers specifically to an author's recollections of his public life, far more than to his rendering of personal history as literary form or metaphor. This former kind of portrait is, of course, exactly what Brown gives us in his narrative.

The narrative is, as I have indicated, bereft of authorship. Brown rarely renders in fresh language those incidents of which he has written elsewhere; he simply quotes himself. His posture as the editor and not the author of his tale disallows any true expression of intimacy with his personal past. This feature is reinforced by certain objectifying and distancing qualities created by third-person narration. Brown's 1847 narrative begins, "I was born in Lexington, Ky. The man who stole me as soon as I was born, recorded the births of all the infants which he claimed to be born his property, in a book which he kept for that purpose. . . ." Thus, it inaugurates the kind of personal voice and hardboiled prose which is Brown's contribution to early Afro-American letters. In contrast, the opening of the 1852 narrative is flat, without pith or strength: "William Wells Brown, the subject of this narrative, was born a slave in Lexington, Kentucky, not far from the residence of the late Hon. Henry Clay." These words do not constitute effective writing, but that is not Brown's goal. The goal is, rather, authentication, and the seemingly superfluous aside about Henry Clay—which in another narrative might very well generate the first ironic thrust against America's moral blindness—appears for the exclusive purpose of validation. In this way Brown commences an authentication strategy which he will pursue throughout the tale.

The tale or memoir is eclectic in its collection of disparate texts; however, very few of the collected texts merit discussion. I will simply list their types to suggest both their variety and their usefulness to Brown:

1. The scrap of verse, usually effusive, always saccharine, culled from antislavery poets known and unknown. The verse expresses high sentiment and deep emotion when the text requires it, engages the popular reading public, and suggests erudition and sensitivity.
2. Quotation from Brown's speeches at famous institutions like Exeter Hall and from "addresses" bestowed on him after such speeches. These advance the memoir, embellish Brown's résumé, and authenticate his claim that he was where he said he was.
3. Quotations from Brown's travel book, *Three Years in Europe*, and from the book's reviews. The passages of personal history advance the memoir and validate "The energy of the man," as well as call attention to the book. The reviews call further attention to the book, and authenticate Brown's literacy and good character.
4. Testimonies and testimonials from various abolitionist groups in the United States and England, white and colored. These texts profess the success of Brown's labors as a lecturing agent, "commend him to the hospitality and encouragement of all true friends of humanity,"

and, upon his departure for England, provide him with what Douglass would have termed a "protection" for his travels. These are, in
short, recommending letters attached to Brown's résumé validating
his character and the fact that he is a fugitive slave.
5. Two letters from a former master, Enoch Price of St. Louis, dated
before and after the Fugitive Slave Law was passed in 1850.

The Enoch Price letters are undoubtedly the most interesting documents in Brown's compendium, and he makes good narrative use of
them. While the other assembled documents merely serve the authenticating strategy, Price's letters, in their portrait of a slaveholder ironically
invoking the dictates of fair play while vainly attempting to exact a bargain price for Brown from his benefactors, actually tell us something
about Brown's circumstances. Despite the lionizing illustrated by the
other documents, Brown is still not a free man. He is most aware of this,
and for this reason the narrative concludes, not with another encomium,
but with the second of Price's letters once again requesting payment—
payment for lost property, payment for papers that will set Brown free.
All Brown can do under the circumstances is refuse to acknowledge
Price's supposed right to payment, and order his present condition by
controlling not so much his tale, which is his past, as the authentication
of himself, which is his present and possibly his future. As the editor of
his résumé—his present circumstance—Brown must acknowledge slavery's
looming presence in his life, but he can also attempt to bury it beneath a
mountain of antislavery rhetoric and self-authenticating documentation.
Through the act of self-authentication Brown may contextualize slavery
and thereby control it. In these terms, then, the heroic proportions to
Brown's editorial act of including and manipulating Enoch Price's letters
become manifest.

Brown's personal narrative most certainly authenticates himself, but
how does it also authenticate *Clotel?* The answer takes us back to Brown's
"Preface," where he outlines the extraliterary goals of both narratives,
and forward to the concluding chapter of *Clotel*, where he writes:

> My narrative has now come to a close. I may be asked, and no doubt
> shall, Are the various incidents and scenes related founded in truth? I
> answer, Yes. I have personally participated in many of those scenes.
> Some of the narratives I have derived from other sources; many from the
> lips of those who, like myself, have run away from the land of bond-
> age. . . . To Mrs. Child, of New York, I am indebted for part of a short
> story. American Abolitionist journals are another source from whence
> some of the characters appearing in my narrative are taken. All these
> combined have made up my story.

Brown's personal narrative functions, then, as a successful rhetorical device, authenticating his *access* to the incidents, characters, scenes, and

tales which collectively make up *Clotel.* In the end, we witness a dynamic interplay between the two narratives, established by the need of each for resolution and authentication within the other. Since *Clotel* is not fully formed as either a fiction or a slave narrative, it requires completion of some sort, and finds this when it is transformed into a fairly effective antislavery device through linkage with its prefatory authenticating text. Since Brown's personal narrative is not fully formed as either an autobiography or a slave narrative, it requires fulfillment as a literary form through intimacy with a larger, more developed but related text. *Clotel* is no more a novel than Brown's preceding personal narrative is autobiography, but together they represent a roughly hewn literary tool which is, despite its defects, a sophisticated departure from the primary phases of slave narration and authentication.

Brown's personal narrative is hardly an aesthetic work, but that is because Brown had other goals in mind. He is willing to forsake the goal of presenting personal history in literary form in order to promote his books and projects like the Manual Labor School for fugitive slaves in Canada, to authenticate *Clotel,* and to authenticate himself while on British soil. He is willing to abandon the goals of true authorship and to assume instead the duties of an editor in order to gain some measure of control over the present, as opposed to illuminating the past. Brown's narrative is present and future oriented: most of his anecdotes from the past are offered as testimony to the energy and character he will bring to bear on future tasks. In short, just as Douglass inaugurates the autobiographical mode in Afro-American letters, Brown establishes what curiously turns out to be the equally common mode of the authenticating narrative. To see the popularity and great effect of the Afro-American authenticating narrative—once it assumes a more sophisticated form—one need look no further than Booker T. Washington's *Up from Slavery.*

Autobiographical Acts and the Voice of the Southern Slave

HOUSTON A. BAKER, JR.

The southern slave's struggle for terms for order is recorded by the single, existential voice engaged in what Elizabeth Bruss calls "autobiographical acts."[1] How reliable are such acts? Benedetto Croce called autobiography "a by-product of an egotism and a self-consciousness which achieve nothing but to render obvious their own futility and should be left to die of it." And a recent scholar of black autobiography expresses essentially the same reservations: "Admittedly, the autobiography has limitations as a vehicle of truth. Although so long an accepted technique toward understanding, the self-portrait often tends to be formal and posed, idealized or purposely exaggerated. The author is bound by his organized self. Even if he wishes, he is unable to remember the whole story or to interpret the complete experience."[2] A number of eighteenth- and nineteenth-century American thinkers would have taken issue with these observations. Egotism, self-consciousness, and a deep and abiding concern with the individual are at the forefront of American intellectual traditions, and the formal limitations of autobiography were not of great concern to those white authors who felt all existent literary forms were inadequate for representing their unique experiences. The question of the autobiography's adequacy, therefore, entails questions directed not only toward the black voice in the South, but also toward the larger context of the American experiment as a whole.

Envisioning themselves as God's elect and imbued with a sense of purpose, the Puritans braved the Atlantic on a mission into the wilderness. The emptiness of the New World, the absence of established institutions and traditions, reinforced their inclination to follow the example of their European forebears and brothers in God. They turned inward for reassurance and guidance. Self-examination became the *sine qua non* in a world where some were predestined for temporal leadership and eventual heavenly reward and others for a wretched earthly existence followed by the fires of hell. The diary, the journal, the meditation, the book of evidences drawn from personal experiences were the literary results of this preoccupation with self, and even documents motivated by religious controversy often took the form of apology or self-justification. A statement from Jonathan Edwards's *Personal Narrative* offers a view of this tradition: "I spent most of my time in thinking of divine things, year after year: often walking alone in the woods, and solitary places, for meditation, soliloquy, and prayer, and converse with God; and it was always my manner at such time, to sing forth my contemplations."[3]

The man alone, seeking self-definition and salvation, certain that he has a God-given duty to perform, is one image of the white American writer. Commenting on Edwards and the inevitable growth of autobiography in a land without a fully articulated social framework, Robert Sayre writes: "Edwards could and had to seek self-discovery within himself because there were so few avenues to it outside himself. The loneliness and the need for new forms really go together. They are consequences of one another and serve jointly as inducements and as difficulties to autobiography."[4] This judgment must be qualified, since Edwards's form does not differ substantially from John Bunyan's, and his isolated meditations fit neatly into a Calvinistic spectrum, but Sayre is fundamentally correct when he specifies a concern with solitude and a desire for unique literary expression as key facets of the larger American experience.

Despite the impression of loneliness left by Edwards and the sense of a barren and unpromising land for literature left by comments like those of Hawthorne in his preface to *The Marble Faun* or James in *Hawthorne*, there were a number of *a priori* assumptions available to the white American thinker. They developed over a wide chronological span (the original religious ideals becoming, like those treated in the discussion of black writers above, increasingly secular) and provided a background ready to hand. There was the white writer's sense that he was part of a new cultural experience, that he had gotten away from what D.H. Lawrence calls his old masters and could establish a new and fruitful way of life in America. There was the whole panoply of spiritual sanctions; as one of the chosen people, he was responsible for the construction of a new earthly paradise, one that would serve as a holy paradigm for the rest of the world. There was the white writer's belief, growing out of the liberal, secular thought of Descartes, Locke, and Newton, that the individual was unequivocally responsible for his own actions; a man was endowed with inalienable rights, and one of these was the right to educate himself and strive for commercial success. There was also the feeling that America offered boundless opportunities for creative originality: a unique culture with peculiar sanctions should produce a *sui generis* art.

Thus, while James's "extraordinary blankness—a curious paleness of colour and paucity of detail" was characteristic for some early white Americans, there were also more substantial aspects or qualities of the American experience that stood in contrast to this "blankness." The writer could look to a Puritan ontology and sense of mission, to conceptions of the self-made man, or to a prevailing American concern for unique aesthetic texts as preshaping influences for his work. The objective world provided both philosophical and ideological justifications for his task. When Emerson wrote, "Dante's praise is that he dared to write his autobiography in colossal cipher, or into universality," he optimistically stated the possibilities immanent in the white author's situation. The writer of comprehensive soul who dared to project his experiences on a broad plane would stand at the head of a great tradition. According to Emerson, the world surrounding such a person—that supposedly void externality—offered all the necessary supports. The permanence and importance of works such as Edwards's *Personal Narrative,* Whitman's *Leaves of Grass,* and Adams's *The Education of Henry Adams* in American literature confirm his insight. As the American autobiographer turned inward to seek "the deepest *whole* self of man" (Lawrence's phrase), he carried with him the preexistent codes of his culture. They aided his definition of self and are fully reflected in the resultant texts—self-conscious literary autobiographies.

This perspective on white American autobiography highlights the distinctions between two cultures. Moved to introspection by the apparent "blankness" that surrounded him, the black, southern field slave had scarcely any *a priori* assumptions to act as stays in his quest for self-definition. He was a man of the diaspora, a displaced person imprisoned by an inhumane system. He was among alien gods in a strange land. Vassa describes his initial placement in the New World:

> We were landed up a river a good way from the sea, *about Virginia country,* where we saw few or none of our native Africans, and not one soul who could talk to me. I was a few weeks weeding grass and gathering stones in a plantation; and at last all my companions were distributed different ways, and only myself was left. I was now exceedingly miserable, and thought myself worse off than any of the rest of my companions, for they could talk to each other, but I had no person to speak to that I could understand. In this state, I was constantly grieving and pining, and wishing for death rather than anything else. [*Life,* p. 34]

For the black slave, the white externality provided no ontological or ideological certainties; in fact, it explicitly denied slaves the grounds of being. The seventeenth- and eighteenth-century black codes defined blacks as slaves in perpetuity, removing their chance to become free, participating citizens in the American City of God. The Constitution re-affirmed the slave's bondage, and the repressive legislation of the nine-teenth century categorized him as "chattel personal." Instead of the ebullient sense of a new land offering limitless opportunities, the slave, staring into the heart of whiteness around him, must have felt as though he had been flung into existence without a human purpose. The white externality must have loomed like the Heideggerian "nothingness," the negative foundation of being. Jean Wahl's characterization of Heideg-ger's theory of existence captures the point of view a black American slave might justifiably have held: "Man is in this world, a world lim-ited by death and experienced in anguish; is aware of himself as es-sentially anxious; is burdened by his solitude within the horizon of his temporality."[5]

There were at least two alternatives to this vision. There was the recourse of gazing idealistically back to "Guinea." Sterling Stuckey has shown that a small, but vocal, minority of blacks have always employed this strategy.[6] There was also the possibility of adopting the God of the enslaver as solace. A larger number of blacks chose this option and looked to the apocalyptic day that would bring their release from cap-tivity and vengeance on the oppressors. (Tony McNeill's words, "be-tween Africa and heaven," come to mind.) Finally, though, the picture that emerges from the innumerable accounts of slaves is charged with anguish—an anguish that reveals the black bondsman to himself as cast into the world, forlorn and without refuge.

And unlike white Americans who could assume literacy and familiar-ity with existing literary models as norms, the slave found himself with-out a system of written language—"uneducated," in the denotative sense of the word. His task was not simply one of moving toward the requisite largeness of soul and faith in the value of his experience. He first had to seize the word. His being had to erupt from nothingness. Only by grasping the word could he engage in the speech acts that would ultimately define his selfhood. Further, the slave's task was pri-marily one of creating a human and liberated self rather than of project-ing one that reflected a peculiar landscape and tradition. His problem was not to answer Crèvecoeur's question: "What then is the American, this new man?" It was, rather, the problem of being itself.

The *Narrative of the Life of Frederick Douglass*, one of the finest black American slave narratives, serves to illustrate the black autobiog-rapher's quest for being.[7] The recovered past, the journey back, repre-sented in the work is a sparse existence characterized by brutality and uncertainty:

> I have no accurate knowledge of my age. The opinion was . . . whis-
> pered about that my master was my father; but of the correctness of this
> opinion, I know nothing. [Pp. 21-22]

> My mother and I were separated when I was but an infant. [P. 22]

> I was seldom whipped by my old master, and suffered little from any-
> thing else than hunger and cold. [P. 43]

> Our food was coarse corn meal boiled. This was called *mush*. It was put
> into a large wooden trough, and set down upon the ground. The chil-
> dren were then called, like so many pigs, and like so many pigs they
> would come out and devour the mush. [P. 44]

Unlike David Walker who, in his *Appeal*, attempts to explain why
blacks are violently held in bondage, the young Douglass finds no explanation for his condition. And though he does describe the treatment
of fellow slaves (including members of his own family), the impression
left by the first half of the *Narrative* is one of a lone existence plagued
by anxiety. The white world rigorously suppresses all knowledge and
action that might lead the narrator to a sense of his humanity.

The total process through which this subjugation is achieved can be
seen as an instance of the imposed silence suggested by Forten's address.
Mr. Hugh Auld, whom Douglass is sent to serve in Baltimore, finding
that his wife—out of an impulse to kindness rare among whites in the
Narrative—has begun to instruct the slave in the fundamentals of language, vociferously objects that "learning would *spoil* the best nigger
in the world." Not only is it illegal to teach slaves, but it is also folly. It
makes them aspire to exalted positions. The narrator's reaction to this
injunction might be equated with the "dizziness" that, according to
Heidegger, accompanies a sudden awareness of possibilities that lie
beyond anguish:

> These words sank into my heart, stirred up sentiments within that lay
> slumbering, and called into existence an entirely new train of thought.
> It was a new and special revelation, explaining dark and mysterious
> things, with which my youthful understanding had struggled, but
> struggled in vain. I now understood what had been to me a most per-
> plexing difficulty—to wit, the white man's power to enslave the black
> man. [*Narrative*, p. 49]

Douglass had come to understand, by the "merest accident," the
power of the word. His future is determined by this moment of revelation: he resolves, "at whatever cost of trouble, to learn how to read." He
begins to detach himself from the white externality around him,
declaring:

What he [Mr. Auld] most dreaded, that I most desired. What he most
loved, that I most hated. That which to him was a great evil, to be carefully shunned, was to me a great good to be diligently sought; and the
argument which he so warmly urged, against my learning to read, only
served to inspire me with a desire and determination to learn. [*Narrative*, p. 50]

The balanced antithesis of the passage is but another example—an explicit and forceful one—of the semantic competition involved in culture
contact. Mr. Auld is a representation of those whites who felt that by
superimposing the cultural sign *nigger* on vibrant human beings like
Douglass, they would be able to control the meanings and possibilities
of life in America. One marker for the term *nigger* in Auld's semantic
field is «subhuman agency of labor». What terrifies and angers the
master, however, is that Douglass's capacities—as revealed by his response to Mrs. Auld's kindness and instructions—are not accurately defined by this marker. For Douglass and others of his group are capable
of learning. Hence, the markers in Auld's mapping of *nigger* must also
include «agent capable of education». The semantic complexity, indeed the wrenching irony, of Auld's "nigger" is forcefully illustrated by
the fact that the representation of Auld and *his* point of view enters the
world of the learned by way of a narrative written by a "nigger." Douglass, that is to say, ultimately controls the competition among the various
markers of *nigger* because he has employed meanings (e.g., agent having the power of literacy) drawn from his own field of experience to
represent the competition in a way that invalidates «subhuman agency
of labor». The nature of the autobiographical act, in this instance, is one
of self-enfolding ironies. Douglass, the literate narrator, represents a
Douglass who is perceived by Auld as a "nigger." Certainly the narrator
himself, who is a learned writer, can see this "nigger" only through Auld,
who is the "other." And it is the "otherness" of Auld that is both repudiated and controlled by the narrator's balanced antithesis. By converting the otherness of Auld (and, consequently, his "nigger") into discourse, Douglass becomes the master of his own situation. And the white
man, who wants a silently laboring brute, is finally (and ironically)
visible to himself and a learned reading public only through the discourse of the articulate black spokesman.

Much of the remainder of the *Narrative* counterpoints the assumption
of the white world that the slave is a brute[8] against the slave's expanding
awareness of language and its capacity to carry him toward new dimensions of experience. Chapter seven (the one following the Auld encounter), for example, is devoted to Douglass's increasing command of the
word. He discovers *The Columbian Orator*, with its striking messages of

human dignity and freedom and its practical examples of the results of
fine speaking. He also learns the significance of that all-important word
abolition. Against these new perceptions, he juxtaposes the unthinking
condition of slaves who have not yet acquired language skills equal to
his own. At times he envies them, since they (like the "meanest reptile")
are not fully and self-consciously aware of their situation. For the narrator, language brings the possibility of freedom but renders slavery intolerable. It gives rise to his decision to escape as soon as his age and the
opportunity are appropriate. Meanwhile, he bides his time and perfects
his writing, since (as he says in a telling act of autibiographical conflation) "I might have occasion to write my own pass" (*Narrative*, p. 57).

Douglass's description of his reaction to ships on the Chesapeake
illustrates that he did, effectively, write his own pass: "Those beautiful
vessels, robed in purest white, so delightful to the eye of freemen, were
to me so many shrouded ghosts to terrify and torment me with thoughts
of my wretched condition" (*Narrative*, p. 76). He continues with a
passionate apostrophe that shows how dichotomous are his own condition
and that of these white, "swift-winged angels."

> You are loosed from your moorings, and are free; I am fast in my chains,
> and am a slave! You move merrily before the gentle gale, and I sadly
> before the bloody whip! You are freedom's swift-winged angels, that fly
> around the world; I am confined in bands of iron! O that I were free!
> O, that I were on one of your gallant decks, and under your protecting
> wing! Alas! betwixt me and you, the turbid waters roll. Go on, go on.
> O that I could also go! Could I but swim! If I could fly! O, why was I
> born a man, of whom to make a brute! The glad ship is gone; she hides
> in the dim distance. I am left in the hottest hell of unending slavery.
> O God, save me! God, deliver me! Let me be free! Is there any God?
> Why am I a slave? I will run away. I will not stand it. Get caught, or
> get clear, I'll try it. [*Narrative*, p. 76]

When clarified and understood through language, the deathly, terri-
fying nothingness around him reveals the grounds of being. Freedom,
the ability to chose one's own direction, makes life beautiful and pure.
Only the man free from bondage has a chance to obtain the farthest
reaches of humanity. From what appears a blank and awesome backdrop, Douglass wrests significance. His subsequent progression through
the roles of educated leader, freeman, abolitionist, and autobiographer
marks his firm sense of being.

But while it is the fact that the ships are loosed from their moorings
that intrigues the narrator, he also drives home their whiteness and places
them in a Christian context. Here certain added difficulties for the black
autobiographer reveal themselves. The acquisition of language, which

leads to being, has ramifications that have been best stated by the West Indian novelist George Lamming, drawing on the relationship between Prospero and Caliban in *The Tempest:*

> Prospero has given Caliban Language; and with it an unstated history of consequences, an unknown history of future intentions. This gift of language meant not English, in particular, but speech and concept as a way, a method, a necessary avenue towards areas of the self which could not be reached in any other way. It is in this way, entirely Prospero's enterprise, which makes Caliban aware of possibilities. Therefore, all of Caliban's future—for future is the very name for possibilities—must derive from Prospero's experiment, which is also his risk.[9]

Mr. Auld had seen that "learning" could lead to the restiveness of his slave. Neither he nor his representer, however, seem to understand that it might be possible to imprison the slave even more thoroughly in the way described by Lamming. The angelic Mrs. Auld, however, in accord with the evangelical codes of her era, has given Douglass the rudiments of a system that leads to intriguing restrictions. True, the slave can arrive at a sense of being only through language. But it is also true that, in Douglass's case, a conception of the preeminent form of being is conditioned by white, Christian standards.

To say this is not to charge him with treachery. Africa was for the black southern slave an idealized backdrop, which failed to offer the immediate tangible means of his liberation. Moreover, whites continually sought to strip Africans of their distinctive cultural modes. Vassa's isolation and perplexity upon his arrival in the New World, which are recorded in a passage previously cited, give some notion of the results of this white offensive. Unable to transplant the institutions of his homeland in the soil of America—as the Puritans had done—the black slave had to seek means of survival and fulfillment on that middle ground where the European slave trade had deposited him. He had to seize whatever weapons came to hand in his struggle for self-definition. The range of instruments was limited. Evangelical Christians and committed abolitionists were the only discernible groups standing in the path of America's hypocrisy and inhumanity. The dictates of these groups, therefore, suggested a way beyond servitude. And these were the only signs and wonders in an environment where blacks were deemed animals, or "things." Determined to move beyond a subservient status, cut off from the alternatives held out to whites, endowed with the "feeling" that freedom is the natural condition of life, Douglass adopted a system of symbols that seemed to promise him an unbounded freedom. Having acquired language and a set of dictates that specified freedom and equality as norms, Douglass becomes more assured. His certainty is reflected by the roles he projects for himself in the latter part of his *Narrative*. They are all in harmony with a white, Christian, abolitionist framework.

During his year at Mr. Freeland's farm, for example, he spends much of his time "doing something that looked like bettering the condition of my race" (*Narrative*, p. 90). His enterprise is a Sabbath school devoted to teaching his "loved fellow-slaves" so they will be able "to read the will of God" (*Narrative*, p. 89). His efforts combine the philanthropic impulse of the eighteenth-century man of sympathy with a zeal akin to Jupiter Hammon's.

Having returned to Mr. Auld's house after an absence of three years, he undertakes a useful trade and earns the right to hire out his own time. All goes well until he attends a religious camp meeting one Saturday night and fails to pay the allotted weekly portion of his wages to his master. When Auld rebukes him, the demands of the "robber" are set against the natural right of a man to worship God freely. Once again, freedom is placed in a Christian context. Infuriated, Douglass decides that the time and circumstances are now right for his escape. When he arrives in New York, he feels like a man who has "escaped a den of hungry lions" (a kind of New World Daniel), and one of his first acts is to marry Anna Murray in a Christian ceremony presided over by the Reverend James W.C. Pennington. It would not be an overstatement to say that the liberated self portrayed by Douglass is firmly Christian, having adopted cherished values from the white world that held him in bondage. It is not surprising, therefore, to see the narrator moving rapidly into the ranks of the abolitionists—that body of men and women bent on putting America in harmony with its professed ideals. Nor is it striking that the *Narrative* concludes with an appendix in which the narrator justifies himself as a true Christian.

In recovering the details of his past, then, the autobiographer shows a progression from baffled and isolated existent to Christian abolitionist lecturer and writer. The self in the autobiographical moment (the present, the time in which the work is composed), however, seems unaware of the limitations that have accompanied this progress. Even though the writer seems to have been certain (given the cohesiveness of the *Narrative*) how he was going to picture his development and how the emergent self should appear to the reader, he seems to have suppressed the fact that one cannot transcend existence in a universe where there is *only* existence. One can realize one's humanity through "speech and concept," but one cannot distinguish the uniqueness of the self if the "avenue towards areas of the self" excludes rigorously individualizing definitions of a human, black identity.

Douglass grasps language in a Promethean act of will, but he leaves unexamined its potentially devastating effects. One reflection of his uncritical acceptance of the perspective made available by literacy is the *Narrative* itself, which was written at the urging of white abolitionists who had become the fugitive slave's employers. The work was written to prove that the narrator had indeed been a slave. And while autobiographical conventions forced him to portray as accurately as possible the existentiality of his original condition, the light of abolitionism is always implicitly present, guiding the narrator into calm, Christian, and publicly accessible harbors. The issue here is not simply one of intentionality (how the author wished his utterances to be taken). It is, rather, one that combines Douglass's understandable desire to keep his job with more complex considerations governing "privacy" as a philosophical concept.

Language, like other social institutions, is public; it is one of the surest means we have of communicating with the "other," the world outside ourselves. Moreover, since language seems to provide the principal way in which we conceptualize and convey anything (thoughts, feelings, sensations, and so forth), it is possible that no easily describable "private" domain exists. By adopting language as his instrument for extracting meaning from nothingness, being from existence, Douglass becomes a public figure.

He is comforted, but also restricted, by the system he adopts. The results are shown in the hierarchy of preferences that, finally, constitute value in the *Narrative*. The results are additionally demonstrated by those instances in the *Narrative* where the work's style is indistinguishable from that of the sentimental-romantic oratory and creative writing that marked the American nineteenth century. Had there been a separate, written black language available, Douglass might have fared better. What is seminal to this discussion, however, is that the nature of the autobiographer's situation seemed to force him to move to a public version of the self—one molded by the values of white America. Thus Mr. Auld can be contained and controlled within the slave narrator's abolitionist discourse because Auld is a stock figure of such discourse. He is the penurious master corrupted by the soul-killing effects of slavery who appears in poetry, fiction, and polemics devoted to the abolitionist cause.

But the slave narrator must also accomplish the almost unthinkable (since thought and language are inseparable) task of transmuting an authentic, unwritten self—a self that exists outside the conventional literary discourse structures of a white reading public—into a literary representation. The simplest, and perhaps the most effective, way of proceeding is for the narrator to represent his "authentic" self as a figure embodying the public virtues and values esteemed by his intended audience. Once he has seized the public medium, the slave narrator can construct a public message, or massage, calculated to win approval for himself and (provided he has one) his cause. In the white abolitionist William Lloyd Garrison's preface to Douglass's *Narrative*, for example, the slave narrator is elaborately praised for his seemingly godlike movement "into the field of public usefulness" (*Narrative*, pp. v-vi). Garrison writes of his own reaction to Douglass's first abolitionist lecture to a white audience:

> I shall never forget his first speech at the convention—the extraordinary emotion it excited in my own mind—the powerful impression it created upon a crowded auditory, completely taken by surprise—the applause which followed from the beginning to the end of his felicitous remarks. I think I never hated slavery so intensely as at that moment; certainly, my perception of the enormous outrage which is inflicted by it, on the godlike nature of its victims, was rendered far more clear than ever. There stood one, in physical proportion and stature commanding and exact—in intellect richly endowed—in natural eloquence a prodigy—in soul manifestly "created but a little lower than the angels"—trembling for his safety, hardly daring to believe that on the American soil, a single white person could be found who would befriend him at all hazards, for the love of God and humanity. Capable of high attainments as an intellectual and moral being—needing nothing but a comparatively small amount of cultivation to make him an ornament to society and a blessing to his race—by the law of the land, by the voice of the people, by the terms of the slave code, he was only a piece of property, a beast of burden, a chattel personal, nevertheless! [*Narrative*, p. vi]

Obviously, a talented, heroic, and richly endowed figure such as Garrison describes here was of inestimable "public usefulness" to the abolitionist crusade. And the Nantucket Convention of 1841 where Garrison first heard Douglass speak may be compared to a communicative context in which the sender and receiver employ a common channel (i.e., the English language) to arrive at, or to reinforce for each other, an agreed-upon message. Douglass transmits the "heroic fugitive" message to an abolitionist audience that has made such a figure part of its conceptual, linguistic, and rhetorical repertoire.

The issue that such an "autobiographical" act raises for the literary analyst is that of authenticity. Where, for example, in Douglass's *Narrative* does a prototypical black American self reside? What are the distinctive narrative elements that combine to form a representation of this self? In light of the foregoing discussion, it seems that such elements would be located in those episodes and passages of the *Narrative* that chronicle the struggle for literacy. For once literacy has been achieved, the black self, even as represented in the *Narrative*, begins to distance itself from the domain of experience constituted by the oral-aural community of the slave quarters (e.g., the remarks comparing fellow slaves to the meanest reptiles). The voice of the unwritten self, once it is subjected to the linguistic codes, literary conventions, and audience expectations of a literate population, is perhaps never again the authentic voice of black American slavery. It is, rather, the voice of a self transformed by an autobiographical act into a sharer in the general public discourse about slavery.

How much of the lived (as opposed to the represented) slave experience is lost in this transformation depends upon the keenness of the narrator's skill in confronting both the freedom and the limitations resulting from his literacy in Prospero's tongue. By the conclusion of Douglass's *Narrative*, the represented self seems to have left the quarters almost entirely behind. The self that appears in the work's closing moments is that of a public spokesman, talking about slavery to a Nantucket convention of whites:

> while attending an anti-slavery convention at Nantucket, on the 11th of August, 1841, I felt strongly moved to speak, and was at the same time much urged to do so by Mr. William C. Coffin, a gentleman who had heard me speak in the colored people's meeting at New Bedford. It was a severe cross, and I took it up reluctantly. The truth was, I felt myself a slave, and the idea of speaking to white people weighed me down. I spoke but a few moments, when I felt a degree of freedom, and said what I desired with considerable ease. From that time until now, I have been engaged in pleading the cause of my brethren—with what success, and with what devotion, I leave to those acquainted with my labors to decide. [*Narrative*, pp. 118-19]

The Christian imagery ("a severe cross"), strained reluctance to speak before whites, discovered ease of eloquence, and public-spirited devotion to the cause of his brethren that appear in this passage are all in keeping with the image of the publicly useful and ideal fugitive captured in Garrison's preface. Immediately before telling the reader of his address to the Nantucket convention, Douglass notes that "he had not long been a reader of the 'Liberator' [Garrison's abolitionist newspaper]" before he got "a pretty correct idea of the principles, measures and spirit of the anti-slavery reform"; he adds that he "took right hold of the cause . . . and never felt happier than when in an anti-slavery meeting" (*Narrative*, p. 118). This suggests to me that the communication between Douglass and Garrison begins long before their face-to-face encounter at Nantucket, with the fugitive slave's culling from the white publisher's newspaper those virtues and values esteemed by abolitionist readers. The fugitive's voice is further refined by his attendance and speeches at the "colored people's meeting at New Bedford," and it finally achieves its emotionally stirring participation in the white world of public discourse at the 1841 Nantucket convention.

Of course, there are tangible reasons within the historical (as opposed to the autobiographical) domain for the image that Douglass projects. The feeling of larger goals shared with a white majority culture has always been present among blacks. We need only turn to the writings of Hammon, Wheatley, and Vassa to see this. From at least the third decade of the nineteenth century this feeling of a common pursuit was reinforced by men like Garrison and Wendell Phillips, by constitutional amendments, civil rights legislation, and perennial assurances that the white man's dream is the black man's as well. Furthermore, what better support for this assumption of commonality could Douglass find than in his own palpable achievements in American society?

When he revised his original *Narrative* for the third time, therefore, in 1893, the work that resulted represented the conclusion of a process that began for Douglass at the home of Hugh Auld. *The Life and Times of Frederick Douglass Written by Himself* is public, rooted in the language of its time, and considerably less existential in tone than the 1845 *Narrative*. What we have is a verbose and somewhat hackneyed story of a life, written by a man of achievement. The white externality has been transformed into a world where sterling deeds by blacks are possible. Douglass describes his visit to the home of his former master who, forty years after the slave's escape, now rests on his deathbed:

> On reaching the house I was met by Mr. Wm. H. Buff, a son-in-law of Capt. Auld, and Mrs. Louisa Buff, his daughter, and was conducted to the bedroom of Capt. Auld. We addressed each other simultaneously, he called me "Marshal Douglass," and I, as I had always called him, "Captain Auld." Hearing myself called by him "Marshal Douglass," I instantly broke up the formal nature of the meeting by saying, "not *Marshal*, but Frederick to you as formerly." We shook hands cordially and in the act of doing so, he, having been long stricken with palsy, shed tears as men thus afflicted will do when excited by any deep emotion. The sight of him, the changes which time had wrought in him, his tremulous hands constantly in motion, and all the circumstances of his condition affected me deeply, and for a time choked my voice and made me speechless.[10]

A nearly tearful silence by the black "Marshal" (a term repeated three times in very brief space) of the District of Columbia as he gazes with sympathy on the body of his former master—this is a great distance, to be sure, from the aggressive young slave who appropriated language in order to do battle with the masters.

A further instance of Douglass's revised perspective is provided by his return to the home plantation of Colonel Lloyd on the Wye River in Talbot County, Maryland:

> Speaking of this desire of mine [to revisit the Lloyd Plantation] last winter, to Hon. John L. Thomas, the efficient collector at the Port of Baltimore, and a leading Republican of the State of Maryland, he urged me very much to go, and added that he often took a trip to the Eastern Shore in his revenue cutter *Guthrie* (otherwise known in time of war as the *Ewing*), and would be much pleased to have me accompany him on one of these trips. . . . In four hours after leaving Baltimore we were anchored in the river off the Lloyd estate, and from the deck of our vessel I saw once more the stately chimneys of the grand old mansion which I had last seen from the deck of the *Sally Lloyd* when a boy. I left there as a slave, and returned as a freeman; I left there unknown to the outside world, and returned well known; I left there on a freight boat and returned on a revenue cutter; I left on a vessel belonging to Col. Edward Lloyd, and returned on one belonging to the United States. [*Life and Times,* pp. 445-46]

The "stately chimneys of the grand old mansion" sounds very much like the Plantation Tradition, and how different the purpose of the balanced antithesis is in this passage from that noted in the delineation of the slave's realization of language as a key to freedom ("What he most dreaded, that I most desired . . ."). This passage also stands in marked contrast to the description of ships on the Chesapeake cited earlier ("those beautiful vessels . . . so many shrouded ghosts"). The venerable status of the *Guthrie* is now matched by the eminence of the marshal of the District of Columbia.

Douglass, in his public role, often resembles the courteous and gentlemanly narrator of Vassa's work—a man determined to put readers at ease by assuring them of his accomplishments (and the sterling company he keeps) in language that is careful not to offend readers' various sensibilities. It is strikingly coincidental that *The Life and Times of Frederick Douglass* was reprinted in 1895, the year in which its author died and Booker T. Washington emerged as one of the most influential black public spokesmen America had ever known.

In 1901, Washington's *Up from Slavery* appeared, and it offers a perfect illustration of the black autobiographer's assumption of the public mantle. Unlike Douglass's 1845 *Narrative* (but like the 1893 version), Washington's work is primarily a life-and-times account that views the self within the larger American social current. Instead of apology, or the justification of rebellion, one finds in *Up from Slavery* gratitude—even joy—that the self has been swept along by the current and acknowledged for aiding its progressive flow. Moral uplift and financial success quickly run together as Washington accepts Economic Man as the norm in his own ascent from ignorance, poverty, and vice to property ownership and a sound bank account. Of course, the first president of Tuskegee Institute cannot be immediately denounced for portraying himself in this manner, since such a condemnation would require censuring the entire age in which he lived. Situated in the Gilded Age and surrounded by a set of conditions that the historian Rayford Logan has called the "nadir" in American race relations, Washington adopted a public mask that displayed a black self in harmony with its era. The problem with this strategy was that it forced the narrator to violate the governing conventions of autobiography at the very outset. He set truth aside from the beginning and simply ignored facts that did not agree with his mask.

Washington, therefore, is no bold historian who has surveyed chaos and given us the verifiable details of his journey. We cannot grasp the uniqueness of a black self because a self distinguishable from those of Huntington, Carnegie, Vanderbilt, and other white capitalists never emerges. Further, the sense that black being can emerge only by erupting through a white nothingness is contradicted by the countless white friends who aid Washington on his way to language, education, and financial stability. Rebecca Chalmers Barton has defined Washington and all black autobiographers who followed his lead as "accommodators," i.e., pseudoidealists who concealed their ambitiousness and feelings of inferiority in religious rhetoric and oratory dedicated to a cause.[11] Given the nature of *Up from Slavery*, this assessment seems just. It is difficult to understand how a more recent writer[12] has set such store by those turn-of-the-century black autobiographies which, time and again, reveal their narrators drawn into the linguistic prisons—the confining public discourse—of the white world.

Difficult, but not impossible. For if one takes language in a broad social sense and treats *Up from Slavery* as a social document, then Washington was simply an imitator of the commercial, industrial utterances that guided his age. His narrative is filled with the kind of observation one would expect to find in a primer devoted to principles of success in business and the conduct of the moral life in an industrialist society:

> One thing I was determined to do from the first, and that was to keep the credit of the school high, and this, I think I can say without boasting, we have done all through these years. I shall always remember a bit of advice given me by Mr. George W. Campbell, the white man to whom I have referred as the one who induced General Armstrong to send me to Tuskegee. Soon after I entered upon the work Mr. Campbell said to

me, in his fatherly way: "Washington, always remember that credit is capital."[13]

On the subject of soliciting contributions for Tuskegee:

> Such work gives one a rare opportunity to study human nature. It also has its compensation in giving one an opportunity to meet some of the best people in the world—to be more correct, I think I should say *the best* people in the world. When one takes a broad survey of the country, he will find that the most useful and influential people in it are those who take the deepest interest in institutions that exist for the purpose of making the world better. [P. 127]

On interaction with the wealthy:

> I have found that strict business methods go a long way in securing the interest of rich people. It has been my constant aim at Tuskegee to carry out, in our financial and other operations, such business methods as would be approved of by any New York banking house. [P. 132]

Two of his improving maxims read:

> In meeting men, in many places, I have found that the happiest people are those who do the most for others; the most miserable are those who do the least. I have also found that few things, if any, are capable of making one so blind and narrow as race prejudice. [P. 152]

> I have a strong feeling that every individual owes it to himself, and to the cause which he is serving, to keep a vigorous, healthy body, with the nerves steady and strong, prepared for great efforts and prepared for disappointments and trying positions. [P. 171]

Finally, one of the most infamous examples of Washington's employment of the language and concepts of the commercial industrial estate of his era appears in his speech to the Atlanta Cotton States and International Exposition, which was delivered in 1895, and which is set down in full in *Up from Slavery*. He advises his recently emancipated fellow blacks:

> when it comes to business, pure and simple, it is in the South that the Negro is given a man's chance in the commercial world, and in nothing is this Exposition more eloquent than in emphasizing this chance. Our greatest danger is that in the great leap from slavery to freedom we may overlook the fact that the masses of us are to live by the productions of our hands, and fail to keep in mind that we shall prosper in proportion as we learn to dignify and glorify common labour and put brains and skill into the common occupations of life. . . . It is at the bottom of life we must begin, and not at the top. [*Up from Slavery,* p. 147]

Founded on the assumption that only through hard work and abundant evidence that one has something to contribute to the white community can the black American rise, Washington's statement implicitly sanctioned the violently racist practices of his day. When Governor Bullock of Georgia introduced him at the Exposition as "a representative of Negro enterprise and Negro civilization," he surely had a clear idea of the type of representation of black life and culture Washington would present. The occasion, as it appears in *Up from Slavery,* is yet another instance of the coming together of a white audience and a black speaker who has molded a publicly useful "autobiographical" self. In Washington's case, unfortunately, Governor Bullock (and not William Lloyd Garrison) was the exemplary member of the white audience. Thus Washington, as a black public spokesman, became the compromiser of his own people's rights, and the Barton view of the author of *Up from Slavery* is reinforced by an analysis of the work as a social document.

But if language is considered not in the broad social sense but in the more restricted context of fictive discourse, then Washington's narrative, as a fictive account, presents a coherent structure signaling a particular domain of meaning. Rather than the "pseudoidealism" deplored by Barton, it implies propositions of the form "If X then Y."[14] For example, the world of the slave is one of unlimited opportunity; the black man can, if only he will. This amounts to a tacit agreement between the propositions governing *Up from Slavery* and the professed ideals of the larger white American culture. The work is designed as a validation of what the psychologists Hans Vaihinger and Alfred Adler called "fictional ideas" or "fictional finalism."[15] The notion captured by these phrases is that human beings are motivated in their present actions by their expectations of the future, by their orientation toward a goal which has no counterpart in reality. "This final goal may be a fiction, that is, an ideal that is impossible to realize but which is nonetheless a very real spur to human striving and the ultimate explanation of conduct."[16] Statements such as "all men are created equal," that is to say, or "honesty is the best policy," govern conduct. Washington's work, under the aspect of fictive discourse, can be interpreted as saying: "The propositions are analytic (basic, beyond question). Here is a story to prove it." In this light, *Up from Slavery* offers a stirring account. The differences between black and white fade; the disruptions of the triangular trade and chattel slavery are excusable failings of a past that is best forgotten. The motivation is directed entirely toward the future.

The problem with this interpretive strategy, however, is that while it provides one means of apprehending and valuing the text, it also ignores the significant conventions surrounding the genre that Washingtion and his cohorts chose to employ. Autobiography—the recounting of the self's or the selves' history—does not presuppose analytic propositions. It is, rather, a gathering together of synthetic propositions—factual statements whose truth-value is assumed to be historically determinate. Its statements are taken to accord with an actual past that is amenable to investigation. The difference between the fictive and the autobiographical can be suggested by the responses each entails to a statement like the following:

> The "Ku Klux" period was, I think, the darkest part of the Reconstruction days. I have referred to this unpleasant part of the history of the South simply for the purpose of calling attention to the great change that has taken place since the days of the "Ku Klux." To-day there are no such organizations in the South, and the fact that such ever existed is almost forgotten by both races. There are few places in the South now where public sentiment would permit such organizations to exist. [*Up from Slavery*, p. 71]

The truth-value of this assertion if it appeared in a novel would not be a very fruitful analytical issue to pursue. In an autobiography, however, the statement must be set against historical evidence as we know it. Only then can a reader judge the author's relationship to fundamental conventions, or rules, of the autobiographical genre.[17] And in the example cited, the narrator's assertion is a patent falsification.

One cannot dismiss Washington's work, however, as simply the effort of a writer confused about two realms of discourse, the fictive and the autobiographical. There is no more justification for such a course than there is for ignoring Wheatley because she used heroic couplets. What is demanded from the literary investigator is an analysis that will reveal the intersections between the two worlds of discourse. This discovery might lead, in turn, to a wider inquiry into the nature of black narrative. The school of "accommodators" can serve as a starting point, that is to say, in the search for higher-order rules that condition the fictionalizing of the self in autobiography and the construction of an autobiographical self in fiction that mark such narratives as Richard Wright's *Black Boy* and James Weldon Johnson's *The Autobiography of an Ex-Colored Man*. The question is how such works achieve their effects and eventually come to hold valued positions in Black intellectual and literary history.

Though Washington's voice is surely not the one Forten had in mind when he spoke of the slaves who might trouble their masters' quiet, it is nonetheless a distinctive voice and raises its own set of problems about Caliban's presence in the New World. *Up from Slavery*, like Wheatley's poetry and Vassa's narrative, stands as a verbal structure that compels our attention. If it falsifies details of the journey, it promises much for our understanding of the voyage into language. The wholeness of the self, the self as public man, the autobigraphical self engaged in fictive discourse—these, too, represent attempts to find terms for order in a complex world.

The culturally unique aspects of *Up from Slavery* reside, like those in the works of the authors already discussed, at a level of functional oppositions. In this case, the disparity is between a graphically depicted hell of rural, impoverished, illiterate black southern life and an intriguingly displayed heaven of black southern urbanity, thrift, and education. Two distinct modes of discourse sustain this opposition—the autobiographical self exists in the former, while the fictive self lives in (and testifies to the possibility of) the latter.

Notes

1. *Autobiographical Acts* (Baltimore: Johns Hopkins University Press, 1976). "All reading (or writing) involves us in choice: we choose to pursue a style or subject matter, to struggle with or against a design. We also choose, as passive as it may seem, to take part in an interaction, and it is here that generic labels have their use. The genre does not tell us the style or construction of a text as much as how we should expect to 'take' that style or mode of construction—what force it should have for us" (p. 4). Professor Bruss is drawing on a speech-act theory as delineated by J. L. Austin, Paul Strawson, and John Searle. The nature, or force, of the speech act combines context, conditions, and intentions; it is called by the philosophers of language mentioned above the *illocutionary force* of an utterance. If the illocutionary force of a speech act is one involving certain rules, contexts, and intentions of self-revelation, the act can be called autobiographical. What I shall be investigating in the next few pages is the peculiar illocutionary force of certain black autobiographies produced during the nineteenth century. For an account of black autobiography, see Stephen Butterfield, *Black Autobiography in America* (Amherst: University of Massachusetts Press, 1974).
2. Rebecca Chalmers Barton, *Witnesses for Freedom* (New York: Harper, 1948), p. xii.
3. George McMichael, ed., *Anthology of American Literature* (New York: Macmillan, 1974), 1:228.
4. *The Examined Self* (Princeton: Princeton University Press, 1964), p. 39.
5. *A Short History of Existentialism* (New York: Philosophical Library, 1949), p. 31. See also Jean Wahl, *Philosophies of Existence: An Introduction to the Basic Thought of Kierkegaard, Heidegger, Jaspers, Marcel, Sartre* (New York: Schocken, 1959).
6. *The Ideological Origins of Black Nationalism* (Boston: Beacon, 1972).
7. *Narrative of the Life of Frederick Douglass, an American Slave. Written by Himself* (New York: Signet, 1968), p. 21.
8. In a fine analysis of the *Narrative* ("Animal Farm Unbound," *New*

Letters 43 [1977]: 25-48), H. Bruce Franklin explores the significance for American literature of white assumptions that blacks are outside the human family. But cf. my own treatment of animal imagery in Douglass, which appeared in my collection of essays *Long Black Song* (Charlottesville: University Press of Virginia, 1972); and Albert Stone, "Identity and Art in Frederick Douglass' Narrative," *CLA Journal* 17 (1973): 192-213.

9. Quoted from Janheinz Jahn, *Neo-African Literature* (New York: Grove, 1969), p. 240.

10. *The Life and Times of Frederick Douglass Written by Himself* (New York: Collier, 1973), p. 442.

11. *Witnesses for Freedom*, pp. 3-40.

12. John Blassingame, "Black Autobiographies as History and Literature," *Black Scholar* 5 (1973-74): 2-9.

13. *Up from Slavery*, in Franklin, ed., *Three Negro Classics*, p. 107. Unless otherwise specified, all citations refer to this edition.

14. The concept of "fictive discourse" is drawn from the work of Barbara Herrnstein Smith. Professor Smith makes a distinction between "natural discourse" and fictive discourse. While "a natural utterance is an historical *event* [and] like any other event, it occupies a specific and unique point in time and space," a fictive utterance is historically indeterminate. It is possible, therefore, for it to postulate and explore propositions that are considered "timeless." Works of imaginative literature, that is to say, may be thought of as discourse structures that imply analytical propositions. An analytical proposition, according to philosophy, is one of the conditions of possibility of reason. All men of reason understand that "If *X* then *Y*." The truth-value of such propositions is not contingent upon empirical reference, but upon reason, operating in a timeless dimension. See "Poetry as Fiction," in Cohen, ed., *New Directions in Literary History*, pp. 165-87. See also her book *On the Margins of Discourse* (Chicago: University of Chicago Press, 1978). For a discussion of analytic propositions in relation to speech acts, see Searle, *Speech Acts*.

15. The discussion here is based on C. S. Hall and Gardner Lindzey, *Theories of Personality* (New York: Wiley, 1978), pp. 160-61.

16. Ibid., p. 161.

17. Bruss, in stating her rules, or appropriateness conditions, for autobiographical acts of discourse says: "(a) under existing conventions, a claim is made for the truth-value of what the autobiography reports—no matter how difficult that truth-value might be to ascertain, whether the report treats of private experiences or publicly observable occasions. (b) The audience is expected to accept these reports as true, and is free to 'check up' on them or attempt to discredit them" (*Autobiographical Acts*, p. 11).

Text and Contexts of Harriet Jacobs' Incidents in the Life of a Slave Girl: Written by Herself

JEAN FAGAN YELLIN

> Your proposal to me has been thought over and over again, but not without some most painful remembrance. Dear Amy, if it was the life of a heroine with no degradation associated with it! Far better to have been one of the starving poor of Ireland whose bones had to bleach on the highways than to have been a slave with the curse of slavery stamped upon yourself and children. I have tried for the last two years to conquor . . . [my stubborn pride] and I feel that God has helped me, or I never would consent to give my past to anyone, for I would not do it without giving the whole truth. If it could help save another from my fate, it would be selfish and unChristian in me to keep it back.[1]

With these words, more than a century ago, the newly-emancipated fugitive slave Harriet Jacobs expressed her conflicting responses to a friend's suggestion that she make her life story public. Although she finally succeeded in writing and publishing her sensational tale, its authenticity—long questioned—has recently been denied. Jacobs' *Incidents in the Life of a Slave Girl: Written by Herself* has just been transformed from a questionable narrative to a well-documented pseudonymous slave narrative, however, by the discovery of a cache of her letters.[2]

This correspondence establishes Jacobs' authorship and clarifies the role of her editor. The letters present a unique chronicle of the efforts of a female fugitive slave to write and publish her autobiography in antebellum America. In doing so, they recount her involvement with an unlikely grouping of mid-century writers: litterateur Nathaniel P. Willis, best-selling author Harriet Beecher Stowe, black abolitionist William C. Nell and white abolitionist L. Maria Child.

Authenticating Jacobs' authorship of *Incidents* sparks the need for a reexamination of this book within multiple contexts: black history and letters, women's history and letters, and American history and letters. But while identifying *Incidents* as the work of black Harriet Jacobs—and not her editor, white L. Maria Child—presents an occasion for exploring its place within these contexts, it does not change this text or make it any less peculiar either in content or in form. And it is peculiar. *Incidents* is, to my knowledge, the only slave narrative that takes as its subject the sexual exploitation of female slaves—thus centering on sexual oppression as well as on oppression of race and condition; it is, to my knowledge, the only slave narrative that identifies its audience as female; it is, to my knowledge, the only slave narrative written in the style of sentimental fiction; and my work suggests that it may be the first full-length slave narrative by a woman to be published in this country. *Incidents* requires students of the narrative to examine the significance of gender in relation to the content and the form of this entire genre. Further, as an antebellum Afro-American female autobiography, *Incidents* requires students of American women's literature to examine the significance of race in women's writings; and as the work of a fugitive slave, it requires an examination of the significance of condition in women's writings. Because it is, to my knowledge, the only pre-Civil War American female autobiography written for publication that renders a first-person account of sexual nonconformity, it requires students of American women's literature to examine the issue of sexual nonconformity in women's writings. All of this makes *Incidents* of interest to students of Afro-American, women's and American culture. This book is at once the plea of an erring American female, the heroic recital of a valiant black slave mother, and a woman's vindication of her life.

The first half of this essay presents evidence establishing Jacobs' authorship of *Incidents* and discusses the history of the text. The second half tentatively explores some of the issues involved in locating *Incidents* within its multiple contexts.

I

The discovery of Jacobs' letters has made it possible to trace her life. She was born near Edenton, North Carolina, about 1815. In *Incidents*, she writes that her parents died while she was a child and that at the death of her beloved mistress (who had taught her to read and spell) she was sent to a licentious master. As she grew into adolescence, he subjected her to unrelenting sexual harassment. In her teens she bore two children to another white man. When her jealous master threatened her with concubinage, Jacobs ran away. Aided by sympathetic black and white neighbors, she was sheltered by her family and for years remained hidden in the home of her grandmother, a freed slave. During this time her children, whose father had bought them from her master, were allowed to live with her grandmother. But despite their father's repeated promises to free them—and although he later took their little girl to a free state—they were not emancipated.

About 1842, Harriet Jacobs finally escaped to the North, contacted her daughter, was joined by her son, and found work in New York. Because the woman who hired her as a nursemaid was the wife of magazinist Nathaniel P. Willis, it has been possible to use Willis' materials to piece out—and to corroborate—Jacobs' story.[3] Harassed as a fugitive in New York, Jacobs escaped to Massachusetts. After returning, when again threatened, she confided in Mrs. Willis. Explaining that she and her children were fugitives Jacobs enlisted Mrs. Willis' aid and fled to Boston to live. The following spring, Mrs. Willis died. Willis prevailed upon Jacobs to accompany his little girl when he took her to visit her grandparents in England. Upon returning to America, Jacobs learned that in her absence her son had left his apprenticeship and had shipped out to sea; instead of resuming her life in Boston, Jacobs enrolled her daughter in a boarding school and joined her brother in Rochester, New York.

In 1849, this prospering canal city was a seed bed of reform. Frederick Douglass' *North Star* was published there each week, and the Women's Rights convention had met only months earlier. With her brother, John S. Jacobs, a fugitive active in the abolitionist movement, Jacobs ran an anti-slavery reading room where she met other reformers. She made the Quaker Amy Post, a feminist and abolitionist, her confidante; her letters to Post date from this period. In September 1850, Jacobs returned to New York and resumed work in the Willis household. When again hounded by the slaveholders who claimed them as property, she and her children were purchased and manumitted by Willis.

It was following this—between 1853 and 1858—that Jacobs acquiesced to Post's urgings; after a brush with Harriet Beecher Stowe, she wrote out the story of her life by herself. In 1859, with letters of introduction from American abolitionists to British anti-slavery leaders, she travelled to England in an unsuccessful effort to arrange for publication of her book. Finally, with the help of black abolitionist writer William C. Nell and white abolitionist writer L. Maria Child (whose correspondence, too, corroborates that of Jacobs), her narrative was published at Boston early in 1861. As the national crisis developed into civil war, Jacobs worked for emancipation by publicizing and circulating her slave narrative. During the war, she left her job with the Willis family and went to Washington, D.C. as a nurse for black troops. She later returned South, making at least one trip back to Edenton. Jacobs remained actively engaged in work among the freed people for the next thirty years. When she died in Washington, D.C., in 1897, she was eulogized by another prominent black abolitionist, Rev. Francis J. Grimke.[4]

In addition to providing overwhelming evidence establishing Jacobs' authorship and defining Child's role as editor, this correspondence yields a new perspective on several antebellum writers.

Jacobs' letters consistently express the conviction that, unlike both his first and his second wife, Nathaniel P. Willis was "pro-slavery." Because of this—although she repeatedly sought help in obtaining the time and privacy to write, even requesting introductions to public figures in the hope they would aid the publication of her book—Jacobs consistently refused to ask for Willis' aid. She did not even want him to know that she was writing. For years, while living under his roof, she worked on her book secretly and at night. A recent reading of Willis' picturesque 1859 account of slave life entitled "Negro Happiness in Virginia" helped me understand Jacobs' attitude.[5]

Jacobs' negative assessment of Harriet Beecher Stowe is not based on the woman's attitudes toward slavery, however, but on her views on the issue of race. Her brief involvement with Stowe was decisive in the genesis of *Incidents.* When Jacobs first agreed to a public account of her life, Jacobs did not plan to write it herself, but to enlist Stowe's help in producing a dictated narrative. To this end, Jacobs asked Post to approach Stowe and suggest that she meet Jacobs and hear her story. Then—reading in the papers that Uncle Tom's author planned a trip to England—Jacobs persuaded Mrs. Willis to write suggesting that Stowe permit Jacobs' daughter Louisa to accompany her to England. Jacobs explained that this would yield triple results: Louisa could interest Stowe in Jacobs' story; Stowe's patronage would benefit Louisa; and "Louisa would make a very good representative of a southern slave" for the English to meet.[6]

Harriet Beecher Stowe evidently responded by writing to Mrs. Willis that she would not take the child with her, by forwarding to Mrs. Willis Post's sketch of Jacobs' sensational life for verification, and by proposing that if it were true, she herself would use Jacobs' story in *The Key to Uncle Tom's Cabin,* which she was rushing to complete. Reporting all of this to Post, Jacobs suggests that she felt denigrated as a mother, betrayed as a woman, and threatened as a writer by Stowe's action.

> [Mrs. Stowe] said it would be much care to her to take Louisa. As she went by invitation, it would not be right, and she was afraid that if . . . [Louisa's] situation as a slave should be known, it would subject her to much petting and patronizing, which would be more pleasing to a young girl than useful; and the English were very apt to do it, and . . . [Mrs. Stowe] was very much opposed to it with this class of people. . . .
> I had never opened my life to Mrs. Willis concerning my children. In

the charitableness of her own heart, she sympathized with me and never asked their origin. My suffering she knew. It embarrassed me at first, but I told her the truth; but we both thought it wrong in Mrs. Stowe to have sent your letter. She might have written to inquire if she liked.

Mrs. Willis wrote her a very kind letter begging that she would not use any of the facts in her *Key*, saying that I wished it to be a history of my life entirely by itself, which would do more good, and it needed no romance; but if she wanted some facts for her book, that I would be most happy to give her some. She never answered the letter. She [Mrs. Willis] wrote again, and I wrote twice, with no better success. . . .

I think she did not like my objection. I can't help it.[7]

Jacobs later expressed her racial outrage:

Think, dear Amy, that a visit to Stafford House would spoil me, as Mrs. Stowe thinks petting is more than my race can bear? Well, what a pity we poor blacks can't have the firmness and stability of character that you white people have![8]

Jacobs' distrust of Willis and disillusionment with Stowe contrast with her confidence in William C. Nell and L. Maria Child. After the Stowe episode, Jacobs decided to write her story herself. She spent years on the manuscript and when it was finished, more years trying to get it published in England and in America. Finally, in a letter spelling out what the lack of an endorsement from Willis or Stowe had cost her, she broke a long silence by reporting to Post that Nell and Child were helping to arrange for the publication of her autobiography.

Difficulties seemed to thicken, and I became discouraged. . . . My manuscript was read at Phillips and Sampson. They agreed to take it if I could get Mrs. Stowe or Mr. Willis to write a preface for it. The former I had the second clinch from, and the latter I would not ask, and before anything was done, this establishment failed. So I gave up the effort until this autumn [when] I sent it to Thayer and Eldridge of Boston. They were willing to publish it if I could obtain a preface from Mrs. Child. . . .

I had never seen Mrs. Child. Past experience made me tremble at the thought of approaching another satellite of so great magnitude . . . [but] through W.C. Nell's ready kindness, I met Mrs. Child at the anti-slavery office. Mrs. C. is like yourself, a whole-souled woman. We soon found the way to each other's hearts. I will send you some of her letters. . . .[9]

Accompanying this correspondence are two letters from L. Maria Child to Harriet Jacobs. These, I believe, resolve the questions historians have repeatedly raised concerning the editing of Jacobs' manuscript. Child begins the first letter by describing her editorial procedures in much the same way she later discussed them in her Introduction to *Incidents*.

> I have been busy with your M.S. ever since I saw you; and have only done one-third of it. I have very little occasion to alter the language, which is wonderfully good, for one whose opportunities for education have been so limited. The events are interesting, and well told; the remarks are also good, and to the purpose. But I am copying a great deal of it, for the purpose of transposing sentences and pages, so as to bring the story into continuous *order*, and the remarks into *appropriate* places. I think you will see that this renders the story much more clear and entertaining.

Here Child makes two editorial suggestions that Jacobs evidently followed. She proposes that the description of the anti-black violence after the Nat Turner rebellion be more fully developed, and she advises that a final chapter on John Brown be omitted. Child's second letter is a detailed explanation of the publisher's contract, which provided that *Incidents* be published pseudonymously, with only Child's name listed as editor.[10]

Jacobs' letters are most interesting, however, not for their comments about other writers, but as the unique running account of the efforts of this newly-emancipated Afro-American woman to render her life in literature. The decision to write her own story evidently prompted Jacobs to follow the long-standing practice of sending apprentice pieces to the newspapers. Both the subject and the style of her first published letter, which appeared in the *Tribune* under the headline "Letter from a Fugitive Slave," suggest her book. Here—as in her narrative—Jacobs' subject is the sexual exploitation of women in slavery. Here—as in her narrative—her form reflects the conventions of polite letters. She begins by announcing that she will tell her tale herself.

> . . . Poor as it may be, I had rather give . . . [my story] from my own hand, than have it said that I employed others to do it for me. . . .

Then—as in her private letters and in her book—she expresses the pain she feels as she recalls and writes about her life.

> I was born a slave, raised in the Southern hot-bed until I was the mother of two children, sold at the early age of two and four years old. I have been hunted through all of the Northern States—but no, I will not tell you of my own suffering—no, it would harrow up my soul. . . .[11]

Encouraged by the publication of this letter, Jacobs secretly composed others. Her private correspondence during this period reveals that she was at once determined to write, apprehensive about her ability to do so, and fearful of being discovered.

> No one here ever suspected me [of writing to the *Tribune*]. I would not have Mrs. W. to know it before I had undertaken my history, for I must write just what I have lived and witnessed myself. Don't expect much of me, dear Amy. You shall have truth, but not talent.[12]

The letters record other pressures. During the years Jacobs composed her extraordinary memoirs, Mr. and Mrs. Willis moved into an eighteen room estate and added two more children to their family; Jacobs' work load increased accordingly. Writing to Post, she voiced the frustrations of a would-be woman writer who earned her living nursing other people's children.

> Poor Hatty's name is so much in demand that I cannot accomplish much; if I could steal away and have two quiet months to myself, I would work night and day though it should all fall to the ground.

She went on, however, to say that she preferred the endless interruptions to revealing her project to her employers.

> To get this time I should have to explain myself, and no one here except Louisa knows that I have ever written anything to be put in print. I have not the courage to meet the criticism and ridicule of educated people.[13]

Jacobs' letters do not suggest that she felt this reticence because of formal problems. Written in the genteel manner of the period, the literary style of *Incidents*—which seems to echo writers like Willis and Child—has been judged an incongruous mode of expression for an emancipated slave. Yet the discovery of Jacobs' correspondence shows that the style of *Incidents* is completely consistent with her private letters. For example, none of its narrative asides is as mannered as Jacobs' private comment about her manuscript:

> Just now the poor book is in its chrysalis state, and though I can never make it a butterfly, I am satisfied to have it creep meekly among some of the humbler bugs.[14]

The letters reveal that Jacobs was more troubled about the content of her book than about its form. As her manuscript neared completion, she articulated her concern about its sensational aspects and her need for acceptance from another woman in a letter asking Post to identify herself with the book.

I have thought that I wanted some female friend to write a preface or some introductory remarks . . . yet believe me, dear friend, there are many painful things in . . . [my book] that make me shrink from asking the sacrifice from one so good and pure as yourself.[15]

II

Jacobs' fullest private statement about her autobiography—her clearest presentation of her conflicts, her problems, her hopes for the book—is in the letter she composed in response to Post's agreement to write the endorsement she wanted. Jacobs focuses first on the personal aspects of her work: its truthfulness and its confessional quality.

> I have, my dear friend, striven faithfully to give a true and just account of my own life in slavery. God knows I have tried to do it in a Christian spirit. There are some things that I might have made plainer, I know. Woman can whisper her cruel wrongs into the ear of a very dear friend much easier than she can record them for the world to read. I have left nothing out but what I thought the world might believe that a slave woman was too willing to pour out, that she might gain their sympathies. I ask nothing. I have placed myself before you to be judged as a woman, whether I deserve your pity or contempt.

Only after this does she discuss her social purpose.

> I have another object in view: It is to come to you just as I am, a poor slave mother—not to tell you what I have heard, but what I have seen and what I have suffered, and if there is any sympathy to give, let it be given to the thousands of slave mothers that are still in bondage, suffering far more than I have. Let it plead for their helpless children, that they may enjoy the same liberties that my children enjoy.[16]

This letter illuminates the complexities of *Incidents*. Narrated by Jacobs' alter ego Linda Brent, it is at once the confession of a female narrator who presents herself "to be judged as a woman" deserving either "pity or contempt"; the triumphant recital of the heroic freedom fight of "a poor slave mother" told to aid the "helpless children" of other slave mothers; and the testimony of a woman who—struggling to maintain a Christian spirit as she acknowledges her failures and her victories—has "striven faithfully to give a true and just account of my own life in slavery."

It is precisely this last point, Jacobs' careful adherence to fact, which William C. Nell stressed in announcing the publication of *Incidents* in Garrison's *Liberator*.

It presents features more attractive than many of its predecessors pur-
porting to be histories of slave life in America, because, *in contrast with
their mingling of fiction with fact, this record of complicated experience
in the life of a young woman, a doomed victim to America's peculiar institution . . . surely need[s] not the charms that any pen of fiction, however gifted and graceful, could lend.* They shine by the lustre of their
own truthfulness—a rhetoric which always commends itself to the wise
head and honest heart. . . .
My own acquaintance, too, with the author and her relatives, of whom
special mention is made in the book, warrants an expression of the hope
that it will find its way into every family. . . .[17] (italics mine)

Like the perspective of other slave narratives, the angle of vision in
Incidents is revolutionary.[18] Like the other narrators, Jacobs asserts her
authorship in her subtitle (*Written by Herself*), uses the first person, and
addresses the subject of the oppression of chattel slavery and the struggle
for freedom from the viewpoint of one who has been enslaved. But in
her title she announces that her book is not—like most—the narrative of
a life but of incidents in a life, and she identifies herself by gender; and
in her Preface, while asserting the truthfulness of her tale, she announces
that she has written pseudonymously. The later assertion that "Slavery
is terrible for men; but it is far more terrible for women" announces her
special subject. *Incidents* is a woman's pseudonymous account of her
struggle against her oppression in slavery as a sexual object and as a
mother.

Jacobs' *Anglo-African* reviewer instantly recognized that this book
represented something new. *Incidents,* he wrote, recounts

the 'oft-told tale' of American slavery, in another and more revolting
phase than that which is generally seen: More revolting because it is of
the spirit and not the flesh. In this volume, a woman tells . . . not,
how *she* was scourged and maimed, but that far more terrible sufferings
endured by and inflicted upon women, by a system which legalizes concubinage, and offers a premium to licentiousness.[19]

Because its subject is the sexual oppression of women in slavery, *Incidents* presents a double critique of nineteenth-century American ideas
and institutions. It inevitably challenges the institution of chattel slavery
and its supporting ideology of white racism; just as inevitably, it challenges traditional patriarchal institutions and ideas. In *Incidents* Jacobs'
Linda Brent dramatizes the success of her struggle to liberate herself and
her children. She prevents her master from raping her, arranges for her
children to be rescued from him, hides, escapes, and finally achieves freedom. Simultaneously, Jacobs' narrator dramatizes the failure of her
efforts to adhere to the sexual patterns she had been taught to endorse.

She reveals that although unmarried, she is intimate with a man, and that in consequence, she is condemned by her grandmother and suffers terrible guilt. But Jacobs' narrator also questions the adequacy of this judgment and tentatively reaches toward an alternative moral code. At the conclusion she dramatizes her daughter's acceptance, which at least partially assuages her conflict. In this narrative, Jacobs' Linda Brent yokes the success story of the life of an heroic slave mother to the confession of a young woman who mourns that she is not a storybook heroine—but who nevertheless, in struggling to announce her own experience, affirms herself a new kind of heroic female figure.[20]

The account of Linda Brent's battle for freedom follows patterns standard to the genre. As in other slave narratives, this struggle is seen as recurrent. Despite her escape from her master midpoint in the book and her flight north a dozen chapters later, she does not achieve her goal of freedom until the final pages. The pattern of repeated struggle is underscored by her efforts to free her children. While apparently their purchase by their white father rescues them from tyranny, it actually presents a new threat; though later sent north, they are not out of danger until the end of the book.

Here, as in other narratives, the effort to achieve freedom is not only presented as recurrent; it is seen as ubiquitous. One group of interpolated chapters discusses the attempts, over several generations, of Linda Brent's relatives—an uncle, a brother, an aunt—to free themselves and their families. Another group establishes a larger framework for this rebelliousness by presenting general discussions of various aspects of slave life in America—such as ideological indoctrination and religious practices—and by commenting on the consequences of pertinent historical events—such as the Nat Turner insurrection and the 1850 Fugitive Slave Law. The resulting text is a densely patterned fabric which locates the protagonist's efforts to free herself and her children within the context of similar attempts by her family, and presents these within the larger configuration of an ongoing struggle for freedom undertaken by an entire black community.

Incidents recalls other slave narratives in locating the battles of its heroic protagonist within the framework of a society at war. But its special focus and its confessional aspects—the account of sexual error, guilt, rejection and at least partial acceptance—are, I think, unique. Jacobs' decision to create a pseudonymous narrator, instead of revealing herself the author of her book, can perhaps be explained by this sensational aspect of her autobiography. An early chapter chronicling Linda Brent's sexual harassment by her master also sketches a thwarted romance with a free black man, whom she is forbidden to marry. Although she reminds us that a slave marriage had no legal status, obviously to her it promised home, husband and children. Her master not only forbade her to marry; he made clear that he intended to use her as his concubine. It was in an attempt to prevent this, she writes, that she decided to involve herself sexually with another man.

Although she characterizes this as "a headlong plunge," the narrator notes that at the time she had seen it as a successful act of defiance:

> It was something to triumph over my tyrant even in that small way.[21]

Whatever elation she felt, however, quickly turned to guilt, especially after her grandmother condemned her. Although the older woman later took her back, she offered pity—not forgiveness. Linda Brent reports that her grandmother's judgment was not unique; the social condemnation of her status as an unwed mother was, she writes, unyielding. Years later, after escaping north, she was warned not to reveal her situation lest she be treated with contempt. And long afterward, although she confided to her sympathetic employer that she and her children were fugitives, she feared revealing her sexual history.

> I valued her good opinion, and I was afraid of losing it, if I told her all the particulars of my sad story.[22]

It is, in fact, only a dozen pages before the end of the book, in a chapter called "The Confession," that the narrator suggests that this problem is even partially resolved. Despite "a shrinking dread of diminishing my child's love," she describes confessing to her young daughter.

> I began to tell her how . . . [my sufferings in slavery] had driven me into a great sin, when she clasped me in her arms, and exclaimed, "O, don't, mother! Please don't tell me any more. . . . I know all about it. . . . All my love is for you."[23]

This acceptance by her daughter balances her grandmother's condemnation and marks a dramatic resolution of Linda Brent's guilt. Her ongoing comments remain inconclusive, however. Repeatedly, throughout the text, she endorses a sexual standard that condemns her actions while she dramatizes her contention that enslaved women are not permitted to adhere to this norm; although once—in a unique passage—she asserts that an alternative standard should be applied in judging the actions of slave women like herself.

Linda Brent's sexual crisis is most fully presented in a chapter melodramatically entitled "A Perilous Passage in a Slave Girl's Life." Here—

at the emotional center of her book—the narrator appeals directly to her "happy" female readers

> whose purity has been sheltered from childhood, who have been free to choose the objects of your affection, whose homes are protected by law, *do not judge the poor desolate slave girl too severely!*[24] (italics mine)

Written in a Latinate vocabulary, couched in clichés, this confession of sexual error and plea for forgiveness seem themselves to be clichés.

Yet they are not. Despite her language (and what other, one wonders, was available to her?) this narrator does not characterize herself conventionally as a passive female victim. On the contrary; she asserts that she was—even when young and a slave—an effective moral agent, and she takes full responsibility for her actions.

> And now, reader, I come to a period in my unhappy life, which I would gladly forget if I could. The remembrance fills me with sorrow and shame. It pains me to tell you of it; but I have promised to tell you the truth, and I will do it honestly, let it cost me what it may. I will not try to screen myself behind the plea of compulsion from a master; for it was not so. Neither can I plead ignorance or thoughtlessness. . . . I knew what I did, and I did it with deliberate calculation.[25]

Nor does this narrator mouth the standard notion that a woman's self-esteem is a simple function of her adherence to conventional sexual mores. Although she discusses her efforts to preserve her virginity in connection with her struggle to maintain her self esteem, she presents these as related, not identical, goals.[26]

Denied the protection of the laws, denied even an extra-legal marriage to a man she loved, she writes that in a desperate attempt to prevent her hated master from forcing her into concubinage, she relinquished her "purity" in an effort to maintain her "self-respect"; she abandoned her attempt to avoid sexual involvements in an effort to assert her autonomy as a human being, to avoid being "entirely subject to the will of another." Expressing her mature estimate of her situation when young and enslaved, the narrator shifts to the present tense:

> It seems less degrading to give one's self, than to submit to compulsion. There is something akin to freedom in having a lover who has no control over you, except that which he gains by kindness and attachment.[27]

She concludes this passage with one of the most interesting sentences in the book. Having recounted her sexual history, the narrator shifts to the present tense to assert a radical alternative to the apparently conventional sexual ideology that has informed her confession and her plea.

> Still, in looking back, calmly, on the events of my life, I feel that the slave woman ought not to be judged by the same standard as others.[28]

Does the narrator here suggest, upon reflection, that women like herself should be judged (like men) on complex moral grounds—rather than (like women) on the single issue of their compliance with accepted sexual behavior? Does Harriet Jacobs, the black fugitive slave author who writes as Linda Brent the black fugitive slave narrator, here propose a new definition of female morality grounded in her own experience? This extraordinary sentence invites analysis and examination both in relation to equivalent assertions of autonomy in the speeches and writings of the other slave narrators, and in relation to equivalent assertions of autonomy in the speeches and writings of other nineteenth century women. To my ear, this quiet comment resonates with Sojourner Truth's ringing interrogatives that redefined womanhood.[29]

Like the treatment of sexual issues, characterizations in *Incidents* which at first appear merely conventional later reveal themselves as challenges to convention. For example, Jacobs' narrator Linda Brent seems to present herself as representative of a stock racial and sexual character, the "tragic mulatto" figure, a woman of mixed race who is betrayed by the white man she adores, the father of her children. But a careful examination reveals something more complex. While Linda Brent reports that she was indeed discarded by the white father of her children, she does not focus on his rejection of her, but on his betrayal of their son and daughter. She writes that although he granted her plea to end their enslavement to her tyrannical master by buying them himself, he repeatedly broke his promises to emancipate them. It is when she finally recognizes this that she resolves to free them herself. Asserting again and again that all her efforts are directed toward achieving freedom for her children, this narrator presents herself not as a cast-off lovesick mistress but as an outraged loving mother; and in doing so, she counters a second racial and sexual stereotype. Linda Brent is a black mother committed to the welfare of her own children, not a "mammy" devoted to her mistress' white babies.

Like the account of her sexual experiences in slavery—her description of her efforts to frustrate the designs of her master and to assert at least some choice about the identity of the man who will use her sexually, and her conclusion that slave women should not be condemned for violating conventional sexual mores—the recital of Linda Brent's experiences as a slave mother merits careful examination. This should be read on its own terms; in relation to similar speeches and writings by other Afro-Americans; and in relation to speeches and writings by freeborn white women on this subject. For example, while the account of Jacobs' narrator describing her battle to liberate her children from the power of their master-father is unique, it has parallels in other narratives; and because (in contrast to statutes regulating slaves) laws governing free Americans denied the authority of the female parent and entrusted children to their fathers, it also has parallels in the writings of freeborn women. Let me be clear. I do not here propose that Jacobs' narrative be collapsed into the writings of the male slave narrators; I do not suggest that it be collapsed into the writings of other Afro-American women (both free and slave); I do not suggest that it be collapsed into the writings of freeborn white women. On the contrary. What I am suggesting is a multiple examination of Jacobs' pseudonymous female slave narrative: of its text and of the relationship of this text to a series of relevant contexts.

For example, viewed from a feminist perspective *Incidents* is a major text. During the years Jacobs was working on her manuscript, a small group of women—most of them white—were developing a critique of sexism modeled on the Garrisonian analysis of chattel slavery. Reflecting this model in their rhetoric, they wrote of "the slavery of woman." The most committed white abolitionists in this group—like Jacobs' editor Child and her sponsor Post—did not confuse their own experience with the triple oppression of sex, condition, and race to which they knew slave women were subjected. It was nevertheless a sense of their own oppression that spurred these freeborn white feminists to identify with black fugitive slave woman like Jacobs.[30]

This feminist consciousness is pertinent to *Incidents*. In this book, Jacobs' Linda Brent presents a closed community split by chattel slavery into two warring camps. Given her primary groupings—blacks who oppose slavery and whites who support it—this narrative is surprising. We expect to encounter the fiendish neighboring female slaveholder and the jealous mistress. But how are we to explain the presence of the white women who defect from the slaveholders' ranks to help Linda Brent? How can we account for the lady who, at the request of the young slave's grandmother, tries to stop her master from molesting her? Even more strange, how can we account for the female slaveholder who hides the runaway female slave for a month? How can we account for the northern employer who entrusts Linda Brent with the baby, so she can flee slavecatchers by traveling as a nursemaid rather than as a fugitive? One explanation is that these women are responding to Linda Brent's oppression as a woman exploited sexually and as a mother trying to nurture her children. That is, viewed from this feminist perspective, what we are watching is women betraying allegiances of race and class to assert their stronger allegiance to the sisterhood of all women.

In her signed preface Jacobs' narrator Linda Brent invites this reading by the way in which she identifies her audience and announces her purpose:

> I do earnestly desire to arouse the women of the North to a realizing sense of the condition of two millions of women at the South, still in bondage. . . .[31]

Seen from this angle of vision, Jacobs' book—reaching across the gulf separating black women from white, slave from free, poor from rich, reaching across the chasm separating "bad" women from "good"—represents an attempt to establish an American sisterhood and to activate that sisterhood in the public arena.

Further, *Incidents* was published in the face of taboos prohibiting women from discussing their sexuality—much less their sexual exploitation—in print. Yet between its covers Harriet Jacobs, a black American woman, pseudonymously presents her shocking narrative in defiance of the rules of sexual propriety; and she is supported in this effort by L. Maria Child, a prominent white American woman. Almost thirty years earlier, Child had made an indelible mark in American letters by discussing the forbidden subject of slavery. Now, in presenting this narrative by a pseudonymous "impure woman" on the "forbidden subject" of the sexual exploitation of women in slavery, she again challenged custom. In her introduction, Child announces that this defiance is deliberate.

> I am well aware that many will accuse me of indecorum for presenting these pages to the public; for the experiences of this intelligent and much-injured woman belong to a class which some call delicate subjects, and others indelicate. This peculiar phase of Slavery has generally been kept veiled; but the public ought to be made acquainted with its monstrous features, and I willingly take the responsibility of presenting them with the veil drawn.[32]

Both the composition and the publication of *Incidents* marked special moments in the history of women's literature in America.

Further examination of *Incidents* within its multiple contexts—including the other narratives and the writings and speeches of other Afro-American women—will, I believe, further demonstrate the importance of this book. In her generation, Jacobs was one of a small group of

Afro-American women who could create a narrative alter ego capable of addressing an audience called "Reader." Because most lacked access to polite English letters, their literary contributions were made within the oral tradition. As the study of Harriet Jacobs' complex pseudonymous narrative proceeds, I think scholars will conclude that—like other slave narrators, like other black authors, like other female writers working within the nineteenth century American literary tradition—Harriet Jacobs not only used the conventions of polite letters, she also challenged them. Although I find her book conflicted—with the confessions undercutting the hero-tale, with neither confession nor hero-tale at ease with the style, with its conventional forms inadequate to express its unconventional perspective and content—this very criticism measures my estimate of the importance of Jacobs' book. These formal problems suggest that new forms were needed, new language, new structures, new characters, new narrative voices, if literature was to express the fullness of Jacobs' new point of view and her new content. In this regard, I think students of the narratives will want to look closely at Linda Brent, the pseudonymous narrator of *Incidents*. It is in and through this literary construct that Jacobs managed—in however conflicted a fashion—to tell a tale that is new: not "the life of a heroine with no degradation associated with it," but a woman's "true and just account of my own life in slavery."

Notes

1. This passage comes from one of thirty letters from Harriet Jacobs to Amy Post in the Isaac and Amy Post Family Papers recently acquired by the University of Rochester Library. Numbered n.d. #84, it was probably written at the end of 1852 or the beginning of 1853. All of the letters cited from Jacobs to Post are in this collection in the Department of Rare Books, Manuscripts and Archives, and are reprinted by permission. Most note only day and month; my attempts to supply missing dates may be in error. Editing Jacobs' letters, I have regularized paragraphing, capitalization, punctuation, and spelling, but have not otherwise tampered with text.

I hasten to record my considerable debt to Dorothy Sterling who includes some of Jacobs' letters in *A Woman and Black* (in press) and with whom I am writing a book on Jacobs; to Karl Kabelac of the University of Rochester Library; and to Patricia G. Holland, co-editor of *The Collected Correspondence of Lydia Maria Child, 1817-1880* (New York, 1980). Without them, this study could not have been made. I am in addition indebted to Bernard Crystal of the Columbia University Libraries, Phil Lapsansky of the Philadelphia Library Company, James Lawton of the Boston Public Library, and Mary-Elizabeth Murdock of the Sophia Smith Collection at Smith College.

I am further beholden to Dorothy Sterling, and to Frederick C. Stern, Milton R. Stern, and Marilyn T. Williams for criticizing an early version of this manuscript; to Elizabeth V. Moore for her cogent remarks; and to Quandra Prettyman Stadler, Elizabeth Fox Genovese, and Hazel Carby, whose comments pushed my thinking forward. Partial discussions of this material have been presented in *American Literature*, vol. 53, no. 3 (Nov. 1981), 479-86; at a meeting of the Modern Language Association in 1981; and at the Columbia University Seminar on Women and Society in 1982.

2. [Harriet Jacobs], *Incidents in the Life of a Slave Girl, Written by Herself*. Ed. L. Maria Child (Boston, 1861). An English edition appeared the following year: [Harriet Jacobs], *The Deeper Wrong: Or, Incidents in the Life of a Slave Girl. Written by Herself*. Ed. L. Maria Child (London, 1862). A paperback edition with introduction and notes by Walter Teller was published at New York in 1973; page numbers in my notes refer to this edition.

Examining *Incidents* in a discussion of "fictional accounts . . . [in which] the major character may have been a real fugitive, but the narrative of his life is probably false," John Blassingame judged that "the work is not credible." See *The Slave Community* (New York, 1972), 233-34.

Professor Blassingame is not the first to question the validity of *Incidents;* see also for example *The Negro Caravan*, ed. Sterling A. Brown, Arthur P. Davis and Ulysses Lee (New York, 1941); and Arna Bontemps, "The Slave Narrative: An American Genre," *Great Slave Narratives* (Boston, 1969). In his more recent study, *Slave Testimony* (Baton Rouge, 1977), instead of repeating this judgment, Professor Blassingame has treated the question of the authenticity of *Incidents* ambiguously; as do, for example, George P. Rawick in *The American Slave: A Composite Autobiography*. Vol. I: *From Sundown to Sunup: The Making of the Black Community* (Westport, 1972); and Russell Brignano in *Black Americans in Autobiography* (Chapel Hill, 1974). Many scholars, however, have accepted Jacobs' narrative as authentic. These include Vernon Loggins, *The Negro Author* (New York, 1931); Marion W. Starling, *The Slave's Narrative: Its Place in American Literary History*, unpublished dissertation (New York University, 1946); Charles Nichols, "Slave Narratives and the Plantation Legend," *Phylon*, 10 (1949); and Nichols' *Many Thousand Gone: The Ex-Slaves' Account of their Bondage and Freedom* (Leiden, 1963); Gilbert Osofsky, *Puttin' On Ole Massa* (New York, 1969); and Stanley Feldstein, *Once a Slave: The Slaves' View of Slavery* (New York, 1971).

3. Willis referred to Jacobs directly—though not by name—in a *House and Home* column reprinted in *Outdoors at Idlewild* (New York, 1855), 275-76. Jacobs' escape from slavery and her emancipation are sketched in Henry C. Beers' biography of Willis in the American Men of Letters Series (Boston and New York, 1885), 284-86. Beers does not mention *Incidents*. The single factual discrepancy between his account and Jacobs' narrative is that he writes that she spent five years in hiding and she says it was seven. Beers' characterization of Jacobs, however, does not tally with her own. Although in her letters Jacobs expresses affection for Willis' wife, she does not speak warmly of Willis, and she does not even mention him in her autobiography. Yet Beers sees her as a stereotypical devoted family servant. Other published references to Jacobs in nineteenth century volumes include *Memorial of Sarah Pugh: A Tribute of*

Respect from her Cousins (Philadelphia, 1888), 100; L. Maria Child, *Letters,* ed. John G. Whittier (Boston, 1883), 204-05; and *History of Woman Suffrage,* ed. Elizabeth C. Stanton, *et. al.,* 6 vols. (New York, 1881-1922), I, 334.

4. While confident of the validity of the large outlines of this biographical sketch, I am aware that it may contain inaccuracies. I am continuing to work on Jacobs' life and can, at this writing, identify most of the individuals she presents pseudonymously in *Incidents.* Grimke's eulogy of Jacobs is in the Francis J. Grimke Papers, Moorland-Spingarn Collection, Howard University.

5. For Jacobs on Willis, see Jacobs to Post, Cornwall, Orange County (late 1852-early 1853?) n.d. #84. Child commented on Jacobs' relationship with Willis in a letter to John G. Whittier dated April 4, 1861, now in the Child Papers, Manuscript Division, the Library of Congress. An endorsement by the Columbus, Georgia *Times* and the Savannah, Georgia *News* judging Willis' *Home Journal* one of only three northern literary publications worthy of southern support was noted in *The Liberator* March 29, 1861. Willis' article was anthologized in *The Convalescent* (New York, 1859), 410-16.

6. This discussion of Jacobs and Stowe is based on five letters from Jacobs to Post: Cornwall, Orange County (late 1852-early 1853?) n.d. #84; Feb. 14 (1853?); April 4 (1853?); New Bedford, Mass. (Spring, 1853?) n.d. #80; July 31 (1854?) n.d. #88. The quotation is from Jabobs to Post, Feb. 14 (1853?). I have been unable to locate any letters to Stowe from Post, Cornelia Willis, or Jacobs, or from Stowe to Cornelia Willis.

7. Jacobs to Post, April 4 (1853?).

8. Jacobs to Post, New Bedford, Mass. (Spring, 1853?) n.d. #80.

9. Jacobs to Post, Oct. 8 (1860?) I have not been able to document a second attempt to gain Stowe's backing. The firm of Phillips, Sampson & Co., c/o S. C. Perkins and A. K. Loring, Booksellers, is listed in the Boston *City Directory* for 1859; it is not listed in the 1860 edition. Jacobs discusses her efforts to publish her book abroad in letters to Post dated June 21 (1857?) n.d. #90; New Bedford, Aug. 9 (1857?); March 1 (1858?); and Cambridge, May 3 (1858?) n.d. #87; also see an important letter in the Boston Public Library from Jacobs to abolitionist Anne Warren Weston, dated June 28 (1858?).

10. Child to Jacobs, Wayland, Aug. 13, 1860; the balance of the text of the letter quoted follows:

> I should not take so much pains, if I did not consider the book unusually interesting, and likely to do much service to the Anti-Slavery cause. So you need not feel under great personal obligations. You know I would go through fire and water to help give a blow to Slavery. I suppose you will want to see the M.S. after I have exercised my bump of mental order upon it; and I will send it wherever you direct, a fortnight hence.
>
> My object in writing at this time is to ask you to write what you can recollect of the outrages committed on the colored people, in Nat Turner's time. You say the reader would not believe what you saw "inflicted on men, women, and children, without the slightest ground of suspicion against them." What *were* those inflictions? Were any tortured to make them confess? And how? Were any killed? Please write down some of the most striking particulars, and let me have them to insert.
>
> I think the last chapter, about John Brown, had better be omitted.

It does not naturally come into your story, and the M.S. is already too long. Nothing can be so appropriate to end with, as the death of your grandmother.

Mr. Child desires to be respectfully remembered to you.

Very Cordially your friend,

L. Maria Child

Jacobs' responses are evidently in "Fear of Insurrection," 65; and "Free at Last," 207-08.

The full text of the second letter, dated Wayland, Sept. 27, 1860, follows:

Dear Mrs. Jacobs,

I have signed and sealed the contract with Thayer & Eldridge, in my name, and told them to take out the copyright in my name. Under the circumstances *your* name could not be used, you know. I inquired of other booksellers, and could find none that were willing to undertake it, except Thayer & Eldridge. I have never heard a word to the disparagement of either of them, and I do not think you could do better than to let them have it. They *ought* to have the monopoly of it for some time, if they *stereotype* it, because that process involves considerable expense, and if you changed publishers, their plates would be worth nothing to them. When I spoke of limiting them to an edition of 2000, I did not suppose that they intended to stereotype it. They have agreed to pay you ten per cent on the retail price of all sold, and to let you have as many as you want, at the lowest wholesale price. On your part, I have agreed that they may publish it for five years on those terms, and that you will not print any abridgement, or altered copy, meanwhile.

I have no reason whatever to think that Thayer & Eldridge are likely to fail. I merely made the suggestions because they were *beginners*. However, several of the *oldest* bookselling firms have failed within the last three years; mine among the rest. We must run for luck in these matters.

I have promised to correct the proof-sheets, and I don't think it would be of any use to the book to have you here at this time. They say they shall get it out by the 1st of Nov.

You had better let me know before hand if you want to come to Wayland; because when I leave home, I generally stay over night, and in that case you would lose your time and your money. I saw your daughter a few minutes, and found her very prepossessing.

Write to me whenever you want to; and when I have time, I will answer.

I want you to sign the following paper, and send it back to me. It will make Thayer and Eldridge safe about the contract in *my* name, and in case of my death, will prove that the book is *your* property, not *mine*.

Cordially your friend,

L. Maria Child

Mr. Child desires a very friendly remembrance.

Any remaining doubts concerning Child's role must, I think, rest on an undated plea for secrecy from Jacobs to Post:

My Dear Friend:

You will please let no one see these letters. I am pledged to Mrs. Child that I will tell no one what she has done, as she is beset by so many people, and it would affect the book. It must be the slave's own story—which it truly is.

Yours always,

H

To my mind, this reflects an effort to shield Child from interruption while she edits the manuscript, not an attempt to hide editorial improprieties. Also see Child to Lucy [Searle] Feb. 4, 1861, in the Lydia Maria Child Papers, Anti-Slavery Collection of Cornell University Libraries.

For the organizational role undertaken by the abolitionists in aiding publication and distribution of *Incidents*, see Child to Wendell Phillips, Dec. 2, 1860; and Dec. 9, 1860, in the Wendell Phillips Collection, Houghton Library, Harvard University. For Jacobs' efforts to distribute her book, see Jacobs to R. Smith, Philadelphia, Jan. 14 (1861); and Jacobs' inscription to Smith in a copy of *Incidents;* both items are in the collection of the Library Company of Philadelphia.

11. New York *Tribune*, June 21, 1853. Another of Jacobs' letters appeared on July 25, 1853.

12. Jacobs to Post, Oct. 9 (1853?) n.d. #85. Also see Jacobs to Post, Cornwall, June 25 (1853?).

13. Jacobs to Post, Cornwall, Jan. 11 (1854?).

14. Jacobs to Post, Cornwall, March (1854?).

15. Jacobs to Post, May 18 and June 8 (1857?).

16. Jacobs to Post, June 21 (1857?) n.d. #90. In the rest of this letter, Jacobs suggests the outline Post used in her testimonial. Testifying in her signed statement, which was published as an Appendix to *Incidents*, to her acquaintance with Jacobs and to the conditions under which the narrative was conceived and written, Post quotes one sentence directly from this letter. Post's testimonial is accompanied by a second statement testifying to the truth of Jacobs' narrative which is signed by George W. Lowther, a black "resident of Boston" who later served in the House of Representatives of the Commonwealth of Massachusetts.

17. Nell's letter appeared under the heading, "Linda, the Slave Girl," Jan. 25, 1861; he ran ads offering the book for sale for the next six months.

18. A standard critical comment is that the slave narrator's perspective makes this inevitable; see, for example, my own *Intricate Knot* (New York, 1972). H. Bruce Franklin makes this observation about *Incidents* and identifies Jacobs' special subject in *The Victim as Criminal and Artist* (New York, 1978).

19. *The Weekly Anglo-African*, April 13, 1861. A letter from Jacobs to Post

dated Oct. 8 (1860?), suggests that this review may have been written by George W. Lowther. The letter also discusses plans for a review in the *National Anti-Slavery Standard;* this appeared on Feb. 23, 1861.

20. I am indebted to Hazel Carby, who commented on an earlier version of this paper and generously permitted me to read the chapter "Slave and Mistress" from her unpublished manuscript, *Black Women Writers in the Diaspora,* for helping me clarify this analysis.

21. *Incidents,* 56.

22. *Incidents,* 184.

23. *Incidents,* 193.

24. *Incidents,* 54.

25. *Incidents,* 54.

26. In her choice of tense, the narrator here indicates that she had made this distinction even when young: "I wanted to keep myself pure; and, under the most adverse circumstances, I tried hard to preserve my self-respect . . ." 54. Later, however, she writes that she was unable to maintain it consistently: "But now that the truth was out, and my relations should hear of it, I felt wretched. . . . My self-respect was gone. . . . I had resolved that I would be virtuous. . . . And now, how humiliated I felt!" 57.

27. *Incidents,* 55.

28. *Incidents,* 56.

29. My reference is of course to Sojourner Truth's classic speech, "Ain't I a Woman?" delivered at the Akron, Ohio Woman's Rights Convention in May, 1851, and reported in reminiscences by Frances D. Gage, in *History of Woman Suffrage,* ed. Elizabeth C. Stanton, *et al.,* 6 vols. (New York, 1881-1922), I, 115-117.

30. See, for example, the discussion of women in slave-holding societies in L. Maria Child, *History of the Condition of Women,* 2 vols. (New York, 1835). Amy Post worked for decades in the anti-slavery movement and was instrumental in organizing the second Woman's Rights Convention in 1848; for Frederick Douglass' appreciation of Post, see *Life and Times* (1892, New York, 1962), 263. Also see the writings of feminist abolitionist lecturers and polemicists Angelina and Sarah Grimke; public statements issued by the three Conventions of American Women Against Slavery; and reports of the various Female Anti-Slavery Societies. This identification had become standard by the time Elizabeth Cady Stanton began her *History of Woman Suffrage* with the sentence, "The prolonged slavery of woman is the darkest page in human history."

31. *Incidents,* xiv.

32. *Incidents,* xii. Child's 1833 *Appeal in Favor of that Class of Americans Called Africans* had resulted in her ostracism from polite literary circles; following this, much of her writing was done for the anti-slavery cause. By 1861, she had touched on various aspects of Jacobs' subject; see for example her treatment of the enslavement of women in *History of the Condition of Women,* 2 vols. (New York, 1835); and of the social victimization of women who do not conform to sexual mores in *Fact and Fiction* (New York, 1846).

The Slave Narrators and the Picaresque Mode: Archetypes for Modern Black Personae

CHARLES H. NICHOLS

Early picaresque fiction like *Lazarillo de Tormes*[1] and *Guzman de Alfarache,* have profoundly influenced the development of European fiction. It is not surprising, therefore, that there are illuminating parallels between Afro-American narrative modes and a work like *Lazarillo de Tormes.* In all these narrative forms we are struck by the self consciousness of the personality whose awareness seizes our attention. The early slave narratives,[2] the autobiographies of Henry Bibb, or William Wells Brown, or Frederick Douglass or Josiah Henson present personae reminiscent of the picaro, Lazarillo. Like the Spanish "rogue," the slave narrators tell their life story in retrospect, after having triumphed over the brutalizing circumstances of their youth. William W. Brown and Frederick Douglass are internationally known orators and reformers. Josiah Henson has become the founder of a refugee colony and celebrated as Harriet Beecher Stowe's "Uncle Tom." Lazaro tells us that at the time he is writing, he has saved money and, having become his wife's pimp and the agent of the Arch priest of San Salvador, has become the town crier. The accounts they have given us of their lives as slaves, servants and scullery boys operate, therefore, on at least two levels of consciousness. In each account the writer presents a welter of realistic detail designed to drive home the brutality and inhumanity of his experience as a victim, a commodity, a rootless, alienated soul without hope or future. His origin is obscure, his masters heartless and treacherous. The episodic march of events in the narrative, its loose disregard of causality, its frequent use of coincidence and chance dramatize the chaos and decadence of the world here depicted. With bitter irony the picaro-slave underlines his contempt for the illusions, the chivalric pretensions and the folly of the master class. Spain in the sixteenth century is in decline; the *antebellum* South is in crisis. The servant sees his master's nakedness and human weakness as well as his power and wealth.

The other level of consciousness is the mask which a corrupt society and desperate need force on the picaro. Lazarillo's mother has offered her favors to a black slave in return for stolen food and firewood. Lazarillo becomes the servant of a blind master whose first act is to dash the boy's head against a stone statue. The boy escapes one vicious and niggardly master only to fall into the hands of another—a hypocritical and heartless priest. Similarly Lazarillo's connection with the idle and indigent squire or that consummate con-man, the pardoner, create in him a personality ruled by selfishness, deceit and trickery. The desperate jeopardy of his condition forces upon the servant-slave-picaro the urgency of his search for an identity, for survival. He looks out on the chaos and moral decay of a social order which denies his humanity. But being human the slave astonishes us by the ingenuity of his means of survival. "I was obliged," writes Lazarillo, "to draw upon my weakness for strength." Henry Bibb is more candid: "The only weapon of self defense that I could use successfully was that of deception." [*Narrative*, p. 17]

The picaresque mode is therefore the achievement of a necessarily devious and subtle consciousness. The individual is engaged in a desperate struggle for survival; the ego rests on a shaky foundation. Like a trapped animal, the picaro is alert to every possible avenue of escape. His effective means of expression are comic modes—irony, satire, paradox, sarcasm, exaggeration, innuendo. He survives by stratagems; a trickster, he adopts protean roles—stage presence. For as Emerson wrote, "Surely no one would be a charlatan who could afford to be sincere!" Indeed as the tone and form of the genre develop in masters like Cervantes, Fielding or Mark Twain, the world of the picaro is characterized by an intriguing burlesque. The life of the ruling class is stripped of its pretensions in a wild masquerade. And the servant-trickster-con-man forces new kinds of perception on the reader. We are moved by a sense of compassion for the suffering individual; we cannot deny him some degree of spiritual triumph in his rise from bondage to freedom. What emerges is a many-colored light, fresh angles of vision, an epistemology which creates a dynamic awareness of the vital interaction of society's outcasts with powers whose religion, philosophy and claims to civilization seem vain indeed.

Lazarillo's whole consciousness is riveted on the problem of survival, for he is literally starving and homeless. Even when he attempts to serve his master faithfully he is subject to constant abuse. Nothing in his experience creates in him a sense of responsibility. Gil Blas was a valet; Moll Flanders, a felon and a prostitute with middle class ambitions.

The slave narrators are neglected (often abandoned) children constantly subject to physical punishment and hounded by fear. "I believed myself to have been cruelly wronged in some way, I could not clearly decide whether by the neighbors or by the world or by the laws of the land, and I became morose, quarrelsome and vengeful," writes Ralph

Roberts. "Like Cain, my hand was against every man and every man's hand against me. I avoided much communication for several years with my fellow slaves and became careless and reckless." ["A Slave's Story" *Putnam's* IX, 618] The isolation and deprivation of these slaves gave rise to an instability of personality which manifests itself in aggression, violence and superstition. They lose the capacity for love; the soul in them virtually dies. For the mental anguish of the picaro-slave is greater than his physical suffering. After being whipped, William Grimes wrote "It seems as though I should not forget this flogging when I die; it grieved my soul beyond the power of time to cure." [*Life of William Grimes*, p. 15]

The slave's stratagems for survival, his ingenuity in playing out the roles his situation demanded is the leitmotif of the narratives. Henry Watson stowed away on a ship bound from Mississippi to Boston. Frederick Douglass escaped slavery in a sailor's uniform. Henry "Box" Brown was shipped by express from Richmond to Philadelphia. Ellen Craft dressed like a master travelling with his slave (her darker husband, William). Many ran literally hundreds of miles by night, hiding by day until they reached free territory. Some seized by uncontrollable rage whipped their overseers; a few plotted the murder of their oppressors. In short the picaresque mode with its accounts of "social disorder and psychic disintegration" creates one of the most popular forms of characterization in western fiction—the trickster, the rogue, the con-man, the street man, the spy. And even the pattern of the early narrators carries us through the psychic underground and the brutality and absurdity of the modern city into the never-never land of fantasy toward which these battered souls yearn.

It is noteworthy that the slave narrators (like the protagonists of modern fiction) relentlessly examine their own motives and the psychological conflicts which their condition creates. Fear, hate, aggression and guilt stalk them all. And their moral and psychic regeneration—their attainment of manhood—is achieved by immense effort and staunch devotion to the ideals of personal freedom in a just society.

Such picaresque fiction as *Don Quixote, Candide,* and *Tom Jones* are satires, employing comic modes: exaggeration, innuendo, mistaken identity and ridicule. The slave narrative is rarely comic, but its personae have a curious double vision and a tendency to employ comic modes. Even the duller slaves perceived the irony of the slaveholders' loud boasts of a superior knowledge and love of liberty. While pretending to accept the religion which exhorted them to obedience, they embrace the God who delivered the Israelites from Egyptian bondage. Henry Bibb—a chronic runaway—had ready-made answers for patrols who might dis-

cover him in the woods. When asked what he was doing, he would be
seeking a mare or a cow which had wandered off. "For such excuses I
was let pass." (*Narrative of Henry Bibb*, p. 7). William Wells Brown was
sent by his irate master with a note and a dollar to be whipped by the
town jailer. He cleverly gave the note and the money to another slave
and sent him in his place. By fawning and deceit, William Hayden got
unusual rewards for a slave. But when his master attempted to cheat
him out of $300 he had paid for his freedom, he produced the papers
and a pass his master had given him before witnesses and exposed the
slaveholder's dishonest dealing. Josiah Henson writes of "midnight visits
to apple orchards, broiling stray chickens, and first-rate tricks to dodge
work." (*Father Henson's Story*, p. 20). Henson wooed and won over his
girl friends with his stolen "stray chickens." Far from feeling apologetic
about stealing he felt it was his "training in the luxury of doing good . . .
in the righteousness of indignation against the cruel and oppressive."
And Frederick Douglass insisted that theft by a slave was only a question of *removal*—"the taking of his meat out of one tub and putting it in
another . . . At first he [the master] owned it in the *tub* and last he
owned it in me." (*My Bondage*, p. 189) When Henry Bibb rode off on
his master's donkey, he opined: "I well knew that I was regarded as
property, and so was the ass; and I thought if one piece of property took
off another, there could be no law violated in the act; no more sin committed in this than if one jackass had rode off another." (Bibb, p. 122)
Milton Clarke describes the slave, Aunt Peggy, who was a "master at
stealing little pigs."

> With a dead pig in the cabin and the water all hot for scalding, she was
> at one time warned by her son that the Phillistines were upon her. Her
> resources were fully equal to the sudden emergency. Quick as thought,
> the pig was thrown into the boiling kettle, a door put over it, her
> daughter seated upon it, and a good thick quilt around her, the overseer
> found little Clara taking a steam bath for a terrible cold. The daughter,
> acting well her part, groaned sadly; the mother was busy in tucking in
> the quilt and the overseer was blinded, and went away without seeing
> a bristle of the pig.
>
> (*Narratives of Lewis and Milton Clarke*, p. 26)

The narrators' resistance to the slave system invariably manifests itself in subtle and ironic turns of speech. For they were conscious victims
of a violent and rapacious society. The master exclaims angrily: "You
scoundrel, you ate my turkey." The slave replies, "Yes, sir, Massa, you
got less turkey but you sho' got mo' nigger." Peter Randolph tells of a
slaveholder who dressed himself up for a fight and asked his favorite
body servant how he looked:

" 'Oh, massa mighty!' 'What do you mean by mighty, Pompey?'
'Why, Massa, you look noble.' 'What do you mean by noble?' 'Why, sir,
you look just like a lion.' 'Why, Pompey, where have you ever seen a
lion?' 'I seen one down in yonder field the other day, massa.' 'Pompey,
you foolish fellow, that was a *jackass!*' 'Was it, Massa? Well, you look
just like him.' "

(From Slave Cabin to Pulpit, p. 199)

As we have seen the picaresque tradition was often an attack on the
chivalric ideal. The slave narrative performed the same function: it
punctured the inflated rhetoric and empty boasts of the slavocracy. It
destroyed the idyllic setting and cultivated setting created by southern
romance. It portrayed the rude and violent behavior of the master class
and the inhumanity of the plantation system.

It is clear, then, that the slave narratives established a tradition
for black autobiography and black fiction. An examination of Richard
Wright's *Black Boy, The Autobiography of Malcolm X* and Wright's existential novel, *The Outsider* will suggest the authors' debt to our own
tradition.

A study of the autobiographies of Afro-Americans enables the reader
to grasp the bitterness and intensity of their lives and the humanity of
those who wrestle so mightily against cynicism and destruction. For the
literary critic this study is an essential step as we analyze the ways in
which the existential experience is transmuted into smoother and more
creative fictional forms.

Autobiographical writings like *Black Boy* and *The Autobiography of
Malcolm X* are intense, passionate revelations of the deepest conflicts in
the black experience—an experience which, when translated into fiction
assumes the form of the picaresque. The distinguishing mark of the black
picaroon is that his fate is determined not only by class but more importantly by *caste* status. *Black Boy* is the modern archetype of the life
of an American "freedman." It illustrates vividly how effectively the
South restored the *status quo ante* by an elaborate system of taboos,
restraints and invidious distinctions sanctioned by law and enforced by
ruthless violence against the posterity of the ex-slaves. The Southern
politicians and their white constituents not only wished to ensure their
own political and economic supremacy: they set out to destroy the black
man's identity and individuality to reduce him to a pre-individual state,
to rob him of his humanity. The system insisted on total obedience and
submission.

Richard Wright's account of his childhood, *Black Boy,* achieves its
stunning impact by dramatizing the collision of a vigorous, imaginative
and daring youth with a family and a society which set out to stamp out

his individuality. His first awareness is of a family setting so cramping and lacking in spiritual nourishment that he is driven to outrageous acts of defiance by its cold hostility. His humble origins with his parents do not spare him the jeopardy of the picaroon (like Lazarillo). For he is hungry, cold and deprived. Indeed his experience is the more alienating precisely because his own mother and the father (who soon abandons the family) are the first to repress his normal curiosity and assertiveness. From the very outset his contact with his environment is traumatic. He is beaten and robbed by gangs, insulted and terrified by whites and sharply restricted in all his movements. At the age of six he finds himself drunk in a local tavern and a frightened observer of the ghetto's underworld life. The next phase of his life is spent with an austere Calvinistic grandmother whose stern admonitions against sin turn his guilt and hostility against himself and alienate him completely from any human warmth or affection. By the time he was compelled to confront the public school and his vicious white employers in cities like Jackson and Memphis, he was a lost soul, bitterly estranged from his relatives, the black community and the larger society. Each day's ordeals brought him to the brink of that vast chasm beyond which lay humiliation, terror, rage and death. Like the picaresque hero, he learned to mask his anger, to repress his natural instincts, to dissemble and conform. The price he paid was dear: a bitter alienation, a lack of identity and an incapacity for love. He writes:

> Again and again I vowed that someday I would end this hunger of mine, this apartness, this eternal difference; and I did not suspect that I would never get intimately into their lives, that I was doomed to live with them but not of them, that I had my own strange and separate road, a road which in later years would make them wonder how I had come to tread it.
>
> I now saw a world leap to life before my eyes because I could explore it, and that meant not going home when school was out, but wandering, watching, asking, talking. (p. 111)

The cruelty of these surroundings could not stamp out the searching intelligence, the critical awareness, the love of life welling up inside this black boy. He discovered newspapers, books, the beauty of the land and the sunset and even a few friends. Like the picaro and the fugitive slave, Richard Wright dreamed "of going north and writing books, novels. The North symbolized to me all that I had not felt and seen; it had no relation whatever to what actually existed. Yet by imagining a place where everything was possible, I kept hope alive in me." (p. 147) This utopian dream was severely tested by the reality of discrimination, insult, lynching and violence. But the boy continued his rootless wandering and heart-breaking quest. "In me was shaping a yearning for a kind of conscious-ness, a mode of being that the way of life about me had said could not be, must not be and upon which the penalty of death had been placed."

The chaos in his life continued, however. He knocked about from one menial job to another. He remained on guard against attack by hostile whites. He avoided stealing only out of fear. As a bellboy he learned to peddle bootleg liquor. "I no longer felt bound by the laws which white and black were supposed to obey in common. I was outside those laws; the white people had told me so. Now when I thought of ways to escape from my environment I no longer felt the inner restraint that would have made stealing impossible, and this new freedom made me lonely and afraid." The brutality of the system affected him in a thousand ways. He was forced to watch his employers attack and beat a Negro woman while he (and the police) stood by and merely watched. He was forced out of a job with a firm of opticians for daring to entertain the hope of learning to be a technician. He was struck down for failing to say "sir" to white men. He is forced into a boxing match for the entertainment of whites. At last he escaped to new uncertainties in Chicago. "Not only had the southern whites not known me," he writes, "but, more important still, as I had lived in the South I had not had the chance to learn who I was." Indeed the world he had known had tossed away "the best and deepest things of heart and mind" in "blind ignorance and hate." (p. 228)

Richard Wright, compelled to preserve some rag of honor in the face of the barbarism of the South, was a "bad boy" and a rogue to his family and acquaintances. But the fact is he was a conscious rebel against an inhuman environment. Chicago led him down the road to revolution and black nationalism.

The *Autobiography of Malcolm X* is probably the most influential book read by this generation of Afro-Americans. For not only is the ac-count of Malcolm Little an absorbing and heart-shattering encounter with the realities of poverty, crime and racism. It is a fantastic success story. Paradoxically, the book designed to be an indictment of American and European bigotry and exploitation, is a triumphant affirmation of the possibilities of the human spirit. Malcolm X presents us with a manifesto, a call to arms, a revolutionary document. At the same time he reveals an incredible and dogged perseverance in the face of soul-destroying limita-tions, a passionate eagerness to learn, a love of life, an ingenious and re-sourceful capacity for survival. In him the picaresque mode is given a new psychic dimension, a sense of history and a tragic force. The chaos which would engulf the protagonist here extends in ever widening cir-cles from the hunger, squalor and petty thievery of the street-corner to the crises in international relations and colonialism and, at last, to the vexed questions involving men's faith and their ultimate relation to the cosmos. The journey of the picaroon, Malcolm X, is from ragged obscurity to world spokesman, to charismatic leader, to martyred saint—a long, sordid, yet visionary, quest through the underworld to a vision of some just and ordered millennium. Thus the black picaresque characteristically presents us with the religious agonist whose search out of poverty, deprivation and despair leads him through dreams of liberation to a transcendent sense of community.

This then is the essential meaning of *The Autobiography of Malcolm X.* He was born into a family of eight children in Omaha, Nebraska on May 19, 1925. He knew poverty, hunger and deprivation. But above all his family lived surrounded by a ring of hate—constant threats by the Ku Klux Klan and innumerable forms of insult and indignity. Malcolm's father, a proud, militant man and Baptist preacher, propagated the Black Nationalism of Marcus Garvey. The bigots responded by burning down the Littles' house and, at last, murdering their father. Malcolm and his brothers were separated and farmed out to relatives and friends. His mother suffered a mental breakdown and had to be hospitalized. Malcolm was sent to Lansing, Michigan and then to Boston, Massachusetts. His schooling was sporadic.

The next phase of his life led him into petty crimes—truancy, thievery, dope peddling, pimping. Like the picaroon he survived by trickery and deceit, by out-smarting others, by "hustling" his way through a vicious underground existence. At last, apprehended by the police for one of his crimes, he landed in jail by the time he was sixteen or seventeen. Then came his conversion to the Black Muslim religion of Elijah Muhammad—a curious amalgam of myth, faith, asceticism and revolutionary doctrine. The Black Muslims' over-riding goal is the liberation of black people from the thralldom and exploitation of dominant white racists. They sought not only to prepare blacks for an inevitable confrontation with the power structure, but to give them a new self-esteem and pride and the determination to establish their own nation. The experience of conversion to the Muslim faith transformed Malcolm's character. Upon his release from prison, he turned from crime and self-indulgence to reading, learning and proselytizing for the group. His first exposure to the history of slavery, discrimination and imperialism convinced him that the "white man is a devil" and that black men must not only cast off the corrupting influence of western society, but work toward a separate black state, The Nation of Islam. One is amazed by Malcolm X's zeal for learning, by the range of his intellectual interests and the far-reaching character of his organizing effort for the cause. Malcolm listened as Elijah Muhammed railed against integration and reconciliation. He dedicated himself to the same cause and represented his great leader's ideas in innumerable speeches. Then came the break. Disillusioned by evidences of immorality and adultery charged against Elijah Muhammed, Malcolm X was silenced by the man who plainly felt threatened by his disciple's popularity. For Malcolm X understood the mentality of the ghetto—the stirrings and conflicts of the black masses. "The black man in North America was spiritually sick because for centuries he had accepted the white man's Christianity—which asked the black so-called Christian to expect no true Brotherhood of man but to endure the cruelties of the white so-called Christians. Christianity had made black men fuzzy, nebulous, confused in their thinking. . . ." he wrote. "The black man in North America was economically sick . . . as a consumer he got less than his share, and as a producer gave least . . . In New York City with over a million Negroes, there aren't twenty black-owned businesses employing over ten people. It's because black men don't own and control their own community's retail establishments that they can't stabilize their own community." (p. 313) These ideas got a wide hearing throughout the black world. The bitter disillusionment of the Negroes who had tried moral suasion, peaceful protest and non-violence only to confront dogs, clubs, guns and unjust imprisonment seized upon this new black nationalism. The assassination of Martin Luther King and Malcolm X himself changed radically the whole climate of race relations in America.

What many black nationalists and followers of Malcolm X seem to have forgotten, however, is Malcolm's pilgrimage to Mecca and the subsequent widening of his horizons. Though indefatigable in his struggle for the liberation of black America, he saw the world-wide implications of oppression and exploitation. He sensed that the wretched of the earth have a common cause and that in our struggle we need allies. The life of Malcolm Little outdoes the fantasies, the jeopardy, the rush of events and accident which we associate with the picaroon. The personalized essays of Eldridge Cleaver and Le Roi Jones have the same stark, rebellious impact. Even fiction can hardly recapture its intensity and tragic dimension. But the imaginative writer could not fail to be enticed by the power of the black picaresque and the creative possibilities of the theme which destroyed the American union and still threatens the foundations of our national life.

It is apparent, then, that the black experience itself suggested to some Afro-American writers the picaresque form when they turned to fiction. For they were conscious victims of fortuitous circumstance, rootless and lonely men forced to survive by various stratagems and Protean roles. Indeed their immersion in a bitter underground life robbed them of the kind of aesthetic distance which could use the picaresque mode creatively in fiction until the twentieth century. Two factors explain the flourishing of a more creative and experimental use of this fictional form in recent times: (1) the pilgrimage of the plantation Negro to the urban setting with its richer cultural contact and growing group solidarity; (2) the refinement of his sensibility and the deepening of his perception which resulted from closer contact with Western literary tradition. We have seen how the slave narrative created its own picaresque forms. Works like *Don Quixote, Moll Flanders, Tom Jones* and *Huckleberry Finn* suggested further variations on familiar themes. Yet these works scarcely appealed to the black writer as having the depth and serious-ness of the Negro experience in America. Even *Moll Flanders* seemed contrived and somewhat frivolous, and Tom Jones, though a bastard abandoned by his benefactors and making a shaky adjustment to a merciless London world, is never convincingly a lower class character. Huck Finn provided the most useful model in his outcast status, his perilous flight, his ingenuity in shifting roles and his subversion of the established values of the society. Yet the odor of the plantation stereo-types clung to Huck and Jim and their adventures could scarcely seem relevant to the industrial setting of twentieth century ghetto life.

When we turn to the black writers, it is plain that none of them is consciously imitating the western picaresque mode but is more influ-enced by the black experience (as we have seen it in autobiographies). Hence in structuring the action, character and language of their novels, they have taken for granted the essential elements of the picaresque. What they have created are comic modes and fictional forms which achieve the intensity, tension and bitter rebellion characteristic of the group's life. For the black picaroon never can escape the iron ring of his caste status. His alienation and struggle for survival are more intensely felt. He must be capable of playing numerous exacting roles, for he is the victim of accident, chaos and irrational caprice. His world conspires to oppress and unsettle him. The maxim of the society is summed up in the directive: "Keep this nigger running." The instability of his emo-tional life leads him into the agony and conflict of a damaged ego. Yet he has developed considerable resilience and ingenuity. His speech, his blues, his jazz, his double vision and sophisticated awareness provide a rich cultural dowry, and he is able by improvisation, disguise, irony, paradox and word play to explore means of escape to a spiritual freedom which even the traditional picaroon could not know.

The early efforts in the black picaresque were trial flights, like Claude McKay's *Home to Harlem*. In this novel the protagonist, Jake, is a lonely wanderer stranded in Europe who goes AWOL to get back home to Harlem. He is somewhat reminiscent of Tom Jones in his irrepressible good spirits, his episodic career, his furious and hedonistic pursuit of pleasure. Drink, sex, dancing and gambling seem to fill his life, and he wastes no time in dour reflection. He spends his time looking for his lost love, Felice. He works because he must. But he is free of self hatred or self pity. Especially when contrasted with his foil, the educated Ray, he seems a stereotyped portrait of the happy-go-lucky darky. But on closer examination we discover that his roguery goes beyond mere lasciviousness and folly. For he is a fugitive and a rebel, resisting the police and refusing to serve as a scab. The picaresque characters' status is symbolized here by the persona of the Pullman Car porter and Dining Car waiter who must perform a daily balancing act on a shaky train while hurtling toward some uncertain destination. The hysterical and feverish search of Jake and Ray for some haven, some lasting human relationship now ends, and they are part of that flotsam and jetsam which the late tides will, at last, float to some abandoned shore.

It is Richard Wright, of course, who establishes the tradition and reveals something of the range of possibilities of the form. As we have seen in *Black Boy* he lived through the anguish of the black picaroon and could depict the extent of his estrangement and the revolutionary implications of the theme. Generally speaking, critics have described *Native Son* as a naturalistic novel—a bold and candid revelation of lower class life in a rat-infested ghetto, a harsh indictment of an exploitative society, a picture of those victimized by impersonal and pre-determined forces. All this is true. Yet there is more to *Native Son* than that. For the achievement of the novel is in Wright's success in humanizing the murderer and bully, Bigger Thomas, and giving him a tragic dimension. Bigger's humanity strikes us first of all in the nature of his roguish adjustment to this world. His obscure origins, his thievery, his pretenses and dreams, his Protean roles (gang leader, chauffeur, servant, kidnapper, black nationalist) are picaresque. But Bigger stands out in contrast to the traditional picaroon in the intensity, stark reality and revolutionary character of his role. But his is a perilous lack of any adjustment. His behavior is plainly moving toward the pathological. He is the archetype of the Black Militant who has discovered that he is willing to pay any price for freedom—even murder and death. And his fantasies of a Black Nation, his expanding awareness of his powers and of his world raise the novel to a new order of consciousness.

In "The Man Who Lived Underground," a long, short story, Richard Wright turns from realism to surrealism and symbolism, from the episodic tale to the interior conflicts of the psyche. For Wright's contribution is his fearful anticipation of the psychic (as well as social) perils the rebel black picaroon faces. Yet again there are elements of the picaresque which anticipate Le Roi Jones's System of *Dante's Hell* and that master of the black picaresque, Ralph Ellison. "The Man Who Lived Underground" is named, but we learn nothing of his origins. But he is fleeing from the police and drops down a manhole into the sewer underneath the city. Though apparently innocent of any crime, he has signed a confession of murder and feels guilty. In his wanderings underground he finds a cave, a church, an undertaker's establishment, a movie house, a coal bin, a safe, a butcher shop, an office and a jeweller's. He establishes himself in a cave where he installs lights and stores the dollars, diamonds and rings that he has stolen. For a time he has a deceptive euphoria: "He had triumphed over the world above ground! He was free . . . He wanted to run from his cave and yell his discovery to the world." When he emerges into the street no one notices him. Compulsively he goes to the police to assure them he *is* a criminal and he urges them to see his underground cave and his stolen goods. The officers of the law think him insane. But finally they follow him to the manhole entrance and when he has descended into the maelstrom one of them shoots him. "He sighed and closed his eyes, a whirling object rushing alone in the darkness, veering, tossing, lost in the heart of the earth."

The story operates on two symbolic levels: the psychological and the social. The protagonist, like Dostoevsky's underground man, is fearful, unstable, masochistic, aggressive and somewhat paranoid. His descent into the sewer brings him face to face with his own conflicts and nightmares—the awful squalor and degradation into which his ego is drowning. At the same time the offal, the dead bodies, the abortions and decay of the acquisitive and wasteful society are poorly concealed below the surface of our cities. Here the anguish and chaos of the picaroon, the outcast, cry out his indictment against the barbarism of the society which defines him as a criminal and robs him of his manhood.

Richard Wright's novel *The Outsider* (1953) has received little critical attention and has been dismissed by those who refer to it as an inept and poorly written novel. The book's importance to our contemporary sensibility, its prophetic and ideological significance, have been much underestimated. *The Outsider*, written under the influence of Satre's existentialism, is nevertheless a powerful sequel to Richard Wright's central theme as we have seen it in *Black Boy*, *Native Son* and "The Man Who Lived Underground." It adds a new dimension to the black picaresque genre in its inexorable pursuit of the conflicts in the soul of the outcast, the brutalized and oppressed Negro. Wright's early writings found heroic elements in the victim-turned-assailant, by convincing us that those who challenged oppression and were defined as criminals by an unjust society had proved that the only possible stance for the Black masses is one of rebellion. I am convinced that this idea owes more to his black nationalism than to Marxist ideology. In *The Outsider* the narrative power of the novel stems not only from the perilous and protean career of the protagonist, but from his attempt to confront the chaos about him by seizing the initiative and fashioning his own destiny. Cross Damon, a thirty-three-year-old Negro is divorced, has 3 children whom he loves and is surrounded by his friends and fellow postal workers. He has a love affair with a young girl who gets pregnant. Yet he is alone, rootless and alienated. His bitter quarrels with his wife, his drinking and extra-curricular sex adventures are symptomatic of his passionate but fruitless quest to find wholeness and health, for a way out of his debts, his shattered marriage and the humiliations of a racist society. The opening scenes of the novel in which he is walking in the snow and constantly fleeing the cold are symbolic in this regard. Then Cross Damon is in a subway accident, his coat containing his identification papers, which he has taken off in attempting to extricate himself from the wreck, falls near a Negro who resembles him. To his amazement he discovers that the next day's newspapers report him among the dead. He reads his own obituaries and watches his own funeral from a safe distance. It is then that he decides to seize the opportunity to blot out his miserable past and create a new identity. "All of his life he had been hankering after his personal freedom, and now freedom was knocking at his door, begging him to come in. He shivered in the cold. . . ." The numerous disguises and changing roles of the picaroon suggest how hungrily the search for a new identity characterizes these persons. Not only is this symptomatic of the instability of the personality concerned (which is deeply involved in an identity crisis) but it suggests the chaos and jeopardy which haunts them. Cross Damon flees to New York, adopts various names and stolen credentials. He commits four murders to protect his real self from discovery and suffers the constant agony and fear of the fugitive. "Now depending only upon his lonely will, he saw that to map out his life entirely upon his own assumptions was a task that terrified him, just to think of it, for he knew that he first had to know what he thought life was . . . the question summed itself up: What's a man? He had unknowingly set himself a project of no less magnitude than contained in that awful question." (p. 83) Cross Damon thinks that in abandoning his old identity he is free to choose to be anyone he likes. But he eventually discovers that he has greatly increased the chaos and sickness in his own heart. For he is not a man at all without an identity; he is a ghost, a spook.

Moreover, he determines not only to manipulate and fashion his own life, but that of others. He assumes God-like prerogatives over others.

His association with the Communist Party enlarges his opportunities for
violating coldly the rights of others. In short, Cross Damon's mental state
is pathological. He is suffering from paranoia: delusions of persecution
followed by delusions of omnipotence. *The Outsider* is often referred to
as an existentialist novel. It is, more accurately, an attack on existentialism, a daring flirtation with its tenets and a final rejection of the selfish
and sick view of existentialism which Cross Damon represents. For
Damon believes in nothing. "God is dead and everything is allowed."
Man is a futile passion. A man is only what he makes of himself. Cross
Damon says: "We 20th century westerners have outlived the faith of our
fathers; our minds have grown so skeptical that we cannot accept the
old scheme of moral precepts which once guided man's life. In our modern industrial society we try to steer our hearts by improvised, prag-
matic rules which are, in the end, no rules at all. . . ." Cross Damon's
career dramatizes the risks faced by the black picaroon: personality disintegration, lack of identity, brutalization and at last paranoia or paranoid schizophrenia. He is shot by another communist. Having stripped
himself of all illusions, having dared everything to preserve himself and
create his own identity and his own law, he achieves some new insights
on his death bed—insights as old as our first exploration of ethics. "I wish
I had some way to give the meaning of my life to others . . . To make a
bridge from man to man . . . Starting from scratch every time . . . is
no good. Tell them not to come down this road . . . Men hate themselves and it makes them hate others . . . We must find some way of
being good to ourselves . . . Man is all we've got . . . I wish I could
ask men to meet themselves . . . Man is returning to the earth . . . The
real men, the last men are coming. . . ." (pp. 437-440)

No doubt Ralph Ellison is the author who has made the most creative
use of the picaresque mode. *Invisible Man* presents us with a protagonist
who is on a lonely journey to the discovery of the self and the world
which surrounds him. He is overwhelmed by the rush of events; he is a
protean figure—a student, a trucker, a confidence man, a laborer, a rab-
ble rouser, a political organizer. He goes through rehearsals of chaos
and harrowing events. With a marvelous use of language, satire, symbols and comic modes the writer carries his character through a series of
epiphanies—revelations. The book is an epistemological novel, dealing as
it does with our ways of perceiving and knowing truth. Ellison's character grows from naive acceptance and passive conformity, through social protest, revolution and anarchy to discover at last the way to his
identity. He becomes at last a man of principle. His pilgrimage through

chaos, violence and hate brings him to a wholeness, a health which is based on idealism and hope.

Ellison, who was a jazz musician, employs the quality of improvisation, daring and intensity characteristic of jazz. Richard Wright tells us that "blue jazz" became the Outsider's "only emotional home." "Blue jazz was the scornful gesture of men turned ecstatic in their state of rejection, it was the musical language of the satisfiedly amoral, the boastings of the contentedly lawless, the recreations of the innocently criminal." (*The Outsider*, p. 140) As such, jazz and blues are surely a vivid evocation of the picaresque mode.

In this story Ellison, by these ironies, reverses the stereotypes and forces us to see the absurdity and injustice of them. Thus the concealment of the main character in a coal cellar suggests not the darkness of the Anglo-Saxon connotation, but "a voice issuing its wisdom out of the substance of its own inwardness—after having undergone the transformation from ranter to writer." (*Partisan Review*, Vol. xxv [Spring, 1958], p. 212ff.) The main character's movement downward is, in keeping with the reverse English of the plot, a process of *rising* to an understanding of his human condition. The main character is, in a sense, *running* throughout the story like many of us today. His is trying to fulfill other people's views of himself. And in the complexity of modern life he is lost—as when working in a factory he allows the paint to overflow and cannot find the right valve which shuts off the vast machinery. The novel suggests alternatives to the violence of one of the demagogues in the book through the use of mistaken identity: the main character discovers great freedom of action in his various disguises. But his most significant discovery is of his own possibilities. "Life is to be lived, not controlled, and humanity is won by continuing to play in face of certain defeat. Our fate is to become one, and yet many—this is not prophecy, but description. Thus one of the greatest jokes in the world is the spectacle of the whites busy escaping blackness and becoming blacker every day, and the blacks striving toward whiteness, becoming quite dull and gray. None of us seems to know who he is or where he's going." (p. 499)

The main character in *Invisible Man* experiences the indignities and cruelties caused by prejudice, but these are familiar to most literate people. The contribution of these books lies in their concern with the problem of identity. Each individual's self-realization which is the goal and glory of free society—is the heart of the matter. "If I were asked what I considered to be the chief significance of *Invisible Man*," said Ralph Ellison, "I would reply its attempt to return to the mood of personal moral responsibility for democracy which typified the best of our 19th century fiction."

In John A. Williams, Clarence Major, Amiri Baraka and, above all, Ishmael Reed, the black picaresque has reached its most complex forms. The individual's consciousness reflects in its comic modes, its anachronisms, its contradictions and absurdities the actual perils, the vast possibilities in our modern world.

[1] The *Life of Lazarillo de Tormes: His Fortunes and Adversities:* Translated by J.G. Markley, Library of Liberal Arts, N.Y., Bobbs-Merrill, 1954.

[2] For a bibliography of slave narratives, see: Charles H. Nichols, *Many Thousand Gone: the Ex-Slaves' Account of Their Bondage and Freedom,* Indiana University Press, 1969.

Singing Swords:
The Literary Legacy of Slavery

MELVIN DIXON

The fabric of tradition in Afro-American literature is woven from slave narratives and Negro spirituals, the earliest and most significant forms of oral and written literature created by blacks during slavery. Not only did the spirituals identify the slave's peculiar syncretistic religion, sharing features of Protestant Christianity and traditional African religions, but they became an almost secretive code for the slave's critique of the plantation system and for his search for freedom in *this* world. Similarly, the narratives identified the slave's autobiographical and communal history as well as his active campaign against the "peculiar institution." Both forms of cultural expression from the slave community create a vision of history, an assessment of the human condition, and a heroic fugitive character unlike any other in American literature.

Critical studies of this material as literature or history have been slow to appreciate its distinctive cultural voice. Marion Starling has argued that slave narratives are of "sub-literary quality" and that their chief importance lies "in their genetic relationship to the popular slave novels of the 1850s," most notably Harriet Beecher Stowe's *Uncle Tom's Cabin.*[1] And historians, until recently, have ignored them as genuine documents because of their subjectivity and possible "inauthenticity."

Further scholarship, such as Charles Nichols' *Many Thousand Gone*, has produced important reconsiderations of the slave community and of the relations between masters and slaves by using slave literature as a primary source. Through the study of black and white autobiographies, folklore, music, religion and art by such historians as John Blassingame, Eugene Genovese, and Lawrence Levine,[2] the black past is now recognized as an active, vital, creative element in American history and literature. Furthermore, we are finding that "slavery was never so complete a system of psychic assault that it prevented slaves from carving out independent cultural forms" that preserve some degree of personal autonomy and a range of positive self-concepts.[3]

Through American slave culture we uncover the roots of the many recurring images and metaphors used to describe the black experience on both a group and individual level. The spirituals and the narratives constitute a literature in that they are deliberate creations of the slaves themselves to express their moral and intellectual universe. These forms of communication, what W.E.B. Du Bois called "the sorrow songs," what Benjamin Mays referred to as "mass" literature, and what Saunders Redding has identified as a "literature of necessity,"[4] remind us that they were created out of the practical need to adjust to the American environment with a burning passion to be free.

Slave narratives were published from 1703 until the first forty years of the twentieth century, when former slaves, interviewed in the Federal Writers' Project, furnished volumes of historical testimony and when men such as Booker T. Washington and George Washington Carver published autobiographies drawn from their childhood experiences during slavery. Published in single volumes both in England and the United States and reaching a height of popularity and commercial success after 1840 when antislavery sentiment was strongest, narratives and autobiographical sketches of slaves appeared in abolitionist newspapers such as Garrison's *Liberator, The National Anti-Slavery Standard, The Quarterly Anti-Slavery Magazine* in New York, *The National Enquirer* in Philadelphia, and *The Observer* in St. Louis. Narratives also appeared in judicial records, broadsides, and church records. Slave songs were less widely popularized, and no major effort to collect them was made until after the Civil War when William Francis Allen and Lucy McKim Garrison published *Slave Songs of the United States* in 1867.

Both narratives and songs are seminal to the development of Afro-American autobiography, fiction, and poetry. By infusing the dynamic vestiges of an oral tradition and culture into a more formal written literary mode, they create an important slave literature in the United States. This literature has been called native, naive and childlike by critics who wish to limit the songs and narratives to one dimensional meaning. Granted the "native imagery and emphasis in the spirituals are selected elements that helped the slave adjust to his particular world,"[5] but it is precisely in the slave's pattern of acculturation that the student of black history and culture finds specific ideologies for survival. That Christianity is easily recognizable in the language of the songs and narratives has led many critics to emphasize the spiritual docility and otherworldliness of slave thought. However, a deeper study of the dual aspects of culture contact and acculturation between European and African belief structures reveals that slaves needed a language and a flexible vocabulary more for communication than for belief. Thus it is more realistic to examine how Christianity was "the nearest available, least suspect, and most stimulative system for expressing their concepts of freedom, justice, right and aspiration." In the literature, that Christian imagery becomes "an arsenal of pointed darts, a storehouse of images, a means of making shrewd observations."[6]

Revolutionary sentiments, plans for escape, and insurrection were often couched in the religious imagery which was the slave community's weapon against despair and moral degradation. This literature contained ideas that reached the masses of slaves primarily through the "church" within the slave community and the men and women preached, testified, and told God all their troubles.

Using the Bible as a storehouse of myth and history that could be appropriated for religious syncretism and a practical philosophy based on historical immediacy, the slave community identified with the children of Israel; but they did not stop there. Slaves knew that deliverance would come, as proven by their African assurance of intimacy and immortality with the Supreme Being, and by the wider implications of the biblical past. Both systems of belief helped the slave know that he could actively participate in deliverance and judgment by joining God's army, singing with a sword in his hand, or walking in Jerusalem just like John. The slave was sure he was experiencing all of history: the past, present and future. Moses very often came to slaves in the person of Harriet Tubman and other ex-slaves who went back into Egypt, heard the children "yowlin'," and led them to the promised land in the North. Historical immediacy created and sustained through the oral tradition that healing moment of deliverance and salvation:

> O Mary don' you weep don' you moan
> Pharaoh's army got drownded.

Upon the rock that was traditional African religion as well as American Christianity, the slave community built a church. Out of religious syncretism and an oral literature they established an active contemporary apocalypse in the realm of their own daily experiences. The historical moment for the slave was never abstract, but imminent. The time for deliverance and witness was now. The complexity of the religious experience, as well as the complexity of the day-to-day social experience in the slave quarters, centered in a conversion-like initiation, became further testing grounds for individual and corporate faith in the possibility of freedom. And as the slave lived, he would reckon with time, community, and his own life journey. He sang:

> God dat lived in Moses' time
> Is jus' de same today.

Slavery had brought black men and women face to face with the extreme fact of their wretchedness as individuals. Conversion to an inner cult, an in-group morality, provided the very real awareness that individual loneliness and despair could be resolved in group solidarity. The conversion experience emphasized a person's recognition of his own need for deliverance from sin and bondage into a holy alliance with God as the avenging deity:

> My God He is a Man—a Man of War,
> An' de Lawd God is His name.
>
> I'm a soljuh in the Army of thuh Lawd,
> I'm a soljuh in this Army.
>
> Hold out yo' light you heav'n boun' soldier
> Let yo' light shine around the world.
>
> We are the people of God.

Conversion also provided for socio-religious mobility and status within the slave community. Conversion also confirmed an African orientation of personal duty on both a ritualistic and humanistic level. Ritual, duty, and creative expression all served as outlets for individual expression without disturbing communal solidarity. Song and personal testimony, as forms of an oral literature, allowed for individual interpretation while they "continually drew [the slave] back into the communal presence and permitted him the comfort of basking in the warmth of the shared assumptions of those around him."[7] Conversion to these shared assumptions provided a basis for self-esteem, new values, and an important defense against degradation. Slaves were initiated through the spiritual potency of personal testimony. They prepared themselves to fight for freedom by becoming morally free of an intrusive and debilitating white out-group and by becoming more responsible to the inner slave community.

Slaves demanded of each other explicit principles of character and right living: for the "soul" to be a "witness for my Lord." This was no mystical yearning, but a real test of character and conviction. As realists, slaves demanded that they be struck dead to sin in order to live again in freedom. In order for this transformation to be real enough to connect with the vital image of deliverance, "conversion had to be in the nature of a stroke of lightning which would enter at the top of their head and emerge from their toes." Slaves, as Paul Radin continues, "had to meet God, be baptized by him in the river of Jordan, personally, and become identified with him."[8]

The status slaves gained as a result was both inward and outward, sometimes manifesting itself in change of behavior from mild submission to active resistance. Here it is necessary to distinguish an important feature of the slave's conversion. Knowing the deep need for community and the deprived sense of belonging for slaves isolated in bondage, and knowing the utter contempt with which whites regarded black spiritual welfare (despite a very false "Christian" religious education), it is obvious that through the religious organization in the slave quarters, the slaves were not converting themselves to God, but *were converting themselves to each other*. As a result, slaves converted God to their new identity and community in the New World and made God active in their struggle for freedom. This syncretic African-Christian God became "a fixed point within and without [the slave] and all that God commanded was unqualified faith and throwing away of doubt,"[9] which was what slaves demanded of each other. Both God and man experienced conversion. Together they struggled for self-expression and the fulfillment of human destiny. "The sins would take care of themselves," Radin has argued, but more importantly a socio-religious mobility has been set in motion, unifying the community. Frederick Douglass himself confirmed, "we were generally a unit, and moved together."[10]

Conversion as rebirth or transformation was a central event in the slave's recorded life. In this way it gave individuals an outline of personal history and made them aware of their part in the larger history of the racial group. In fact, by achieving a personal witness (a personal historical sense or vision in which man is the essential binder of time and space), individual men and women could participate in the larger history and further regenerate themselves by attaining freedom and salvation. Testimonies in the narratives speak directly to this transformation and regeneration:

> I was born a slave and lived through some very hard times. If it had not been for *my God,* I don't know what I would have done. Through his mercy I was lifted up. My soul began singing and I was told that I was one of the elected children and that I would live as long as God lives. . . . A building is waiting for me way back in eternal glory and I have no need to fear. He stood me on my feet and told me that I was a sojourner in a weary land. I came from heaven and I am now returning.[11]

And he sang:

> I'm er rollin', I'm er rollin'
> Through an unfriendly world.

When slaves came to write their formal autobiographies they emphasized a conversion-like model of personal experience and testimony to construct their own "witness" to the horrors of slavery and the regenerative joy of freedom. The conversion experience helped to organize the individual life and unite it with time and the eternal presence of God. As one slave testified to this historical pattern:

> The soul that trusts in God need never stumble nor fall, because God being all wise and seeing and knowing all things, having looked down through time before time, foresaw every creeping thing and poured out His spirit on the earth. The earth brought forth her fruits in due season. In the very beginning every race and every creature was in the mind of God and we are here, not ahead of time, not behind time, but just on time. It was time that brought us here and time will carry us away.[12]

The use of historical and religious language and symbol is seen most clearly in the escape episode in slave narratives. The nearby woods or the wilderness into which the fugitive escapes becomes the testing ground of his faith in God and in himself:

> If you want to find Jesus, go in de wilderness
> Go in de wilderness, go in de wilderness
> Mournin' brudder, go in de wilderness
> To wait upon de Lord.

The scenes of self-revelation and the experience of grace and a final rebirth become as characteristic to the narratives as they are to the songs. What is developed from this imagery, shared between oral and written

modes, is a literature of struggle and fulfillment. The thematic transformation in the text parallels the transformation in its creators. The change
is from chattel status, unholiness, and damnation in the hell which was
slavery to the integrity of being a man and a saved child of God now
walking the paved streets of a heavenly city, the promised North. The
slave has been delivered. Conversion was the correlative for a subjective
synthesis of history; earning freedom through escape (or insurrection)
was heroic action.

That religion and freedom went hand in hand is evidenced by the
entire experience of the fugitive slave. Often poorly equipped for long
journeys and with few geographic aids, he was alone with only God to
help him endure the wilderness. Often leaders of fugitive parties were
ministers themselves. One preacher, a Methodist, tried to persuade John
Thompson to join his band of runaways. Thompson was unwilling to
escape with them, and only several months later did he attempt his escape alone, once he was assured of God's presence. Thompson described
the occasion and method of that first fugitive group and his own skepticism:

> The Methodist preacher . . . urged me very strongly to accompany
> them, saying that he had full confidence in the surety of the promises
> of God . . . he believed he was able to carry him safely to the land of
> freedom, and accordingly he was determined to go. Still I was afraid
> to risk myself on such uncertain promises; I dared not trust an unseen
> God.
>   On the night on which they intended to start . . . they knelt in
> prayer to the great God of Heaven and Earth, invoking Him to guard
> them . . . and go with them to their journey's end.[13]

Most often the slave's idea of freedom was a consequence of his
recognition of his slave status. He needed little outside influence to convince him of the advantages of freedom. Even as far south as Louisiana
and in as isolated a region as Bayou Boeuf to which Solomon Northup
was kidnapped, the idea of freedom was a regular topic among the
slaves, as Northup writes:

> They understand the privileges and exemptions that belong to it—that it
> would bestow upon them the fruits of their own labor, and that it would
> secure to them the enjoyment of domestic happiness. They do not fail
> to observe the difference between their own condition and the meanest
> white man's and to realize the injustice of the laws.[14]

Thus, freedom, an essential aspect of human development, was a value
within the slave community which also outlined a socio-religious mobil-

ity for its attainment. The mobility established in the slave's conversion experience became the philosophical model for further initiation into free status and identity.

The first step in this mobility on the personal level involved a recognition of one's wretchedness as a slave, a realization that one is different and deprived. "I was born a slave," wrote Harriet Jacobs, "but I never knew it till six years of happy childhood had passed away . . . When I was six years old, my mother died; and then, for the first time, I learned by the talk around me, that I was a slave."[15]

Henry Bibb of Kentucky had a similar rude awakening; "I knew nothing of my condition as a slave. I was living with Mr. White, whose wife had died and left him a widower with one little girl, who was said to be the legitimate owner of my mother and all her children. This girl was also my playmate when we were children." When he was eight or ten years old Bibb discovered that his wages were being spent for the education of his playmate. It was then that he realized his slave labor was profitless for himself. "It was then I first commenced seeing and feeling that I was a wretched slave."[16]

Former slave Thomas Jones began his narrative with the following recognition: "I was born a slave. My recollections of early life are associated with poverty, suffering and shame. I was made to feel in my boyhood's first experience that I was inferior and degraded and that I must pass through life in a dependent and suffering condition."[17]

The Negro spirituals speak to the same sense of wretchedness in slavery as the singers sought deliverance:

> Oh, wretched man that I am;
> Oh, wretched man that I am;
> Oh, wretched man that I am,
> Who will deliver poor me?
>
> I am bowed down with a burden of woe;
> I am bowed down with a burden of woe;
> I am bowed down with a burden of woe;
> Who will deliver poor me?
>
> My heart's filled with sadness and pain;
> My heart's filled with sadness and pain;
> My heart's filled with sadness and pain;
> Who will deliver poor me?

The moment of self-discovery has been one of the more dramatic turning points in the personal history of every black American. The moment called for new tactics or behavior that would help the individual come to grips with his feelings of difference and alienation from the society at large. William Du Bois once wrote of his own experience that:

> Then it dawned upon me with a certain suddenness that I was different from the others; or like, mayhap in heart and life and longing, but shut out from their world by a vast veil. I had therefore no desire to tear down that veil, to creep through; I held all beyond it in common contempt, and lived above it in a region of blue sky and great wandering shadows.[18]

That crucial self-discovery, which can happen suddenly and by accident, is nonetheless the beginning of a collective consciousness and group identity. As poet Margaret Walker once wrote in her more contemporary account, it was a bitter hour "when we discovered we / were black and poor and small and different and / nobody cared and nobody / wondered and nobody understood."[19]

By the force of this personal alienation the individual began to see himself as a member of an oppressed group. Within the group experience, perhaps because of it, the individual resolved to remedy the situation for himself and the others who were joined to him by the extreme pressures of racial oppression. The slave could openly rebel or secretly escape. He could also accommodate himself to the subservient role slavery defined for him, as no doubt some slaves did. Whatever action the slave finally took was considered not the end of experience, but the beginning of a long confrontation from which he hoped to wrench his freedom.

Black religion told the slave where to seek liberation: "Jesus call you, go in the wilderness." There a man will be tested, tried and "be baptized." Religion agitated the slave's search. Preachers like Nat Turner and Denmark Vesey conspired to gain it. Other leaders urged slaves to run away. Turner himself often secreted himself in the woods where he communed with the Spirit and returned with the fresh assurance that his struggle had divine sanction:

> . . . I saw white spirits and black spirits engaged in battle, and the sun was darkened—the thunder rolled in the heaven, and blood flowed in streams—and I heard a voice saying, "Such is your luck, such you are called to see, and let it come rough or smooth, you must surely have it." I now withdrew myself as much as my situation would permit, from the intercourse of my fellow servants, for the avowed purpose of serving the Spirit more fully—and it appeared to me and reminded me of the things it had already shown me, and that it would then reveal to me the knowledge of the elements. After this revelation in the year of 1825 . . . I sought more than ever to obtain true holiness before the great day of judgement should appear, and then I began to receive the true knowledge of faith.[20]

On the night of his rebellion, Turner met again in the woods with his co-conspirators, where they shared cider and roasted pork as sacraments to their mission.

Other slaves often secreted themselves in the woods, even if only to meditate on their condition. In the wilderness of nature, freedom was revealed as a man's right in the natural harmony of God's created world. Henry Bibb meditated in the woods and wrote: "I thought of the fishes of the water, the fowls of the air, the wild beasts of the forest, all appeared to be free to go where they pleased, and I was an unhappy slave."[21] Nature furnished the slave with examples of freedom and the harmony of all life with God just as his African religious tradition continued to inform him. In the new American environment, the harmony of the natural world was easily given religious significance. Natural imagery was analogous to freedom and revealed a point of contact between man and God. The slave resolved to seek that contact and unity in the wilderness. Frederick Douglass once described this communion: "I was in the wood, buried in its somber gloom and hushed in its solemn silence, hidden from all human eyes, shut in with nature and with nature's God, and absent from all human contrivances. Here was a good place to pray, to pray for help, for deliverance."[22]

From the slave's point of view, the life pilgrimage of man was possible only through a renewed contract with nature, and by so doing he could effect a new covenant with God. This qualification of the life experience is evident in the ordinary day-to-day struggle of the slave in the hot fields and dramatized vividly in the plight of the fugitive. In nature the slave found a guide for the fulfillment of his identity; once he saw himself as a wretched slave, then too, even as he saw himself as a child of God, for the power of God as reflected in the world around him was strong enough to deliver him from slavery. This was one basic element of the slave's belief pattern, and he responded accordingly when Jesus called him into the woods. Thus the slave felt himself converted to the community of believers and to the mission of freedom. In this same wilderness, Henry Bibb stood on the bluff of the Ohio River, perhaps knowing then that in African beliefs, water, as well as the wilderness, was a place of divine power: wells, springs, rivers and streams.[23] There he meditated and formed his resolution to seek freedom. He wrote:

> Sometimes standing on the Ohio River bluff, looking over on a free State, and as far north as my eyes could see, I have eagerly gazed upon the blue sky of the free North, which at times constrained me to cry out from the depths of my soul, Oh Canada, sweet land of rest—Oh! that I had the wings of a dove, that I might soar away to where there is no

slavery; no clanking of chains, no captives, no lacerating of backs, no parting of husbands and wives; and where man ceases to be the property of his fellow man.[24]

In a similar way Douglass resolved to seek freedom. He cried: "O God save me! God deliver me! Let me be free. . . . Only think of it: one hundred miles north, and I am free. . . . It cannot be that I shall live and die a slave. I will take to the water. This very bay shall yet bear me into freedom."[25] For Josiah Henson, freedom in the North was heaven. He resolved: "Once to get away with my wife and children, to some spot where I could feel that they were indeed *mine*—where no grasping master could stand between me and them, as arbiter of their destiny—was a heaven yearned after with insatiable longing."[26] Henry "Box" Brown felt called to escape with the same fervor that he felt called upon to serve God. The revelation also told him how he could escape successfully:

> One day, while I was at work and my thoughts were eagerly feasting upon the idea of freedom, I felt my soul called out to Heaven to breathe a prayer to Almighty God. I prayed fervently that he who seeth in secret and knew the inmost desires of my heart would lend me his aid in bursting my fetters asunder and in restoring me to possession of those rights of which men had robbed me; when suddenly, the idea flashed across my mind of shutting myself *up in a box,* and getting myself conveyed as dry goods to a free state.[27]

The impulse for freedom was very often the beginning of a change in the slave's character. He began to strengthen himself for the difficulties which he would have to endure. Gustavas Vassa, one of the earliest narrators who vividly remembered his African heritage, wrote that in the midst of his thoughts on slavery and freedom his immediate impulse was to look "up with prayers anxiously to God for my liberty; and at the same time [use] every honest means and [do] all that was possible on my part to obtain it."[28]

James W.C. Pennington, the fugitive "blacksmith," had a clear idea of what lay beyond his resolution to be free. He knew that the time had come for him to act:

> . . . and then when I considered the difficulties of the way—the reward that would be offered—the human bloodhounds that would be set upon my track—the weariness—the hunger—the gloomy thought of not only losing all one's friends in one day, but of having to seek and make new friends in a strange world. . . . But, as I have said, the hour was come, and the man must act or forever be a slave.[29]

The moment of decision and action was sometimes taken in flight from cruel treatment. William Parker once fought his master when the master tried to whip him: "I let go of my hold—bade him goodbye, and ran for the woods. As I went by the field, I beckoned to my brother, who left work and joined me at rapid pace." Parker's escape brought him to the verge of a new era in his life, one that would sustain him over many years because of the very impulse of freedom:

> I was now at the beginning of a new and important era in my life. Although upon the threshold of manhood, I had, until the relation with my master was sundered, only dim perceptions of the responsibilities of a more independent position. I longed to cast off the chains of servitude because they chafed my free spirit, and because I had a notion that my position was founded in injustice . . . The impulse of freedom lends wings to the feet, buoys up the spirit within, and the fugitive catches glorious glimpses of light through rifts and seams in the accumulated ignorance of his years of oppression. How briskly we traveled on that eventful night and the next day.[30]

The same impulse for freedom was so strong in Henry Bibb that he "learned the art of running away to perfection." He continues: "I made a regular business of it and never gave it up until I had broken the bonds of slavery and landed myself in Canada where I was regarded as a man and not as a thing."[31]

Often the fugitives' only companion was God, and they believed that it was He alone who could deliver man from the death and hell experience of slavery and escape. One recalls John Thompson's reluctance to escape with the Methodist preacher because he doubted an unseen God. But because membership in the community of believers, in God's army, required an unconditional faith in God's power and willingness to deliver his children, Thompson had to be converted. He had to hear God's voice and believe. When saved from a dangerous situation, Thompson began to believe in God's presence and then, started his life pilgrimage toward the salvation and freedom slaves felt was theirs to achieve. Thompson's personal witness united him to his community and to the cause of freedom that he now has the strength and guidance to seek alone:

> I knew it was the hand of God, working in my behalf; it was his voice warning me to escape from the danger towards which I was hastening. Who would not praise such a God? Great is the Lord, and greatly to be praised.
>
> I felt renewed confidence and faith, for I believed that God was in my favor, and now was the time to test the matter . . . I fell upon my knees, and with hands uplifted to high heaven, related all the late circumstances to the Great King, saying that the whole world was against me without a cause, besought his protection, and solemnly promised to

serve him all the days of my life. I received a spiritual answer of approval; a voice like thunder seeming to enter my soul, saying, I am your God and am with you; though the world be against you, I am more than the world; though wicked men hunt you, trust in me, for I am the Rock of your Defense.

Had my pursuers then been near, they must have heard me, for I praised God at the top of my voice. I was determined to take him at his word, and risk the consequences.

I retired to my hiding place in the woods.[32]

Once united with God, man shared in a specific moral code that sanctioned his escape and other tactics to insure success. The ethos of the fugitive was as practical as it was unique. In describing the tactics of Harriet Tubman, Sarah Bradford recognized this aspect of the fugitives' experience as perhaps a consequence of fear during their dangerous plight. "They had a creed of their own," Bradford writes, "and a code of morals which we dare not criticize till we find our own lives and those of our dear ones similarly imperiled."[33] It was this moral code that helped the fugitive identify people along the escape route who could be trusted to help.

William Wells Brown once indicated his indictment of all people as victims of slavery and found most of them unworthy of his trust:

> I had long since made up my mind that I would not trust myself in the hands of any man, white or colored. The slave is brought up to look upon every white man as an enemy to him and his race; and twenty-one years in slavery had taught me that there were traitors, even among colored people.[34]

The slave on the run was constantly on his guard. John Thompson used his unique "Christian" experience as a criterion for seeking help from others. He was referred to people of *true* Christian character, meaning those who would aid a fugitive. Of one man who offered his aid, Thompson writes: "I knew this man was a Christian, and therefore that it was safe to trust him, which is not true of all, since there are many treacherous colored, as white men." In another instance Thompson inquired, "I asked what I should do; to which he replied he could not tell, but pointing to a house nearby, said 'There lives Mrs. R., a free woman, and one of *God's true children,* who has travelled there many times and can direct you. You can depend upon what she tells you' "[35] (emphasis mine). When suddenly accosted by a party of potentially dangerous white men, Thompson passed among them unharmed and calm. He attributed this to God's grace:

. . . they did not molest us, although they followed us with their eyes, as far as they could see us. This was another Ebeneezer for us to raise, in token of God's deliverance, we knelt and offered up our thanksgiving to God for this great salvation.[36]

Slaves believed that God moved through nature to help the fugitive. Moreover, through nature, God made his presence known by presenting obstacles and avenues for deliverance during the fugitive's journey. Most often the same natural force, such as a wide river, was both obstacle *and* aid. The dual quality of nature in the slave's thought makes it more crucial for man to take an active part in seeking deliverance, for he must be capable of identifying the voice as he did through his conversion experience and those good people who share in God's word: the children of God, the *true* believers. These barriers become an important test of man's faith in the power of God to make possible the freedom and salvation the slave seeks. Again, man must earn his freedom.

When Henry Bibb attempted escape alone, nature was his guide: "I walked with bold courage, trusting in the arm of Omnipotence; guided by the unchangeable North Star by night, and inspired by an elevated thought that I was fleeing from a land of slavery and oppression, bidding farewell to handcuffs, whips, thumbscrews and chains."[37] Once having gained freedom for himself, he returned to rescue his wife and child. Caught again in slave territory, he felt he had to renew his covenant with God; he "passed the night in prayer to our Heavenly Father, asking that He would open to me even the smallest chance for escape."[38]

In the woods following their escape, Bibb and his wife and child encounter nature at its harshest level:

So we started off with our child that night, and made our way down to Red River swamps among the buzzing insects and wild beasts of the forest. We wandered about in the wilderness for eight or ten days. . . . Our food was parched corn . . . most of the time we were lost. We wanted to cross the Red River but could find no conveyance to cross it. I recollect one day of finding a crooked tree which bent over the river. . . . When we crossed over on the tree . . . we found that we were on an island surrounded by water on either side. We made our bed that night in a pile of dry leaves. . . . We were much rest-broken, wearied from hunger and travelling through briers, swamps and cane breaks. . . .[39]

Then Bibb encountered the wolves who lived there and who came howling out of the night close to them:

The wolves kept howling. . . . I thought that the hour of death for us was at hand . . . for there was no way for our escape. My little family

were looking up to me for protection, but I could afford them none.
. . . *I was offering up my prayers to that God who never forsakes those
in the hour of danger who trust in him.* . . . I was surrounded by those
wolves. But it seemed to be the will of a merciful providence that our
lives should not be destroyed by them. I rushed forth with my bowie
knife in hand. . . . I made one desperate charge at them . . . making
a loud yell at the top of my voice that caused them to retreat and scatter
which was equivalent to a victory on our part. *Our prayers were answered,* and our lives were spared through the night.[40] (Emphasis mine.)

Through prayer Bibb was able to unite himself to the greater force of
God and thus renew his own life force. However, his escape with his
family had further complications and eventually they were recaptured.
Once again Bibb escaped alone and began a new life in free territory
without them. This last escape found Bibb secreted aboard a ship which
conveyed him out of the waters of slavery and trial and into the promised North:

When the boat struck the mouth of the river Ohio, and I had once
more the pleasure of looking on that lovely stream, my heart leaped up
for joy at the glorious prospect that I should again be free. Every revolution of the mighty steam-engine seemed to bring me nearer and
nearer the "promised land."[41]

Henry Bibb's narrative is characteristic of the many slave autobiographies in which the protagonist confronts and is confronted by the challenge of survival and deliverance from the wilderness. Man, here, en-
dures the test of the wilds in order to reap his reward of freedom, which
is a direct result of his alliance with God. In the end he will be delivered
on foot or aboard a particular conveyance which will provide a secret
cover for his rebirth.

The escape episode in nature or secreted aboard a ship is an experience of the womb, the woods, or a dark cover that will give birth to a
new man. Escape, then, is the central transforming episode in the death-
rebirth cycle of life as viewed by the slave. By dint of his escape and his
hiding, man becomes enlightened about his condition and reborn through
his confrontation fighting his own fear, the wolves, the deep water of
Jordan or the slave "patrollers."

The Reverend Thomas Jones recorded in his narrative that he hid
aboard a ship until the time was right, until nature intervened by making
the tide flow in his favor, and he gained his free identity:

Here [in the hold of the ship] I was discovered by the Captain. He
charged me with being a runaway slave, and said he should send me
back by the first opportunity that offered. That day a severe storm came

on and for several days we were driven by the gale. I turned to and cooked for the crew. The storm was followed by a calm of several days; and then the wind sprung up again and the Captain made for port at once. . . . While the Captain was in the city . . . I made a raft of loose board as I could get and hastily bound them together, and committing myself to God, I launched forth upon the waves. The shore was about a mile distant; I had the tide in my favor.[42]

In the *Life and Adventure of Robert* . . . the narrator hid in a "cave surrounded by a thick hedge of wild briars and hemlock" in Fox Point, Providence, Rhode Island, when his life in free territory was further complicated by slave catchers. Robert was a slave in Princeton, New Jersey, and engineered his escape by secreting himself aboard a sloop bound for Philadelphia. When his family was threatened and then separated by slave catchers, Robert made a final retreat into the wilderness. He returned to the womb of nature, his cave; as he told his amanuensis, "I felt but little desire to live, as there was nothing then to attach me to this world—and it was at that moment that I formed the determination to retire from it—to become a recluse, and mingle thereafter as little as possible with human society."[40]

Henry "Box" Brown made more poignant use of the death-rebirth theme. He nailed himself up in a box and shipped himself to free territory as cargo. During the long journey he experienced the physical effects of dying: "I felt a cold sweat coming over me which seemed to be a warning that death was about to terminate my earthly miseries; but as I feared even that less than slavery, I resolved to submit to the will of God, and, under the influence of that impression, I lifted up my soul in prayer to God, who alone was able to deliver me. My cry was soon heard."[44] When the box arrived at its destination a friend knocked to see if Brown was still alive inside. Brown's rebirth began: "The joy of the friends was very great. When they heard that I was alive they soon managed to break open the box, and then came my resurrection from the grave of slavery. I rose a free man; but I was too weak, by reason of long confinement in that box, to be able to stand, so I immediately swooned away."[45]

By all accounts the God of the fugitive is a God who offers immediate freedom and deliverance to his chosen people. But this deliverance is on the condition of man's trial—man's willingness to be struck dead and achieve enlightenment through his despair, fear and solitude. Man with God conquers Egypt and death so that a freeman can be born.

In their long search for freedom, as in their religion and literature, slaves defined life as a pilgrimage. Just as life for the African was a continual practice of maintaining harmony and force within the ontological hierarchy established between man, the ancestors, and natural phenomena, so too was life for the Afro-American a pilgrimage toward renewed contact with God. The slave narrators preserve the dualism between the African and the Christian components in black religious syncretism, and we find through their emphasis on the escape experience that the narrators and bards gave the wilderness confrontation a central place in recounting the progress of their lives. For the narrators, this crucial moment of escape is also symbolic of the fusion of the two divergent cultural modes: the African and the American. Out of this cultural confrontation and, in some cases, moral entanglement the slave is converted and reconverted to himself, his community, his God. By engaging the wilderness the slave, as fugitive, renews his primal covenant with God through nature and becomes a freeman. From this primary connection with spiritual and natural forces, man derives his creativity, his freedom, and his spiritual redemption. His self and soul are strengthened.

In song and narrative, through the unifying image and actual experience of deliverance and survival—a life-affirming ideology—the slaves themselves have defined heroic value as an essential aspect of human character. The journey of the fugitive is but a microcosm of the entire life experience of men in search of freedom, which is also salvation. Samuel Ringgold Ward, himself a fugitive when just a child, has written that men entrusted with such a mission grow with it heroically, and thus the fugitive becomes an exemplar of individual and group ideals:

> The fugitive exercises patience, fortitude, and perseverance, connected with and fed by an ardent and unrestrained and resistless love of liberty, such as cause men to be admired everywhere . . . the lonely toiling journey; the endurance of the excitement from constant danger; the hearing the yell and howl of the bloodhound, the knowledge of close hot pursuit. . . . All these furnaces of trial as they are, purify and ennoble the man who has to pass through them. . . . All these are inseparable from the ordinary incidents in the northward passage of the fugitive; and when he reaches us, he is, first, what the raw material of nature was; and secondly, what the improving process of flight has made him.[46]

Thus, the life of man that the spirituals and the narratives create for us is one which is grounded in concrete action and one which follows the highest moral persuasions. Man, as conceived within the slave's mythos and ethos, progresses toward spiritual regeneration. Through the test and trial of his faith he has fixed time and space in his quest; he has conquered the future by realizing it now; he has gained free territory by stepping forth from bondage; he has conquered life as a slave by being struck dead. Rebirth and immortality are his rewards. What gave the slave the surety of his life convictions and what made real the possibility of regeneration in this life and a positive, functional immortality in the next, was religion. The slave's religion, indeed his corporate faith that joined one to the other by the example of trial and the witness of death, was a joy and a healing fortune. And the slave has become free by first singing with a sword in his hand.

Notes

1. Marion Starling, "The Slave Narrative: Its Place in American Literary History." Unpublished dissertation, New York University, 1946. For a further discussion of the narratives' relation to American literature, see Edward Margolies, "Ante-bellum Slave Narratives: Their Place in American Literary History," *Studies in Black Literature* 4:3 (Autumn, 1973), 1-8.

2. John Blassingame, *The Slave Community* (New York: Oxford, 1972).

3. Lawrence W. Levine, "Slave Songs and Slave Consciousness," in *American Negro Slavery*, 2nd ed., edited by Allen Weinstein and Frank Otto Gatell (New York: Oxford, 1973), p. 161. See also Sterling Stuckey, "Through the Prism of Folklore: The Black Ethos in Slavery," in the same edition; and Eugene Genovese, *Roll, Jordan, Roll* (New York: Pantheon, 1974).

4. Benjamin Mays, *The Negro's God as Reflected in his Literature* (New York: Atheneum, 1968), p. 1. J. Saunders Redding, *To Make a Poet Black* (Maryland: McGrath, 1968), p. 3.

5. G.R. Wilson, "The Religion of the American Negro Slave: His Attitude Toward Life and Death," *Journal of Negro History* VII (January, 1923), 43.

6. John Lovell, Jr., "The Social Implications of the Negro Spiritual," in *The Social Implications of Early Negro Music in the United States,* ed. Bernard Katz (New York: Arno Press, 1969), 135. See also Lovell's fuller treatment of the spirituals in *Black Song: The Forge and the Flame* (New York: Macmillan, 1972).

7. Levine, pp. 162-3. See also Lawrence W. Levine, *Black Culture and Black Consciousness* (New York: Oxford, 1977).

8. Fisk University, *God Struck Me Dead* (Nashville: Social Science Institute, Fisk University, 1945), vii. Note particularly Paul Radin's introduction, "Status, Phantasy, and the Christian Dogma." Narratives collected in this edition hereafter cited as Fisk.

9. Ibid., p. vi. See also Albert Raboteau, *Slave Religion* (New York: Oxford, 1978).

10. Quoted in Blassingame, p. 210. See also his discussion of group solidarity, 75-76, and George Rawick, *From Sundown to Sunup: The Making of the Black Community* (Westport, Ct.: Greenwood Press, 1972).

11. Fisk, p. 23.

12. Ibid., 209.

13. John Thompson, *The Life of John Thompson* (1856; rpt. Negro Universities Press, 1968), p. 76.

14. Solomon Northup, "Twelve Years A Slave," in *Puttin' On Ole Massa,*

ed. Gilbert Osofsky (New York: Harper Torchbooks, 1969), p. 370. This collection contains the narratives of Henry Bibb and William Wells Brown in addition to Northup. Citations of their narratives by last name refer to this edition.

15. Harriet Jacobs, in *Black Men in Chains*, ed. Charles Nichols (New York: Lawrence Hill, 1972), p. 269. Contains also narrative sketches from William Parker, Henry "Box" Brown, et al. and are cited hereafter by author.

16. Bibb, pp. 64-5.

17. Thomas Jones, *The Experience of Thomas H. Jones* (Boston: Bazin & Chandler, 1862), p. 5.

18. William E.B. Du Bois, *The Souls of Black Folk* (1903; rpt. New York: New American Library, 1969), p. 44.

19. Margaret Walker, *For My People* (New Haven: Yale, 1947).

20. Nat Turner, *The Confessions of Nat Turner*, ed. Thomas Gray; rpt. in *Nat Turner's Slave Rebellion*, ed. Herbert Aptheker (New York: Grove Press, 1968), p. 136.

21. Bibb, p. 72.

22. Frederick Douglass, *Life and Times of Frederick Douglass* (1881; New York: Bonanza Books, 1962), p. 135.

23. Geoffrey Parrinder, *Religion in Africa* (Baltimore: Penguin, 1969), p. 56.

24. Bibb, p. 72.

25. Douglass, p. 125.

26. Josiah Henson, *Father Henson's Story of His Own Life* (1858; New York: Corinth Books, 1962), pp. 60-1.

27. Henry "Box" Brown, p. 194.

28. Gustavas Vassa, *The Interesting Narrative of Olaudah Equiano, or Gustavas Vassa, the African. Written by Himself*, 1791; rpt. in *Great Slave Narratives*, ed. Arna Bontemps (Boston: Beacon Press, 1969), p. 87. Also contains narratives of James Pennington and William and Ellen Craft.

29. Pennington, p. 216.

30. William Parker, pp. 290-1.

31. Bibb, p. 165.

32. Thompson, pp. 80-81.

33. Sarah Bradford, *Harriet—The Moses of Her People* (New York: Lockwood, 1886), p. 72.

34. William Wells Brown, p. 216.

35. Thompson, pp. 85-86.

36. Ibid., p. 87.

37. Bibb, p. 85.

38. Ibid., p. 96.

39. Ibid., pp. 125-126.

40. Ibid., pp. 126-128.

41. Ibid., p. 151.

42. Thomas Jones, p. 46.

43. Robert Voorhis, *Life and Adventures of Robert, The Hermit of Massachusetts, Who has lived Fourteen Years in a Cave, Secluded from Human Society, Taken from His Own Mouth* (Providence: Henry Trumbull, 1829), n.pag.

44. Henry "Box" Brown, p. 196.

45. Ibid., p. 197.

46. Samuel Ringgold Ward, *Autobiography of a Fugitive Negro* (London: Snow, 1865), pp. 165-166. Recent scholarship has expanded the study of the fugitive hero in Afro-American autobiography. See Stephen Butterfield, *Black Autobiography in America* (Amherst: University of Massachusetts Press, 1974); Sidonie Smith, *Where I'm Bound: Patterns of Slavery and Freedom in Black American Autobiography* (Westport, Ct.: Greenwood Press, 1974); and in a broader literary and cultural context, Houston Baker, *Long Black Song: Essays in Afro-American Culture and Literature* (Charlottesville: University of Virginia Press, 1972).

A Selected Bibliography

Black Narratives, 1760-1865:

This bibliography lists in chronological order the autobiographical narratives and slave narratives dictated or written by persons of African descent between 1760 and 1865. We have used 1865 as an end date because in that year the American Civil War came to an end, as did slavery in the United States. With the ending of slavery, certain generic expectations disappeared from black autobiographical narratives. Whereas scores of black ex-slaves published autobiographical accounts of their bondage and their freedom from 1865 until well into this century, these texts are beyond the scope of this book and so are not listed here.

We have also chosen not to include the demonstrably fictional narratives that imitated and sometimes even pretended to be the written testaments of ex-slaves. Richard Hildreth's *The Slave; or Memoirs of Archy Moore* (1836) and Mattie Griffiths's *The Autobiography of a Female Slave* (1857) are only familiar examples of a curious narrative tradition that began as early as 1749, when the Reverend William Dodd published *The Royal Slave; or Memoirs of the Young Prince of Annamboe* in London in 1749. While these fictional slave narratives are anathema to the historian seeking to reconstruct the past utilizing the first-person accounts of slaves, they serve to elucidate by resemblance and difference the contours of the genre of the slave narrative. A comparative study of these fictional narratives, dictated narratives, and written narratives published before 1865 is most certainly a promising pursuit for the student of narrative theory in general, and of the slave's narrative in particular. Similarly, Allan Austin's bibliography of "Narratives of African Muslims in Antebellum America" serves to unlock a lost cache of data for the historian and literary critic about this seldom studied and little understood group of slaves and ex-slaves.

The editors completed this bibliography with the invaluable assistance of Darby Tench, Hazel Carby, David A. Curtis, William Luis, James Olney, and especially William L. Andrews.

1760

Hammon, Briton. *A Narrative of the Uncommon Sufferings, and Surprizing [sic] Deliverance of Briton Hammon, a Negro Man,—Servant to General Winslow, of Marshfield, in New England: Who Returned to Bos-*

ton, after having been absent almost Thirteen Years. Containing An
Account of the many Hardships he underwent from the time he left his
master's house, in the year 1747, to the Time of his Return to Boston.—How he was cast away in the Capes of Florida:—the horrid
Cruelty and inhuman barbarity of the Indians in murdering the whole
Ship's Crew:—the Manner of his being carried by them into captivity.
Also, An Account of his being Confined Four Years and Seven Months
in a close Dungeon—and the remarkable Manner in which he met with
his good old Master in London: who returned to New-England, a Pas-
senger, in the same Ship. Boston: Green and Russell.

1770

Gronniosaw, James Albert Ukawsaw. A Narrative of the Most Remarkable
Particulars in the Life of James Albert Ukawsaw Gronniosaw, An African Prince, as Related by Himself. Bath: S. Hazzard.

1785

Marrant, John. A Narrative of the Lord's Wonderful Dealings with John Marrant, a Black (Now going to Preach the Gospel in Nova Scotia) Born
in New York, in North America. Taken down from his own relation,
Arranged, Corrected, and Published by the Reverend Mr. Aldridge.
London: by the author.

1787

Cugoano, Ottobah. Thoughts and Sentiments on the Evil of Slavery. London:
for the author.

1789

Equiano, Olaudah. The Interesting Narratives of the Life of Olaudah Equiano,
or Gustavus Vassa, the African, written by Himself. London: for the
author.

1790

Mountain, Joseph. Sketches of the Life of Joseph Mountain, a Negro, Who
Was Executed at New Haven, on the 20th Day of October, 1790, for
a Rape, Committed on the 26th Day of May Last. New Haven: T. and
S. Green.

1798

Smith, Venture. A Narrative of the Life and Adventures of Venture, a Native
of Africa; but Resident above Sixty Years in the United States of America. Related By Himself. New London: C. Holt.

1799

Sierra Leone Company. Substance of the Reports Delivered by the Court of
the Sierra Leone Company, to the General Court of Proprietors to
Which is Prefixed Memoirs of Laimbanna, an African Prince. Philadelphia: Dobson.

1810

Prentiss, Benjamin F. The Blind American Slave or Memoirs of Boyrereau
Brincho. St. Albans, Vt.: Harry Whitney.

White, George. *Account of Life, Experience, Travels, and Gospel Labours of George White, an African, Written by Himself and Revised by a Friend.* New York: J. C. Tottle.

1815

Jea, John. *The Life, History, and Unparalleled Sufferings of John Jea, The African Preacher.* Portsea: for the author.

William. *The Negro Servant: An Authentic Narrative of a Young Negro, Showing How He Was Made a Slave in Africa, and Carried to Jamaica, Where He was Sold to a Captain in His Majesty's Navy, and Taken to America, Where He Became a Christian, and Afterwards Brought to England and Baptised.* Kilmarnock: H. Crawford.

1818

Joyce, John. *Confession of John Joyce. Related to Richard Allen.* Philadelphia: n.p.

1820

Bayley, Solomon. *Incidents in the Life of Solomon Bayley.* Philadelphia: Tract Association of Friends.

1824

Grimes, William. *Life of William Grimes, the Runaway Slave. Written by Himself.* New York: by the author.

1825

Bayley, Solomon. *Narrative of Some Remarkable Incidents in the Life of Solomon Bayley, Formerly a Slave in the State of Delaware, North America, Written by Himself.* London: Richard Hunard.

1829

Voorhis, Robert. *Life and Adventures of Robert Voorhis, the Hermit of Massachusetts, Who Has Lived Fourteen Years in a Cave, Secluded from Human Society. Comprising an account of his Birth, Parentage, Sufferings, and Providential Escape from Unjust and Cruel Bondage in Early Life—and His Reasons for Becoming a Recluse. Taken from his own mouth by Henry Trumbull, and published for his benefit.* Providence: for Henry Trumbull.

1831

Prince, Mary. *The History of Mary Prince, a West Indian Slave, Related by Herself, With a Supplement by the Editor, to Which is Added the Narrative of Asa-Asa, A Captured African.* London: F. Westley and A. H. Davis.

Strickland, Simon, ed. *Negro Slavery Described by a Negro: Being the Narrative of Ashton Warner, a Native of St. Vincent's.* London: S. Maunder.

1832

Spear, Chloe. *Memoir of Chloe Spear, a Native of Africa, Who Was Enslaved In Childhood. By a "Lady of Boston."* James S. Loring, ed. Boston: James S. Loring.

1833

Allen, Richard. *The Life, Experience, and Gospel Labors of the Right Reverend Richard Allen.* Philadelphia: Martin Boden.

1834

Blake, Jane. *Memoirs of Margaret Jane Blake.* Philadelphia: n.p.
Boen, William. *Anecdotes and Memoirs of William Boen, a Colored Man, Who Lived and Died Near Mount Holly, New Jersey. To Which is added the Testimony of Friends of Mount Holly Monthly Meeting Concerning Him.* Philadelphia: John Richards.

1835

Stewart, Maria W. *Productions of Mrs. Maria Stewart.* Boston: n.p.

1836

Fisher, Thomas. *Slavery in the United States: a Narrative of the Life and Adventures of Charles Ball, a Black Man, Who Lived Forty Years in Maryland, South Carolina, and Georgia as a Slave. Prepared by Fisher from the verbal narrative by Ball.* Lewiston, Pa.: J. W. Schugert.
James, John Ismael Augustus. *A Narrative of the Travels, etc. of John Ismael Augustus James, an African of the Mandingo Tribe, Who was Captured, Sold into Slavery, and subsequently liberated by a Benevolent English Gentleman.* Truro: n.p.
Lee, Jarena. *The Life and Religious Experiences of Jarena Lee, A Coloured Lady, Giving an Account of Her Call to Preach the Gospel. Revised and Corrected from the Original Manuscript, Written by Herself.* Philadelphia: for the author.

1837

Roper, Moses. *A Narrative of the Adventures and Escape of Moses Roper from American Slavery, with a Preface by the Reverend T. Price.* Thomas Price, ed. London: Darton, Harvey, and Darton.
Williams, James. *A Narrative of Events Since the First of August, 1834, by James Williams, an Apprenticed Labourer in Jamaica.* London: William Ball.
Williams, James. *Narrative of the Cruel Treatment of James Williams, a Negro Apprentice in Jamaica.* Glasgow: n.p.

1838

Greene, Frances Whipple. *Memoirs of Eleanor Eldridge.* Providence: B. T. Albro.
Joanna. *Narrative of Joanna, an Emancipated Slave of Surinam (From Stedman's Narrative of Five Years' Expedition Against the Revoluted Negroes of Surinam).* Boston: I. Knapp.
Williams, James. *Narrative of James Williams, An American Slave; Who Was for Several Years a Driver on a Cotton Plantation in Alabama.* Dictated to J[ohn] G[reenleaf] Whittier. New York: American Anti-Slavery Society.

1839

Greene, Frances Whipple. *Eleanor's Second Book.* Providence: B. T. Albro.

Lester, Charles E., ed. *Chains and Freedom: or, The Life and Adventures of Peter Wheeler, a Colored Man Yet Living as told by Charles Edward Lester*. New York: E. S. Arnold and Company.

1840

Manzano, Juan Francisco. *Poems by a Slave in the Island of Cuba, recently liberated; translated from the Spanish, by R. R. Madden, M.D., with the History of the Early Life of the Negro Poet, written by Himself; to which are prefixed two pieces descriptive of Cuban Slavery and the Slave-Traffic by R.R.M.* London: Thomas Ward and Co.

1842

Joseph and Enoch. *Narrative of the Barbarous Treatment of Two Unfortunate Females, Natives of Concordia, Louisiana, by Joseph and Enoch, Runaway Slaves. As told by Mrs. Todd and Miss Harrington.* New York: by the authors.

Lane, Lunsford. *The Narrative of Lunsford Lane, Formerly of Raleigh, N.C.; Embracing an Account of His Early Life, the Redemption by Purchase of Himself and Family from Slavery and His Banishment from the Place of His Birth for the Crime of Wearing a Colored Skin.* William G. Hawkins, ed. Boston: Hewes and Watson, for the author.

1843

Aaron. *Light and Truth of Slavery. Aaron's History of Virginia, New Jersey, and Rhode Island.* Worcester, Mass.: for the author.

Grandy, Moses. *Narrative of the Life of Moses Grandy, Late a Slave in the United States of America.* London: C. Gilpin.

1844

Armstrong, Archer. *Compendium of Slavery As it Exists in the Present Day. To Which is Prefixed, a Brief View of the Author's Descent.* London: by the author.

1845

Clarke, Lewis. *Narrative of the Sufferings of Lewis Clarke, during a Captivity of More than Twenty-Five Years among the Algerines of Kentucky. Dictated by Himself, Written by Joseph C. Lovejoy.* Boston: D. H. Eli.

Douglass, Frederick. *Narrative of the Life of Frederick Douglass, an American Slave. Written by Himself.* Boston: Boston Anti-Slavery Office.

1846

Clarke, Lewis and Milton. *Narratives of the Sufferings of Lewis and Milton Clarke, Sons of a Soldier of the Revolution, during a Captivity of More than Twenty Years among the Slave-Holders of Kentucky, One of the So Called Christian States of North America; Dictated by Themselves.* Joseph C. Lovejoy, ed. Boston: B. Marsh.

Hayden, William. *Narrative of William Hayden, containing a Faithful Account of His Travels for a Number of Years, Whilst a Slave in the South. Written by Himself.* Cincinnati: by the author.

Meachum, John B. *An Address to the Colored Citizens of the United States, Prefaced by a Narrative of the Author as a Slave in Virginia.* Philadelphia: King and Baird.

1847

Black, Leonard. *Life and Sufferings of Leonard Black, a Fugitive from Slavery. Written by Himself*. New Bedford: Benjamin Lindsey.

Brown, William Wells. *Narrative of William Wells Brown, a Fugitive Slave, Written by Himself*. Boston: Boston Anti-Slavery Office.

Hammond, Jabez D., ed. *Life and Opinions of Julius Melbourn; with Sketches of the Lives and Characters of Thomas Jefferson, John Quincy Adams, John Randolph, and Several Other Eminent American Statesmen*. Syracuse: n.p.*

Jackson, Andrew. *Narrative and Writings of Andrew Jackson of Kentucky Containing an Account of His Birth and Twenty-Six Years of His Life While a Slave. Narrated by Himself, Written by a Friend*. Syracuse: Daily and Weekly Star Office.

Zamba. *The Life and Adventures of Zamba, an African Negro King; and His Experiences of Slavery in South Carolina. Written by Himself. Corrected and Arranged by Peter Neilson*. London: Smith, Elder, and Company.

1848

Brown, William Wells. *Narrative of the Life of William Wells Brown*. Boston: Bela Marsh.

Joseph, John. *The Life of John Joseph*. Wellington: for the author.

Watson, Henry. *Narrative of Henry Watson, a Fugitive Slave*. Boston: Henry Holt.

1849

Bibb, Henry. *Narrative of the Life and Adventures of Henry Bibb, an American Slave. Written by Himself*. New York: by the author.

Brown, Henry Box. *Narrative of Henry Box Brown, Who Escaped from Slavery in a Box Three Feet Long, Two Wide, and Two and a Half High. Written from a Statement of Facts Made by Himself. With remarks upon the remedy for slavery by Charles Stearns*. Boston: Brown and Stearns.

Henson, Josiah. *The Life of Josiah Henson, Formerly a Slave, Now an Inhabitant of Canada, as Narrated by Himself*. S. A. Eliot, ed. Boston: A. D. Phelps.

Jones, Thomas H. *The Experiences of Thomas H. Jones, Who Was a Slave for Forty-Three Years. Written by a Friend as Given to Him by Brother Jones*. Boston: n.p.

Lee, Jarena. *Religious Experience and Journal of Mrs. Jarena Lee, Giving an Account of Her Call to Preach the Gospel. Revised and Corrected from the Original Manuscript, Written by Herself*. Philadelphia: by the author.

Pennington, James W. C. *The Fugitive Blacksmith; or, Events in the History of James W. C. Pennington, Pastor of a Presbyterian Church, New York, Formerly a Slave in the State of Maryland, United States*. London: Charles Gilpin.

---

* The editors believe this title to be a fictional slave narrative. John Blassingame, however, believes it to be "authentic."

1850

Prince, Nancy. *A Narrative of the Life and Travels of Mrs. Nancy Prince. Written by Herself*. Boston: for the author.

Truth, Sojourner. *Narrative of Sojourner Truth, a Northern Slave, Emancipated from Bodily Servitude by the State of New York in 1828. Narrated to Olive Gilbert, including Sojourner Truth's Book of Life, and a dialogue*. Leeds, Mass.: for the author.

1851

Asher, Jeremiah. *Incidents in the Life of the Reverend J. Asher, Pastor of the Shiloh (Colored) Baptist Church, Philadelphia, U.S. With an Introduction by Wilson Armstead*. London: C. Gilpin.

Brown, William Wells. *Illustrated Edition of the Life and Escape of William Wells Brown*. London: C. Gilpin.

Smallwood, Thomas. *Narrative of Thomas Smallwood, Written by Himself*. Toronto: J. Stephens.

1852

Watkins, James. *Narrative of the Life of James Watkins, Formerly a Chattel in Maryland, United States, Dictated to H.R.* Boston: Kenyon and Abbott.

1853

Brown, William Wells. *Clotel; or, the President's Daughter: A Narrative of Slave Life in the United States, with a sketch of the Author's Life*. London: Partridge and Oakey.

Green, William. *Narrative of Events in the Life of William Green (Formerly a Slave), Written by Himself*. Springfield, Mass.: L. M. Guernsey.

Northup, Solomon. *Twelve Years a Slave; Narrative of Solomon Northup, a Citizen of New York, Kidnapped in Washington City in 1841, and Rescued in 1853, from a Cotton Plantation near the Red River, in Louisiana*. David Wilson, ed. Auburn, Buffalo, and London: Derby and Miller.

Tilmon, Levin. *A Brief Miscellaneous Narrative of the More Early Part of the Life of Levin Tilmon, Pastor of a Colored Methodist Church, New York City*. Jersey City, N.J.: W. and L. Pratt.

1854

Anderson, Thomas. *Interesting Account of Thomas Anderson, a Slave, "Taken from his Own Lips."* Dictated to J. P. Clark. n.p.

Anderson, William J. *Life and Narrative of William J. Anderson; or, Dark Deeds of American Slavery Revealed, Written by Himself*. Chicago: Daily Tribune Book and Job Printing Office.

Baquaqua, Mahommah G. *Biography of Mahommah G. Baquaqua. Written and Revised from his own words by Samuel Moore*. Detroit: G. E. Pomeroy.

Jones, Thomas. *The Experience and Personal Narrative of Uncle Tom Jones: Who Was for Forty Years a Slave; also, the Surprising Adventures of Wild Tom, a Fugitive Negro from South Carolina*. New York: C. G. Holbrook.

Peterson, Daniel H. *The Looking Glass: Being a True Narrative of the Life of the Reverend D. H. Peterson, a Colored Clergyman.* New York: Wright.

1855

Brown, John. *Slave Life in Georgia: a Narrative of the Life, Suffering, and Escape of John Brown, a Fugitive Slave, Now in England.* Louis A. Chamerovzow, ed. London: W. M. Watts.

Douglass, Frederick. *My Bondage and My Freedom. Part I. Life as a Slave. Part II. Life as a Freeman.* New York and Auburn: Miller, Orton, Mulligan.

Grimes, William. *Life of William Grimes, the Runaway Slave, Brought Down to the Present Time. Written by Himself.* New Haven: by the author.

Randolph, Reverend Peter. *Sketches of Slave Life; or, Illustrations of the "Peculiar Institution." By Peter Randolph, an Emancipated Slave.* Boston: by the author.

Ward, Samuel Ringgold. *Autobiography of a Fugitive Negro: His Anti-Slavery Labours in the United States, Canada, and England.* London: J. Snow.

1856

Steward, Austin. *Twenty-Two Years a Slave and Forty Years a Freeman, Embracing a Correspondence of Several Years While President of Wilberforce Colony.* Syracuse: W. T. Hamilton.

Still, Peter. *The Kidnapped and the Ransomed: Being the Personal Recollections of Peter Still and His Wife "Vina," after Forty Years of Slavery. Related to Kate Pickard.* Syracuse: W. T. Hamilton Press.

Thompson, John. *The Life of John Thompson, a Fugitive Slave: Containing His History of Twenty-Five Years in Bondage, and His Providential Escape: Written by Himself.* Worcester: by the author.

1858

Ball, Charles. *Fifty Years in Chains; or, the Life of an American Slave.* New York: Dayton and Asher.

Henson, Josiah. *Truth Stranger than Fiction: Father Henson's Story of His Own Life; with an Introduction by Mrs. H. B. Stowe.* Boston: J. P. Jewett and Company.

Roberts, James. *Narrative of James Roberts, Soldier in the Revolutionary War and Battle of New Orleans.* Chicago: by the author.

Williams, Sally. *Aunt Sally; or The Cross the Way to Freedom. Narrative of the Life and Purchase of the Mother of Revered Isaac Williams of Detroit, Michigan.* Cincinnati: American Reform Tract and Book Society.

1859

Davis, Noah. *A Narrative of the Life of Reverend Noah Davis, a Colored Man, Written by Himself.* Baltimore: J. F. Weishampel, Jr.

Loguen, Jermain W. *The Reverend Jermain W. Loguen, as a Slave and as a Freeman. A Narrative of Real Life.* Syracuse: Office of the Daily Journal.

Platt, Reverend Smith H. *The Martyrs and the Fugitive, or a Narrative of the Captivity, Sufferings and Death of an African Family and the Escape of Their Son.* New York: Daniel Fanshaw.

Wilson, Harriet E. Adams. *Our Nig; or, Sketches from the Life of a Free Black, In a Two-Story White House, North. Showing that Slavery's Shadows Fall Even There By "Our Nig."* Boston: George C. Rand and Avery.

1860

Brown, Jane. *Narrative of the Life of Jane Brown and Her Two Children. Related to the Reverend G. W. Offley.* Hartford: for G. W. Offley.

Craft, William. *Running a Thousand Miles for Freedom; or, the Escape of William and Ellen Craft from Slavery.* London: W. Tweedie.

Offley, Reverend G. W. *Narrative of the Life and Labors of the Reverend G. W. Offley, a Colored Man and Local Preacher, Written by Himself.* Hartford: by the author.

1861

Anderson, Osborne P. *A Voice from Harper's Ferry.* Boston: by the author.

Brent, Linda. [Harriet Jacobs.] *Incidents in the Life of a Slave Girl. Written by Herself.* Boston: by the author.

Campbell, Israel. *Bond and Free; or, Yearnings for Freedom, from My Green Briar House; Being the Story of My Life in Bondage and My Life in Freedom.* Philadelphia: by the author.

Pennington, James W. C. *A Narrative of Events of the Life of J. H. Banks, an Escaped Slave.* Liverpool: n.p.

Wilkerson, James. *Wilkerson's History of His Travels and Labors in the United States, as a Missionary, in Particular that of the Union Seminary, Located in Franklin County, Ohio, since He Purchased His Liberty in New Orleans, Louisiana.* Columbus, Ohio: n.p.

1862

Asher, Jeremiah. *An Autobiography, with Details of a Visit to England, and Some Account of the Meeting Street Baptist Church, Providence, R.I., and of the Shiloh Baptist Church, Philadelphia, Pa.* Philadelphia: n.p.

1863

Anderson, John. *Story of John Anderson, Fugitive Slave.* Harper Twelvetrees, ed. London: W. Tweedie.

Dinah. *The Story of Dinah, as Related to John Hawkins Simpson, after Her Escape from the Horrors of the Virginia Slave Trade, to London.* London: A. W. Bennett.

Fedric, Francis. [Charles Lee.] *Slave Life in Virginia and Kentucky, or, Fifty Years of Slavery in the Southern States of America. By Francis Fedric, an Escaped Slave.* London: Wertheim, MacIntosh, and Hunt.

1864

Green, J. D. *Narrative of the Life of J. D. Green, a Runaway Slave from Kentucky, Containing an Account of His Three Escapes, in 1839, 1846, and 1848.* Huddersfield, Ky.: Henry Fielding.

Mars, James. *Life of James Mars, a Slave Born and Sold in Connecticut, Written by Himself.* Hartford: Case, Lockwood and Company.

1846 Addendum

Elaw, Zilpha, *Memoirs of the Life, Religious Experiences, Ministerial. Travels and Labours* . . . London. Dudley.

Narratives of African Muslims in Antebellum America:

COMPILED BY ALLAN AUSTIN

Ali, Mohammed. "A Native of Bornoo." *Atlantic Monthly* (October 1867): 485–95. Autobiography.

Bluett, Thomas. *Some Memoirs of the Life of Job, the Son of Solomon, the High Priest of Boonda in Africa, Who was a Slave about two Years in Maryland, and afterwards being brought to England, was set free, and sent to his native land in the Year 1734.* London: Richard Ford, 1734. Portrait Biography (63 pages).

Brown, David. "Old King, a 'Mahomedan.' " In *The Planter, on Thirteen Years in the South by a Northern Man*. Philadelphia: H. Hooker, 1853, pp. 120–27. Fiction.

Brown, David. "Condition and Character of Negroes in Africa." *Methodist Quarterly Review* (January 1864): 77–90. Biographical fragments on Kebe and Omar ibn Said.

Cockrane, Benjamin. Two autobiographical fragments. In Madden, *Twelve Months*, Vol. I, pp. 99–102.

Couper, James Hamilton. "Letter of. . . ." In William Brown Hodgson, *Notes on Northern Africa, the Sahara, and the Soudan*. New York: Wiley and Putnam, 1844, pp. 68–71. Biography of Salih Bilali of Massina.

Dwight, Theodore, Jr. "Remarks on the Sereculehs, an African Nation, accompanied by a Vocabulary of their Language." *American Annals of Education and Instruction* V (1835): 451–56. Biographical fragments on "Lamen Kebe."

Gallaudet, Thomas. *A Statement with Regard to the Moorish Prince Abduhl Rahahman*. New York: Committee to Solicit Subscriptions in New York for Abduhl Rahahman, 1828. Biographical fragments.

Grier, Mathew B. "Uncle Moreau." *Fayetteville North Carolina Presbyterian*, 23 July 1859. Biography of Omar ibn Said.

Griffin, Cyrus. "Abduhl Rahahman's History." *African Repository* (May 1828): 79–81. Autobiography.

Griffin, Cyrus. "Prince Abduhl Rahahman." *Natchez Southern Galaxy*, 29 May, 5 June, 12 June, 5 July 1828. Biography.

Harris, Joel Chandler. *Aaron in the Wildwoods*. Boston: Houghton Mifflin, 1897. Fiction.

Harris, Joel Chandler. *The Story of Aaron (So Named) the Son of Ben Ali*. Boston: Houghton Mifflin, 1896. Fiction.

Kaba, Mohammed. Biographical fragment. In Madden, *Twelve Months*, Vol. II, pp. 133–37.

McDougall, Frances Harriet W. G. *Shammah in Pursuit of Freedom, or the Branded Hand*. New York: Thatcher and Hutchinson, 1858. Fiction.

"The man who prayed five times a day." In *Slavery in the United States: a Narrative of the Life and Adventures of Charles Ball, a Black Man*, 3rd ed. Pittsburgh: John T. Shyrock, 1854, pp. 145–60. Autobiography.

Meade, William. "Selim, the Algerian." In *Old Churches, Ministers and Families of Virginia*, Vol. I. Philadelphia: Lippincott and Co., 1857, pp. 341–48. Portrait p. 333. Biography.

Moore, Francis. *Travels into the Inland Parts of Africa . . . with a Particular Account of Job Ben Solomon . . .* London: 1738, pp. 202–211, 217, 223–4, 230–1. Biographical fragments.

Moore, Samuel. *Biography of Mahommah G. Baquaqua, a Native of Zoogoo, in the Interior of Africa*. Detroit: Author, 1854. Portrait Biography and autobiography. 65 pages. Second portrait in A. T. Foss and E. Mathews. *Facts for Baptist Churches*. Utica: American Baptist Free Mission Society, 1850. Frontispiece.

Peale, Charles Willson. "Diary—1819." Unpublished, pp. 45–49. Biographical sketch of Yarrow Mamout.

Peale, Charles Willson. "Diary—1819." Portrait by Peale in Historical Society of Pennsylvania.

Rahahman, Abdul. Manuscript dated 10 October 1828, in John Trumbull Papers, Yale University. Short autobiography in Arabic and author's own translation.

Rahahman, Abdul. Dictated letter to Thomas Gallaudet, 7 June 1828. In *Freedom's Journal* (New York), 20 June 1828, p. 109.

Rahahman, Abdul. Extracts from dictated letters from Philadelphia, 2 July and 13 July 1828. In *Natchez Statesman and Gazette*, 23 October 1828.

Rahahman, Abdul. Extract from dictated letter from Monrovia, Liberia, 5 May 1829. In *African Repository* (July 1829): 158.

Rahahman, Abdul. Letter to Timbo, Futa Jallon, Africa. Translated, an extract. In *Freedom's Journal* (New York) 28 May 1829, p. 406.

Rahahman, Abdul. Portrait by Henry Inman in *The Colonizationist and Journal of Freedom*. Boston: Light, 1834. Frontispiece.

ibn Said, Omar. "Autobiography of Omar ibn Said, Slave in North Carolina, 1831" (translated from the original Arabic). *American Historical Review* XXX (July 1925): 791–95.

ibn Said, Omar. "Autobiography of Omar ibn Said, Slave in North Carolina, 1831." Portrait available from daguerreotype in Davidson College, Davidson, North Carolina.

ibn Said, Omar. "Autobiography of Omar ibn Said, Slave in North Carolina, 1831." Extract from letter in "Secretary's Report." *African Repository* XIII (July 1837): 203–5.

al-Siddiq, Abu Bakr. "The History of Abon Becr Sadiki, known in Jamaica by the name of Edward Donlan." In Richard Robert Madden, *Twelve Months Residence in the West Indies*. Philadelphia: Carey, Lea & Blanchard, 1835. Vol. II, pp. 126–30. Autobiography translated from Arabic, dated 20 September 1834, by al-Siddiq and Madden.

al-Siddiq, Abu Bakr. "The History of Abon Becr Sadiki." Another version of this autobiography, in G[eorge] C. Renouard, "Routes in North Africa, by Abu Bekr es Siddik," *Journal of the Royal Geographical Society* VI (1836): 99–113. Translated by Renouard from a second manuscript in Arabic, dated 29 August 1834 [1835].

al-Siddiq, Abu Bakr. "The History of Abon Becr Sadiki." A third version, reprinted in *Journal of Negro History* (July 1936): 52–55. Translated by an unknown hand. Dated 29 August 1834.

al-Siddiq, Abu Bakr. "The History of Abon Becr Sadiki." See also al-Siddiq
    letter translated from Arabic in Madden, *Twelve Months*, Vol. II,
    pp. 136–37.
Washington, John. "Some Account of Mohammedu Sisei, a Mandingo of Nyani-
    Maru on the Gambia." *Journal of Royal Geographical Society* VIII
    (1838): pp. 449–54.

Index